Karl Barth's
Christological Ecclesiology

Karl Barth's
Christological Ecclesiology

KIMLYN J. BENDER

New Paperback Edition

with a foreword by D. Stephen Long

and a new preface by the author

CASCADE *Books* · Eugene, Oregon

Cascade Books
An Imprint of Wipf and Stock Publishers
199 W. 8th Ave., Suite 3
Eugene, OR 97401

www.wipfandstock.com

ISBN 13: 978-1-62564-043-7

Cataloguing-in-Publication data:

Bender, Kimlyn J., 1969–

    Karl Barth's christological ecclesiology / Kimlyn J. Bender ; foreword by D. Stephen Long.

    xvi + 304 pp. ; 23 cm. Includes bibliographical references and index.

    ISBN 13: 978-1-62564-043-7

    1. Barth, Karl, 1886–1968. 2. Jesus Christ—History of doctrines—20th century. 3. Church—History of doctrines—20th century. I. Long, D. Stephen, 1960–. II. Title.

BV600.3 .B46 2013

For Trudy

Contents

CD I.2, 348) (12). His argument is convincing. Barth interpreters who fail to acknowledge it will miss something significant in Barth's work. Already in his defense of this main thesis, Bender points in an important direction in Barth's ecclesiology. The church is the body of Christ. Such a statement explains why Barth left his unsatisfying ecclesiology of the *Romans* period behind when he embarked on his *Church Dogmatics*. Bender's analysis and comparison of these two different epochs in Barth's work should also put an end to any interpretation that finds too much continuity between them such that it cannot account for the "Church" in Barth's *Church Dogmatics*. There are continuities between his criticisms of the church in both epochs. Bender reminds us of Barth's vigilance against "cultural Christianity" and "an ecclesiastical triumphalism." But with his move to Münster Barth begins to take on, and take more seriously, Roman Catholic ecclesiology.

Because Barth's theology was not reactive, he did not dismiss what he learned of Roman Catholic ecclesiology; nor did he take it on without a critical 'reformation' of what he found objectionable in it. Bender puts it well: "What Barth opposed in Catholicism was its transformation of revelation into historical and temporal realities so that revelation could be identified with the dogma of the church or grace with the sacramental elements" (56). For this reason, Barth never relented of his dismissal of the Roman Catholic claim that the church is an extension of the incarnation. As is well known, he called such a teaching "blasphemous." Bender helps us understand why. Barth did not deny the church is the body of Christ. Bender points out the importance of the *totus Christus* in Barth's theology. In his "mature ecclesiology" Barth's "reconceptualization of election" grounded ecclesiology "in election and thus in an eternal decision." The church, he notes, " is viewed as part of God's eternal covenantal intention" (101). Why then did Barth refer to the Catholic teaching as blasphemous? For a simple reason: only if Jesus is absent does his presence need to be mediated through an institution that stands in his place. Because Christ is already fully present in his church, the church need not "continue" his body. The church effects a witness that is Christ's own words.

Bender offers important criticisms of Barth's ecclesiology. He notes:

> Barth's strength is preserving the distinction and irreversibility between the divine and human agency, as well as that between the work of Christ and the church. He is less successful in describing their relation and inseparability. Especially in the final volumes of the *Church Dogmatics*, Barth often speaks of a parallelism of action, rather than an embodied action, so that divine and human activity are portrayed as in conjunction rather than in terms of the divine acting in and through the human, Christ acting in and through the church. The point might be illustrated by asking whether Christ comes to us *through* the proclamation of the church or *along side* of it. (279-280)

That is an important criticism. He also notes that Barth takes up Joseph rather than Mary as an image for the church, and asks why must it be an either-or? Nonetheless, Bender shows us what Barth set out to do in his response to Georg Wobbermin. Here is a Protestant ecclesiology founded upon the confidence that God has spoken fully and definitively in Jesus and continues to do so in and through the Holy Spirit in the gathered community that is the church. It is both event and institution. Barth's ecclesiology may not be fully satisfying. His answers may not be our answers, but he returned theology to questions that mattered and to a conversation worth having. Bender's work is a must read for anyone who desires to join in that conversation.

D. Stephen Long
Professor of Systematic Theology
Marquette University

Preface to the Paperback Edition

As any author would naturally say with reference to a work produced with hard labor and long hours, I am very grateful to see this book receive second life in a new form. With this in mind, I am grateful to Cascade Press for bringing this new paperback edition into print. I would like to thank Charlie Collier especially for his help with this endeavor. Charlie has been a wonderful editor, and I am thankful not only for his insight and wisdom but also for his flexibility and patience through the entire process of bringing this book into existence. I am also thankful to Christian Amondson, Diane Farley, Patrick Harrison, and Jim Tedrick at Cascade for their help along the way.

Many of my other grateful recognitions remain the same as those found in the original Acknowledgements included herein. In addition to those there mentioned, I am appreciative to D. Stephen Long, who has written the Foreword to this new edition.

Finally, changes in my life since the original appearance of the book bring with it other new thanksgivings. I am thankful to Truett Seminary (and Baylor University), my new academic home, for the wonderful place it is and the context it provides in which to teach and think and write. My colleagues here are a gift to me, providing not only intellectual conversation but also true fellowship. I am particularly grateful to David Garland, Dean of Truett Seminary, and Dennis Tucker, Associate Dean, both who have worked to make my transition to Truett a smooth one and who, with all of my colleagues here, are a constant source of encouragement and support.

Finally, there is one last change of note. Since the Ashgate edition first appeared, there is a new addition to our household. Andrew, Stephen, and now Karalyn, continue to fill my life with joy, as does my wife, Trudy. My thanks to all of them continues on from those originally given.

Acknowledgments

In producing this study, a revised version of my doctoral dissertation written at Princeton Theological Seminary, I have become indebted to many. While some debts are no doubt overlooked, and most must go unmentioned, the greatest ones merit special recognition.

I thank first my advisor, Daniel Migliore, for his wisdom and patience in overseeing the original dissertation. His wealth of insight into Barth's thought and careful direction were invaluable for the completion of the project and kept me from many errors. My work has benefitted greatly from his sound guidance. Similarly, special thanks are extended to Bruce McCormack for providing valuable insight as well as ongoing encouragement and support. Recognition is also extended to Ellen Charry for her helpful advice during the writing of the dissertation. My debt to these members of the dissertation committee is great and extends beyond the pages of this study.

As Director of the Center for Barth Studies, George Hunsinger helped in obtaining access to materials therein and has provided ongoing support. I also extend my thanks to the editors of *Barth Studies*, Dr. Hunsinger, John Webster, and Hans-Anton Drewes, for choosing to include this work in the series, as well as to Sarah Lloyd, Ann Newell, and Pete Coles of Ashgate for providing gracious help in numerous areas and oversight of the project. Dr. Drewes and the members of the Nachlaß Kommission of the Karl Barth-Archiv granted permission to cite from unpublished materials from Barth's Göttingen lectures that have only recently come into print. Clifford Anderson assisted in obtaining bibliographical information, and his friendship reminds me of the truism that 'iron sharpens iron.' Dieter Heinzl provided much appreciated help in German translation. Stanley Grenz and Lee McDonald provided helpful and gracious advice on the publication process.

In my new institutional home, the University of Sioux Falls, I greatly enjoy the friendship and encouragement of my colleagues in theology, John Hiigel, Christina Hitchcock, and Dennis Thum. They have not only patiently listened to litanies of ideas, but have sacrificed time and energy to allow me to undertake this endeavor. Judy Clauson, Laura Olson, and Katie Pelzel of Mears Library provided ongoing, cheerful assistance in obtaining materials. Larry Ort, Kirby Wilcoxson and Beth Jernberg in their administrative leadership roles have also supported the project in numerous ways. The members of the Karl Barth Society of Sioux Falls always provide stimulating discussion as well as encouragement to me. These conversations are a highlight of every week.

Finally, my deepest thanks are reserved for my family members to whom I owe the most. My parents, Clarence and Sadie Bender, and my brother, Kerry Bender, have supported me all along the journey. My two wonderful sons, Andrew and

Stephen, fill my life with joy, happiness, and laughter. My greatest earthly debt and gratitude is due to my wife Trudy, whose love, friendship, and encouragement helped me to stay the course through good and bad alike. With her unfailing support, she has truly borne, believed, hoped, and endured the most of all (....πάντα στέγει, πάντα πιστεύει, πάντα ἐλπίζει, πάντα ὑπομένει – I Corinthians 13:7).

Abbreviations

CD	*Church Dogmatics*
ET	English Translation
GD	*Göttingen Dogmatics*
NRSV	New Revised Standard Version
Römerbrief/ *Romans*	*Der Römerbrief.* 2nd ed. (München: Chr. Kaiser Verlag, 1923). ET: *The Epistle to the Romans.* (Oxford: Oxford University Press, 1968).

Chapter One

Introduction

Even the most superficial reading of Barth's *Church Dogmatics* reveals its massive scope and ambitious attempt to leave no theological stone unturned. Yet only a careful and extensive examination discloses its equally impressive coherence and deeply-woven structure in which each doctrinal strand of this gigantic theological tapestry is intertwined with others, so that no thread is entirely independent of another. Barth's doctrine of the church is no exception in this regard.

In dialogue with his students, Karl Barth once described Christian truth as 'a globe, where every point points to the centre,' and asserted that dogmatics may in theory begin with any doctrine, including that of the church.[1] In fact, however, Barth began his dogmatics proper with the doctrine of God's revelation as the triune God, and the doctrine of the church followed discussions of revelation, the Trinity, and Christology. These prior discussions were not peripheral but integral to Barth's understanding of ecclesiology. Even from a developmental standpoint, while the question of the church arose for Barth early in his theological career, it was always inextricably entwined in a web of related questions.

These observations are not surprising, for ecclesiology itself is a derived system, dependent upon other theological doctrines and their attendant propositions and principles to provide it with shape and substance.[2] This is especially true with regard to ecclesiology's relation to Christology, for the identity of the church is intimately connected to that of Christ. The inclusive and complex nature of the doctrine of the church poses a problem for any study in ecclesiology, for such an investigation cannot limit itself to an examination of the question of the church *per se*, but must also take into consideration these pertinent theological presuppositions and convictions. A further related difficulty is posed by the fact that ecclesiology is a synthetic doctrine — it includes within it many aspects of theology. It is therefore impossible to say that it is either purely dogmatic or ethical, for ecclesiology includes both aspects, with

---

[1] *Karl Barth's Table Talk*, ed. John D. Godsey, (Edinburgh: Oliver & Boyd, 1963), 13. George Hunsinger has likened Barth's understanding of the interconnectedness of Christian theology to the examination of a multi-faceted crystal, where each doctrine serves as a facet through which to view the whole structure of dogmatics (*How To Read Karl Barth: The Shape of His Theology*, [New York/Oxford: Oxford University Press, 1991], 28-29).

[2] See Maurice B. Schepers, 'The Work of the Holy Spirit: Karl Barth on the Nature of the Church,' in *Theological Studies*, 23 (1962): 625.

either coming to the fore depending upon whether one is focusing on the church's nature or activity.[3]

Both of these difficulties are present when one attempts to examine the ecclesiology of Karl Barth. As has been noted, Barth's concept of the church is greatly influenced by other theological doctrines and convictions. Furthermore, Barth's ecclesiology, like his theology as a whole, is comprised of both dogmatic and ethical elements, joined together in an intimate way. Indeed, it is misleading to say that for Barth ethics follows ecclesiology — it is much more accurate to say that ecclesiology *is* ethical, a point that will become evident in the course of this study.[4] Many missteps in the interpretation of Barth's ecclesiology (both past and present) can be traced back either to a failure to place Barth's doctrine of the church within his larger dogmatic framework, or to understand its implicitly ethical nature. I hope to show how these missteps have been made, and also how they can thus be avoided. Indeed, the present work is nothing less than a re-narration of the historical development and re-presentation of the inner logic of Barth's doctrine of the church.

To fulfill this task, this study will attempt to explicate Barth's ecclesiology by drawing attention to the Christological logic that governs its inner shape, structure, and content. Other theological patterns will be discerned as well, but these are subordinate to the distinctive Christological ones, for it is the Christological patterns that are in general inclusive of the others, not surprising in light of the centrality of Christology in Barth's theology. So, while Barth's ecclesiology will be examined in light of other central doctrines such as election and reconciliation, it is preeminently the Christological aspects of these doctrines that influence and shape Barth's ecclesiology.

It has in fact often been said that Barth's theology is Christocentric, but what does this mean? Perhaps with some careful qualification one could even say that Schleiermacher was a Christocentric theologian, but this of course should not be taken to imply that Barth and Schleiermacher shared a similar theological method. To say that a theology is Christocentric may mean a number of things — what we must understand is what it meant for Barth.

---

[3]Ibid, 625.

[4]Barth can therefore claim in his discussion of the ethics of creation that 'the active life of man willed and demanded by God is primarily and decisively the active life of the community of Christ' (*CD III.4*, 486). Likewise: 'In other words, the obedient action of man consists basically in joining the community' (ibid, 493; cf. 515). For the relation between ecclesiology and ethics in Barth's theology, see Robert E. Willis, *The Ethics of Karl Barth* (Leiden: E. J. Brill, 1971), 97-102; 273-427; also Reinhard Hütter, *Evangelische Ethik als kirchliches Zeugnis: Interpretationen zu Schlüsselfragen theologischer Ethik in der Gegenwart* (Neukirchen-Vluyn: Neukirchener Verlag, 1993), 25-105.

The short answer is that for Barth theology *is* Christology.[5] To say this is to affirm that every Christian doctrine must be determined and shaped by God's revelation in Jesus Christ. This does not entail that every doctrine need be strictly deduced from Christology, or that all theology becomes Christology so that all other doctrines are excluded. But it does mean that no doctrine can be formulated independently from Jesus Christ. For Barth, to consider and formulate a Christian doctrine in isolation from the revelation given in Christ results in an abstract doctrine that has lost its moorings and can be regarded only as speculative. To say that Christology is the center of Barth's theology will be examined further in the coming chapters, but for now it is sufficient to say that for Barth, every Christian doctrine must be determined in light of the particular person of Jesus Christ, and this holds true for ecclesiology.

Three primary elements comprise the Christological logic that shapes Barth's ecclesiology and provides its inherent principles of reasoning.[6] This logic is the formal and internal skeletal structure upon which the material substance of Barth's doctrine of the church is hung. These elements are related in an inclusive fashion, in that the second element serves as a further detailed explication of an aspect of the first, and the third as a further detailed explication of an aspect of the second. They are therefore unfolding elements, each intricately related to the other.

The first and most comprehensive element is what George Hunsinger has identified as the Chalcedonian pattern.[7] This pattern serves as the constitutive paradigm for understanding the formal relation, itself unique and irreplaceable, between the divine and human natures of Christ in the incarnation. In Barth's thought, however, it also serves as the regulative pattern for all divine and human relationships

---

[5]See *CD I.2*, 123; 883; also *CD II.1*, 148-149.

[6]To say that Christological logic rules Barth's ecclesiology is not to say that every aspect of Christology directly applies to ecclesiology. For instance, while Barth can discuss the church's mission in terms of its prophetic task and at times can allude to a priestly one, Barth does not allow for any lordship within the church, i.e., there is no strong correlation between the kingly aspect of Christ's *munus triplex* and the mission of the church, which is always that of a servant, though Barth can provide a very qualified and brief discussion of how the Christian and the community do indeed participate not only in the prophetic and priestly aspects of the office of Christ, but also in the kingly one (see *CD III.3*, 287-288). Nevertheless, Barth does not like to speak of offices within the church at all; Christ alone holds the three-fold office of prophet, priest, and king, and the church simply witnesses to the Lord who fulfills this unique office, as will be seen below.

[7]See Hunsinger, *How to Read Karl Barth*, 85; 173-180; 185-187; 204f.; 286-287; et al. See also *Barth, Barmen, and the Confessing Church Today: Katallegete*, James Y. Holloway, ed. (Lewiston: Edwin Mellen Press, 1992/1995), 289-292. I am greatly indebted to these works for the current discussion. Barth himself described the decisions of the ecumenical councils as 'guiding lines' for an understanding of Christ's existence and action, (*CD IV.1*, 127).

that stand in analogy to the incarnation itself, as well as for a few carefully qualified relationships between created entities.[8] The Chalcedonian pattern is comprised of a unity, a differentiation, and an asymmetrical relation between the divine and human natures in Christ, and by analogy between the members, or terms, of the other designated relations. The unity of the natures entails that they cannot be thought of as severed so that the intimacy of their relation is lost — in the language of Chalcedon, they are 'without division or separation.' The distinction of the natures entails that they cannot be thought of as mingled so that the integrity of either is sacrificed — in the language of Chalcedon, they are 'without confusion or change.' The asymmetry between the natures signifies that they exist in an ordered and irreversible relation whereby the first is independent and superior in relation to the second, whereas the second is dependent and subordinate to the first, the first being different from the second in kind, not merely in degree. Just as the distinction between the natures or terms guards against an identification of them, protecting the integrity of each, so also the asymmetry of the natures or terms ensures that there is no parity between them.[9] The Chalcedonian pattern is used by Barth to guard against mistaken positions on the left and the right, those that either exalt humanity by granting it autonomy, or those that denigrate humanity by positing a divine determinism or monism.[10]

The second element of the Christological logic follows from this final aspect of the Chalcedonian pattern. In essence, it may be described as a further exposition clarifying the nature of the asymmetrical relation itself with primary reference to the personal union of Word and flesh in Christ and then to the communion of the natures, and with secondary application to defining the relationship between divine and human subjects. This element is articulated in terms of the patristic *anhypostasia/enhypostasia* formula in Christology.[11] This doctrine, as Barth

---

[8]Hunsinger states that 'there is virtually no discussion of divine and human agency in the *Church Dogmatics* which does not conform to this scheme' (*How to Read Karl Barth*, 187).

[9]Hunsinger, *How to Read Karl Barth*, 177.

[10]'The Chalcedonian pattern is used to specify counter positions that would be doctrinally incoherent (and also incoherent with scripture). "Without separation or division" means that no independent human autonomy can be posited in relation to God. "Without confusion or change" means that no divine determinism or monism can be posited in relation to humanity. Finally, "complete in deity and complete in humanity" means that no symmetrical relationship can be posited between divine and human actions (or better, none that is not asymmetrical). It also means that the two cannot be posited as ultimately identical' (ibid, 204).

[11]*CD I.2*, 163; cf. *CD IV.2*, 49-50; 90-91. For a discussion of the place of this couplet in Barth's Christology, see Thomas F. Torrance, *Karl Barth, Biblical and Evangelical Theologian* (Edinburgh: T & T Clark, 1990), 198-201; also 125. In reference to this couplet, Torrance writes: 'As Barth used it...this was a technically precise way of speaking of the

understood and articulated it, made two statements, one negative and one positive. The negative assertion (expressed by the *anhypostasis*) is that the human nature of Christ has no independent existence apart from the Word in the incarnation. This safeguards both the divine freedom and initiative as well as the utter dependence of the creature upon the Creator. It therefore protects against any form of adoptionism. The positive assertion (expressed by the *enhypostasis*) is that the human nature does have a real, true, and complete existence in the Word. This ensures the integrity and wholeness of the creature, that Jesus was a complete human being. The Christological couplet preserves both the sovereign freedom and benevolent goodness of the divine self-giving in the incarnation, as well as the wholeness and bestowed dignity of the creature, thus expressing 'the essential logic in the irreversible movement of God's grace.'[12]

When applied by analogy to designated divine and human relationships, then, this Christological formula entails that the human partner and work has no independent existence apart from the divine initiative, but at the same time ensures that the human subject does have a real and true existence and activity as established by and in relation to the divine Subject and activity. The human activity is not abolished or denigrated but established and dignified by the divine activity, even though it cannot supplement or replace the divine work and exists on an entirely different plane. Barth's anhypostatic-enhypostatic Christological formula allows him to speak of a true unity of the Word and flesh in Christ and of the Creator with the creature, without sacrificing the distinction and superiority of the divine to the human on the one hand or the integrity of the creature on the other. It is the ontological complement to the soteriological 'justification by grace alone.'

The final element of the Christological logic follows from the two preceding. It further describes the nature of the human life of Christ in relation to his divine life, and thus describes the character of the real, true, and whole human existence that is established by the divine Word in material rather than purely formal terms. Barth answers the question as to the positive relation of the second term to the first, of Christ's human life to his divine life, by positing the notion of correspondence [*Entsprechung*].[13] Correspondence itself includes both ontological and ethical aspects

---

reality, wholeness and integrity of the human nature of Jesus Christ in the incarnation, without lapsing into adoptionism, and of speaking of its perfect oneness with the divine nature of Christ without lapsing into monophysitism' (ibid, 200).

[12]Torrance, *Karl Barth, Biblical and Evangelical Theologian*, 199; cf. 125.

[13]For a discussion of Barth's concept of correspondence (and the accompanying concepts of 'parable' [*Gleichnis*] and 'analogy' [*Analogie*], see Helmut Gollwitzer, 'Kingdom of God and Socialism in the Theology of Karl Barth,' in *Karl Barth and Radical Politics*, ed. George Hunsinger (Philadelphia: Westminster Press, 1976), 97-99.

and is related to the epistemological concept of the analogy of faith [*analogia fidei*].[14] It is a specifically Christological notion, however, for it is defined by and refers first and preeminently to the manner in which Christ's human life mirrors and indeed re-presents the divine life of God in its own proper sphere of being and activity.[15] It is then applied by analogy to obedient human activity that reflects the divine will as established by grace.

The concept of correspondence speaks neither of an identity, continuity, and cooperation between divine and human action, nor of a purely radical separation, opposition, and contradiction between them. It is neither univocal nor equivocal, but analogical, in nature. On the one hand, it guards against any type of identification or conflation of divine and human activity, excluding any synergistic or cooperative understandings of salvation. Divine and human activity remain distinct and do not exist on the same plane. Positively, it entails that human activity not contradict but reflect the divine will and activity in a manner appropriate to the creature, neither replacing nor supplementing the divine activity.[16] And it is for this positive affirmation that the negative judgment is made: human activity is relativized and limited not so that it is to be set aside as irrelevant or purely sinful, but so that human activity might be given its own proper place as a truly *human* work, rather than the work of God. The eschatological reservation gives rise, and does not destroy, an ethical and historical affirmation of human life and activity.[17]

This human life and activity corresponds, or lives in analogy to, the divine life, but does so only in light of the previous logic whereby the radical asymmetry between the partners and their work is affirmed, and the complete and utter dependence of the human upon the divine is safeguarded. Barth's notion of correspondence describes the character of the human life and activity that exists enhypostatically in the divine Word in the incarnation, and by analogy the character of the life of the church and the

---

[14]Correspondence may be thought of as the ontological and ethical parallel to the epistemological 'analogy of faith' [*analogia fidei*] in Barth's theology. Referring to the concept of correspondence and to the related one of parable in Barth's theology, Gollwitzer concludes: 'It is indicative of academic theology's idealist way of thinking that it is not these concepts, but their correlate from the theory of knowledge — the concept of analogy — which has held the center of attention in the discussion and interpretation of Barth....*Analogia fidei* corresponds at the theoretical level to "parable" at the level of social praxis; the former is necessary in that it grounds and secures the correct occurrence of the practice of the Christian life,' (97).

[15]See *CD IV.2*, 166.

[16]Gollwitzer, 97-99.

[17]Gollwitzer writes: 'Here the eschatological reservation loses the paralyzing effect it has exercised for so long,' (98). Likewise: 'Eschatology does not brake, but propels, our activity,' (99).

Christian established by God within the covenant of grace. It thus ties the theological and the ethical, the vertical and the horizontal, together. An analogous relationship of being and a correspondence of activity are made possible by divine grace rather than a natural human capacity. The action of the human partner does not replace nor supplement the divine activity, but does have a real, true, and important place that reflects and bears witness to God's salvific work. There is nothing insufficient in the divine activity that requires completion in a human act, but the human act does by grace accompany and serve the divine activity as a witness, taking the form of obedience rather than disobedience.

Once again, correspondence is first and foremost a Christological principle before it is an ethical one, however, in that the correspondence of the creature to the Creator finds its ultimate and normative example in the obedience of Jesus Christ to God, the life of the New Adam lived in conformity to the Father's will. This is seen preeminently in the fact that Jesus Christ is not only the electing God but also the elect human being, not only the humble and obedient Son of God but also the exalted and glorified Son of Man. Yet this Christological correspondence is complemented by an ecclesiological one, in that the church is to attempt and bear within its life and in the life of each member 'an imitation and representation [*Nachahmung und Darstellung*] of the love with which God loved the world.'[18]

These Christological elements of the Chalcedonian pattern, the *anhypostasia/enhypostasia* formula, and the motif of correspondence, serve both a critical and constructive purpose. They are critical in that they help to criticize and avoid mistaken positions whether conceived on the theological left or right. The close affiliation between Christology and ecclesiology in Barth's thought is made evident in that these mistaken ecclesiological positions are construed by Barth in terms of Christological heresies. For Barth, to consider the true church to be an invisible reality behind the visible institution, and indeed opposed to and in contradiction with it, was to succumb to a docetic ecclesiology. On the opposite side, to conceive of the church solely and purely as a historical phenomenon and as one human society among others, without regard to its grounding in the activity of the Holy Spirit as an eschatological event, was to fall into an ebionitic heresy. While Barth explicitly identified these errors as docetic and ebionitic, he also implicitly speaks of a third error: that of confusing the historical institution, life, and practices of the church with revelation itself, what might be termed a Eutychian heresy. Here the dialectical relation itself is sacrificed so that history is divinized and revelation is historicized in a confused and amalgamated relation. The first error sacrifices the historical form to the divine event, thus failing to account for the enhypostatic character of the church. The second sacrifices the divine event to the historical form, thus failing to account for the anhypostatic character of the church. The third sacrifices the dialectical

---

[18]*CD III.4*, 502.

character and confuses the realities, so that the asymmetrical and irreversible character of the relation is lost, the correspondence of the church giving way to a synergism of cooperation.[19]

Barth's own position is to speak of the church as both divinely constituted and historically situated, a reality comprised of both an inner mystery of the Spirit and a society of human persons in fellowship and joint activity. The church is for Barth both invisible and visible, so that the inner mystery is not sacrificed to the external form, nor vice versa, maintaining the integrity of each. Barth seeks neither to confuse nor separate the divine event and the historical and sociological form, presented in a highly dialectical construal of the relation between divine action and historical duration.[20] He regularly defines the church dialectically with reference to rejected and opposing dyads — the church is neither docetic nor ebionitic, neither idealized nor historicized, neither antinomian nor legalistic, neither sacralized nor secularized.

The Christological patterns are not only critical but also constructive, and are so in two senses. First, they are constitutive for Christology itself, describing the real and irreducible aspects and relations of the incarnation — the unity, differentiation, and irreversible ordering of the divine and human natures, the irreversible relation of the Word and flesh of Christ, as well as the positive relation between them. They are constructive in another sense, however, in that they are also the regulative patterns that both govern and illustrate other complex divine and human relations.

With specific regard to the question of the church, Barth's Christological logic, as comprised of these three elements, is witnessed in three specific relationships, each closely though not exclusively tied to three aspects of the church's existence. The

---

[19]For an insightful description of ecclesiology in terms of the relationship between divine event and historical form and duration, see Martin Honecker, 'Kirche als Gestalt und Ereignis: Die sichtbare Gestalt der Kirche als dogmatisches Problem,' in *Forschungen zur Geschichte und Lehre des Protestantismus*, ed. Ernst Wolf, No. 10, v. 25 (München: Chr. Kaiser Verlag, 1963), 1-238; esp. 11-15. I am indebted to this study for the current discussion of this problem. Honecker identifies this relationship between eschatological event [*Ereignis*] and historical form [*Gestalt*] as central to the Reformation understanding of the church, and states that the central theological problem pertaining to this relationship can be stated succinctly: 'the church stands in history but does not originate from history,' ['*die Kirche in der Geschichte besteht, aber nicht aus der Geschichte stammt*'], (12). In Biblical parlance, the church is in, but not of, the world. Honecker's analysis and description of the problem is better than his assessment of Barth's own position, however. He concludes that Barth sacrifices visible form to invisible event (see 157-204; esp. 201-204). This is a common criticism of Barth's ecclesiology, but one that is either mistaken or, at best, one-sided, as will be seen in due time below.

[20]As we shall see, Barth perceived a mistaken docetic position in Brunner and Sohm, a mistaken ebionitic position in much of Protestant liberalism and in German nationalism, and a Eutychian confusion in Roman Catholicism.

first aspect, that of the church's *origin and nature*, pertains to the overarching relationship between the Spirit and the church and to the question of the church's reality as both an event called into existence by the Spirit and an institution existing as a human society within time. Barth can speak of this two-fold nature of the church as comprising a mystery, and he also designates these two aspects in his idiosyncratic understanding of the relationship between the invisible and the visible church. This relationship constitutes the reality of the church itself.

The second aspect is that of the church's *order and form*, pertaining to the overarching relationship between Christ and the church and to the question of the church's structure as this is expressed in a concrete rule of law. Here Barth speaks of the church as a community that possesses a definite form and order within the world. He speaks of this form primarily in terms of the concept and imagery of the body of Christ, and of its order as Christologically-derived.

The final aspect is that of the church's *ordination and mission*, pertaining to the overarching relationship between the church and the world and to the question of the church's commission to a specific and divinely-entrusted task. This relationship between the church and the world is both similar and different from the previous two, for now the church takes the place of the first term in the relation. This entails a modification, though not an abandonment, of the Christological patterns found in the two previous relations.

These three aspects of the church's nature, form, and mission constitute Barth's ecclesiology, which is determined by the distinctive relationships between the Spirit and the church, Christ and the church, and the church and the world. These primary and dialectical relationships are in turn ruled by the Christological logic we have outlined, and are also complemented by other sub-relationships, represented by but not limited to the relation between the invisible and visible church and the relation between the providence of God and the confusion of humanity. The Christological logic therefore holds not only *within* the terms themselves (Jesus Christ as both divine and human; the church as both invisible and visible; world-occurrence as marked both by the providence of God and the confusion of humanity), but also *between* the terms (between Christ and the church, and between the church and the world).

Christ, church, and world thus exist in a relation of concentric circles, with Christ as the center of both the church and the world, and with Christ and the church together comprising the center of world-occurrence and its history.[21] In each relation, there is a unity of the terms, a differentiation between them, and an asymmetrical relation in which the second term has no independent existence apart from the first term, but has a true existence as established by the first. This relation of the second

---

[21]Hunsinger notes that the 'root metaphor' of the *Church Dogmatics* may be thought of as 'the metaphor of the circle comprising center and periphery — a metaphor which is constantly employed to bring out the centrality of Jesus Christ' (*How to Read Karl Barth*, 59).

term to the first is marked by a correspondence which is neither univocal nor equivocal, but rather analogous, to the being and activity of the first term. This correspondence is therefore both theologically grounded and ethically oriented.

All of these relations together fall within the larger framework of Barth's Trinitarian dogmatics. Barth's doctrine of the church, in all of its varied and multi-faceted complexity, is best understood when its Christological logic is delineated and understood, and its strengths and deficiencies can be assessed more fairly and accurately when the deep substructure of Barth's doctrine of the church is more accurately mapped. Such is the claim and justification of this study.

The purpose of this work therefore influences its organization. Barth's ecclesiology (like his Christology and theology as a whole) did not arise *ex nihilo* in his thought, but was the result of theological development in a concrete historical and intellectual context of reflection, activity, and debate. Chapter two recounts the development of Barth's theology of the church in his early writings and as it came to expression in conflict with theological opponents on the left and on the right, Neo-Protestantism and Roman Catholicism. Here it will become evident that it is precisely the lack of an adequate Christology in Barth's early theology that led to defects in his early ecclesiology. In chapter three, the emergence of Barth's Chalcedonian Christology is examined and its effect upon Barth's first dogmatic ecclesiology, articulated in his Göttingen lectures, is assessed. These two chapters form the historical backdrop of the following systematic investigation, a backdrop necessary to cast light upon Barth's mature ecclesiology, for his later thought was rooted in earlier struggles and never escaped their influence.[22] In chapters four and five we turn from primarily historical to systematic investigation, describing the close relationship between the doctrines of election and reconciliation within the *Church Dogmatics* and their bearing upon Barth's mature ecclesiology.[23] Chapter four examines the doctrine of election as the foundation of Barth's mature ecclesiology, with particular attention to the interrelation of election and Christology and their significance for Barth's ecclesiology. In chapter five the doctrine of reconciliation is examined as the context of Barth's mature ecclesiology, with particular attention to Barth's conception of

---

[22]These chapters do not pretend to be exhaustive in presenting Barth's thinking on all church-related questions in his early years, but are only intended to present the early development of Barth's *doctrine* of the church, thus providing the historical background necessary for understanding Barth's mature ecclesiology. The same may be said for all the chapters that follow. For this reason, limited space and a definite purpose have required that various significant episodes pertaining to the question of the church, such as Barth's involvement in the German church struggle and his role in the ecumenical movement, be left largely unexamined.

[23]For the relationship between Barth's doctrines of election and reconciliation with particular regard to ecclesiology, see Hütter, *Evangelishe Ethik*, 25-105.

correspondence and understanding of history, and to their bearing upon ecclesiology. Chapters six, seven, and eight form the heart of this study and examine the questions of the nature, form, and mission of the church, respectively, with the first of the three focusing upon the relationship between the Spirit and the church, the second, upon the relationship between Christ and the church, and the third, upon the relationship between the church and the world. Barth himself divided his ecclesiology in the fourth volume of the *Church Dogmatics* into three sections, speaking of the gathering, the upbuilding, and the sending of the Christian community.[24] While each of our three chapters roughly corresponds to each of Barth's three ecclesiological sections, respectively, the relationships and issues described in each chapter are not exclusively limited to one of Barth's sections but cross their boundaries. After these three chapters, this study comes to a close with a final concluding chapter summarizing the strengths and weaknesses of Barth's doctrine of the church in light of recent evaluations of his ecclesiology and an assessment of these evaluations themselves.

Here an initial objection might be raised and should be addressed. Barth can state that the hypostatic union has no analogies.[25] If this be true, then an analogical application of Christological categories like the Chalcedonian pattern and the anhypostatic-enhypostatic formula to ecclesiology as here presented may be deemed questionable. In response, a number of points must be made.

First, Barth's statement itself must be clearly understood. Barth's insistence that the hypostatic union has no analogy means that there is no analogy for the incarnation in the created order such that it be construed as merely a type or exemplification of a more fundamental union of God and humanity. The hypostatic union of Christ is unique, singular, and irreplaceable, and therefore it must be understood solely on its own terms. One only knows Jesus Christ, Barth states, if one begins with the acknowledgment that no analogy exists to express 'his own being and becoming.'[26] The incarnation is therefore not an illustration of a more fundamental union between God and humanity (mystical, ethical, or other), but is itself the ground and basis for God's relationship with the world and thus for all other interactions between the Creator and the creature. In this sense, the hypostatic union can truly be said to have no analogy.

It would be incorrect, however, to conclude from this that Barth does not extend Christological patterns of thought beyond Christology proper. Barth does not negate, but reverses, analogical predication. While no analogy exists for the hypostatic union

---

[24] *CD IV.1*, §62 — 'The Holy Spirit and the Gathering of the Christian Community'; *CD IV.2*, §67 — 'The Holy Spirit and the Upbuilding of the Christian Community'; *CD IV.3.2*, §72 — 'The Holy Spirit and the Sending of the Christian Community.'

[25]See, for example, *CD IV.2*, 57-58.

[26]*CD IV.2*, 58.

in the created order, Barth does believe that this unique union serves as the source, foundation, and paradigm for all of God's ways with the world, and therefore is reflected in those relations. Make no mistake — the union of God and humanity in Christ for Barth is *sui generis* and has no true parallel. Yet, precisely because this singular relation is God's self-elected means to establish a covenant with all of creation, the incarnation is the pattern on which all other divine-human relations are predicated, though they stand on a different plane and exist only in subservience to and as shadows of this unsubstitutable event.

Barth therefore can say that the relation between Christ and the Christian stands 'in analogy to the mystery and miracle of Christmas,'[27] and that Christians exist in 'proximity to Him and therefore in analogy to what He is.'[28] Furthermore, Barth can explicitly attribute Christological formulas, such as the language of *anhypostasia* and *enhypostasia*, to ecclesiological concerns such as the relation between Christ and the church.[29] Ecclesiology is thereby construed along Christological lines, and mistaken ecclesiologies likened to Christological heresies. Hence, the formal Christological patterns described above are not read into Barth or superimposed upon his thought, but arise out of his own concrete depictions of the church, and the remainder of this study will attempt to highlight the formal patterns by examining them in the actual material content of Barth's ecclesiology. The final refutation of this initial objection is therefore something that must await the end of our investigation. If such patterns are valid and useful, they are so only insofar as they arise out of Barth's own ecclesiological descriptions and in turn help us better understand them. The proof of the pudding is in the eating, so to speak.

One final clarification is in order. We must define what Barth means when he speaks of the 'church.' For Barth, the referent for the church is first and foremost the congregation of believers in a specific place and time, gathered by God in Christ through the Holy Spirit, built up together into a common life of fellowship, entrusted with the task of worship, witness, and service, and sent into the world to fulfill this task. Barth thinks of the church more in terms of a *people* than an *institution*, as a personal congregation rather than as a bureaucratic organization, and this leads to his favoring of the term 'community' [*Gemeinde*] over the term 'church' [*Kirche*], the latter in German referring more to the polity and organization than to the personal

---

[27] *CD IV*.3.2, 542; cf. 554.

[28] *CD IV*.3.2, 532. Barth later writes: 'Their new and distinctive being as Christians is their being in this real similarity, for all the dissimilarity, to His being as the Son of God' (*CD IV*.3.2, 533; see also 532-533).

[29] *CD IV*.2, 59-60; cf. *CD I*.2, 348.

fellowship that the first term expresses.[30] Barth could, however, use the latter term to express or include the concept of the former, and for this reason, in conjunction with the lack of such a nuanced distinction in English, these terms are here used interchangeably, their meaning to be interpreted by context.[31]

Barth could speak of the church not only as a local congregation (his primary manner of speaking of the church), or as an institution (a much more rare occurrence), but also as a universal fellowship, as the corporate body of God's people across spatial and temporal boundaries. The referent for Barth's term must be determined by context. For this reason, the words 'community' and 'church' will consistently be used in the lower-case, rather than in the upper-case (which in normal use generally refers to the universal church), though quotations will never change the capitalization of any translation cited. A similar rule applies to the use of inclusive language — while I have attempted to use gender-neutral terminology as much as possible, I have not changed any translations that follow more traditional usage. All quotations cited are from the standard English translations of Barth's works unless expressly noted to be my own, though references to the original German works are frequently included as deemed appropriate. Finally, this work came into existence through a slow process. Readers are gently encouraged to read slowly, and to read the notes.

---

[30]See, for example, Barth's discussion of the difference between the terms in *Evangelical Theology: An Introduction*, trans. Grover Foley (New York: Holt, Rinehart and Winston, 1963), 37. Barth could elsewhere write: 'We assume that by the Christian community or Church is not meant an establishment or institution organised along specific lines, but the living people awakened and assembled by Jesus Christ as the Lord for the fulfillment of a specific task,' (*CD III.4*, 488). Barth's conception of the church was distinctively non-hierarchical — Barth had little regard for strong distinctions between clergy and laity, or for distinctive 'offices,' favoring an emphasis upon the ministry of service and witness entrusted to each member of the Christian community, extending even to the discipline of theology itself (see *CD III.4*, 488-490; 497-499; 505; cf. *CD IV.2*, 690-695).

[31]Barth speaks of the 'church' [*Kirche*] when he is discussing the church as a problem of theological prolegomena (*CD I.2*), whereas he speaks primarily of the 'community' [*Gemeinde*] when providing his formal ecclesiology. Whether this difference is due to the different topic at hand, or due to the time lapse between the writing of Volumes I and IV, is not entirely clear. See Sheldon W. Sorge, *Karl Barth's Reception in North America: Ecclesiology as a Case Study* (Unpubl. Ph.D. Diss., Duke University, 1987), 66-67. For a discussion of the multivalent character of the term 'church,' see Erwin Fahlbusch, 'Church,' in *The Encyclopedia of Christianity: Volume 1 A-D*, ed. Erwin Fahlbusch, Jan M. Lochman, et al., trans. Geoffrey W. Bromiley (Grand Rapids: Eerdmans, 1999; and Leiden: Brill, 1999), 477-478.

Part One

Barth's Early Ecclesiology

I believe the Church as the place where honour is given to God and where therefore divine honour for the Church is repudiated, and therefore I believe the Church as the instrument of grace. I believe the Church as the divine institution and therefore that it must be not so much God's palace as God's shanty among men until the world's end. I believe the church as the communion of saints, that is the communion of sinners set apart and called by God, which yet is the communion of saints. I believe the Church as the proclaimer and the hearer of the divine Word. I believe it also as the people of God on earth, who — precisely as the people of God — shall live from God's mercy (and that is not to be counted as a small thing!) until the kingdom of glory where the transitory, even the transitoriness of this community, of the earthly body of the heavenly Lord, shall put on eternity, where here also what is sown in weakness shall be raised in strength.

Karl Barth, 'The Concept of the Church,' July, 1927

Chapter Two

Barth's Early Theology:
Battles on the Left and on the Right

1. The Setting — Wilhelm Herrmann and the Legacy of Liberalism

The early treatises of theology that flowed from the pen of Karl Barth during his pastorate in the Swiss village of Safenwil display a feeling of restlessness, a restlessness that arose from disillusionment with the cultural and social order. This disillusionment became wedded to dissatisfaction with the theology of his former teachers, the heritage of Protestant liberalism. Barth's work among the labor class in the small village of Safenwil fostered such discontentment with the status quo, but Barth's final divorce from theological liberalism itself came with the outbreak of the first World War. Many of Barth's former professors openly supported the German war effort through an explicit subscription to a manifesto supporting Wilhelm II and his war policy, an action Barth found to betray an underlying theological and ethical failure.[1] Barth would later look back upon this event as marking his official break with the theology of his teachers.[2] The most highly esteemed of these teachers, and one of the signatories of the manifesto, was Wilhelm Herrmann.

Barth had studied with Herrmann in Marburg and could rightly be called a disciple of his at the time. Barth's break with liberalism in 1914 was thus specifically

---

[1] For a history of Barth's development and activities during the years of his pastorate in Safenwil leading up to this event, see Eberhard Busch, *Karl Barth: His Life from Letters and Autobiographical Texts*, trans. John Bowden (Grand Rapids: Eerdmans, 1994), chapter three. See also the detailed account of Barth's theological development and activities during this time in Bruce McCormack, *Karl Barth's Critically Realistic Dialectical Theology: Its Genesis and Development 1909-1936* (Oxford: Clarendon Press, 1995), chapters one and two.

[2] See Karl Barth, 'Evangelical Theology in the 19th Century,' in *The Humanity of God*, trans. Thomas Wieser (Atlanta: John Knox Press/C. D. Deans, 1960), 14. Even a month before the appearance of the manifesto Barth wrote to Eduard Thurneysen that in Germany the Gospel was being substituted with a 'German war-theology' and stated: 'It is truly sad! Marburg and German civilization have lost something in my eyes by this breakdown, and indeed forever' (*Revolutionary Theology in the Making: Barth-Thurneysen Correspondence, 1914-1925*, trans. James D. Smart [Richmond: John Knox Press, 1964], 26).

a break with Herrmann and his own brand of Schleiermacherian Ritschlianism.[3] Barth nonetheless never completely abandoned the teaching of Herrmann, at least not in every respect, and could still say in 1925 that 'I could never inwardly agree that I had really turned away from my teacher,' despite the fact that Barth had chosen an uncharted and revolutionary theological course.[4] Barth's rejection of metaphysics and historicism, as well as his rejection of natural theology and apologetics, were life-long commitments that he owed to Herrmann. Along with these convictions, Barth's early theology reveals another inheritance from his former teacher.

In his work *Ethik* of 1901, Herrmann had identified the family, cultural life, and the state as the three most influential spheres of Christian activity.[5] Granting the fact that this is a work in ethics, and not overlooking the fact that Herrmann had indeed provided a discussion of the ethical task of the Christian with particular reference to membership in the Christian church,[6] it is nonetheless curious that the church is not given as significant a place for ethical activity as these other spheres. Barth had read Herrmann's work in 1905 and called Herrmann '*the* theological teacher of my student years.'[7] Herrmann's position concerning the church could not have escaped him. It is therefore not without a bit of irony that just as Barth was to begin his ministry in the church, five minutes, in fact, before he was to ascend to the pulpit, he received in the mail the fourth edition of Herrmann's *Ethik* as a gift from the author, the coincidence of which Barth viewed as a 'dedication of my whole future.'[8]

---

[3]For an account of Herrmann's influence upon Barth, see McCormack, *Barth's Theology*, 49-68; see also Hendrikus Berkhof, *Two Hundred Years of Theology: Report of A Personal Journey*, trans. John Vriend (Grand Rapids: Eerdmans, 1989), 179-207. Barth himself critically appraised the theology of his former teacher in the 1925 essay 'The Principles of Dogmatics according to Wilhelm Herrmann,' in *Theology and Church: Shorter Writings 1920-1928*, trans. Louise P. Smith (New York: Harper & Row, 1962), 238-271. That Barth found Herrmann's signature on the manifesto particularly disconcerting is documented by McCormack, *Barth's Theology*, 112-114.

[4]Barth, 'Wilhelm Herrmann,' 239.

[5]Herrmann, *Ethik*, 5th ed. (Tübingen: J.C.B. Mohr, 1913), 180ff. Cited in Klaus Scholder, *The Churches and the Third Reich - Volume 1: Preliminary History and the Time of Illusions 1918-1934*, trans. John Bowden (Philadelphia: Fortress Press, 1988), 38.

[6]Herrmann, *Ethik*, §25 'Die Aufgabe des Christen in der Welt.' Barth would later credit Herrmann for recognizing a relationship between ethics and ecclesiology (*CD III.4*, 516). This is one of the very few remarks concerning his former revered teacher that Barth would make in later years.

[7]Barth, 'Wilhelm Herrmann,' 238.

[8]Ibid., 238.

Herrmann's attitude toward the church was an ambivalent one, evidenced not simply in the limited discussion of the church in his ethical work.[9] Like Harnack, Herrmann rejected any form of doctrinal orthodoxy as contrary to Christian faith, and he opposed any enforced subscription to a traditional creed or even to the Scriptures, maintaining that faith cannot be prescribed but must be personally experienced. To see faith as the assent of the intellect and will to dogmas of the church was to live through the faith of others — a religious impossibility. Such an attempt was, to borrow an anachronistic term, inauthentic faith. It was also, according to Herrmann, a transgression of Luther's *sola fide*, in that beside faith as personal trust in Christ was set the knowledge of and assent to doctrines as necessary for salvation. In this sense, Herrmann was a strong opponent of any form of ecclesiastical authority or traditionalism.[10]

Yet on the other hand, Herrmann did not consider himself a liberal, a person Herrmann defined as one who sought God in human existence through an appeal to reason, history, or mysticism, while taking flight from Christ, Scripture, and church altogether. He opposed mysticism as strongly as orthodoxy, for while orthodoxy is the attempt to live through the faith of others expressed in doctrine, mysticism is the attempt to experience God directly apart from Jesus' mediation of God through his personal life, a course of action which Herrmann contended leads into pure subjectivism. In both cases, an experience of Christ himself is absent, as both

---

[9]For the following account, see Wilhelm Herrmann, *The Communion of the Christian with God*, ed. Robert T. Voelkel, trans. J. S. Stanyon and R. W. Stewart (Philadelphia: Fortress Press, 1971); and Herrmann's posthumously published *Dogmatik*, (Gotha/Stuttgart: Verlag Friedrich Andreas Perthes, 1925); ET: *Systematic Theology*, trans. Nathaniel Micklem and Kenneth A. Saunders (New York: Macmillan, 1927); see also James D. Smart, *The Divided Mind of Modern Theology: Karl Barth and Rudolf Bultmann 1908-1933* (Philadelphia: Westminster Press, 1967), 33-36; McCormack, *Barth's Theology*, 49-68; Gary Dorrien, *The Barthian Revolt in Modern Theology: Theology Without Weapons* (Louisville: Westminister John Knox Press, 2000), 15-27; 168-173.

[10]Herrmann's *Dogmatik* for this reason was not a true dogmatics in the traditional sense, i.e., a presentation of the church's dogma and doctrine to be confessed and taught. Dogmatics for Herrmann was rather a *Religionswissenschaft*, a science of religion, that attempted to define religion over against other intellectual and cultural forces as well as present the distinctive quality of the Christian religion in relation to its faith and explicate the ideas that originate from this faith. See Herrmann, *Dogmatik*, 1-2; ET 15-16. Herrmann states: 'It is for the science of religion in every such community to make clear and defend from distortion the religious experience of its members, and the expression of religion common to them all' (*Dogmatik*, 4; ET 19).

orthodoxy and mysticism are ultimately attempts to escape from history, either into timeless and eternal dogmas or into unmediated experience.[11]

For Herrmann, 'personal Christianity' was 'the communion of the soul with the living God through the mediation of Christ.'[12] He thus affirmed the transcendence of God and the uniqueness of the revelation of God in Jesus, which he declared to consist in the redemptive power of Jesus' ethical character, his 'inner life.' This 'inner life' is communicated through a succession of persons who have experienced this living reality of Jesus' inner life, as well as through Scripture, which places persons in immediate contact with this personal life. So Herrmann's theology rejected both ecclesiastical authority and traditional church doctrine (he repudiated Chalcedonian Christology),[13] while yet retaining a place for the community as the medium of Jesus' inner life and even for doctrine if it was seen not as prescriptive for faith but as expressive of a community's experience of faith itself (and in this he differed from Harnack).

It should be noted that while Herrmann retained a significant place for the church in his theology, it is primarily a formal place, in that the church is solely the collective community of those who have experienced faith and the means of communicating that faith in history. Herrmann's ecclesiology was quite thin and undeveloped. The section of the *Dogmatik* dedicated to the church in its own right is given a few scant pages of discussion and comes second to last of all topics discussed (the last topic was the Trinity, in true Schleiermacherian fashion).[14] The church for Herrmann serves a simple mediatorial function between the individual believer and Christ, as it preserves the 'portrait' or 'picture' of Christ [*Bild*] that is the impression that Christ's ethical character made upon the first disciples. This 'picture' was transmitted from them to others and is carried by the Christian community throughout history, and the perception of this picture of Jesus in the community is the ground for the inception of religious faith in the individual.[15] Herrmann states:

---

[11]'The real facts of the case, then, are that ecclesiastical dogma and the piety which culminates in mysticism are bound up the one with the other, and that the Christian Church can abide by neither. For she cannot allow herself to be placed permanently in a position where she must be separated from Christ if she is to be lifted into communion with God. The Christian cannot cut himself loose from that history in which he has found the revelation of God to himself' (Herrmann, *Communion*, 36).

[12]Ibid., 9.

[13]*Dogmatik*, 93-97; ET 139-145. As shall be seen, it was Barth's recovery of Chalcedonian Christology which led to a revitalization of his ecclesiological thought.

[14]Ibid., 100-102; ET 148-151; cf. Herrmann, *Communion*, 189-195.

[15]Herrmann maintained, however, that morality, and specifically inner moral conflict, is a precondition for a saving encounter with Christ. See *Ethik*, 90-96.

In the Christian fellowship we are made acquainted, not merely with the external course of Jesus' lot in life and of His work in history, but we are also led into His presence and receive a *picture* of His inner life. For this we are certainly dependent, in the first instance, upon other men. For the *picture* of Jesus' inner life could be preserved only by those who had experienced the emancipating influence of that fact upon themselves....We need communion with Christians in order that, from the *picture* of Jesus which His church has preserved, there may shine forth that inner life which is the heart of it.[16]

This understanding of the church as the bearer of the picture, or portrait [*Bild*], of Christ that it communicates to others in order to effect redemption was not unique to Herrmann. It originated with Schleiermacher[17] and would continue in the liberal tradition through Tillich.[18] It was this understanding of the church as the bearer of Christ, the subjectivity of the church replacing Christ's own, along with the conception of revelation as the portrait of Christ and a permanent possession of the community, that Barth would completely reject, as will be seen.

In the end, it was the individual and the individual's faith, not the church, that was of utmost interest and the true value-holder in Herrmann's understanding of religion. Herrmann was a true citizen of the nineteenth century and exemplified its religious individualism. Nevertheless, he could, or would, not abandon the church, a corollary of the fact that he could not abandon the historical figure of Jesus. In this sense Herrmann refused to let go of a historically-mediated revelation in the particular person of Jesus, though of course he understood 'history' in a unique sense, for the

---

[16]Herrmann, *Communion*, 72-73 (emphasis added). Herrmann could also attribute the communication of this 'picture' to the direct perception of it in Scripture. See Herrmann, *Dogmatik*, 27-29; ET 49-52.

[17]Schleiermacher states that 'the individual even to-day receives from the picture of Christ, which exists in the community as at once a corporate act and a corporate possession, the impression of the sinless perfection of Jesus, which becomes for him at the same time the perfect consciousness of sin and the removal of the misery' (Friedrich Schleiermacher, *Der christliche Glaube*, vol. 2, ed. Martin Redeker [Berlin: Walter de Gruyter, 1960], 21-22; cf. 138; ET: *The Christian Faith*, ed. H. R. Mackintosh and J. S. Stewart, trans. Macintosh, Stewart, et al. [Edinburgh: T & T Clark, 1989], 364; cf. 467).

[18]'The appearance of the Christ in an individual person presupposes the community out of which he came and the community which he creates. Of course, the criterion of both is the picture of Jesus as the Christ; but, without them, this criterion never could have appeared' (Paul Tillich, *Systematic Theology: Vol. 2 – Existence and The Christ* [Chicago: University of Chicago Press, 1957], 136).

portrait of Christ that gave rise to faith was not determined by historical science but was a constant possession of the Christian community.

It became more and more difficult, however, for Herrmann to maintain the uniqueness of Jesus for revelation and faith when revelation itself was defined in terms of the power of Christ's ethical character. Such ethical character could be found in others, even if to a lesser degree, and this quality of humanity's inner life thereby would have to be seen as a presence of God in humanity itself. This danger of immanentalism threatened the uniqueness of the historical figure of Jesus for Herrmann's theology. Herrmann had opened himself to this danger by placing the moral conscience beside Christ as a second objective fact that provided the ground for the consciousness of the communion of the Christian with God.[19] Yet Herrmann, like Schleiermacher before him, firmly clung to the absolute significance of Jesus for the genesis of faith, and this in turn entailed a commitment to the church as the community and communicator of faith in history. The tenaciousness of Herrmann's grip upon Jesus and his importance for faith was a legacy passed on not only to Barth but also, though in a very different way, to Herrmann's other famous student, Rudolf Bultmann.

Herrmann's example illustrates the intricate relation between Christ and the church and the ambiguity of this relation that was passed on to Barth. Herrmann's own *Ethik* left little place for the church as a sphere of significant Christian ethical action, and it is not unwarranted to say that Barth's own early Christian activity in the main revolved around socialist and political involvements as much as or more than around church activities, even considering that he was a pastor and the seriousness with which he took this calling. At the same time, such socialist activity did demonstrate Barth's early movement away from Herrmann's ethical and religious individualism, as well as Herrmann's conservative and broad acceptance of the existing social order.

More importantly, the danger of sacrificing the uniqueness of the particular revelation in Christ to a general revelation given in moral conscience was an implicit though constant danger in Herrmann's theology, even though he himself rejected any such reduction. Such a move would, of course, make the historical person of Jesus superfluous for faith. It would also render the church irrelevant, as revelation would not be historically mediated from Jesus through a Christian community but would be a universal datum of human existence. Barth's early theology was dedicated to overcoming these problems and attempted to do so by ultimately rejecting the liberal program and the inheritance that Herrmann bequeathed to Barth. From the outbreak of the first World War onward, Barth's theology increasingly focused on a critical

---

[19] '*The second objective ground* of the Christian's consciousness that God communes with him *is that we hear within ourselves the demand of the moral law*' (Herrmann, *Communion*, 103; cf. 102-103).

examination of theological liberalism and the search for a new starting point for theology in a revelation of the Word. It might even be said that Barth's theological travels were the search for a true Christology as the basis of revelation, and thus an attempt to overcome Herrmann's own problematic Christology.[20] Barth also inherited from Herrmann an ambiguous ecclesiology, and the solutions to this ecclesiological problem followed solutions to the other and came later in time. At this point it is simply worth noting that for Barth ecclesiological solutions followed Christological ones.

One is certainly justified in maintaining that Barth in fact did not develop a complete ecclesiology until the latter volumes of the *Church Dogmatics*. Barth's early treatises on the church were certainly more critical and occasional than constructive and systematic. Yet it would of course be untrue to claim that only in the *Church Dogmatics* has Barth addressed the issue of the church. For while Barth's early theology centered upon the topics of revelation, Christology, and the Trinity, as well as the questions of natural theology and theological method, the question of the church was never far behind. For this reason, it is important to recognize that the constructive ecclesiology of the *Church Dogmatics* and its underlying convictions and principles find their origin in the critical battles and constructive work of Barth's early years as he traveled from Switzerland to Germany and back again. These battles were carried on at two fronts, with opponents on the left and on the right. Barth's early struggles were taken up with the opponent on the left, Neo-Protestantism and the liberal tradition. Increasingly, however, it was the opponent on the right that was to interest and engage Barth, that of Roman Catholicism. As will become clear, Barth's own constructive work in ecclesiology would be carried out with an eye on each opponent, and Barth's intent was to avoid the errors that he perceived were endemic to each. It is therefore appropriate to view Barth's early writings on the church within the context of his engagement in these conflicts.[21]

---

[20]See, for example, Barth's own assessment of Herrmann's Christology, 'Wilhelm Herrmann,' 263-266.

[21]It is true that Barth later also battled on a third front, namely, against National Socialism, and that this battle also shaped his thought on the church. This point may be granted, but a crucial difference must be noted. Barth's battles with liberalism and Catholicism were battles with *Christian* traditions that possessed their own ecclesiologies against which Barth developed his own understanding. Barth's battle with National Socialism was a battle not with a rival Christian tradition but with a pagan one.

2. The Struggle against Neo-Protestantism and Its Church Concept

A. Revolt Against the Church-Culture Synthesis and the Romans Commentary

As has been noted, Barth's early theology was marked by a restlessness and dissatisfaction with the prevailing cultural situation and the theological justification that undergirded it.[22] Barth despised this cultural synthesis of Christianity and culture, of church and state, of religion and political establishment, though this outlook was widespread and shared by conservative and liberal alike.[23] As early as 1916 he could decry those who would attempt to possess the righteousness of God through appeals to reason, morality, or even through religion and Christianity itself.[24] All were 'towers of Babel,' vain attempts to reach God and exercises in self-deception. In the midst of the problems of Europe, Barth contended, some may attempt to escape through appeals to the church's preaching and morality or to national religious life, but this

---

[22]McCormack states: 'On a conscious level certainly, Barth's break with liberal theology can be traced to the events of August 1914. But on a deeper level, the break had already been underway for some time. For several years, the "social question" had been for Barth and Thurneysen a primary source of their unrest and it was in socialism that they saw the most effective protest against all that which exists. Since academic theology in Germany — whether in its liberal or positive form — was a most important prop for the maintenance of the political and economic *status quo*, Barth's socialism already placed him on a collision course with the reigning theology. To put the matter more concretely, if Barth's disappointment over the ethical failure of his theological teachers was the impetus which sent him in search of *a new theology*, his search for *a new world* had been set in motion much earlier' (McCormack, *A Scholastic of a Higher Order: The development of Karl Barth's theology, 1921-31* [Ann Arbor: UMI, Ph.D Diss.,1989], 22-23; see also 32-33).

[23]Scholder notes: 'Although there were nearly unbridgeable differences in German Protestantism between the conservative majority and the liberal minority in understanding what specifically was the religious and moral task of the present, there was no doubt that there was a task. Conservatives and liberals were united in stressing that the present crisis did not alter religious and moral values, and that on the contrary their significance was much more recognizable. While the content of moral and religious standards might be argued over by conservatives, nationalist Protestants and liberals, the principle that religion was the means and object of moral development and renewal remained intact. Only if we keep this in mind as the only absolutely self-evident and undisputed common ground and foundation of German Protestantism will we understand the weight and significance of a theology [i.e., dialectical theology] which fundamentally and radically challenged precisely this premise' (*The Churches and the Third Reich*, Vol. 1, 39-40; cf. 37-40).

[24]Karl Barth, 'Die Gerechtigkeit Gottes,' in *Das Wort Gottes und die Theologie* (München: Chr. Kaiser Verlag, 1925), 5-17. ET: Karl Barth, 'The Righteousness of God,' in *The Word of God and the Word of Man*, trans. Douglas Horton (Gloucester: Peter Smith, 1978), 9-27.

was an exercise in delusion. 'And we are Christians! Our *Volk* is a Christian *Volk*! A wonderful illusion, but an illusion, a self-deception!'[25]

Barth's references to the church during this early period are marked by strong criticism.[26] The church stands on the side of religion, a human construct of *hubris*, and the church is a form of religion itself.[27] As such, it stands under the divine judgment of a 'Wholly Other' God who opposes a sinful world. Barth's charges against the church parallel his general indictment of the prevailing theology of culture which, he argues, seeks to domesticate God and lay claim to God's revelation for the purposes of furthering its own aspirations and programs. In the process, religiosity is set up as an idol in the place of God. For this substitution, the church itself stands guilty before God and falls under judgment in the same manner as the rest of the world so that there can be no absolute, or even strong, distinction between the church and the world. The apex of this critical phase of Barth's judgment on the church is the second edition of the *Römerbrief*.[28]

Already in the first edition of *Romans*, Barth's earlier sense of social unrest was eclipsed by a preoccupation with the otherness of the Kingdom of God. This theological unrest was not based on the vagaries of changing social conditions, but upon the eternal distinction between God and the world that sets all human achievements in question. Such was an absolute and eschatological unrest rather than

---

[25]Ibid., 12 (my translation); ET 20.

[26]See, for example, Barth's 1920 article, 'Biblische Fragen, Einsichten und Ausblicke,' in *Das Wort Gottes und die Theologie* (ET: 'Biblical Questions, Insights, and Vistas,' in *The Word of God and the Word of Man*), where Barth states that the church has done more harm than good in relation to the question of the knowledge of God, 72; ET 54. Cf. 83-84; ET 72. See also Busch, *Karl Barth*, 86-87.

[27]Ibid., 81; ET 68-69.

[28]The first edition of the *Römerbrief* was published in 1919; the second edition in 1922. The second edition is here discussed. While from the standpoint of Barth's understanding of revelation the development between the two editions is significant, Barth's understanding of the church changes little between them. Barth could say in the first edition: 'The church has crucified Christ. The way of Christ and the way of the church are from now on two separate ways' (*Der Römerbrief [Erste Fassung] 1919*, ed. Hermann Schmidt, [Zürich: Theologischer Verlag Zürich, 1985], 361). He would reiterate this criticism in the later edition. Such criticisms of the church would not lessen but intensify in the second edition, which stands as the apex of Barth's critical phase. The greatest difference between the editions is seen in the fact that Barth replaces the concepts of 'Tribulation,' 'Guilt,' and 'Hope' in the first commentary with 'The Tribulation of the Church,' 'The Guilt of the Church,' and 'The Hope of the Church,' marking Barth's recognition not only of the church's failure but also its promise and necessity, as will be seen below. Such a recognition marks the hinge between Barth's critical and constructive ecclesiological thought, though Barth would not retract his criticisms.

a relative and cultural one in that this condition could not be alleviated through transforming social conditions but required a divine solution.[29] This perspective was sharpened in Barth's second edition of the *Romans* commentary.[30]

Gary Dorrien maintains that Barth's radical eschatological perspective of this period made systematic theology impossible, and it is true that the *Romans* commentary cannot be considered a systematic work in any real sense.[31] If anything, it is an expressionistic polemic against current theological trends rather than a systematic treatise presenting a fully developed theological program.[32] Recognition of this fact, however, should not lead one to conclude that the *Romans* commentary is without a consistent theological viewpoint. In the preface to the second edition Barth stated: 'If I have a system, it is limited to a recognition of what Kierkegaard called the "infinite qualitative distinction" between time and eternity, and to my regarding this as possessing negative as well as positive significance.'[33] Such an approach is indeed more standpoint than system,[34] and such a standpoint is perhaps most accurately characterized as an infinite distinction between God and the world articulated in an eschatological dialectic of time and eternity. On this account, the Gospel does not proclaim the divinization of humanity, but a God who is utterly distinct [*ganz anders*] from the world, and upon whom humanity is entirely dependent for revelation, for no knowledge of God is possible apart from God himself. This revelation comes in the form of Jesus Christ, who is the Gospel in his person, the point at which the two worlds of God and humanity meet and pull apart, where two planes intersect. One is the known plane of creation, fallen in sin, the world of humanity, time, and things. This plane is intersected by another, unknown plane, the world of the Father, primal creation, and final redemption. The intersection of these two planes, these two worlds, is Jesus Christ, the point of contact between them. In Christ the *Deus absconditus* is the *Deus revelatus*.[35]

---

[29]McCormack, *Scholastic*, 64-65.

[30]For the shift to a 'consistent eschatology,' see McCormack, *Barth's Theology*, 207-240.

[31]Gary Dorrien, *The Barthian Revolt*, 68.

[32]Cf. McCormack, *Barth's Theology*, 244-245; McCormack, *Scholastic*, 114-115.

[33]*Der Römerbrief*, 2nd ed. (München: Chr. Kaiser Verlag, 1923), XIV. ET: *The Epistle to the Romans*, trans. Edwyn C. Hoskyns (Oxford: Oxford University Press, 1968) 10.

[34]Barth would later state in an address of 1922 that 'what I might conceivably call "my theology" becomes, when I look at it closely, a single point, and that not, as one might demand as the least qualification of a true theology, a *stand*point, but rather a *mathematical* point upon which one cannot stand — a *view*point merely' (Barth, 'Not und Verheißung der christlichen Verkündigung,' in *Das Wort Gottes und die Theologie*, 99; ET: 'The Need and Promise of Christian Preaching,' in *The Word of God and the Word of Man*, 97-98).

[35]*Römerbrief*, 4; also 408; ET 28; also 422.

Barth contends that from our side of the chasm between time and eternity, however, this revelation in Christ is imperceptible. Only in the resurrection is the revelation in Christ made known to humanity: 'The Resurrection is the revelation: the disclosing of Jesus as the Christ, the appearing of God, and the apprehending of God in Jesus...In the Resurrection the new world of the Holy Spirit touches the old world of the flesh, but touches it as a tangent touches a circle, that is, without touching it.'[36] The revelation in Christ is in no way a self-evident truth, and revelation is in fact a paradox, the veiling of God in human flesh, and the concealing of God in the act of disclosure itself.[37]

Such a view of revelation, it should be noted, leaves little place for a true incarnation. Indeed, God's revelation is not the person of Jesus as a historical figure, but neither is it revealed in his historical life. Revelation pertains only to the resurrection event, through which God is revealed in the person of Christ, and such revelation is an entirely eschatological event.[38] This limitation of revelation does not entail that Barth denied that revelation ever encountered history, but it does point to the fact that there is no historical content to the revelation event. Barth's struggle in the *Römerbrief* was to retain a place for revelation that was in but not of history, i.e., occurring within history but not arising from the stream of history and its matrix of causes. Barth's emphasis was certainly upon the latter to the endangerment of the former, threatening to lose any reality of a historical revelation whatsoever. As an eternal point between two worlds, as a tangent touching a circle, the revelation here articulated makes a true incarnation in time extremely problematic, if not impossible.

Yet apart from this revelation, no matter how isolated, God cannot be known. For Barth, God is a hidden God, though, paradoxically, it is precisely on account of this fact that he 'bestows life and breath and all things.'[39] God's power set forth in the resurrection of Christ cannot be identified with a power of history, nature, or the human soul. It is because and not in spite of this, Barth states, that God can be a

---

[36]Ibid., 5-6; ET 29-30.

[37]Ibid., 70-74; cf. 261-263; ET 96-99; cf. 278-280.

[38]Ibid., 182-186; ET 202-205.

[39]Barth's concept of the 'hiddenness' of God is a complex idea, involving Lutheran and Calvinistic theological convictions pertaining to God's transcendence and human sinfulness, Kantian epistemological presuppositions, and Kierkegaardian philosophical notions, as well as Barth's own unique understanding of the dialectic of judgment and grace and of time and eternity. To explicate these ideas would go beyond the bounds of this study, but they are addressed by Eberhard Busch in 'God is God: The Meaning of a Controversial Formula and the Fundamental Problem of Speaking About God,' *Princeton Seminary Bulletin* N.S. 7 (1986): 101-113.

saving God.[40] This is often overlooked when Barth's work is considered.[41] Barth's message in *Romans* is certainly a negative one, as he takes aim and shoots down any attempt to find a revelation of God in historical events, nature, human self-awareness, or moral conscience. He presents a radical critique of a compromised church and complacent social order and the natural theology that legitimated them. Nevertheless, Barth's negation undermines all human attempts at salvation only in order to make room for God's salvation, the salvation that God alone can provide. True, even in God's salvation the world remains the world — the present reality of existence continues, as the world and all persons remain under the 'burden of sin and the curse of death.'[42] Knowledge of God and of this salvation is therefore never accessible without a direct act of God. But the human impossibility can be overtaken by a divine possibility, and this is a message of hope. Barth thus sets two movements against one another, that from humanity to God (religion), and that of God to humanity (revelation), seeing the second as succeeding where the former can only fail.

Barth's rejection of all attempts to discern divine revelation in the movements of history, culture, or the human soul is therefore an attempt to end the confusion between God and humanity that results in the manipulation of God for the furtherance of human goals and aspirations, whatever these causes may be — whether church, state, or family life, whether individualism or collectivism, nationalism or internationalism, humanitarianism or ecclesiasticism. Barth contends that by safely assuming that we know who God is, we place God in our world as its highest principle and thereby place him on our side of the line between time and eternity. In so doing we reveal our own unrighteousness and attempt to control God and be master of the relationship between God and ourselves. This can only end in idolatry, as we substitute ourselves for God, and thus a 'No-God' for the true God.[43]

Barth's consistent eschatological perspective, emphasizing the radical *diastasis* between God and the world and the complete non-temporality of the Kingdom of God, is an attack upon such idolatry. Barth constantly reiterates that no historical movement or event can be identified as God's revelation. Revelation, he maintains, touches history only as a tangent touches a circle, and this point of the tangent is the resurrection of Christ, which is not a historical event. All historical events and realities stand on the worldly side of the God-world divide, and as such, fall under God's judgment. The church, standing on this side of the abyss, is therefore not a special exception but a demonstration of this general rule.

---

[40]*Römerbrief*, 11; ET 36.

[41]See Bruce McCormack, 'The Unheard Message of Karl Barth,' in *Word and World*, v. 14 (1994): 59-66.

[42]*Römerbrief*, 13; ET 37-38.

[43]Ibid., 19-20; 25-27; 447; ET 44-45; 49-51; 462-463.

Barth discusses the church in the context of Paul's epistle and its chapters nine through eleven, Paul's apologia for Jewish rejection of Christ and the ongoing place of Israel in redemptive history. Barth's exegesis is original, to say the least, as he identifies the church with Israel's unbelief, and portrays it in terms of disobedience and faithlessness, rather than as a believing community set over against an unbelieving world. Barth equates Israel, the church, and the world of religion in his exposition and states that here religion is at its height, not in a 'debased form,' but as the 'ideal and perfect church.' The church, however, while the apex of human achievement, still stands on this side of the abyss separating the world from God. The church confronts the Gospel as the last human possibility confronting the 'impossible possibility,' the final achievement of humanity facing the divine miracle of grace. It is consequently both the height of human achievement and the height of blasphemy, for the church is the place where 'the eternity of revelation is transformed into a temporal, concrete, directly visible thing in this world.'[44] In essence, the church is the highest attempt to domesticate God: 'The church is the more or less extensive and energetic attempt to humanize the divine, to temporalize it, to make it a thing, to secularize it, to make it a practical "Something," and all for the benefit of persons who cannot live without God, yet cannot live with the living God either.'[45] For this reason, the Gospel and the church are antithetical to one another: 'Here it is clear that the opposition between the Gospel and the church is fundamental and infinite all along the line. Here one standpoint stands against another. Here one is in the right and another in the wrong. The Gospel is the abolition [*Aufhebung*] of the church, as the church is the abolition [*Aufhebung*] of the Gospel.'[46]

The key distinction for Barth is thus not between those who believe the Gospel and those who do not, a distinction between one group of persons and another, but the ultimate and final distinction between God and humanity. All persons in the church share in the guilt and tribulation of the world and of the church itself — in the light of the righteousness of God, all are sinners, and the relative distinction between persons 'more or less' righteous is meaningless.[47]

Since all persons share in sin and guilt, Barth states that the pure Gospel cannot be declared by a human voice, and there can be no identification between the Gospel and the proclamation of the church. Just as the church stands on the side of religion against the Gospel, so does its proclamation, and as there can be no identity between revelation and church proclamation, so the one who proclaims the Gospel remains a person of the church, sharing in its misery and its guilt. All human thoughts, deeds,

---

[44]Ibid., 316; ET 332.

[45]Ibid., 316-317 (my translation); ET 332.

[46]Ibid., 317 (my translation); ET 333.

[47]Ibid., 317, 321; ET 333; 336.

and possessions, even if orthodox, can never be anything more than a parable (*Gleichnis*). Barth states: 'Whenever we fail to discern the immortal in the parable of the transitory, we have served the church and not proclaimed the Gospel — and who besides God can protect us against this great likelihood?'[48] To focus upon the distinction between righteous and unrighteous persons is a mistake: 'We have no opportunity to be in the right against others who stand against us in the wrong. God's standpoint is safeguarded against all other standpoints. He is in the right and we are in the wrong.'[49]

Barth does not, however, simply want to oppose God and creation, and he does not want to eliminate the concept of guilt and substitute a Neoplatonic concept of non-being in its place. He reminds the reader that 'creatureliness is a curse only in virtue of our sin.'[50] Barth's criticisms of the church are harsh and strongly stated yet are directed to the church's tribulation on account of its guilt. This guilt is incurred as the church does not recognize and protect the *diastasis* between God and the world but attempts to encroach upon it. The church looks to identify God with a discernible movement in history or an element of human consciousness. In doing so, the church demonstrates its guilt, and this guilt results from the continual avoidance of the true tribulation which the church itself must acknowledge, its utter separation and reliance upon God. The height of the church's sin and attempt at self-justification is the crucifixion of Christ. Barth proclaims: 'It was the Church, not the world, which crucified Christ.'[51]

Such pronouncements could easily lead one to conclude (and many have so concluded) that in the *Romans* commentary the church is only seen as sinful and without any positive place in God's salvific purposes. Barth, however, states that even in the crucifixion, at the apex of the church's sin, the church is not abandoned to its tribulation and guilt. For Barth the church is not given over to judgment and left without hope, for the church is in fact the locus of hope precisely in being the locus of judgment. It is the hopelessness of the church, its utter failure, that points beyond itself to the hope that is in God alone, as the given reality of the church points beyond itself to the non-givenness of God. It is here in the church, and nowhere else, that such a witness exists: 'It is sentimental liberal self-deception to think that direct roads lead from nature and history, from art, morality, science or even religion to the impossible possibility of God.'[52] Such roads lead rather to the church, and only here, at the failed end of the human and ecclesiastical attempt to reach God, when it is

---

[48]Ibid., 317 (my translation); ET 333.

[49]Ibid., 318 (my translation); ET 334.

[50]Ibid., 346-347; ET 362-363.

[51]Ibid., 370-373; ET 386-389.

[52]Ibid., 321-322; ET 337-338.

realized that one can neither go round, nor go through, the church, can the problem of God be radically and seriously raised. So even in its limitation, and precisely because of it, the church can serve a positive function by pointing beyond itself and its inadequacy and need to God. The church is, however, not a direct way or path to God, but directs attention to the fact that no such path exists. Here, where the human attempt fails, God will succeed, and for this reason the church can be seen not only in negative terms but in a positive light. The church cannot be ignored or left behind precisely because it is there that the relation between God and humanity is addressed. In the stuttering and inadequate speech of the church's proclamation, God himself may choose to speak, and in this divine proclamation the church is both condemned and established, killed and made alive.[53]

As already observed, Barth is concerned with the absolute distinction between God and the world and not with relative distinctions within or without the church among persons. He continues this line of thought in his distinction between the church of Esau and the church of Jacob. The church of Esau, on the one hand, is described as the church where no miracle appears, where in speaking and hearing about God, persons in the church are shown to be liars. The church of Jacob, on the other hand, is the church where the miracle occurs, and where, beyond the lies of persons, the truth of God is revealed.[54] The distinction and relation between these two churches corresponds to Barth's unique conception of the distinction between the visible and invisible church, and this distinction is crucial for understanding Barth's ecclesiology in *Romans*. The church of Esau and the church of Jacob are not two churches that stand over against one another, but two aspects, or realities, of the one church. The church of Esau is the visible church, the church in history and concretely found in specific locations, such as Rome, Wittenberg, or Geneva. It is marked by flaws and failures, by corruption, reform, and schism, and it alone is knowable and observable. It is the subject of the history of the church. The church of Jacob, however, is the invisible church, the unobservable and unknowable church, without name or place or history. It is constituted by God's free grace, his calling and election. We can speak only of the church of Esau, but the theme to which we refer is the church of Jacob. The tribulation of the church is the absolute distinction between these churches which makes all question of improving the visible church and addressing its problems secondary and of only relative importance. The crisis which plagues the church is simply that 'God is God, and that he is the God of Jacob.'[55] In this sentence lies the

---

[53]Ibid., 324-326; ET 340-341. See also McCormack, *Barth's Theology*, 282-288; McCormack, *Scholastic*, 182-194.

[54]Ibid., 326-327; ET 341-342.

[55]For the significance of the phrase 'God is God' in Barth's theology, see Busch, 'God is God,' 101-113.

condemnation and hope of the church. Can the church ever truly be the church of Jacob, or is it condemned forever to be the church of Esau? Should it abandon the attempt to speak of its proper theme, the Gospel, and concede that the church of Jacob exists only in eternity? Barth states that while one must seriously ponder such questions which point to the tribulation of the church, the duty of the Christian is to wrestle with God, knowing that this God, the God of Jacob, is a God who blesses after such struggle. It is precisely where human hope and aspirations end, when the church recognizes itself as the church of Esau, that the miracle of God can enter and realize the church's proper identity as the church of Jacob.[56]

The church therefore denotes all those who, 'touched by the breath of revelation, call earnestly upon God, wait for Him, and keep His commandments.' This is the miracle — when the Word of God is truly spoken and truly heard, then, hidden in that moment of time occurs the eternal 'Moment' of revelation. In that eternal moment, the church of Esau becomes the church of Jacob. This remains, however, only a divine possibility, never a human one.[57] The tragedy comes when the church fails to realize its own weakness and refuses to cast itself upon the mercy of God and instead seeks to strengthen and legitimate itself, its own traditions and customs. Such refusal is itself a failure to realize the church's own tribulation.[58] The hope of the church is the promise of the church, the promise that the Word of God will succeed where the words of men and women fail. The basis of the church's tribulation is its hope, its death to itself is its life to God.[59] In light of this tribulation, the church's proper task is to devote itself to God and to the service of the Word.[60] It is in this proclamation of the Word that God's revelation occurs.

In this revelation that God brings about, however, a crisis exists, for the Word of God is either heard or not heard, and this raises the issue of election. Corresponding to the two-fold nature of the church as the church of Esau and the church of Jacob is a double predestination in which persons either hear or do not hear the Word, and on this account belong either to the church of Esau or Jacob, as the reprobate or the elect. This determination of persons belongs solely to God, and Barth

---

[56]*Römerbrief*, 326-327; ET 341-342. Barth would present this dialectical 'solution' again in 'Das Wort Gottes als Aufgabe der Theologie,' in *Das Wort Gottes und die Theologie*, 156-178. ET: 'The Word of God and the Task of the Ministry,' in *The Word of God and the Word of Man*, 183-217. Barth states: '*As ministers, we ought to speak of God. We are human, however, and so cannot speak of God. We ought therefore to recognize both* our obligation and our inability *and by that very recognition give God the glory*' (158; ET 186).

[57]Ibid., 326; ET 342.

[58]Ibid., 328-329; ET 344.

[59]Ibid., 329; ET 345.

[60]Ibid., 351-353; ET 367-369.

here evidences a highly actualistic understanding of election and reprobation.[61] Yet even in predestination, Barth is ultimately not concerned with a division of humanity into two groups, one elect and the other reprobate, according to traditional Augustinian and Reformed understandings (Barth goes so far as to say that when the Reformers spoke of a quantitative conception of predestination they were speaking 'mythologically'). For Barth, election and reprobation belong to all persons — predestination does not divide persons, but unites them. All people are Esau — yet, in the moment of revelation, all are Jacob. In time, all persons are vessels of wrath, but in eternity, all are vessels of mercy. The election of the church thus occurs only in faith; it cannot be empirically observed. The church that is seen remains always the church of Esau, and the true church lives only through the promise of the Spirit, which is its basis and hope.[62] All persons are thus the objects of wrath and of mercy, of tribulation and hope, and therefore to attempt to divide persons into two discrete classes of individuals is to destroy the dialectic of time and eternity.[63] For this reason, 'church' and 'world' should also not be seen as two discrete entities, but as two aspects, dialectically related, of a single reality. It should be noted that here Barth's future universalistic tendency is already evident.[64]

The church is both the elect and the reprobate, the church of Jacob and the church of Esau, the invisible and the visible church. These realities, however, do not stand apart from one another on equal footing, for they are rooted in the sovereign will of God, and God's will is not divided. A distinct order and specific pattern belong to God's action. God is the God of Esau because he is the God of Jacob, the God of tribulation and rejection because he is the God of help and election. God's 'No' serves God's 'Yes.' Rejection is thus only the shadow side of election. In the language of Luther, God slays in order to make alive.[65] Barth states: 'The tribulation and guilt of the church is a "Moment" in the invisible, divine scheme of advance from rejection to election, from "No" to "Yes," from Esau to Jacob, from Pharaoh to Moses.'[66] So what is united in God and eternity must be perceived in time as a two-fold reality, election and rejection.

Barth's understanding of the hope of the church in revelation and election is related to the fact that however strong his criticism of the church was to be, he never contemplated leaving the church nor advocated an escape from it. Yes, the church

---

[61]Ibid., 328-329; ET 343-345.

[62]Ibid., 330-332; 344-345; ET 346-348; 360-361.

[63]Ibid., 387; ET 402.

[64]Ibid., 390; ET 405.

[65]Ibid., 334; cf. 342-343; ET 350; cf. 358.

[66]Ibid., 386; ET 401.

stands within history and thus against God, but to try to abandon the church for a more righteous perspective and course of action is impossible. To attempt this is in fact to try to realize a higher point of a superior knowledge or method above the sin of the church — but this is what Barth himself denies exists, for every human place stands under sin and judgment. The Christian should not leave the church nor act as if there were no Gospel, but rather serve in the church, which is directed by, or conformed to [*gerichtet durch*], the Kingdom of God, all the while recognizing the eternal opposition between the Gospel and the church, and sharing not only in its task but in its guilt and failure. The one who hears the Gospel does so from within the church, all the while knowing that the church means suffering, never triumph. For this reason, there is no such thing as a non-ecclesiastical relation with God, no more a possibility than the innocence of paradise. The tribulation of the church is the tribulation of the person within the church. The true prophet, Barth states, would rather be in hell with the church than with the pietists in heaven, for it is there in disconsolation that there is the hope of salvation, not where self-assuredness reigns.[67] He concludes:

> The description of the Church which we have just given is often blamed as being typical of those who oppose the Church or who, at least, hold themselves aloof from it. But blame such as this does not affect us. When, however, our critics go on to propose that we ought to leave the Church if we think of it thus, we are bound to state that we could not contemplate such a proposal, and would do our best to dissuade others from even considering it. It would never enter our heads to think of leaving the Church. For in describing the Church we are describing ourselves.[68]

What are we to conclude regarding Barth's ecclesiological thought in the *Romans* commentary? It must first be said that Barth's consistent eschatology expressed in the radical *diastasis* between time and eternity serves to protect against and criticize any direct identification between the church in history and the Kingdom of God, whether made by liberalism or conservatism, and as such, this eschatology fulfilled an important purpose. For Barth, the church in time could in no way be identified with the eternal Kingdom of God, nor its proclamation directly identified with revelation. Such a view was parallel with and analogous to Barth's central conviction that the revelation of God in Christ could not be identified with the

---

[67]Ibid., 318-321; ET 334-337. In a later letter of 1925, Barth noted: 'Naturally it dare not be a *new* church that we want but rather the *church* in distinction to sects or even to our own personal prophesying. Also our *protest* against the church, so far as it was valid, was intended as specifically *by the church*' (Smart, *Revolutionary Theology*, 216).

[68]Ibid., 355; ET 371.

historical person of Jesus. The first dialectic pertained to the subjective pole of salvation; the second pertained to the objective pole.

The relationship between these positions must be carefully considered. In refusing to identify revelation with the historical figure of Jesus, Barth was rebelling against the liberal tradition and its tendency to reduce revelation to ethics with its conception of revelation as the simple message of Jesus determined on the basis of a scientific historical method. The simple message that was derived, Barth maintained, said more about the religious and moral convictions of nineteenth century men and women than about the God of the Bible revealed in Christ. In a similar manner, Barth's refusal to identify the historical church with the Kingdom of God marked a rebellion against a corresponding ecclesiastical triumphalism, whether of the theological left or right, that saw the church either as the pinnacle or as the driving force of society and culture. In both cases the direct identification of history and revelation served to domesticate God and to substitute human conceptions of morality and progress for God's revelation, subsuming revelation into history and fusing church and culture. In other words, Christ and church became ciphers for contemporary religious, ethical, cultural, and political content.[69] Barth's strong dialectic between eternity and time protected against such moves in regard to revelation insofar as it guarded against them in both Christology and ecclesiology.

Barth's dialectic of time and eternity did not come without a steep price, however. While it served well to protect against the attempt to bestow divine sanction upon human cultural norms and programs, it also created significant problems from a theological standpoint. Specifically, it made any conception of the incarnation extremely problematic and indeed rendered any fully developed Christology an impossibility, in that revelation was so opposed to history that a true entrance of revelation into history was excluded.

In a corresponding and derivative manner, the visible church in history was seen by Barth only in terms of sinfulness, and this made any true account of ecclesiology an impossibility as well. Just as no incarnation, or entrance of revelation into history, was possible in any type of enduring fashion, so the church could not be seen as an enduring entity through time but existed only in a non-historical event of revelation wherein the church of Esau became the church of Jacob. In other words, just as revelation touched the world only as a tangent touching a circle, so the invisible church touched the visible church only as a tangent touching a circle. For Barth, the visible and historical church could only be seen as sinful, and as such, the church differed from the world only in that it was the site where the revelation event occurred.

---

[69]Barth's critique of culture Protestantism did not mean, however, that he held that the church possessed no cultural tasks. See McCormack, *Barth's Theology*, 215.

There certainly was no place for a positive evaluation of church history, and there was little appreciation for doctrine.[70]

Such a formal status for the church did provide a positive function to the church in time — Barth's view of the church in the *Romans* commentary was not solely negative, as so often thought. The church's positive role was, however, so limited as to make a coherent ecclesiology impossible.[71] Completely absent in the *Romans* commentary is a positive and constructive account of the church as a new community in the world, or a discussion of the church in the traditional terminology of its being the people of God, the body of Christ, or the fellowship of the Holy Spirit. Nor is there any sustained discussion of the church's teaching, worship, or practices from a positive standpoint. Perhaps most conspicuously absent is any type of connection between the resurrection and the church in the light of this event. In the *Romans* commentary the church seems to be a community of sin that *precedes and opposes* the resurrection more than a new community that is established *in the light of and through* the resurrection. In short, Barth seems to have emphasized the division, or *diastasis*, between the kingdom and the church to such a degree as to have neglected their positive relation, identifying the church's visibility and historicity with its sin in an over-simplified manner.

The weaknesses of the time-eternity dialectic would lead Barth to abandon it, though he did not abandon dialectical thinking, which would come to rest in Christology. Nor did he abandon the infinite qualitative distinction between God and the world.[72] Barth's development of a coherent Christology would make a true ecclesiology possible, as will become evident. Barth's view of the church in *Romans* provided a needed critique of an accommodated church, though the critique in effect undermined a coherent conception of the church. For this reason, Barth would retain the dialectical relation between the church and the kingdom but would seek to find a dialectic that not only preserved the difference between them but that set them in a relation of correspondence and not of contradiction, the latter always in danger of expressing a Platonic conception of the relation of the invisible and visible church rather than a Christian, Christological one. Barth's view of the church in *Romans* indeed subordinated the visible church to the invisible church in such a one-sided manner that it became vulnerable to charges of presenting a docetic ecclesiology.

---

[70]At this time Barth's view of church history was shaped by Franz Overbeck and his view of doctrine remained under the influence of Herrmann. See Eberhard Jüngel, *Karl Barth: A Theological Legacy*, trans. Garrett E. Paul (Philadelphia: Westminster Press, 1986), 54-70; see also McCormack, *Scholastic*, 189; cf. McCormack, *Barth's Theology*, 287.

[71]McCormack articulates this point succinctly: 'Barth's positive valuation of the Church in this phase remains strictly in the vertical dimension. It does not extend to the horizontal' (*Scholastic*, 190).

[72]See McCormack, *Barth's Theology*, 244-245; 327-328.

A solution to this problem was hinted at in Barth's conception of analogy and 'parable' already present in *Romans,* where Barth indicated that human lives such as that of Abraham could be a witness and type, or icon [*Abbild*], of the life of Christ,[73] and that human history and human speech could be a parable [*Gleichnis*] of God's revelation,[74] though all are preceded by the free decision of God. When Barth here speaks of parable, this is certainly a prelude to his concept of the *analogia fidei* as well as his very important later conception of correspondence [*Entsprechung*]. Barth stresses the infinite qualitative difference between God and the world, between the church and Gospel, and between the proclamation of the church and the Word of God. Yet, in the concept of parable Barth allows for a correspondence between human speech and action and God's speech and action. The direction runs not from a general correspondence in the world, or in human language, to God, but from God who makes such action and speech a parable, or analogy, of God's own Word and action. Such analogies prefigure a position that would not be fully developed in relation to ecclesiology until the *Church Dogmatics.*

Barth would leave this critical stage of *Romans* and speak of the church in more positive terms, but he never withdrew or minimized his criticisms of a cultural Christianity or of an ecclesiastical triumphalism, and he could speak with the same criticisms again later when he sensed that the church was failing to discern its dependence upon God and turning instead to triumphant self-congratulation.[75] Barth never retracted his criticisms of a church that was wedded to culture as its highest triumph or legitimizing force. Such criticisms were a lasting achievement of *Romans* and shaped Barth's constructive ecclesiology in the *Church Dogmatics.*

B. *Debate with Schleiermacher, Founder of Liberal Protestantism*

Barth's ongoing debate with Neo-Protestantism led him to a study of the founder of liberalism itself, Friedrich Schleiermacher. Barth's criticism of Schleiermacher's ecclesiology is intricately tied to his criticism of Schleiermacher's Christology and concept of revelation. Barth's central criticism centers upon Schleiermacher's understanding of the relation between the contingency and particularity of revelation in Christ that comes to humanity from without, and the general revelation that

---

[73]*Römerbrief,* 102; 105-108; ET 126; 129-132.

[74]Ibid., 82; 317-318; ET 107; 333.

[75]Barth's essay of 1930 is such an attack upon ecclesiastical triumphalism, '*Quoques Tandem...?*' in *Der Götze Wackelt,* ed. Karl Kupisch (Berlin: Käthe Vogt Verlag, 1961), 27-32; see also Barth's essay of the following year, 'Die Not der evangelischen Kirche,' in idem, 33-62. For the circumstances giving rise to these articles, see Scholder, *The Churches and the Third Reich,* Vol. 1, 120-126; cf. also Timothy Gorringe, *Karl Barth: Against Hegemony* (Oxford: Oxford University Press, 1999), 113-114; 154-155.

humanity possesses within the individual's own self-consciousness. Barth maintains that the correlation of these two forms of revelation results in a redemption that is a *cooperation* of something divine without and something divine within.[76] In this relation, Barth contends, the first is ultimately sacrificed to the second, though not without a valiant attempt by Schleiermacher to retain the two in harmonious peace. This criticism runs as a thread throughout all of Barth's works on Schleiermacher in the 1920s.[77]

Barth's early foray into critically examining Schleiermacher while teaching at Göttingen caused him to shake his head in dismay. In Barth's estimation, Schleiermacher had attempted to explicate the religious self-consciousness of persons as the ground of religion while maintaining a place for the unique revelation in Christ as the origin of faith. In the process, Schleiermacher defined Christ's unique revelation as the perfection and actualization of a human religious ideal. For Barth, however, if classical Christian dogma and Scripture are right in seeing in Christ a final and definitive revelation of God, then, in Schleiermacher's Christology, 'we have a heresy of gigantic proportions.'[78] And if the nineteenth century adopted this Christology without question — well, so much the worse for the nineteenth century.

---

[76]Karl Barth, *The Theology of Schleiermacher: Lectures at Göttingen, Winter Semester of 1923/24*, ed. Dietrich Ritschl, trans. Geoffrey W. Bromiley (Grand Rapids: Eerdmans, 1982), 25. Barth began with an investigation of Schleiermacher's sermons, and then moved on to examine Schleiermacher's *Brief Outline, Hermeneutics, Christian Faith*, and the *Speeches*.

[77]Consider, for example, the following: 'Schleiermacher's doctrine of the person and work of Christ preserves thus the form of the ellipse with two foci, but the figure tends to shift towards a circle with one centre. Consequently it is still doubtful whether the methodological point of departure, the exalted humanity of Christ, is not really the original, and whether Christ himself is not the derivative destined to vanish. Under redemption, Schleiermacher in the last analysis understood only an empowering, and under the Redeemer only a strong helper or a helping power. Therefore there could not be any word of a *founding* of communion in the strict sense, but only of confirming it and of continuing the fulfilment of an already existing communion' (Barth, 'Schleiermacher,' in *Theology and Church*, 189).

[78]Barth, *Theology of Schleiermacher*, 103-104. The accuracy of Barth's assessment of Schleiermacher bears, of course, no overarching significance for a study of the development and themes of Barth's own theology, for even if Barth completely misread Schleiermacher, this would not necessarily undermine Barth's own constructive proposals (though it may call into question his evaluation of Schleiermacher's program). Given Barth's focus upon Schleiermacher's early writings and sermons, his reading, evaluation, and criticisms of Schleiermacher's theology can be defended, though not in every detail. Whether Barth understood Schleiermacher correctly in every respect is a matter of ongoing debate. See, for example, the essays contained in *Barth and Schleiermacher: Beyond the Impasse?*, ed. James O. Duke and Robert F. Streetman (Philadelphia: Fortress Press, 1988).

Schleiermacher would have been more consistent, Barth alleges, had he simply left Christ out of his theology or at least let go of the absolute uniqueness of Jesus and seen in him a religious genius, one among others. As it is, Schleiermacher has attempted to retain the uniqueness of Jesus for revelation and the origin of faith, but has ultimately failed to do so, for the particularity of Jesus is swallowed up in the generality of universal religion. It is, moreover, this general revelation that defines the particular, though Schleiermacher's intention is to retain both focal points, both the particularity of Christ's unique revelation, as well as the general and present religious consciousness. In the end, Barth wryly notes, Schleiermacher's Christ looks very much like a 'cultivated modern Christian who knows how to deal liberally with educated people in any position, who repels nobody, who has a clever word for everybody. In short, he bears a striking resemblance to Schleiermacher himself.'[79] Such is the reflection from Schleiermacher's deep well. Yet, Schleiermacher did cling to Christ and his unique significance for Christian faith, and because of this Barth can declare (only shortly after describing Schleiermacher's Christology as 'heresy') that Schleiermacher was not only a clever man but a 'sincerely devout Christian.'[80] One can only wonder here if Barth's somewhat forgiving spirit following such a strong accusation is in reality influenced by an ongoing if subliminal loyalty to Herrmann.

Schleiermacher's subsumption of the particular into the general in revelation and Christology has a direct bearing upon his view of the church, for the doctrine of the church is shaped by the Christology adopted. Just as Schleiermacher's Christ is not the incarnation of an eternal divine Word but the fulfillment of a human ideal, the perfect exemplar of a quality intrinsic if unactualized in all persons, so the Spirit of the church is not the eternal Holy Spirit who comes from without and calls the church into existence, but is the community's own Spirit. Schleiermacher's church, like Schleiermacher's Christian, Barth contends, is in 'happy possession.'[81] The question whether the community has received the Holy Spirit cannot even arise, for the community per community is the possessor of the Spirit which is passed on as a

---

[79]Ibid., 105.

[80]Ibid., 106. These ambivalent sentiments expressed in both a forceful rejection of Schleiermacher's theology and a sincere admiration for his tenacity in clinging to Christ and his intellectual achievement remained throughout Barth's life, evidenced in Barth's 'Concluding Unscientific Postscript on Schleiermacher,' trans. George Hunsinger, included in *The Theology of Schleiermacher*, 271-272; 274. See also Berkhof, *Two Hundred Years*, 201-204.

[81]'The Christian according to Schleiermacher is in happy possession....He is never told about Christ except with the emphatic promise that what was in Christ can and should be in you too, not excluding the very highest that was in him, but this most of all. Not only will this be in you but it is in you already if only you rightly understand yourself according to the best that you are and do not refuse to grow in this' (ibid., 25).

permanent element of Christian history. Furthermore, because this Spirit is the expression of an actualized human capacity, the distinction between the Christian and the non-Christian is a fluid one. The Christian possesses the Spirit in truth. The non-Christian possesses the Spirit in potentiality, exemplified in a 'real but unconscious love of man for God.'[82] The question of whether one has received the Holy Spirit is on this basis an illegitimate question in the Christian church, for the Spirit is a constant possession of the person *qua* person. Barth concludes:

> The primary thing that makes a Christian a Christian and establishes the church neither is nor has to be an original encounter of God with man but the mediacy of a supposedly Christian history, the continuum of the religious stimulation which runs through this history and in which man can have a bigger or smaller share with no danger in principle....Whether this latitudinarianism can be the last word in the question of the church if God is really God and the Spirit is really the Spirit and not the stream of life, is a very different question.[83]

If it is then true that Christ is the perfection of a human ideal, and if the Spirit is the presence of this ideal in redeemed humanity as communicated from Christ to the church,[84] then the 'dialectic between Christ and the church is dissolved and changed into an identity.'[85] The church takes the place of Christ, for Christ's faith is the church's faith. In a similar manner, the church possesses the Spirit as its own — the Spirit no longer 'blows where it wills,' no longer comes to the church through a sovereign act of divine freedom, but belongs to the church as a permanent expression of its religious life. Finally, the revelation of a transcendent God is replaced by the immediate religious experience of the Christian community.

Barth returned to these themes when he examined Schleiermacher's *Celebration of Christmas* later in 1924, a work that grew out of his earlier study, and here the criticisms outlined in Barth's course on Schleiermacher emerge once again.[86] Christ

---

[82]Ibid., 31.

[83]Ibid., 31.

[84]'The Christian community is the qualified agent of the movement of life or Spirit that derives from the Redeemer' (ibid., 28). Barth adds that the church is founded only on the sharing of this internal religious experience by its members and is thereby not constituted by verbal confession nor subject to any external authority. This is what Schleiermacher champions as the *free* church (ibid., 28).

[85]Ibid., 177. The same ultimately holds true, of course, for the relation between Christ and the Christian.

[86]Barth, 'Schleiermacher's *Celebration of Christmas*,' in *Theology and Church*, 136-158.

is the *Urbild*, the perfect and complete man, with Christians standing over against him and yet in relation to him so that they can approach him in imitation.[87] The church is the community of those whose religious consciousness has been awakened through the communication of the inner religious consciousness of Jesus transmitted through history by the community itself, 'through the spirit of the Church which proceeds from him, "the true Son of Man."'[88] For Barth, these understandings of Christ and the church are problematic, to say the least, and he again raises pointed questions for Schleiermacher's theology:

> Can the unique dignity of the revelation, which has apparently been established, be transformed...into the exact opposite? Into the universal religious dignity of man whose participation in being is guaranteed with his becoming? If 'knowledge' (the awakening of the individual to the self-consciousness of humanity) establishes for men their participation in the Church, and if for somewhat more foolish women 'emotion' achieves the same thing, what remains of the central place of Christ, which for a moment appeared to be a presupposition for setting up the concept of the Church?[89]

In other words, can the Christian, and the church, take the place of Christ? Does the faith of the Christian and of the church arise from Christ, or is Christ an idea, a projection of the church intended as a postulate of its own religious consciousness, and yet in reality a creation of that experience itself, so that Christ is a product of the church?[90] 'Is the "Word become flesh" really anything different from the "elevation of humanity?"'[91] So in the end, do we celebrate Christ at Christmas, or ourselves? Once again, Barth concludes, the particularity of Christ has been swallowed up into the general and universal religious consciousness, and Christ is a predicate of that consciousness and therefore of history itself. The church has given rise to Christ, not Christ the church.

In a later essay of 1926 Barth refined these questions, focusing upon the topic of peace which was already a theme in his earlier lectures on Schleiermacher.[92] What

---

[87]Ibid., 139. Here Barth is referring not to the *Weihnachtsfeier* itself but to a Christmas sermon of 1794.

[88]Ibid., 153.

[89]Ibid., 155.

[90]Ibid., 154-155.

[91]Ibid., 156.

[92]Barth, 'Schleiermacher,' 159-199. Cf. Barth, *The Theology of Schleiermacher*, 4ff., passim.

makes the theme of peace so important to Barth in analyzing Schleiermacher's thought? An answer may be found in Barth's own hand:

> There exists above the antithesis of religiously affecting and being religiously affected a Schleiermacherian Unity, a peace in relation to which this contradiction is relative and evanescent. The goal of religious speaking is therefore the surmounting of this contradiction, the good of salvation is to be sought not in a *relation* between God and man but in their *undifferentiatedness*. And when we remember a sermon of the elderly Schleiermacher on the ultimate inability to distinguish between the impulse of his own heart and the work of the Holy Spirit, we realize again that the speaker in 1799, however different the words he used, remained throughout true to himself.[93]

It would be difficult to find a more succinct passage throwing light upon Barth's final evaluation of Schleiermacher, for here Barth's central criticism is presented in its purest form. In Schleiermacher's conception of peace, the *diastasis*, the infinite qualitative difference, between God and humanity is dissolved. The central truth which Barth strove to present in the *Römerbrief* is here not only absent but abrogated. Barth also, as we shall see, wanted to speak of a union of God and man in Christ. But this union was a differentiated union, a dialectical union, where God does not cease to be God in taking up flesh, just as humanity does not cease to be human. And this relation was an irreversible one, where the initiative always rested upon God's gracious and free activity, never upon a human capacity for or possession of divinity. Schleiermacher's understanding of revelation, and therefore of Christology, according to Barth, fused the divine and the human into a unity of peace where the integrity of each was sacrificed. Such a relation was not only reversible but in fact began not with an act of revelation on the side of God but with an examination of one's own religious consciousness, so that anthropology replaces theology. What Barth said later of Herrmann's Christology he could here have said of Schleiermacher:

> Here no other 'way' whatever exists except the road from above downwards. Orthodox Christology is a glacial torrent rushing straight down from a height of three thousand metres; it makes accomplishment possible. Herrmann's Christology, as it stands, is the hopeless attempt to raise a stagnant pool to the same height by means of a hand pump; nothing can be accomplished with it.[94]

---

[93]Ibid., 173.

[94]Barth, 'Wilhelm Herrmann,' 265.

Schleiermacher's failure was not only a failure of Christology, but of pneumatology. For Barth, the human spirit cannot be mistaken for the Holy Spirit, or vice versa. Yet in Schleiermacher the substitution of the Holy Spirit with humanity's religious consciousness bequeathed to the nineteenth century not only a confusion but an identification of the two, so that the religious aspirations of persons became the political goals and *Geist* of nations, and Christ and culture, and concomitantly church and culture, became fused in an undifferentiated identity. In Schleiermacher, Barth found the root of the vine that he believed had choked true theology and the church so that church and society became indistinguishable, and Barth's rejection of Schleiermacher's psychologism was also a rejection of Schleiermacher's historicism — Barth saw Schleiermacher as the source of each.[95] In Barth's estimation, Schleiermacher's notion of peace was in fact death, the substitution of humanity for God, and therefore the cornerstone of the idolatry of an age.

For Barth, Schleiermacher's failure was wide-ranging — theological, Christological, pneumatological, and ecclesiological. He had collapsed the dialectical relation between God and humanity, grace and sin, the Word and flesh, the Holy Spirit and the human spirit, and the church and the world, into an undifferentiated unity, falsely elevating humanity and humanizing God. 'Religion is the finite with capacity for the infinite.'[96] This is how Barth understood Schleiermacher, and only if we conceive this in the strongest terms possible can we understand both Barth's fascination with Schleiermacher's achievement and his own repudiation of Schleiermacher's program, contending that Schleiermacher could be overcome not by criticism but only with an equally forceful and constructive countermeasure, an entirely new dogmatic achievement:

> The higher one values Schleiermacher's achievement in and for itself, and the better one sees with what historical necessity it had to come and how well...it fitted the whole spirit of Christianity in the 19th and 20th centuries, the more clearly one perceives how easy it is to say No in word but how hard it is to say it in deed, namely, with a positive counterachievement.[97]

To draw the strands of Barth's criticisms of Schleiermacher together with particular regard to their relation to ecclesiology, we might summarize them in the following three points: 1) The distinction between Christ and the church (and the

---

[95]For Barth's understanding of the relation between Schleiermacher's 'mysticism' and 'cultural religion,' see Barth, 'Schleiermacher,' 192-199.

[96]Ibid., 177. In relation to the church, see ibid., 178-179.

[97]Barth, *The Theology of Schleiermacher*, 260; cf. Barth, *Protestant Theology in the Nineteenth Century* (Valley Forge: Judson Press, 1973), 427.

Christian) has been sacrificed in that Christ is no longer the unique revelation of an incarnate God but the perfection of a human ideal, and therefore he may be subsumed into the church. The work of Christ and the work of the community are thus interchangeable and become coextensive. 2) The Spirit is no longer a free Lord but now a permanent possession of the church, and is in fact the community's spirit, the realization of the redemption communicated from Christ. Put more broadly, the distinction between a transcendent God and humanity has been lost, as Christ is the revelation of perfected humanity and the Spirit is the presence of the quality of this perfection in all persons. The church is founded not upon the revelation of the Word of God through the Spirit in proclamation but by the awakening of religious consciousness. 3) Finally, the distinction between church and culture itself has been lost — no longer are these realities dialectically related but are now rather identified. The goals, principles, and task of the church and those of culture are therefore equated. As we have seen, this was Barth's criticism not only of Schleiermacher but of Protestant liberalism as a whole.

Barth would utterly reject Schleiermacher's conception of the church as a 'corporate life,' as a possessor of revelation, the Word, and the Spirit, and as the communicator of Christ's inner life in history.[98] Barth's rejection of such an understanding of the church was also a rejection of the religious individualism upon which it was based,[99] and Barth's revolution in his theological starting point had a direct effect upon his ecclesiological thought. In addition, Barth's growing appreciation for doctrine and its ability to convey true knowledge of God when tested by the Word of God also caused him to view Schleiermacher's relativization of doctrine and emphasis upon the ineffable quality of religion with growing distrust. For Barth, the revelation of the Word communicated a real knowledge of God, and such knowledge was best expressed in doctrines that should be regarded as true (and here his break from Herrmann is apparent). The church's responsibility was to teach doctrine.[100] In Schleiermacher, Barth saw an emphasis not upon knowledge of God but upon the inexpressible quality of religion, evidenced in Schleiermacher's favoring the evocative power of music over the spoken word.[101] Barth understood this to be a

---

[98]Barth, 'Schleiermacher,' 184.

[99]Referring to Schleiermacher, Barth states: 'Revelation is the excitement of feeling in an individual, which, moving, conveys itself to others and thus allows a development from the religious individual to a religious type, a religious species, a religious community, a Church' (*Protestant Theology*, 470).

[100]'The Church should always present the revelation to men in "doctrine".... And it should always present it with the claim that this doctrine "is to be accepted as true"....For that purpose the Church is here; it is that which the Church can do in relation to the revelation; it can teach what man should accept as true' (Barth, 'Wilhelm Herrmann,' 270-271).

[101]Barth, 'Celebration of Christmas,' 156-157; cf. Barth, 'Schleiermacher,' 161-162.

disdain for words mirrored in a disdain for doctrine and knowledge of God as a cognitive reality.[102] In place of the Word, of the Gospel, of Christ, Barth held that Schleiermacher had substituted religion or piety.[103]

Barth would ground the church on an entirely different basis. The church for Barth was not a community of persons in 'happy possession,' full possessors of the reality of Christ and therefore of the Spirit, a group of persons who freely bind themselves to one another as those who share and partake of a common experience. The church, rather, is a community that has been called into existence by God and which never replaces or possesses Christ, for Christ is the eternal Word spoken from above the church. The Spirit is not the community's Spirit but the Spirit of God that calls the church into existence and which exists in relation to the church only as promise, never as possession. Barth's view of the church is thus one where God remains sovereign in his election of the church and is never bound to the church by necessity, where Christ remains Lord and is never replaced by the church, and where the Spirit remains free and is never a possession of the church. Knowledge of God is a free gift, and it is given in revelation communicated through the proclaimed Word and witnessed in the church's doctrine and teaching. To summarize, God's grace is free grace and always remains free. The Christian does not possess it, but it comes as a gift from above.[104] This was the foundation upon which Barth began his own thought on the church. Before we examine this, however, we must turn our attention to see how Barth responded to a new opponent on the right, Roman Catholicism.

3. The Engagement with Roman Catholicism and Its Ecclesiology

Barth's move from Göttingen to Münster in 1925 marked a turn from a consuming engagement with Protestant liberalism to an increasing interest in and dialogue with Roman Catholicism, a shift that had already begun during his final years in Göttingen.[105] The question of the church played a major role in Barth's new debate

---

[102]Barth, 'Schleiermacher,' 172. 'Therefore the speaker and the hearer, although unavoidably making use of words, can forgo (if they do not actually disdain) all knowable truth, all truth apart from religion's ineffable reality — that is, of course, they can dispense with the letter' (ibid., 172). Cf. Barth, *Protestant Theology*, 454.

[103]Barth, *Protestant Theology*, 458. 'In carrying out this programme, in demonstrating that faith and Christ, equated with experience and history, are the foci of an ellipse, Schleiermacher turns the Christian relationship of man with God into an apparent human possibility' (ibid., 463).

[104]Barth, 'The Word in Theology,' in *Theology and Church*, 215.

[105]Consider Barth's expressed appreciation in the preface to the fourth edition of *Romans* (1924) for its reception by Catholic reviewers (*Romans*, 21). Barth's early engagement with Catholicism while in Göttingen is documented by Reinhard Hütter, 'Karl Barth's "Dialectical

with Roman Catholicism, for in Catholicism ecclesiology was a central and not a peripheral concern, in marked contrast to Neo-Protestantism. Two essays written during this period stand out in importance in regard to Barth's understanding of and interaction with the Roman Catholic conception of the church.

In 1927 Barth presented a brief lecture entitled, 'The Concept of the Church.'[106] This essay marked an early attempt by Barth to engage Roman Catholicism directly as a partner in dialogue. Barth's goal in such dialogue was simply to take the other partner seriously and come to an understanding of the reasons for the present disagreement between the parties. Such an understanding required that differences neither be ignored nor papered over to achieve a superficial agreement, but rather that, as during the time of the Reformation, each partner should look the other in the eye and clearly pronounce where agreement could not be reached and the position of the other not followed. It was with this intention in mind that Barth took up a discussion of the nature of the church and the different conceptions of it held by the Roman Catholic and Protestant communions.[107]

Barth begins his discussion by acknowledging that when Catholics and Protestants speak of the church they are referring to the same entity. Escape from disagreement cannot be found by claiming that the two sides are in fact discussing two different realities when they refer to the church. Barth describes the common doctrine that unites Roman Catholic and Protestant thought regarding the church, namely, that the church is one, holy, catholic, and apostolic, and he carefully outlines the broad area of agreement between Catholicism and Protestantism regarding the convictions underlying these affirmations pertaining to the church.[108]

Yet disagreement remains, and Barth's task is to clarify such disagreement, which he locates in the differing conceptions of the phrase, 'By faith only we know' [*fide solum intellegimus*], in the two communions. Barth outlines these differences by examining how Protestantism understands these words. Barth contends that for Protestantism they signify that God's grace is always a gift and never a possession of the church. Faith lays hold of God's gift but never ceases itself to be a gift of God. A person who receives such grace 'does not thereby possess the slightest mastery over the grace as he does over other realities which he perceives, knows, and experiences.'[109] The relation between God and humanity remains one that

---

Catholicity": *Sic et Non,' Modern Theology*, 16 (2000): 137-157, esp. 139-140; 152 (note 7). For the background of Barth's interaction with Roman Catholicism during his years in Münster, see Busch, *Karl Barth*, 164-189; McCormack, *Barth's Theology*, 376-391.

[106]Barth, 'The Concept of the Church,' in *Theology and Church*, 272-285.

[107]Ibid., 272-273.

[108]Ibid., 275-278.

[109]Ibid., 279-280.

presupposes God's inaccessibility by humanity and humanity's sinfulness, and therefore entails an irreversible relationship, one that can be established only from God's side. For this reason, humanity lives moment to moment dependent upon God's grace and can never presume to possess such grace, for no reciprocity exists in the relation between God and the world.

Such a conception of grace has ramifications for how the church is understood. Barth concedes that the church is the 'place and the instrument of the grace of God,' and that the church is the place where the reality of the incarnate Word through the Holy Spirit 'speaks and is heard.'[110] Nevertheless, while the church is the instrument of grace, and thereby has a relative authority over us, the church is not a self-actualized reality that can be claimed as a human possession, but comes into existence only where God alone chooses to speak. True, the church exists in the form of a visible entity existing in the realm of history. Yet, nevertheless, its visible existence in time does not negate the fact that the church only truly comes into existence by a special act of God's grace. Barth writes:

> But this visible actuality does not at all affect the truth that we have it [the church] only as we have God. We so have it that in it and through it the claim of God reaches us, but not so that any claim of ours on God arises from it or any claim on what is reserved for God alone. From every other claim on us, there may arise a corresponding claim of ours, a claim asserting ownership over what is promised us, validating the promise. But from God's claim arises no such counter-claim of ours. Our relation to God is, in distinction to all other relations, irreversible. Therefore the fact that the Church has the 'summons' (*evocatio*) and has the divine promise cannot mean that any claim is put in our hands, that there has been delivered to us human beings in that visible, historical place and instrument of grace some kind of tool with which we can gain control over grace, can make ourselves *secure* in relation to grace.[111]

The church by this account lives solely and continuously dependent upon God's divine initiative, and in this sense the church is a divine institution, established by God's gracious act. Yet at the same time, the church, which exists as the medium between Christ and the sinner, stands on the side of sinful history, for as the sinner lives only under God's judgment and promise, so does the church. The church is therefore never a possession of persons but a gift of God. To reverse this relation between God and the church, Barth says, would not be an exaltation of the church, but

---

[110]Ibid., 280.

[111]Ibid., 281.

its dissolution effected by an attempt of the church to become master in its relation with God. 'The relation between us and God must not be reversed because of our desire to have a Church without degradation or with its degradation covered by a king's robe.'[112]

The church must therefore live in a state of both humility and hope. Its humility arises from the realization that it has no splendor but to listen to the Word that is spoken to it and that it then must proclaim to the world. Its hope consists in the fact that this Word has been spoken and can be expected again, for this Word is free — it cannot be controlled or possessed as material or intellectual goods are possessed. The marks of the church are thereby a result of this hearing of the Word and are established by God, for the church is one, holy, catholic, and apostolic not on the basis of its own nature but by a free act of God's grace.[113] Barth concludes:

> This is the meaning of 'I believe one holy catholic and apostolic Church' (*Credo unam sanctam catholicam et apostolicam ecclesiam*). I believe the Church as the place where honour is given to God and where therefore divine honour for the Church is repudiated, and therefore I believe the Church as the instrument of grace. I believe the Church as the divine institution and therefore that it must be not so much God's palace as God's shanty among men until the world's end. I believe the church as the communion of saints, that is the communion of sinners set apart and called by God, which yet is the communion of saints. I believe the Church as the proclaimer and the hearer of the divine Word. I believe it also as the people of God on earth, who — precisely as the people of God — shall live from God's mercy (and that is not to be counted a small thing!) until the kingdom of glory where the transitory, even the transitoriness of this community, of the earthly body of the heavenly Lord, shall put on eternity, where here also what is sown in weakness shall be raised in strength.[114]

Barth states that such a conception of the church and the words 'by faith we know' is in sharp contradiction to that of Roman Catholicism, but adds that he does not wish to elaborate upon such differences. In an essay of the following year, 'Roman Catholicism: A Question to the Protestant Church,' however, Barth's

---

[112]Ibid., 281-282.

[113]Ibid., 282-284.

[114]Ibid., 284-285.

criticism of the Roman Catholic understanding of the church became both more refined and more explicit.[115]

Barth begins this second essay much as he did the last, stating that the partner that one is addressing must be taken seriously and truly heard. This conviction entails that Protestantism not only question Roman Catholicism, but that Catholicism be allowed to question Protestantism and that these questions be taken seriously, for Catholicism presents a serious alternative to the Protestant church and poses a question that cannot be definitively answered once for all but must be taken up again and again, as witnessed in the Reformers' ongoing debates with Rome.[116] Furthermore, the questions of Catholicism cannot be ignored simply because of the fact that the questions placed to it by Protestantism may themselves not be taken seriously; this would simply mirror a mistaken stance on the Catholic side.[117]

The first question posed to the Protestant church by Catholicism is whether and to what degree the Protestant church is truly a church. The Protestant church in the sixteenth century, Barth states, was not determined to set up a second church, but to reform the one church itself. It attempted to recover the true substance of the church. Now the question is whether modern Protestantism has lost this concern, and has in fact established another church. This question posed from the Catholic side pertains to the substance of the church and asks whether Protestantism has in fact lost this substance. This substance which defines the church's true existence, Barth states, is comprised of the fact that the church is the house of God and not of individual or communal experience or convictions.[118]

Catholicism itself has claimed to guard this substance, that it is '*God's* presence that makes the Church to be the Church.' Whether this is the case with Protestantism needs to be addressed. Still, the question Barth poses to Protestantism from the Catholic side is set against Barth's own understated though clear criticisms of the Catholic position. For while the Catholic position emphasizes that God in Jesus Christ is the true agent in the Church, Barth contends that this agency is offset and in fact relativized by 'earthly human surrogates' such as the papacy, the priest, the sacrificial host, and the visible church itself. However, Barth alleges that even if God's true

---

[115]Barth, 'Roman Catholicism: A Question to the Protestant Church,' in *Theology and Church*, 307-333.

[116]Ibid., 307-310.

[117]Ibid., 310-312.

[118]Ibid., 312-313.

agency is threatened in Catholicism, it is not lost in principle — he doubts that the same can be said of Neo-Protestantism.[119]

In contrast to modern Protestantism, the original protest of the Reformers against the Catholic conception of the church consisted in emphasizing that 'God alone' was the subject of the church, rejecting all 'direct identifications with God in the visible church.' Barth writes: 'The Reformation applied the "Thou alone!" (*Tu solus!*) to Jesus Christ as the Lord in his immutable unlikeness to all his servants, as the Word in ineluctable antithesis to all which we ourselves say, as the Spirit in unalterable contrast to all material things.'[120] The Reformation thereby asserted that God is ever Subject and never object of the church and stressed the deity of Christ and the Spirit over against a confusion of them with the historical media taken up into the event of revelation within the church. The objections against the papacy, the priesthood, and the sacraments were not a denial of the 'real and primary presence and action of God in his Church' but rather an assertion of these in 'a purer, more compelling form.' It is a misunderstanding of Protestantism, Barth writes, to see it as the replacement of God's presence and action with that of human persons and agents.[121]

The Catholic insistence upon God's presence and agency in the church does not preclude but includes the existence of 'actual, earthly, human service of God in the church.' This is rooted in the reality of the incarnation: as God is Subject, so can persons and things be used by God as predicates, and such a conception serves as the foundation for the papacy, the priesthood, and the sacraments. Such human service and material mediation is not to be denied, Barth argues. But here too, his questions to Catholicism become explicit, as Barth alleges that in Catholicism the church is not only the object but an acting subject, leading to a synergistic relation between divine and human action. The Mass is often understood to repeat Christ's unique sacrifice. The priest can effect such a sacrifice and make Christ present on the altar. And the pope is nothing less than Christ on earth. Against such conceptions the Reformers could only protest, as Barth writes:

> Here again the Reformation was clearly restoration, restoration of the knowledge of the absolute uniqueness of the person of the Lord and of the absolute unrepeatability of his work; restoration of the immutable relation

---

[119]Ibid., 313-315. Barth proclaims in a note: 'If I today became convinced that the interpretation of the Reformation on the line taken by Schleiermacher-Ritchl-Troeltsch (or even by Seeberg or Holl) was correct; that Luther and Calvin really intended such an outcome of their labours; I could not indeed become a Catholic tomorrow, but I should have to withdraw from the evangelical Church. And if I were forced to make a choice between the two evils, I should, in fact, prefer the Catholic' (ibid., 314).

[120]Ibid., 315.

[121]Ibid., 316.

of Word and flesh, of subject and predicate; restoration of the interrelation between the divine reality of revelation and the equally divine reality of faith. But in this restoration, the Reformation was affirmation not denial, strengthening and sharpening not weakening; least of all was it obliteration of the idea of mediation, of the concept of the church service, of the insight that the Church is the House of God.[122]

In essence, the Reformers did not deny the historical mediation of revelation, but they attempted to understand it in a manner more consistent with the incarnation of the Word, emphasizing that the mediation is an act of God himself and not an institution within the realm of human manipulation or the actualization of a human possibility. Word and sacraments remain instruments in the hand of God and never pass over into the control of humans, just as God remains master in the church, not humanity. As the Reformers did not deny the historical mediation of revelation, so they did not deny the visible church. They had no intention of bypassing the visible church, nor Word and sacrament. The question, Barth maintains, is whether Neo-Protestantism has not passed beyond these to deny the mediation of revelation through God's gracious action of speaking through the specific media of the church. The Reformers did not deny such a relative mediation and relative service in the church, nor did they attempt an escape from the visible church. Whether the Neo-Protestantism has retained these original convictions is a question that Catholicism rightly raises.[123]

As the Catholic church claims the subjectivity of God regarding the church and human service and mediation in the church, so it also asserts the authority of the church based upon the subjectivity of Christ within it. Barth defends this conviction as he did the others, arguing that the church does have an authority and that Protestantism is misunderstood if taken to entail the denial of such authority. The church's authority is a concomitant of the fact that the church is God's house, the place where God speaks, and this is the basis for the church's own prophetic proclamations. The Protestant, like the Catholic, is bound to a higher authority than subjective conscience, and his or her conscience itself is freely bound by the authority of the church. The existence of the church thus necessarily entails the reality of authority, and Protestantism refuted not its existence but its abuse.[124] Protestantism therefore does not rebel against the very concept of authority *per se*. The question

---

[122]Ibid., 318.

[123]Ibid., 318-319.

[124]Ibid., 319-321. Barth states what still strikes one with force: 'We cannot intelligently condemn the Papacy for exercising power. If that power had remained only churchly, spiritual power, and therefore a God-serving power, and had not become instead a power which displaces and replaces God, we, like Luther, should have no objection to kissing the Pope's feet' (ibid., 321).

today, Barth alleges, is whether this has in fact become the case for contemporary Protestantism, and if it has, the Catholic question to Protestantism is incisive and serious.

If the first question put to the Protestant Church regards its substance, the second question posed by Catholicism is whether it is truly a *Protestant* church. That is to say, can it provide a viable answer to the question as to whether it possesses a unique identity set over against the Roman Catholic church? This identity, Barth insists, must be defined by the dictum that God is and remains the Lord of the church. The Catholic church claims this as well, as the Reformers recognized. But Protestantism asks whether this is truly the case in the Catholic church, whether God remains Lord or shares God's glory with another, whether God alone remains Subject above the church, above the church's service of mediation, above the church's authority. The Protestant church attempts to let this insight shine brighter and purer than in Catholicism, and as it does so stands over against Catholicism as a *Protestant* church.[125]

Does the current situation still merit such separation and distinction between the churches? Not if judged by the achievement of modern Protestantism, Barth concludes, for if the new Protestantism has lost the substance of the church, so also has it lost its restoration: 'It has ceased to be Church and it has ceased to be Protestant — the former more in its rational, the latter more in its pietistic form.'[126] Nevertheless, there still remains reason for separation from Rome, Barth contends, insofar as the Lordship of God in the church remains not entirely clear in Catholicism. The Reformers insisted upon God's subjectivity, and as such established the church upon the Word that comes from without the church, maintaining 'the immutable subjectivity of God, the freedom of God above all instruments, the uniqueness of God's authority.' Barth goes on to assert: 'To declare and establish this truth is the business of Protestantism. We cannot see that this is really done in the Catholic teaching.'[127]

Because the Word creates the relation between God and humanity, the Word that is heard is a word of judgment, as humans remain sinners and servants before God. This is lost in the Catholic church, Barth argues, for even though it speaks of sin, it does not see it as effecting humanity at its core. And, Barth states, such is the case with the new Protestantism, making an ongoing separation from Catholicism questionable for *that* Protestant church.[128]

---

[125]Ibid., 322-323.

[126]Ibid., 323. Barth states that in Schleiermacher rationalism and pietism have 'flowed together until they are indistinguishable' (ibid., 324).

[127]Ibid., 324-325.

[128]Ibid., 326-328.

As the church of the Reformation was the church of the Word, so was it the church of God's mercy, emphasizing the free and unmerited grace of God in justification and sanctification. Here is the third aspect, Barth states, wherein the Protestant church differs from the Catholic one. True, Barth says, the Catholic church also speaks of the prevenient grace of God. But insofar as it also speaks of preparation and merit, the status of grace and mercy as the sole basis for salvation is placed in doubt. Such synergism is evident in the example of the Catholic understanding of Mary as a model of creative cooperation with God's redemptive purposes. Nonetheless, such questions plague not only the Catholic church, but present-day Protestantism as well, Barth argues. Again, this places the question of the continuing separation from Rome before the Protestant church, for if God's Word of grace is to be replaced with the activity and exaltation of humanity, the Roman Catholic way is far more simple and elegant than the dilettantism of contemporary Protestantism.[129]

Barth's interaction with Roman Catholic theology in these two essays is both understated and poignant. While Barth's criticisms of Neo-Protestantism are openly and strongly presented, Barth's criticisms of Catholicism's position are more tempered. Yet, they are nonetheless clear and forceful. What should not be missed is the similarities between the criticisms of both sides. Barth's criticisms of Roman Catholic ecclesiology are tied to its understanding of revelation and grace. Barth maintains that for Catholicism the dialectical relation between God and the world is lost in that revelation becomes directly identified with the historical media that communicate it, whether this be the church itself as an extension of Christ's incarnation in the world, dogma as the Word of God, or the sacraments as the presence of Christ and the Spirit. For Barth, such an undialectical relation between revelation and its historical and earthly medium leads, ultimately, to what is at best a synergistic relation between God and human agents and at worst a replacement of the divine by the human: the church replaces Christ in the ongoing history of redemption, the pope takes the place of Christ in the world, and the priest and the sacrifice of the altar take the place of Christ's unique sacrifice on Calvary. This replacement can occur because the entrance of revelation into history is understood by Catholicism as a historicizing of revelation whereby revelation, grace, and the Spirit become identified with their historical mediation and thereby become a permanent possession of the church. In short, the church here again is in 'happy possession.'

Barth's interaction with Catholicism drew upon many sources, including the Roman Catechism and Roman mass, the writings of Aquinas, and contemporary

---

[129]Ibid., 328-333.

Catholic authors such as Erich Pryzwara and Karl Adam.[130] Barth's criticisms may seem wide of the mark and overly polemical in the light of the Second Vatican Council, though it must be remembered that at the time they addressed a Catholicism very different from the open and progressive one of that assembly and its concomitant documents.[131] This fact must be remembered when one attempts to evaluate the accuracy and fairness of Barth's appraisal of Roman Catholic conceptions of the church. Whether Barth accurately assessed Catholic understandings of revelation, grace, and the church in every detail does not greatly effect a study of Barth's own thought, though a gross distortion by Barth would of course undermine his own evaluation of Catholicism. As with Schleiermacher, and in light of the authors addressed, Barth's reading of the situation and the charges he made are not indefensible. That many Catholic theologians would protest against Barth's criticisms of Catholic theology in these essays cannot be denied.[132] Nevertheless, that Barth's criticisms were not wide of the mark is evidenced by the seriousness with which they

---

[130]Such sources are frequently referenced in the essays here considered. See also McCormack, *Barth's Theology*, 376-391.

[131]Consider the following statement of Catholic theologian Hugo Lang, as quoted by Barth: 'The Catholic Church, as the old (!), as the mother Church is still in possession (*in possessione*).....Protestantism is accountable to her, stands before her tribunal and her seat of judgement; let us say rather, before her motherly, cherishing and demanding eye, to be tested, to justify itself' (Hugo Lang, *Der katholische Gedanke*, vol. 1, 1928, Nr. 2, p. 182 — quoted in Barth, 'Roman Catholicism,' 311). It was of course this claim to be 'in possession' that Barth found so objectionable and that he so strongly repudiated. In regard to the Second Vatican Council, it is also important to remember that many of the theologians prominent in formulating and drafting the documents of that Council, such as Hans Urs von Balthasar and Yves Conger, were in fact greatly influenced by Barth. Catholic theologian Avery Dulles is therefore warranted in stating: 'The change in Barth's attitude toward the Catholic Church [in later years] should be attributed not so much to his own mellowing (though he did mellow) as to the inner transformation of Catholic theology itself in the 1940s and 1950s, partly under the influence of Protestants such as himself' (cited in: Emilien Lamirande, 'The Impact of Karl Barth on the Catholic Church in the Last Half Century,' in *Footnotes To A Theology*, ed. H. Martin Rumscheidt [Corp. for Publ. of Acad. Stud. in Religion, 1974], 127).

[132]The response of Catholic writers to Barth's theology will be addressed in the following chapter. For a general survey of early Roman Catholic responses to Barth's work, see Grover Foley, 'The Catholic Critics of Karl Barth: In Outline and Analysis,' *Scottish Journal of Theology* 14 (1961): 136-155; also Emilien Lamirande, 'Roman Catholic Reactions to Karl Barth's Ecclesiology' *Canadian Journal of Theology* 14 (1968): 28-42; and Lamirande, 'The Impact of Karl Barth,' 112-141. One of the most insightful comparisons of Barth's ecclesiology with that of Roman Catholic theologians remains that of Wendell S. Dietrich, *Christ and the Church, According to Barth and Some of His Roman Catholic Critics* (Unpublished Ph.D. Thesis, Yale University, 1960/1987).

were addressed by many Catholic theologians and by the impact Barth's theology had, whether directly or indirectly, upon Vatican II.[133]

Even though Barth's criticisms would mellow with time, the substance of these protests would be retained by Barth and would in fact shape his later theology in general and his ecclesiology in particular as he developed these in the *Church Dogmatics*. For Barth, the choice between the Catholic and the Protestant conceptions of the church demanded an *either/or* decision.[134] For Protestantism, Barth held, revelation was historically mediated but could never be directly identified with the historical and earthly medium of revelation. For this reason, Scripture stood between the Word revealed in the incarnate Lord and the Word proclaimed and heard in the present church, and the church was thus dependent upon the Word proclaimed in Scripture in order to receive this revelation in Christ. For Catholicism, Barth maintained, no such bridge between Christ and the church was needed, for the church itself was the bridge between the time of Christ and our own time as not only the bearer but the continuation and representation of revelation throughout history, God's revelation and grace being its permanent possession in apostolic succession and church dogma. For Catholicism it can thus be said: 'Where the church *is*, there *is* Christ.'[135] The relation between Christ and the church is thus reversible.

For Protestantism, Barth claims, no such direct relation between Christ and the church exists, as no direct relation between revelation and the historical person of Christ exists.[136] The relation of the church to Christ must be one of permanent differentiation and irreversible subordination.[137] The church is not the continuation

---

[133]Lamirande, 'The Impact of Karl Barth,' 126-127.

[134]For the following, see Barth's account of the differences between Protestant (and specifically Reformed) and Catholic positions on Scripture and the church — Barth, 'Das Schriftprinzip der reformierten Kirche' (1925), in *Vorträge und kleinere Arbeiten, 1922-1925*, ed. Holger Finze (Zürich: Theologischer Verlag Zürich, 1990), 500-544, esp. 520-530.

[135]Ibid., 520-521.

[136]Barth stated in 1925: 'History can indeed become a predicate of revelation, but never *possibly* can revelation become the predicate of history' (Barth, 'Church and Theology,' in *Theology and Church*, 292).

[137]Ibid., 294-296. The authority of the church, in comparison to that of Christ, is therefore relative and formal. Its task is one of witness, not cooperation. See also Dietrich, who writes: 'From the Reformed perspective (and Karl Barth speaks for all Protestants on this point) there is one fundamental, completely impermissible, church-shattering error in the Catholic understanding of the relation of Christ and the church. The Catholic position so describes the participation of Christ and the church in one mystical person that the relation of Christ and the church is reversible. Christ is the church; the church is Christ. Although the Catholic may prefer to put the matter in terms of a structure of mutual participation, he is willing to state the matter in terms of the reversibility of the relation. This in the judgment of the Reformed

of revelation in history, but stands over against and under revelation. It exists only as it is called into existence through a free act of God's grace.

Here again the actualistic conception of the relation between the invisible church and the visible church witnessed in the *Römerbrief* remains evident. What Barth opposed in Catholicism was its transformation of revelation into historical and temporal realities so that revelation could be identified with the dogma of the church or grace with the sacramental elements. Such a view was rooted in a view of the incarnation as revelation *becoming* history in such a manner that it could be passed on historically through apostolic succession and tradition. In such a scheme, the church could be seen as an extension of the incarnation itself and the church's work as an extension of Christ's own sacrifice.[138] Such a conception led, Barth believed, to synergistic understandings of revelation and grace whereby God's subjectivity, the uniqueness of the person and work of Christ, and the freedom of the Holy Spirit, could be transformed into the church's subjectivity displayed through a conception of the church as an extension of the incarnation and the re-presentation of Christ's sacrifice in the sacrament of the altar, as well as the possessor of the Spirit transferred through succession, tradition, and sacramental efficacy. In the worst case, a synergism of divine and ecclesiastical subjectivity leads to the replacement of God's sole subjectivity with that of the church, as the church takes the place of Christ in the world and its visible existence and actions replace the free action of the Spirit. In the end, Barth opposed in Catholicism what he opposed in liberalism, namely, the loss of the qualitative difference between God and the world and the absolute distinction between Christ and the church, as well as the confusion of divine and human agency wherein the human claims the Spirit as a permanent possession so that revelation exists not by divine initiative but human prerogative.[139] Barth's relation with Catholicism would soften in tone, but such strong criticisms would not disappear from his thought.[140]

---

church is a heretical assertion' (*Christ and the Church*, 251). Such certainly was the judgment of Barth.

[138]Ibid., 294-295; cf. Barth, 'Die Not der evangelischen Kirche,' 39-40.

[139]'If one accepts Schleiermacher without blushing, then Thomas Aquinas is equally acceptable. Both are equally far from Luther and Calvin' (Barth, 'Church and Theology,' 288). Whether this assertion is fair to Aquinas is of course another question.

[140]Consider Barth's statement recorded by John Godsey: 'Certainly there is in the Roman Catholic Church a codification of tradition and a hardening of lines. The real error of Rome lies deeper than this, however. Roman Catholicism is a terrible thing, because it means the imprisonment of God Himself! It claims to be the possessor of the Holy Spirit and revelation and Jesus Christ Himself. Can there be anything more terrible than the identification of God and man! This is worse than any pantheism! It is the more terrible because it is so pious, so beautiful' (*Karl Barth's Table Talk*, 43).

Barth never retracted the criticisms he made of Neo-Protestant and Catholic ecclesiologies. Such criticisms against what Barth believed to be two mistaken and paradoxically related positions continued to shape his own ecclesiological thought, and his understanding of the relations between the Spirit and the church, between Christ and the church, and between the church and the world would be developed in opposition to these other alternatives. He would summarize his criticisms of the ecclesiology of liberalism and Catholicism in 1934:

> The Church is not divine revelation institutionalized. It is not an organization into whose possession, disposition, and administration God has resigned His will and truth and grace in the form of a definite sum of supernatural power, insights, and virtues. It is knowledge peculiar to the Church that God's will is the will of a sovereign Lord who does not share his glory with man. The Church is aware that the truth of God is not an object — not even a supernatural object — but the eternal subject which makes itself known to us in a mystery only, and only to faith. And it is peculiar to the Church that it adores the grace of God in the person of Jesus Christ, i.e., a grace so original in character and function that it excludes every thought of cooperation, either of man or any other creature. The Church understands it therefore to be the sovereign act of the Holy Spirit. The Church is not a human way of salvation nor an apparatus for man's salvation with which God identified His own kingdom. We have drawn a line of demarcation against the error of the Roman Catholic Church.
>
> But neither is the Church a voluntary association for the cultivation of impressions, experiences, and impulses which men may have received from divine revelation and by reason of which they have formed definite convictions, condensed them into definite resolutions, rules, and customs of life and made them the center of their piety and morals. The Church is not the result of human election, decision, and disposition toward divine revelation. It arises from the election, decision, and disposition of God toward man. In revelation they have become an event. There God meets men and communicates Himself to men. Men are not gathered into, nor preserved as, the Church by an agreement in sentiments, convictions, and resolutions. Rather, it is the one God, one Christ, one Spirit, one baptism, one faith. The Church is not a religious society. We reject the error of modernistic Protestantism.
>
> Both errors have two misconceptions in common. They magnify the Church while at the same time minimizing it. They magnify it by placing too great a trust in man, and they minimize it by trusting God too little. In the Church, man is neither a vessel of supernatural authority, insight, and

power, as Roman Catholicism teaches, nor is he the free religious personality of modernistic Protestantism. . . .

Rather, the constitution and preservation of the Church rests in this, that man hears God. This is what makes it truly great and truly little.[141]

---

[141]Barth, 'Offenbarung, Kirche, Theologie,' in *Theologische Existenz Heute*, 9 (1934): 24-25; also in *Theologische Fragen und Antworten* (Zollikon: Evangelischer Verlag AG Zollikon, 1957), 166-167. ET: 'The Church,' in *God in Action: Theological Addresses*, trans. E.G. Homrighausen & Karl J. Ernst (New York: Round Table Press, 1936), 20-22. Cf. Barth, *CD* *I.1*, 36-41.

Chapter Three

The Path to the Ecclesiology of the *Church Dogmatics*

1. From Critical to Constructive Ecclesiology — A Shift in Emphasis

As previously seen, Barth's ecclesiology in the *Romans* commentary is marked by a strong distinction between the visible church that stands on the side of human sinfulness and the invisible church that is brought into existence by God's gracious action. The first is touched by the second only as a circle touched by a tangent — the true church does not exist in history but touches it only at a specific point. This sharp division between the visible and the invisible church gave Barth's ecclesiology a Platonic and docetic tendency that came dangerously close to divorcing the true church from history altogether, and it was the corresponding ecclesiology to a Christology that stressed the division rather than the relation between revelation and the historical person of Jesus, a radical distinction that made a true incarnation extremely problematic. Both the Christology and the ecclesiology of the *Römerbrief* (if one is permitted to speak of the existence of such) were determined by this distinction insofar as they were rooted in the time-eternity dialectic that governed the *Romans* commentary. Yet, while Barth clearly placed the visible and historical church on the side of sinful humanity and under God's judgment, his thought on the church did not leave the church in time entirely without hope, and he did not in fact completely separate the church in history from the church of revelation.

That Barth did not do so can be demonstrated when his two arguments for the revelatory function of the visible church are considered. The first argument is a negative one. Barth claimed, as we have seen, that the very sinfulness and hopelessness of the church can serve as a sign pointing to the hope that God alone can give. This was not a self-realized capacity for revelation, but itself pointed to the reality that God could choose to reveal in the church's weakness.[1] The second

---

[1]Such an argument, i.e., that God's victory and strength are revealed precisely through the veil of defeat and weakness, is an ecclesiological analogy to the normative Christological reality of the cross and its place in God's revelation. McCormack can thus write: 'It is at this point that we arrive at Barth's final solution to the problem of the knowledge of God. His solution is that the unintuitable, unhistorical event of the resurrection *becomes, by an act of God's grace, intuitable in the event of the cross.* We see the Resurrected in the Crucified' (*Barth's Theology*, 253; cf. 255-256). In relation to ecclesiology, the true church as the elect of God is revealed in the veil of the sinful and rejected one. There is thus a divinely-actualized (not

argument is a positive one: the proclamation of the church, while not to be identified with God's own Word, could be taken up by God as a vehicle for revelation. Again, the dialectical relation between God and the world was not sacrificed to a conception of a revelatory capacity intrinsic to language in general. Nevertheless, God's free grace was understood to create a correspondence between the proclamation of the church and God's own self-speaking. The church in this case serves a positive function as the site of the revelation event.[2]

While both of these arguments for the revelatory function of the church are present in the *Römerbrief*, the emphasis upon the first overshadows the second as to leave little place for the positive argument and thereby a positive place for the visible church.[3] Yet, the *Romans* commentary marked a turning point from a predominantly critical stance toward the church to a more appreciative one in Barth's thought as he came more and more to emphasize the second, positive argument.[4] This is readily seen in Barth's essay, 'The Tribulation and Promise of Christian Preaching' presented in Schulpforta in July, 1922.[5] In this essay, Barth's growing appreciation for the preaching event as the locus of revelation (and for Scripture, from which preaching arises) was mirrored in a growing appreciation for the church as the locus of this

---

naturally existent) analogy or correspondence (though not identity) between the suffering of Christ and the suffering of the church. This remains a consistent element throughout Barth's ecclesiological thought.

[2]It should be noted that such analogical arguments exist alongside and in dependence upon the time-eternity dialectic. Dialectic and analogical thinking exist together; the latter does not replace the former. For a discussion of the relation between dialectic and analogy in Barth's thought and the history of their interpretation, see McCormack, *Barth's Theology*, 1-28.

[3]Klaus A. Baier has noted that 'Barth's ecclesiology is, during the time of *Romans*, almost without exception a negative ecclesiology in the form of criticism of the church [*Kirchenkritik*]' (Baier, *Unitas ex auditu: des Einheit der Kirche im Rahmen der Theologie Karl Barths* [Bern: Verlag Peter Lang, 1978], 41).

[4]McCormack has described this as a turn from seeing the church as the locus of judgment to seeing it as the locus of authority (*Scholastic*, 374-377).

[5]Barth, 'Not und Verheißung der christlichen Verkündigung,' 99-124; ET: 'The Need and Promise of Christian Preaching,' 97-135. *'Not'* is here translated 'Tribulation' rather than 'Need' in order to remain consistent with the translation in *Romans*, where Barth spoke both of the 'Tribulation [*Not*] of the Church' and the 'Promise of the Church.' In this later essay, Barth still speaks of the church's tribulation, but the emphasis now falls upon the promise of the church. The locus of this tribulation and promise are here rooted in the church's attempt to speak of God, and thus in the church's proclamation. Preaching is the site of the revelation event in the present.

proclamation, a church that exists both as an institution and a gathered people.[6] This newfound appreciation for the church did not entail that Barth ceased to see the visible church as sinful. He did not simply substitute grace for judgment, nor did he leave the dialectical and inextricable relationship between the two outlined in *Romans* behind. Nevertheless, the emphasis began to shift. Barth now began to see the church in time and space as the place where God speaks through the church's own proclamation and that the church itself is called into existence precisely through God's Word spoken through this proclamation. A relation of circularity exists between the church and its proclamation, as the church gives rise to preaching but is in fact called into existence by God's Word spoken through this preaching itself. This circularity is not vicious, however, because God breaks into it, establishing the true church.

Barth's understanding of the relation between the invisible and visible church was that of a relation grounded in the preaching event. In that event, the invisible and visible churches were united. While this was an advance upon the radical diastasis between the invisible and visible church in *Romans*, it still was quite limited in scope and could not be identified as a developed ecclesiology by any means. The visible church served a purely formal function, that of being the site of proclamation. The invisible church touched the visible church in this event, but the true church did not have an ongoing historical duration in time — apart from the preaching event, the church remained a purely historical and sinful institution. In sum, Barth had revolutionized the theological program of Herrmann but had ended with an ecclesiology that was still formal in character — that is to say, the church served primarily a mediatorial function, though now this mediation was not seen as a communication of Jesus' inner life or God-consciousness through a portrait historically transmitted by the Christian community, but as accomplished by a divine Word-event in the church's proclamation wherein God chooses in divine freedom to address humanity through the medium of human speech.

The formal ecclesiology of Herrmann and of Barth in these early years may be largely attributed to the fact that for both the church is treated primarily as a problem of formal method and not as the focus of a material doctrine. Trutz Rendtorff has

---

[6]Ibid., 104-105; ET 104-107. If by the time of this lecture Barth had determined the preaching event as the locus of divine revelation, we are in a position to offer a possible explanation for one of the mysteries of Barth's lectures on Schleiermacher, namely, why he began with an analysis not of the *Speeches* nor of the *Christian Faith*, but with an attempt to analyze and interpret Schleiermacher in light of his sermons, an approach that Barth could comment on at the end of his life as unique to himself (*Theology of Schleiermacher*, 266). If Barth understood preaching as the locus of revelation and therefore the theological task as critical reflection upon it, then it is consistent for him to begin with Schleiermacher's sermons as the focus for critical evaluation of Schleiermacher's theology.

noted that the concept of the church becomes prominent for two different sets of problems: 'in the prolegomena of dogmatics, and therefore as the initial problem in theology; and in ecclesiology as the doctrine of the church.'[7] What is apparent in Barth's early work, and in Herrmann's theology as well, is that the church is predominantly treated in relation to the former question and therefore as a concept of theological prolegomena in general and with regard to the issue of revelation in particular.[8] The church for Barth serves as the locus of the preaching event, and therefore the locus of revelation in the present. Its own dogmas are critical reflection upon this revelation as it comes in preaching, in Scripture, and normatively in the person of Christ. Barth's early theology is thereby marked by an overwhelming emphasis upon the church as a question of theological method with little reflection on the doctrine of the church itself in terms of a developed ecclesiology as a material doctrine of dogmatics.

It was in his Göttingen dogmatic lectures of 1924-25 that Barth took up the question of the church as a material doctrine of theology for the first time. Barth's doctrine of the church was greatly influenced and shaped by a Christology and a Trinitarian framework that were also developed during this lecture cycle. This Christology is marked by a concern to retain a dialectical relation between the revelation of the Word and the humanity of Christ so that they remain irreducibly distinct yet irrevocably united. An example of this concern is already evident in Barth's interaction with Paul Tillich in 1923. Though Barth insisted on distinguishing revelation from its historical medium in the *Romans* commentary, in his debate with Tillich he was compelled to emphasize that revelation was, just as importantly,

---

[7]Trutz Rendtorff, *Church and Theology: The Systematic Function of the Church Concept in Modern Theology*, trans. Reginald H. Fuller (Philadelphia: Westminster Press, 1971), 21; cf. 183.

[8]Barth addressed the question of the church in such a manner in the 'Introduction' to his Göttingen lectures and posed the question of the church in relation to its place as the locus of the preaching event: 'To be sure, the church is also a fellowship of spirit and of faith. It is a fellowship with a distinctive orientation, a fellowship of the sacrament. But what always makes it the church, what distinguishes it from any other fellowship of faith and spirit and distinctive orientation and sacrament, is the vital link between this very specific hearing and making heard, the Word which it receives and passes on. To generate faith God has instituted the preaching office, giving the gospel and the sacrament, so that through them as means he might give the Holy Spirit, who works when and where he will in those who hear the gospel' (Barth, *Unterricht in der christlichen Religion, I: Prolegomena*, ed. Hannelotte Reiffen [Zürich: Theologischer Verlag Zürich, 1985], 30. ET: Barth, *The Göttingen Dogmatics: Instruction in the Christian Religion*, Vol. 1, ed. Hannelotte Reiffen, trans. Geoffrey W. Bromiley [Grand Rapids: Eerdmans, 1991], 24). Rendtorff sees such a formal and hermeneutical conception of ecclesiology as marking not only the early theology of Barth but that of dialectical theology in general. See Rendtorff, *Church and Theology*, 181-184.

inseparable from its historical medium. In other words, Barth was led to insist upon the inextricable relation between revelation and the person of Jesus, and thus upon the integrity of a true incarnation.[9] Against Tillich, who had chastised Barth for locating revelation in a specific historical event, namely, the person of Jesus of Nazareth who walked upon the earth in the years AD 1-30, Barth stressed the specificity and singularity of the revelation in the person of Jesus and called attention to the ongoing validity of the Chalcedonian formula.[10] In doing so he not only recognized the church as possessing a real though circumscribed authority but also upheld the specific importance of the Christology of Chalcedon. It is safe to maintain that from this point Barth's interest in classical Christology only increased as the incarnation became a central fulcrum of his theology.[11]

Barth's rediscovery of the church's historic doctrine, and specifically its Trinitarian formula and Christological foundation in Chalcedon, was complemented by the anhypostatic-enhypostatic Christology of the early church and its distinctly Protestant interpretation.[12] With this doctrine the dialectic between time and eternity

---

[9]For Barth's debate with Tillich, see James M. Robinson, ed., *The Beginnings of Dialectic Theology*, trans. Keith Crim and Louis DeGrazia (Richmond: John Knox Press, 1968), 133-158, esp. 150-154. See also McCormack, *Barth's Theology*, 322-323; McCormack, *Scholastic*, 265-267. A variation of Tillich's criticism had been articulated earlier in Bultmann's review of Barth's second edition of *Romans*. See Robinson, *Beginnings*, 115-118.

[10]Robinson, *Beginnings*, 152.

[11]For Barth's understanding and reformulation of Chalcedonian Christology, see *GD vol. 1*, 160-206; esp. 169-172; ET: 131-167; esp. 138-140; also McCormack, *Barth's Theology*, 327-328; 358-367.

[12]T. F. Torrance defines this doctrine thus: 'By *anhypostasia* classical Christology asserted that in the *assumptio carnis* the human nature of Christ had no independent *per se* subsistence apart from the event of the Incarnation, apart from the hypostatic union. By *enhypostasia*, however, it asserted that in the *assumptio carnis* the human nature of Christ was given a real and concrete subsistence within the hypostatic union — it was enhypostatic in the Word. *Anhypostasia* and *enhypostasia* are inseparable. In the Incarnation the eternal Son assumed human nature into oneness with Himself but in that assumption Jesus Christ is not only real man but a man' (Torrance, 'The Atonement and the Oneness of the Church,' *Scottish Journal of Theology*, 7 [1954]: 249-250). See also Torrance, *Karl Barth, Biblical and Evangelical Theologian*, 198-201. This definition ably describes Barth's own understanding. F. LeRon Shults has challenged Barth's use of this dyad as expressing a genuine patristic doctrine. Shults asserts that Barth has propounded the view of Protestant Scholasticism which (mistakenly) attributed this formula to Leontius of Byzantium, but that patristic theology did not use it in the two-fold form found in Barth ('A Dubious Christological Formula: From Leontius of Byzantium to Karl Barth' *Theological Studies* 57 [1996]: 431-446). Yet Shults' accusation seems in the end not to comprise a criticism of what Barth intended to say with this doctrine, i.e., 'the creature's total reliance on God's grace' (ibid., 446), but of Barth's

gave way to a Christological dialectic rooted in Chalcedonian Christology, a dialectic which stressed both the unity and distinctiveness of the divine and human natures in Christ, as well as of the Word and flesh of the hypostatic union. The anhypostatic-enhypostatic doctrine complemented Barth's Chalcedonian Christology by maintaining that the human nature of Christ existed only through an act of grace, so that the humanity of Christ had no independent existence apart from its union with the Word, which itself entailed that the relation between the Word and the flesh of Christ, like that between the divine and human natures in Christ, was an irreversible one. Yet, in the incarnation, the Logos established the true place of the creature, and specifically, Christ's humanity, his human nature.[13] The adoption of this doctrine along with a recovery of Chalcedonian Christology bears witness to a movement from an eschatological to a Christological dialectic for Barth's theology.[14] In this

---

understanding that the dyad-form was a patristic formula. Shults' criticism thus finally boils down to a question of historical interpretation: 'I conclude by stressing again the importance of distinguishing the following statements: (1) that the human nature of Jesus does not subsist except in its union with the Logos in the one Person of Christ, and (2) that *enhypostasis* and *anhypostasis* are good terms to describe this fact about the human nature of Jesus. If one is compelled to reject the second thesis, and the use of the formula in the way meant by the Protestant Scholastics, Loofs, and Barth, this does not mean that one rejects what they were trying to express by using those terms, namely, the first thesis' (446). Even this criticism of Barth's historical accuracy, however, is not a given. U. M. Lang has ably responded to Shults and demonstrated that, while not present in Leontius, the *anhypostatic-enhypostatic* doctrine itself (though not the technical formula) is found in John of Damascus, and is then legitimately taken up by the Lutheran and Reformed scholastics through a study of the Damascene's writings, and thus also legitimately taken up by Barth (Lang, 'Anhypostatos–Enhypostatos: Church Fathers, Protestant Orthodoxy, and Karl Barth,' *Journal of Theological Studies* 49 [1998]: 630-657; esp. 655-657). Lang's point is that it is not the terminology but the concept that is important (ibid., 631-633). What Shults however is correct to note (and what Lang fails to realize) is that the 'central parable' [Shults, 445] or 'central paradigm' [Lang, 657] that replaces the time-eternity dialectic in *Romans* cannot be the *anhypostasis-enhypostatis* formula, for the latter refers properly not to the relation between God and the world but only to the human nature of Christ. What can be said in response, and what we will consistently maintain throughout this study, is that it is an *actualized Chalcedonian Christology wedded to a Protestant anhypostatic-enhypostatic doctrine* that forms the 'central parable' which replaces the time-eternity dialectic of *Romans*.

[13]'The humanity of Christ, although it is body and soul, and an individual, is nothing subsistent or real in itself. Thus it did not exist prior to its union with the Logos. It has no independent existence alongside or apart from him' (*GD vol. 1*, 193-194; see also 193-197; ET: 157; see also 157-160).

[14]McCormack, *Barth's Theology*, 327-328. See also Thomas F. Torrance, *Karl Barth: An Introduction to His Early Theology* (London: SCM Press, 1962), 79-80. Robert Jenson's observations pertaining to the relation between dialectic and analogy remain valid and were

Christological logic, Barth discovered not only a way to relate the Word and flesh and the divine and human natures in Christ, but a paradigm for understanding all divine and human relations.[15] For while the incarnation was the unique, inimitable, and irreplaceable unity of God and humanity in Christ, the logic of the incarnation serves as a paradigm and provides patterns for analogies regarding other relations, such as that between the invisible and visible realities within one church as well as the relation between Christ and the church. The Christological logic is thereby not only constitutive for understanding the person of Christ, but it is also regulative and paradigmatic for understanding all divine and human relations, though none of these relations can be more than analogous to the definitive one of the incarnation. The following chapters attempt to clarify and untangle the Christological patterns that are involved in the relations between the Spirit and the church, between Christ and the church, and between the church and the world, in Barth's mature ecclesiology as found in the *Church Dogmatics*. These moves were prefigured, however, in Barth's first attempt to address the question of the church systematically as a doctrine of dogmatics in light of his newly-formulated theology of the Trinity and incarnation. This was undertaken in Barth's Göttingen lectures.

---

in fact ahead of their time: 'If one went through the *Commentary on Romans* and replaced the tangential intersection of time and eternity with the story narrated by the second article of the Apostles' Creed, he would obtain the theology of the *Church Dogmatics*. . . . The formal structure of Barth's later doctrine of analogy does not, therefore, differ from that of the *Commentary on Romans* or of the tradition. Barth's later doctrine differs only — but this is a large "only" — in that analogy and dialectic both now become *christology*. . . . So we repeat: the dialectic of the *Commentary on Romans* is not reversed by the christological move, nor is the situation to which it brought us abandoned. Rather, the analogy and dialectic which were in mutual necessity the content of the *Commentary on Romans* have both become *christology*' (Robert Jenson, *God after God: The God of the Past and the God of the Future, Seen in the Work of Karl Barth* [Indianapolis: Bobbs-Merrill, 1969], 71; 77; 78). All that should be added for correction is that this move to a Christological dialectic is already witnessed in the Göttingen period well before the *Church Dogmatics*.

[15]McCormack is right to state that Barth's continuing appreciation for the church was grounded in an ongoing wrestling with and appreciation for classical Christian dogma, and that this appreciation for the church was characterized by a new existential attitude toward the church, a shift from viewing it as the locus of judgment to viewing it as the locus of grace, and not by a new doctrine of the church (*Scholastic*, 374-377). He writes: 'What is at issue is a shift in the way Barth existentially regarded the Church, on a deeply personal level a shift in attitude not in doctrine. This shift in attitude does finally result in a material change but when it comes, it is in Christology, not ecclesiology' (idem, 377). This is true — but what also needs to be said is that it is precisely this material change in Christology that provides the basis and paradigm for a later change in ecclesiology and the patterns on which it is based. In essence, it provides the possibility for a fully developed ecclesiology to come into existence.

2. The Ecclesiology of the *Göttingen Dogmatics*

It has been noted that the dialectic of eternity and time came to rest in the dialectic of Christology and the relation between the Word and flesh, as well as between the divine and human natures, in the person of Christ. This dialectic then subsequently served as the paradigm for understanding other diverse relations between divine and human agency. In a parallel way, the general problem of the relation between revelation and history now took a specific form as the problem of the relation between revelation and the church.[16] Rendtorff has correctly identified a central concern of ecclesiology: 'The concept of the church deals with the question, How can revelation enter into relationship with human reality without losing its proper distinctiveness?'[17] It may be argued that this question is the general problem Barth addressed in *Romans* and that the specific solution to the problem was found in Christology. This claim is true enough — but the question pertains not only to revelation but to the church, and specifically to the relation between the church as a spiritual and as a historical reality. The connection between questions of Christology and those of ecclesiology thereby testifies to the need for related solutions. And just as Barth repudiated both Harnack's (and Roman Catholicism's) identification of revelation and history on the one hand, and Tillich's (as well as Bultmann's) divorce of revelation and history on the other, so also he refused what he took to be the false option of either a positivistic and triumphalistic direct identification of the visible church with the true church or a Tillichian flight from the visible church altogether.[18] Barth could accept neither course, and his alternative solution rested upon a Christological (and soteriological) logic. Barth articulated this connection between Christology and ecclesiology in his debate with Eric Peterson:

> But as the pollution and misery of human nature is taken up in the Word become flesh merged and elevated in the holiness and sinlessness of the

---

[16]See Barth, *Die christliche Dogmatik im Entwurf*, Vol. 1 (Munich: Christian Kaiser Verlag, 1927), 240. Cited in: Rendtorff, *Church and Theology*, 21; see also 185-191. Rendtorff writes: 'The extraordinary importance of the concept of church in relation to theology turns out to be a new form of the theological problem of history. This becomes most obvious in Karl Barth's insistence that in the future we have to deal with "revelation and history" under the rubric "Revelation and Church." His insistence on this shows that the importance of the concept of the church in contemporary theology can be recognized only when it is conceived in connection with the understanding of theology as a whole, and thus released from the confines of purely ecclesiological discussion' (idem, 21). The current study attempts to follow such an approach.

[17]Rendtorff, *Church and Theology*, 181.

[18]See Barth, 'Die Not der evangelischen Kirche,' 43-49.

eternal God, as man without ceasing to be in himself a sinner is in Christ forgiven, justified and made holy; so and in the same sense it can be said of a history qualified by revelation that, without ceasing to be in itself what all history is, yet when qualified by revelation it is not *merely* interim.

Certainly the realm, in which 'chosen sinners' (*peccatores electi*) unified and reconciled by the Word become flesh, await their redemption in the midst of history, is itself in all its aspects history and stands in the same dark shadows with all other historical realities. But that is not all which must be said about it. There is the other and extravagant statement which must be made: this realm even in the midst of the realm of shadows is the kingdom of light, ruled by the heavenly Lord and believed by miserable men who yet are his chosen and called — the one holy, universal, apostolic Church.[19]

The foundation for this (positive) understanding of the church was laid in Barth's first attempt to define the doctrine of the church within a dogmatic framework undertaken during his tenure in Göttingen.

A. Exposition: The Shape and Content of Barth's Ecclesiology in the GD

In accordance with the traditional ordering of dogmatics, Barth took up the doctrine of the church toward the end of his dogmatic cycle of lectures in 1924-25.[20] Barth's greatest creative effort was spent upon the earlier questions of revelation, Trinity, and Christology, and his thinking on the church draws heavily upon other sources as he brings his lectures to a close. Nevertheless, even here at the end, Barth's thought is creative and original, and themes are present that would continue to play a significant role and be further developed in the later *Church Dogmatics*.

Barth opens his discussion of the church by making the striking claim that there is no Christian philosophy of history. Over against such a general view of history, Barth sets the particular doctrine of the church. Here it is evident that his focus has shifted from the problem of the relation between revelation and history to the relation between revelation and the church. Revelation is not an immanent principle of history, but is particular in that it enters time in the incarnation and is made present today in the church's proclamation, thereby giving rise to the church itself. The church therefore is *in* but not *of* history, for its origin lies beyond history itself. The

---

[19]Barth, 'Church and Theology,' 292-293.

[20]Karl Barth, Barth, *Unterricht in der christlichen Religion, III: Die Lehre von der Versöhnung/Die Lehre von der Erlösung*, ed. Hinrich Stoevesandt (Zürich: Theologischer Verlag Zürich, 2003). Hereafter cited in the text as *GD vol. 3*. The section devoted particularly to the church is '§ 34. Die Kirche.'

church is in fact the boundary of history, having its own unique existence (*GD vol. 3*, 350-351).[21]

The church is a community in the world, and as such exists as other communities do, yet its nature and ongoing existence are unlike that of any other community, for of all communities it alone arises from and is bound to God and his grace, living from a power that is not quantitatively but qualitatively different from that of any other (*GD vol. 3*, 352, 353). This raises the question of the basis by which the true church can be recognized in history, for if the true nature of the church is grounded in God's action, how is the church to be perceived? Barth states that when we focus upon the church in history, all becomes unclear: 'Have we not always seen that as soon as our gaze falls upon ourselves, upon humanity, that all becomes relative and uncertain?' (*GD vol. 3*, 353). Only God knows the true nature and extent of the church. And yet, must not the church be identified by us so that it can be both recognized and affirmed? Barth's answer to such a question is unambiguous: 'The church of election and calling, the church of the three-in-one God and of those who belong to him is indeed invisible. There is no infallible characteristic which belongs to it.' (*GD vol.3*, 353). It is misleading, Barth insists, to claim that we can point to a specific reality in time and space and exclaim that here or there is the church, to identify the true church with a specific church in history. The church is an article of faith, so that while it is a community more real than any other, it is perceived, like God's revelation, not by direct observation but must be given in faith in order to be believed. It could not be otherwise for the church to really be the *church*, Barth argues, for how could the church be what it is if it is known and affirmed otherwise than in faith? As God can be revealed and known only by God, so the Spirit can be known only by the Spirit. Because the church is grounded in God and his grace, therefore the true church is invisible, and for this reason we confess, '*Credo ecclesiam*' (*GD vol.3*, 353-354).

The important point Barth is making, and which he explicitly states, is that 'the same eternal ground of its [the church's] reality is also the eternal ground of its knowledge' (*GD vol. 3*, 354). Such language comes from Barth's conception of the Trinity as both the noetic possibility and ontic reality of revelation — in other words, the economic and immanent Trinity are one and the same.[22] The recognition and affirmation of the church's true nature is thus effected by God's grace and revelation just as its origin and existence are grounded in God's grace and decision. In short, the church exists by the Spirit and is recognized by the Spirit, as the church both exists and is revealed to faith by a sovereign divine act.

---

[21]Barth would reflect upon this relation between revelation and history and revelation and the church in his debate with Peterson in 1925. See 'Church and Theology,' 292.

[22]See *GD vol. 1*, 116-134; esp. 123; ET: 95-109; esp. 101.

The traditional Nicene-Constantinopolitan marks of the church on this account belong to its invisible nature and for this reason are not perceptible in history but remain confessions of faith. The church is one [*una*], Barth states, in the midst of the historical plurality of churches and confessions. 'As there is only one God, so only one church, beside which there is no other (*GD vol. 3*, 354). Such visible divisions between individual churches and communions should not disconcert us, for they do not undermine the reality that 'the body of Christ on the earth is one.' For Barth, a person cannot believe in the church or his or her own reconciliation if he or she does not believe that the church is one (*GD vol. 3*, 354-355).

The church is also holy [*sancta*] and infallible [*infallibilis*]. Again, its holiness does not rest upon its visible reality, but rests upon the justification and sanctification of Christ himself. No matter how sinful and fallible the church may be in itself, 'in Christ and through the Spirit the church is considered and preserved magnificent and pure,' so that while the church may stumble and fall, it cannot remain down and defeated. The undeniable fact that the particular churches we see are not holy or infallible should not disconcert us. True, such shortcomings should not be overlooked — Kutter and Kierkegaard have taught us, Barth says, that criticism of the church must be sharp. Yet, this does not negate the fact that the invisible church, the church of faith, in which the miserable concrete churches somehow participate, is holy and infallible, so that while it can be 'poor, wretched, blind, and naked,' lose both faith and obedience, and err in the most grievous way, 'it cannot lose Christ's justification and his Spirit.' For this reason, in criticizing the church one must take care not to overstep the boundary unexpectedly and criticize not only the church but Christ. Kierkegaard occasionally made this mistake, Barth avers, and should not be followed in this regard (*GD vol. 3*, 355-356).

Third, the church is catholic, and this mark of the church is related to the first. Barth notes that the question of separation from the church at large is often a question for serious Christians, and it may at times occur that the minority are in the right against the majority. But this need not be the case, Barth contends, and in fact most often is not — the majority of the time the church at large is in the right against the sects that stand against it. For this reason, 'separation is a matter of final recourse [*ultima ratio*],' and it should be undertaken with fear and trembling. The church catholic is invisible; no absolute rules or prohibitions in relation to the conduct of its visible form are given. Yet, while the visible church is only the form of the invisible one, they are one in content [*Inhalt*]. To attack the church therefore is to attack Christ, to disable his body (*GD vol. 3*, 356-357).

The final traditional mark of the church normally given is apostolic, but Barth instead here replaces this with *perpetua*: 'Beyond the well-known three-fold formula of the Apostles' Creed the old Reformed yet added: "ecclesia est perpetua"' (*GD vol.*

3, 357).[23]   This signifies that the church does not rest upon an accident nor is it grounded upon historical contingencies. The church, rather, rests upon God's will [*Ratschluß*], upon Christ's kingly office [*munus regium*], and upon the Holy Spirit's effectiveness [*Wirksamkeit*]. The church is not at the mercy of the vagaries of history but has an abiding duration [*unvergängliche Dauer*]. Nevertheless, the history of the church is a 'mishmash' of error and the abuse of power, so that to look at the visible church without faith one may well lose sight of the fact that the church is grounded in God and that for this reason there has never been a time when in the *ecclesia perpetua* there were not '7,000 in Israel who have not bowed the knee to the evil spirit of the times' (*GD, vol. 3*, 357-358).

Barth can go so far as to state that the formula of the ancient church remains true: 'the church is the mother of faith, *ecclesia mater fidelium.*' It is not sentimental but true to say that we would as little be Christians without the church as a child would exist apart from his mother. This is tied to the fact that salvation rests upon the predestination that has appeared in Christ, who from the start is not the Savior of this and that private individual, but of his Body as a whole. Therefore, whoever does not belong to this Body, this community, is indeed not saved [*selig*]. This understanding of predestination, Barth admits, no doubt implies a very different conception than is normally taken for granted in Neo-Protestantism and contradicts its religious individualism. In contrast, Barth states that an individual is an object of election and calling only as one who is a member of the corporate Body of Christ. That the church is the mother of faith, Barth declares, does not restrict the immediacy of the relation between God and humanity, but indicates the place where this immediate relation occurs: 'This place is the church, the *communio sanctorum*' (*GD vol. 3*, 358-359).

In the next sub-section, Barth directly addresses the dialectical relation between the invisible and the visible church. 'The same church,' Barth asserts, 'is invisible and visible' (*GD vol. 3*, 359). While in the earlier section Barth emphasized the invisible reality of the church, he now turns to the necessity of its visible existence, asserting that it is impossible to believe in the invisible church without the visible one; anyone who makes such a claim does not believe in the church, not even the invisible one. Barth then puts forth what may be seen as a central tenet of his understanding of the church. Faith in the church, he declares, concerns a double and not only a single dialectical reflection: one must believe in the visibility of the church

---

[23] Why Barth replaces '*perpetua*' for the traditional 'apostolic' as the fourth mark of the church is unclear. It is probable that this substitution is meant to emphasize Barth's distinctive understanding of what it means to say that the church is apostolic, an understanding that Barth sees at variance with a Catholic emphasis upon apostolic succession and the historical transmission of tradition. No matter what Barth's specific intention for this substitution might have been, he did not maintain it for long, evidenced in his discussion of the four traditional marks, including apostolicity, in his lecture of 1927, 'The Concept of the Church,' 284.

in spite of its invisible nature [*Wesen*], and one must believe in its invisibility in spite of its visible appearance [*Erscheinung*]. Neither can be sacrificed. The marks of the church as one, holy, catholic, and perpetual cannot be perceived in its visible appearance but must be believed in faith. 'The true church exists everywhere and at all times only in a veil [*Verhüllung*], just as its true members are what they are only in the hiddenness of a veil' (*GD vol. 3*, 360).[24] Barth reasserts that the true church, the predestined church, the church of Jacob, is invisible. This does not mean that analogies of faith and obedience to the invisible church's justification and sanctification do not manifest themselves in the visible church, but since even hypocrites can mimic these things, one must remember that 'unambiguous manifestations of the church qua invisible church do not exist.' Only the Lord truly knows his own, as the individual churches participate in the one true church only invisibly (*GD vol. 3*, 359-360).

Nevertheless, not only the church's invisible essence belongs to the article of faith on the church, but its visibility does as well. The *one* church is both *invisible* and *visible*. This is not a matter of two different churches, for 'the distinction of the visible and the invisible church is not the difference between two species of one genus, but rather intends to be the definition of one and the same subject according to two different relations of its existence' (*GD vol. 3*, 361).[25] The visible church exists only where the invisible church exists, but the reverse is also true, for as revelation in Christ is a 'flesh-becoming Word,' so the true church exists only in visible form amidst the ambiguities of history (*GD vol. 3*, 361-362). Yet even though the visible church cannot be neglected, it cannot be considered in itself to be the true church, for in itself and apart from grace the visible church is the church of Esau, the church of the Antichrist, belonging to sinful history, and no amount of morality or piety can change this fact for the church even as it cannot do so for individuals (*GD vol. 3*, 362-363).

There is thus a deep-seated tension in Barth's understanding of the church's visibility. On the one hand, the sin and misery of the visible church threatens to undermine its existence and belie its claim truly to be a church at all. 'This is the sword,' Barth says, 'that always and everywhere stands over the visibility of the church' (*GD vol. 3*, 363). Yet, while this ambiguity of the visible church is

---

[24]Note that the language of veiling, already present in the *Römerbrief*, at this point serves as an analogy to its definitive use in the dialectical understanding of the incarnation earlier expounded in the *Göttingen* lectures. See *GD, vol.1*, 166-167; cf. 168; ET: 136; cf. 138. For Barth's dialectic of veiling and unveiling, see McCormack, *Barth's Theology*, 16; 18; 269-270; 327-328; 366-367; 459-460; et al.

[25]Barth references M. Riissen at this point. Notice again the ecclesiological analogy to the Christological doctrine of two natures within one Subject. Barth states that this distinction also relates to that between the Word of God as revelation, Holy Scripture, and preaching.

inevitable, the visible church itself cannot be cast off nor its visibility abandoned. One can and must believe in the visibility of the church precisely because it has pleased and still pleases God to give to the mystical Body of Christ a visible, historical body. The true church does not remain invisible in a Platonic or docetic sense, but rather the true church has assumed and assumes a form in history just as God in Christ took on flesh. There is a right and true visible form of the church — without such a form, there would also be no reconciliation, no incarnate [*fleischgewordenen*] Son of God, no residing of the Holy Spirit within truly sinful persons. The invisible church would be a 'cloud-cuckoo-land' [*Wolkenkuckucksheim*] without the visible church which exists in particular confessions and individual churches (*GD vol. 3*, 363-364).

One cannot, however, have faith in the visible form itself, or in any particular instance of the church, whether Lutheran, Reformed, or so on, as little as one can make the human person of Jesus himself an object of faith and worship. It is meaningless to have faith in what is seen, for faith is never obtained directly from a given historical fact. The visible church in itself, in its form and appearance, is a creature, standing under the rule of the Fall, and one should not have faith in creatures but in the Creator. To believe in God and rightly to believe in the visibility of the church, which is an article of faith, is then to believe in the visibility of the church only as it is established from above, from the grace of God. For the church to believe instead in itself, in its own faith and reconciliation rather than in the Reconciler, is already to fall from grace. The church does not believe in itself and in what is visible, but in the 'invisible-which-becomes-visible,' known and truly understood in this becoming-visible [*Sichtbarwerden*]. Barth states: 'The work praises the Master... The visible testifies to the invisible. The honor of the church consists in giving the honor to God'(*GD vol. 3*, 364). In the end, 'one can only be reformed to the honor of God, not to the honor of the Reformed church' (*GD vol. 3*, 365). Still, the crisis under which all visible churches exist, the sword which hangs over them all, is also the promise under which they stand and by which they live, for the churches live not by their own merit but by the grace of God. 'The church, which in its complete lowliness and poverty in all seriousness hopes in grace, is humanly speaking the best church (*GD vol. 3*, 366).[26]

Barth begins his third subsection by linking the teaching of the invisible and visible church in ecclesiology previously outlined to the larger theological and doctrinal framework. He states: 'The doctrine of the invisible and visible church in ecclesiology is the analogy, so to speak, to the doctrine of justification [*Rechtfertigungslehre*] in soteriology and to the doctrine of the person of Christ in

---

[26]The language of 'crisis' and 'promise' is thus retained from the *Romans* commentary and functions in a similar manner, pointing to the dialectical relation of judgment and grace whereby each exist in a differentiated and irreducible, though inseparable, unity.

Christology,' as well as to the doctrine of Christ's work and to the doctrine of sanctification [*Heiligungslehre*] (*GD vol. 3*, 366). As has been seen, one and the same church is both invisible and visible. As the church is the true church only as it is invisible, this signifies a crisis for the church. But it signifies not only crisis, but also hope, right [*Anspruch*], invitation [*Aufforderung*] and call [*Geheiß*]. The church should be the true church, and this should be reflected in the church's visible life, though the church possesses no means whereby to purge and exclude all hypocrites from its midst. Barth contends that should the church attempt to undertake such a purification, which only God can perform, honesty would necessitate that no one would be allowed to remain in the church and the visible church would be lost (*GD vol. 3*, 366-367).

Such a perfectionism and purification, however, is not what is required by the fact that the church should be the church. The undeniable and unchangeable reality is that the mystical body of Christ as an external body is composed of sinners and hypocrites just as it is both justified and sinful. Nevertheless, just as the justification of individuals does not exist apart from sanctification, so also the identity of the body of Christ with the visible church cannot be without marks of obedience that characterize it. It is true that the church remains sinful, and that the church believes not in itself but in God. Yet this does not alter the fact that the church, even in the ambiguity and relativity of its historical form and appearance, is the true church in this ambiguity and bears visible traits that, though themselves ambivalent, witness to their true source (*GD vol. 3*, 367).

These manifestations of the true church in the visible individual churches by which such churches can be recognized as true churches are the 'so-called *notae ecclesiae*,' the marks of the church. Here Barth speaks not of the traditional Constantinopolitan marks earlier discussed ('one, holy, catholic, apostolic,') but of the distinctive Reformation marks, originating with Melanchthon and followed by Calvin, used to identify an individual church as a true and right church. Such evidence should not be either over- or underestimated, Barth maintains. Yet, such marks do provide a standard whereby the true church may be discerned in individual churches, though only with 'human, earthly, and relative certainty.' Such certainty is thus other than that whereby the Bible is recognized through the self-attestation of the Word of God and the Holy Spirit to be a witness of revelation. The Scripture stands over the church and constitutes the church as a visible church. Just as the mystical Body of Christ [*corpus mysticum*] is gathered by Christ, or by the internal Word [*verbum internum*] of Scripture, so also is every external body [*corpus externum*] gathered by the external word [*verbum externum*] (*GD vol. 3*, 367-368).

For this reason, a true church will stand under and allow itself to be tested by Scripture. The first and foundational mark of a true church is therefore 'the purity of its preaching,' rooted in Scripture. The church is called in order to extend this call to others ['*Die Kirche ist berufen, um zu berufen*']. Where this divine call exists, the visible church will bear a mark that reflects this call and that provides evidence that it is a true church: in its human words of preaching, God's Word is proclaimed. Such pure proclamation is complemented by pure doctrine, for pure doctrine exists where 'the external word of the Bible [*biblische verbum externum*] is the measure [*Maß*] and guiding principle [*Richtschnur*] of the external word of the church [*kirchlichen verbum externum*]' (*GD vol. 3*, 368).

The second mark of a true church, standing beside that of pure preaching and doctrine, is the right administration and use of the sacraments. 'Through the administration of the sacraments the church can recognize itself in a second particular way in its necessary visibility in the sinful earthly and human sphere.' Through the external words and signs of the church, God must speak his own word, for sacraments are indeed *signa visibilia gratiae invisibilis*. The church's word is thus a witness to God's own (*GD vol. 3*, 368-369).

The third and final mark of the church, Barth states, is 'a particularity of the Reformed church [*eine reformierte Besonderheit*]. This is the mark of discipline [*Disziplin*] or an order of confession [*Bußzucht*]. Barth states that the church when viewed 'from above' [*von oben*] is seen as constituted by its Head, Jesus Christ. In this sense it is the church of Word and sacrament. The church is also, however, seen 'from below' [*von unten*], and for this reason, the church, its character as a church of Word and sacrament notwithstanding, must be also considered a church of 'discipline and obedience,' reflecting in its earthly life its divine call. Pure preaching and right preaching must have such an effect of bringing this third mark about (*GD vol. 3*, 369-370).

Barth reiterates that the members of the church are sinners and remain so. But there is a difference, he states, between those who are startled at their sin and commit to battle against it in patience and hope, and those who do not do so. Where this commitment does not occur, Barth maintains, 'where there is no sanctification, there can then also be no justification,' and there is then no church at all. The Word cannot be purely preached and the sacraments rightly administered without the church taking up the task of discipline so that not only the faith but also the obedience of the members of the church are taken seriously (*GD vol. 3*, 370-371). The sinful nature of the church's members must be recognized but not given an autonomy that precludes the necessity of discipline and obedience. The church is not an island of peace but lives in the fray of battle. If it does not, it is not a church. The mark of discipline thus supplies a relative and human proof whereby the true church can be recognized in a visible church. While such a standard is relative, Barth insists that 'a relative standard is better than having none at all.' It thus fulfills its purpose for identifying a concrete church as a true church and for providing a norm for its life and activity (*GD vol. 3*, 371-372).

Barth's fourth and final subsection concerns church service. Barth states that he intentionally will not speak of church offices, for the only true office in the church is held by its Head, Jesus Christ, a three-fold office of prophet, priest, and king. There is no 'vicar or substitute [*Stellvertreter*]' of this office on earth, no prophet, priest, or king below Christ. 'An apostle is as such not a prophet, priest, or prince, but rather an emissary or envoy [*Abgesandter*]' of these, and this apostolic 'office' of being an envoy or legate is the only one that the church continues (*GD vol. 3*, 372). Barth does recognize that the older dogmatics spoke of a *regimen principale* that belonged to Christ alone, and a *regimen ministeriale* that belongs to members of the church, but he says little of this distinction. Barth turns instead to the distinction between clergy and laity, a distinction that he finds, like many Protestant scholastics, to be a false one, while recognizing that the ministry of the Word that is entrusted to all (and which is the proper task of the church) can legitimately be delegated to a specific group that carries out this general vocation (*GD vol. 3*, 372ff.). In discussing these 'offices' Barth follows the traditional Reformed pattern of discussing: 1) pastors; 2) teachers; 3) presbyters, or elders; and 4) deacons (*GD vol. 3*, 375-377). With this, he brings his ecclesiological section to a close.

B. Evaluation: *The Achievement of Barth's Ecclesiology in the* GD

Barth's ecclesiology in the *Göttingen Dogmatics* witnesses a number of marked developments beyond that of his earlier *Romans* period. What is initially striking in Barth's understanding of the church is the positive place which it is assigned and the Trinitarian language in which it is described. The church is of one God and his grace which builds its members up and draws them to him, of one Jesus Christ whose earthly body is the church itself, of one Holy Spirit who makes sinners holy (*GD vol. 3*, 352). This church is grounded in an eternal election, realized through a divine calling, and alive in faith and obedience through the Holy Spirit (*GD vol. 3*, 352). Such descriptions would have been unthinkable in *Romans* but are possible here in light of Barth's newly-formulated Trinitarian and Chalcedonian theology and new-found appreciation for the church's positive place in God's salvific activity.

Another key development is that ecclesiology is now treated as a material doctrine of dogmatics and is shaped by Trinitarian and Christological patterns of thought, themselves newly formulated during the Göttingen lecture cycle. The relation between the invisible and visible church is explicitly likened and analogically related to the doctrines of Christology and soteriology. The church is described as comprised of two irreducible and dialectically related realities, invisible and visible, which do not comprise two separate churches but two aspects of one reality in Chalcedonian fashion. This two-fold reality of the church is grounded and takes its rise from a divine decision of election wherein God's invisible act of constituting the church is given visible form in history so that the mystical Body of Christ, the invisible church, is given historical embodiment in visible concrete communities.[27] Moreover, just as Christ's physical body has no existence apart from, but has a real existence in, the Word, so also the church as a historical body of believers has no independent existence but has a real and visible existence as it is called into being by the Word through the Spirit.

The relation between the two aspects of the invisible and the visible within one church is therefore not symmetrical but disproportionate and irreversible. The initiative for the church's existence always rests in God, and thus the visible church has no independent existence apart from its ground in God's election and the Spirit's call, existing not by human initiative nor as the product of historical contingency but as the result of divine decision and the Spirit's act of constitution. Barth thus understands the invisible church to be the true church of God's election which is one, holy, catholic, and apostolic (or perpetual) and which does not exist apart from but in inextricable unity with the historical and visible church, or churches, which are multiple, marked by sin, local and divided, and historically contingent. The dialectic between the invisible and visible church can also be taken to signify the relation between divine and human agency within the one church, and Barth does not always clarify whether he is using the distinction between the invisible and visible church in the former or the latter sense, though these are of course related.

The true church is not, however, the invisible church in itself, but the 'invisible-becoming-visible' (*GD vol. 3*, 364).[28] Barth does not set a church of faith over against an empirical church but sees these as two facets of a single reality. There is

---

[27]Barth's understanding of election here follows a distinct pattern found earlier in *Romans*, namely, it concerns not two distinct groups of individuals but the corporate church as a whole. If one element of Barth's doctrine of election remained constant from the beginning of his theological career to its end, it was his conviction that election did not signify a separation of elect and reprobate individuals into two defined and determined groups, an idea Barth dismissed in both its traditionally Reformed and liberal Neo-Protestant forms. For Barth, election always concerned two aspects of a single reality (whether this was the church in *Romans*, or Christ as the elect and rejected in the *Church Dogmatics*), wherein election and reprobation do not stand in a symmetrical relationship but where the latter is the means to the end of the former. For Barth's complex and actualistic understanding of election in the Göttingen lectures, see Barth, *Unterricht in der christlichen Religion, II: Die Lehre von Gott/Die Lehre vom Menschen* (Zürich: Theologischer Verlag Zürich, 1990), 166-212. The English translation of this material is contained in *The Göttingen Dogmatics*, 440-475. See also McCormack, *Barth's Theology*, 371-374.

[28]Such an understanding of the church is predicated upon an actualistic ontology in which the church is an event that comes into existence through the agency of God's action. For a discussion of Barth's actualistic ontology, see Eberhard Jüngel, *God's Being Is in Becoming: The Trinitarian Being of God in the Theology of Karl Barth*, trans. John Webster (Grand Rapids: Eerdmans, 2001).

a highly dialectical relationship between the invisible and the visible church whereby they can never be equated or confused but also never separated or divided. This relation bears resemblance to the Chalcedonian formula in that the church is both a divine work and a human reality, wherein the divine initiative gives rise to the historical form in such a manner that the visible church has no independent existence apart from this divine act. There is thus a parallel relation in ecclesiology to the anhypostatic-enhypostatic doctrine in Christology. The inner reality of the church is invisible, yet its form is visible, as the first is veiled in the second in an analogical way to the veiling of the Word in human flesh (*GD vol. 3*, 359ff.). The invisibility *and* the visibility of the church are on this account both aspects of the article of faith on the church, *Credo ecclesiam*. Faith cannot be had in an invisible church apart from the visible church, for this would betray a Platonic and docetic ecclesiology that Barth rejects (though such Platonic and docetic tendencies are evident in the *Römerbrief* and were later recognized by Barth himself to be present in his early work).[29] Nor, however, can faith be had in the visible church in itself, for the church in history remains sinful and is never the object of faith as such, just as faith is not in the humanity of Jesus but in the Word-become-flesh in Jesus Christ. A simple equation of the visible church with the true church would betray an Ebionitic ecclesiology that Barth also rejected.[30]

What must also be emphasized, however, is that while there is a correspondence between the incarnation and the church, it is a similarity in radical difference. The church is not a second incarnation, for while the person of Christ may be described as a single divine Subject in human flesh, the church is not the incarnation of a divine Subject but the unity of divine initiative and human form, of divine and human agency in distinct yet inseparable union. The nature of the church may be described as divine, but only if this is carefully qualified to mean that the origin and reality of the church lies in God's action through the Holy Spirit. It in no way signifies a deification of the church. The church is comprised by divine will and human constitution, wherein divine and human agency are neither confused nor divided. One must thereby speak of two subjects in relation to the church: God, from whose decision and act in Christ the church arises through the Spirit; and the church itself, which remains always a created and historical reality comprised of human persons. Another way of stating the relation of the invisible and visible church is thus to say that the church as event precedes the church as institution.

This dialectical relation between the invisible and visible church in Barth's ecclesiology is complemented by a second dialectical relation, namely, that between

---

[29]See Barth, 'Die Not der evangelischen Kirche,' 43-49.

[30]See ibid., 48-49. Barth saw an example of the second temptation in the triumphant ecclesiasticism of Otto Dibelius (with its concomitant German nationalism). See also Gorringe, *Against Hegemony*, 154-155.

Christ and the church. Whereas the first dialectic may be seen as pneumatological, the second is specifically Christological. The relation between Christ and the church is dialectical in nature and Christological in shape in that the church has no independent role and task apart from that which precedes it in Christ and which is defined and prescribed yet also limited and circumscribed by Christ's own work. Christ is the Head of his earthly body. This explicit formulation entails the implicit corollary that the body does not exist apart from nor independently of its Head (Barth does not here state that the reverse is true, namely, that Christ does not live apart from his earthly body, though this will become an explicit though highly qualified axiom in the *Church Dogmatics*).

There is an irreversible relation between Christ and the church in that Christ establishes the ministry of the church, yet the church's ministry can never be seen as an earthly substitute or prolongation of Christ's work but only as a witness to it (*GD vol. 3*, 372-374). The church never becomes a vicar of Christ upon earth. This Christological dialectic, like the first pneumatological one, will carry into the *Church Dogmatics*. Here it is only a rough sketch of what it will become, though Barth will always stress what here exists in outline, namely: 1) that the church's ministry is established by and united with that of Christ, but is not itself a continuation of Christ's work nor independent of it, and; 2) that the church's own prescribed task is marked not by cooperation in Christ's *munus triplex* but by witness to Christ's complete and sole fulfillment of this office. What Barth here has failed to provide, however, is an account of how Christ's and the church's agency interact and complement one another. Another manner of stating this problem is that Barth has mentioned but skimmed over the relation between the *regimen principale* and the *regimen ministeriale*.

The dialectical relation between the divine constitution and historical manifestation of the church and the dialectical relationship between Christ and the church is complemented by a third dialectic, that between the sanctification and sinfulness of the church. In essence, this is tied to the more general relation between the church and the world, for the tension between the church's sanctification and sinfulness parallels the tension between the church's uniqueness and separation from the world and its commonality and solidarity with the world.

The traditional Constantinopolitan marks of the church, Barth states, are not evident within the visible church but belong to the invisible one. This is not an understanding original to Barth, of course. The Reformers themselves introduced this conception when they criticized the church of Rome for moral laxity and perversion while attempting to uphold God's faithfulness to the church and the church's ongoing reality in the midst of disobedience and sin. Yet Barth, also like the Reformers, is not satisfied to speak only of attributes that define the invisible church, the church of faith, but also attempts to identify the marks that characterize a visible church, an empirical church, as a true church. The marks of faithful preaching and the right administration and use of the sacraments are the visible means whereby the church is constituted from above and which identify a true church. Barth is nevertheless not content with these alone but specifically includes what has often been excluded, namely, the particular mark of discipline.[31] It is this distinct emphasis upon discipline and the importance of the church's obedience that demonstrates that Barth does not intend simply to oppose a holy invisible church over against a sinful visible one, just as he does not intend simply to oppose God and the world. The visible and historical church itself is marked by a dialectical tension between its ongoing sinfulness and its sanctification, or obedience. Barth displays this tension in a dialectical method of statement and counter-statement, now emphasizing the church's intractable sinfulness, now the church's required obedience, and back again.

Barth consistently maintains that no infallible mark exists for identifying the true church in history. Nevertheless, no less important is Barth's equal emphasis upon the necessity of obedience for the church to be a true and real church. Here a significant shift from *Romans* is evident, a shift from seeing the church in time as primarily in opposition to God and his purposes, to a view of the church as corresponding to God and his gracious action of reconciliation, a view which nevertheless does not embrace a moral perfectionism. This theme too is only roughly outlined, as Barth relies simply upon the traditional Reformation marks for describing the shape and form that this obedience might take. Nevertheless, this theme will be carried into the *Church Dogmatics* as well and mature in Barth's concept of *correspondence*. The shift in emphasis from *contradiction* to *correspondence* is a shift in emphasis from the eschatological 'not yet' to the 'already,' from 'crisis' to 'promise,' from 'diastasis' to 'analogy,' from God's 'No' to God's 'Yes,' though never leaving the former terms behind but taking them up in a new positive articulation.[32] So while in one sense this

---

[31]Barth's contention that the mark of discipline is a peculiarity of the Reformed tradition is not entirely accurate. Luther had mentioned such a mark in his 'On the Councils and the Church' under the title of the office of the keys, though this was not emphasized nor included in later Lutheran discussion of the marks, which focused upon purity of preaching and right administration and use of the sacraments. The practice of church discipline was a fundamental mark of the sixteenth century Anabaptist groups as well.

[32]It is a failure to see this development as a shift in emphasis, perspective, and formulation rather than a replacement of one term for another that causes the mistaken view that Barth 'switched' from one position to the next — for example, from dialectic to analogy. Such a view has been soundly refuted by McCormack, who carefully traces the continuity in Barth's thought (*Barth's Theology*, 1-28, passim). But the opposite mistake can also be made, namely, to see the continuity without taking into account the real and significant development along the way. Barth himself could at times emphasize the continuity and at other times the discontinuity of his thought, and Barth's progression of thought is best seen as both strong continuity in the midst of real development, and significant development in the midst of true continuity. For an account emphasizing Barth's self-described continuity of thought, see Barth, 'Brechen und Bauen: Eine Diskussion (1947),' in *Der Götze Wackelt*, 112-113; see also

third dialectic pertains to the tension between the church as simultaneously sanctified and sinful, at a deeper level it demonstrates Barth's intention to retain the infinite qualitative difference between God and the world (and here specifically the church), while setting the church not simply in opposition to God but attempting to find a place for the church that neither deifies it nor leaves it in the sinful morass of history. It therefore pertains to the relation between the church and the world on the horizontal plane as a reflection of its relation to God on the vertical one, though the theme of the church's mission that is so central within the *Church Dogmatics* is absent here, as is a systematic attempt to delineate the formal relation between the church and the world.

This final dialectic, in conjunction with the first two, demonstrates that Barth was determined to hold together the vertical and horizontal axes in relation to ecclesiology: the church was not only an invisible object of faith but a visible subject of obedience, not only an eschatological event of revelation but an institution and people with a particular historical existence and corresponding marks of faithfulness. It is of course true that Barth's overwhelming emphasis was placed upon the first and that the second remained at best underdeveloped and at worst neglected, or even at points distorted. But now (unlike in the *Römerbrief*) the second became an important element to be considered. Faith *and* obedience, justification *and* sanctification, theology *and* ethics, were intertwined in Barth's thought in general, and now became specifically so in determining the relationship between the invisible and the visible church. All such relations from now on were determined in correspondence to the paradigmatic relation between the full divinity and full humanity of Jesus Christ, the mystery of the incarnation.

In sum, one can discern and present Barth's goal in ecclesiology in a three-fold form: 1) to preserve the divine initiative and freedom of the Spirit while making a place for the church as an institution in history; 2) to maintain the uniqueness of Christ's person and work while providing a place for the church as a community with its own proper task; and 3) to protect the infinite distinction between God and the world, as well as between the eschatological kingdom of God and the present realm of sin, while providing a place for the church as a true missionary people of God in

---

CD IV.2, xi. For an account emphasizing Barth's self-described revolutionary development, see Barth, *The Humanity of God*, trans. John N. Thomas & Thomas Wieser (N.C: John Knox Press, 1960), 37-65; esp.41-42. Barth offers there not a reversal but a 'retraction,' a revision that does not negate what was said before but now recognizes that what was said formerly was too one-sided. A retraction thus attempts to preserve the former truth while now articulating it in a better way. Every attempt to trace Barth's development is under the constant danger of falling into a one-sided distortion, either emphasizing the continuity of Barth's thought to the neglect of the progressive and real development over time, or of emphasizing discontinuity as to overlook the constancy of Barth's abiding convictions.

the world, a people which stands not only on this side of the Creator-creature divide, and thus within the realm of sin that opposes God, but which also, as a reconciled people, lives a life of true obedience in correspondence to God's revelation in Christ. Such a life is lived between Christ's first and second advent, and thus in the eschatological tension 'between the times.' Barth's goal is certainly not fulfilled in the *Göttingen Dogmatics*, but it is glimpsed. In light of the previous chapter, Barth did not find it fulfilled in either liberal Protestantism or in Roman Catholicism. What remains to be seen is how it is approached in the *Church Dogmatics* and how these three themes, or relations, are there understood.

Before closing this section, it should noted that Barth's turn to the development of a material doctrine of ecclesiology did not entail that he abandoned the question of the church as a formal problem of method. Barth addressed such questions in his section on authority, and there Barth maintained that the church does possess a real, though 'historical, relative and formal,' authority.[33] Such an authority rests upon the fact that Scripture is read in the church.[34] The nature of this authority takes three forms. First, the church possesses a real authority in determining the text and shape of the canon that comes to us.[35] Second, the church possesses an authority in its doctrinal formulations and individual teachers which interpret revelation, and in the church's determination of which of these authorities are to be heard in the practice of interpreting Scripture.[36] Finally, the church possesses an authority when it speaks to a pressing concern of a specific historical moment. Barth placed this third authority under the general umbrella of the 'teaching office' of the church.[37] For the Word of God to come to us, there must be 'an authoritative canon and text, fathers, dogma, and a teaching office.'[38] Yet, all of these relative authorities, which may be subsumed under the general authority of the church, are not on the same level as Scripture. Scripture stands over them with an absolute authority, and thus stands over the church itself. Yet, it is evident that here the church with its traditional dogmas and doctrines has a true and positive though circumscribed place in relation to God's revelation that it did not have in the *Romans* commentary. It is this positive place that fosters the

---

[33]*GD vol. 1*, 282-305; ET: 232-249. See also McCormack, *Barth's Theology*, 346-350. Barth reiterated these themes in the first volume of the *Church Dogmatics*, 'The Doctrine of the Word of God.'

[34]McCormack states that here Barth for the first time advocates an 'ecclesial hermeneutic' whereby Scripture is read in and under the guidance of the church while yet remaining over the church as the distinct authority it must hear and obey (*Barth's Theology*, 147).

[35]*GD vol. 1*, 283; ET: 232.

[36]Ibid., 288; ET: 237.

[37]Ibid., 296; 297; ET: 242-243; 243.

[38]Ibid., 299; ET: 245.

possibility of an advance from regarding the church as solely a problem of theological method to considering it the focus of a material doctrine in its own right.

3. Reactions to Barth's Early Ecclesiology

It should come as no surprise that the majority of responses to Barth's early ecclesiological thought should be the products of Roman Catholic scholarship given the centrality of the church to Catholic theology. One of the earliest of such studies was the doctoral dissertation of Georg Feuerer, published in the *Freiburger Theologische Studien* in 1933.[39] Feuerer's study focused upon the work of Barth and especially the *Romans* commentary, and it is worthy of consideration for it not only marks the beginning of specialized studies of Barth's ecclesiology in Catholic circles, but also introduces criticisms that were to remain constant charges in later studies of Barth's theology, and especially so among Roman Catholic scholars.

Feuerer's criticisms of Barth's ecclesiology, and Barth's theology in general, hinge upon the so-called 'qualitative difference between God and the world,' and it is the understanding of this difference that Feuerer states is the source of what he denotes as the 'agnosticism in Barth's theology' (Kirchenbegriff, 6). Feuerer's central criticism of Barth might be summarized by saying that for Feuerer Barth has failed to relate the divine and the human in a positive manner, seeing them only in opposition, God standing in judgment over against the world. Barth's corresponding dialectical method, Feuerer claims, allows for no true basis and content for revelation, yet Feuerer curiously can critique Barth not only for a radical dualism that fails to relate God and the world, but also for a monism that is entailed by Barth's negation of the human and the positing of God as the sole reality and subject of all events to the exclusion of any true human subjectivity or agency [*Alleinwirksamkeit*]. The human is subsumed into the divine (Kirchenbegriff, 8-9).

Feuerer thus criticizes Barth for what appear to be two mutually exclusive positions, a radical dualism and an ontological monism. What lies at the heart of this critique, however, is Feuerer's conviction that Barth lacks an adequate conception of the incarnation, and this deeper critique unites the other two. Barth's dualism in ecclesiology, according to Feuerer, may be attributed to the Lutheran dialectic of *homo justus et peccator*, so that Barth sets a visible church [*sichtbare – homo peccator*], a church of sinners [*Sünderkirche*], over against an invisible church [*unsichtbare – homo justus*], a church of the sanctified [*Kirche als Gemeinschaft der Heiligen*]. This duality is rooted in Barth's 'qualitative difference between God and humanity' which fails to relate the visible and invisible church in any positive way (Kirchenbegriff, 20-21).

---

[39]Georg Feuerer, 'Der Kirchenbegriff der dialektischen Theologie,' *Freiburger Theologische Studien*, 36 (1933): 1-133. Hereafter cited in the text as 'Kirchenbegriff.'

Feuerer does recognize, however, that these dualities do not posit two distinct churches but rather a dual reality [*Doppeltheit*] within one church, and he also astutely notes that it is this relationship between the visible and the invisible church, between the church as a 'sociological entity' [*soziologischem Gebilde*] and a 'spiritual community' [*geistlicher Gemeine* (sic)] that constitutes the fundamental problem of Protestant ecclesiology (Kirchenbegriff, 22-23). This relationship is unclear in Barth's thought, according to Feuerer. Barth can relate them only in opposition, and if the visible church is only a church of sinners, Feuerer asks, it is unclear why it is needed at all, especially if God is free to act alone and effect salvation apart from the visible church (Kirchenbegriff, 33). Furthermore, if God takes the place of all human activity, why are human things, such as religion, temporal authority, or historical mediation necessary? Why does it not then follow that one either abandon these human and historical realities altogether and accept only the concept of an invisible church, or take these things as part of revelation itself, as they are testified to be bearers of revelation? If one takes this latter view, Feuerer states, one has arrived at the Catholic solution (Kirchenbegriff, 53-54).

What Barth's theology lacks, according to Feuerer, is 'a human possibility for the taking up, or reception [*Aufnahme*], of revelation, the fundamental relationship of persons to revelation and grace: *potentia oboedientialis*' (Kirchenbegriff, 57). This lack of a concept of *potentia oboedientialis*, accompanied by a lack of a concept of indwelling grace [*gratia inhabitans*] is a serious defect in Barth's theology, Feuerer contends, for such a lack makes a real incarnation impossible, as it is the doctrine of potential obedience that allows for a true relation between God and humanity. Barth can in the end only posit an 'either-or' in relation to God and the world, whereas Catholicism can speak of a true 'both-and' of God and man in the incarnation. This failure to provide for a true incarnation is paralleled by Barth's failure to provide a place for the contingent mediation of revelation through the church and its organs [*Organe*] (Kirchenbegriff, 85-87). Hence, Barth falls into a pure occassionalism that lacks an understanding of secondary causes [*causa secunda*] and thereby sacrifices human and ecclesial agency and mediation as well as any conception of continuity for the church in history (Kirchenbegriff, 69ff; cf. 125).

Feuerer himself does not set revelation over against religion, but sees them as complementary, religion being the historical bearer of revelation. In fact, *revelation has become history*, and this changes the relation between revelation and the church. Because revelation has become history in the incarnation, it can be passed on historically, and the historical mediator of this revelation is the church. The church is the unity of revelation and religion. They exist in an undifferentiated unity, not dialectical tension, as in Barth (Kirchenbegriff, 89-91). For this reason, Feuerer can designate the church as both the absolute religion and as the kingdom of God in the present (Kirchenbegriff, 94-96). The guarantee of the identity of the church with absolute religion and the present kingdom of God is nothing other than the incarnation, which grounds revelation in history and inaugurates its historical mediation through the church, guaranteeing the ongoing and ontological connection [*Zusammenhang*] between the church and Christ. Feuerer states: 'So the unity between religion and revelation, between the kingdom of God and the church is thus not a dialectical, but a real unity' (Kirchenbegriff, 96-97). The freedom of God, which Barth speaks of, is not absolute but has received a self-imposed limitation in the incarnation, for revelation has entered into history and is transmitted through historical mediation. The incarnation thus ensures that revelation and history are not opposed, that the true church does not lie beyond history, but exists in history as the product of the revelation which has now become history. Feuerer can thus assert that the church is itself the continuation [*Fortsetzung*] of the unity of God and man in the incarnation, the prolongation in history of Christ's entire historical life (Kirchenbegriff, 102-103).

For Feuerer, Barth's own insistence upon the indirectness of revelation, i.e., his resolute refusal to identify revelation and its historical medium, ultimately undercuts any true conception of the incarnation. In the end, Barth separates the revelation of God from the humanity of Jesus, entailing that Christ remains only the medium of revelation; he is not himself revelation (Kirchenbegriff, 108-115). Barth's failure to recognize that revelation has become history in the incarnation, along with his mistaken concept of the indirectness of revelation, causes him to fail to realize that the church as the continuation of the incarnation possesses not just relative but absolute authority, for it is the authority of revelation entrusted to it by Christ, the continuation of Christ's earthly authority. This authority does not need to be received ever anew, but is an ongoing possession of the church, passed on through the historical transmission of apostolic succession and tradition, and grounded in the incarnation (Kirchenbegriff, 125-129; cf. 115-129).

In the end, Barth is unable to bring God and man, the divinity and humanity of Christ, the invisible and visible church, the Word of God and the words of humans in Scripture and preaching, and the body and blood of Christ and the elements of the Eucharist, into any true unity. Barth can express the distinctions between these only in dialectical tension, and ultimately as an 'either-or.' For Catholicism, they are 'both-and.' In fact, one can state that the first becomes the second, as God becomes man in revelation, revelation becomes history, the invisible church is the visible church, and the elements of the Eucharist become Christ's body and blood through the power of God (Kirchenbegriff, 125). The identity of all of these realities is established by the fundamental unity of God and man in the incarnation (Kirchenbegriff, 129).

The criticisms of Barth's theology that Feuerer here introduced continued in variant forms in later Catholic studies of Barth's ecclesiology. Such works criticized Barth's occassionalism and his failure to provide an adequate description of the place of human action and mediation in the church, as well as his conception of the church as an eschatological event which failed to address its historical existence, continuity, and duration, charging Barth with an inadequate and problematic understanding of the visible church and its place in the economy of salvation.[40]   They therefore implicitly or explicitly indicted him with the charge of a docetic ecclesiology. Emilien Lamirande accurately summarizes these criticisms:

> The ever-recurring lament among Roman Catholic critics is that, for all his endeavours, Barth does not respect the proper consistency of created being, the relative autonomy of man in his relationship with God; that he does not acknowledge the transformation of man through divine grace or the co-operation which he is called to bring in response to this grace; and finally, that he suppresses the very reality of the church. Not only does he affirm, as he must, that everything comes *from* Christ, but also apparently, that everything remains *in* Christ. Thus no church, in the Roman Catholic sense, exists, but only a purely human world, which God touches tangentially, without ever penetrating it. For some, the source of this position is to be found in an insufficient Christology.[41]

---

[40]Charles Journet, *L'Église du Verbe Incarné: V. 2: Sa Structure Interne et son Unité Catholique* (Desclée de Brower, 1951), 1129-1171; Jerome Hamer, *Karl Barth*, trans. Dominic M. Maruca (Westminster: Newman Press, 1961), esp. 159-203; 207-213; 289-291. (Originally published as *Karl Barth: L'Occasionalisme Théologique de Karl Barth – Étude sur sa méthode dogmatique* [Paris Desclée de Brouwer, 1949]). Some Catholic studies were more sympathetic to Barth's position but nevertheless provided criticisms along similar lines. See Heinrich Fries, 'Kirche als Ereignis: Zu Karl Barths Lehre von der Kirche,' *Catholica* 11 (1956): 81-107; Hans Urs von Balthasar, *The Theology of Karl Barth*, trans. John Drury (New York: Holt, Rinehart and Winston, 1971), 90-93; 289-292; B. A. Willems, *Karl Barth: An Ecumenical Approach to His Theology*, trans. Matthew J. van Velzen (Glen Rock: Paulist Press, 1965), 95-114; and especially Colm O'Grady, *The Church in the Theology of Karl Barth* (Washington-Cleveland: Corpus Books, 1968); and O'Grady, *The Church in Catholic Theology: Dialogue with Karl Barth* (Washington-Cleveland: Corpus Books, 1969). For a survey of early Catholic engagement with Barth's ecclesiology, see Emilien Lamirande, 'Roman Catholic Reactions to Karl Barth's Ecclesiology,' 28-42. Such criticisms were not limited to Roman Catholic thinkers, for similar arguments were made by Protestants as well. See, for example, Jean-Louis Leuba, 'Le Problème de L'Église chez M. Karl Barth,' *Verbum Caro* v.1 (1947): 4-24, esp. 21-24; Leuba, 'Die Ekklesiologie Karl Barths,' in *Unsichtbare oder sichtbare Kirche?: Beiträge zur Ekklesiologie*, ed. Martin Hauser (Freiburg: Universitätsverlag, 1992), 59-82, esp. 77-82; Ernst-Wilhelm Wendebourg, 'Die Christusgemeinde und ihr Herr: Eine kritische Studie zur Ekklesiologie Karl Barths,' *Arbeiten zur Geschichte und Theologie des Luthertums* 17 (Berlin and Hamburg: Lutherisches Verlagshaus, 1967), 1-272, esp. 25-33; 100-108; 241ff.; and Christof Bäumler, 'Die Lehre von der Kirche in der Theologie Karl Barths,' *Theologische Existenz Heute, Neue Folge* 118 (1964): 1-60.

[41]Lamirande, 'Roman Catholic Reactions,' 36.

What can be said of Feuerer's charges (and the related ones of later critics) in light of what we have seen thus far?

First, it must be admitted that Feuerer has rightly identified the central issue for Barth's ecclesiology as the relation between the invisible and the visible church, or otherwise stated, the relationship between revelation and history, between the divine constitution and the historical and sociological existence of the church (Kirchenbegriff, 23). Furthermore, Feuerer and others have pointed out a real weakness in Barth's developing theology by correctly concluding that Barth's lack of a positive place for the visible church (though this must be qualified, even in regard to *Romans*) is related to his failure to provide an adequate basis for the incarnation. In other terms, the negative and ultimately inadequate ecclesiology of the *Romans* commentary is the result of an inadequate Christology, and the failure to provide a positive grounding for the relation of God and man in the incarnation. This was mirrored in Barth's inability to understand and construe the relation between faith and history, between the kingdom of God and the church, in any manner other than strong opposition and contradiction.

What Feuerer and many others did not see, however, was the positive side of Barth's harsh judgment upon the church, namely, that the judgment that fell upon the church did not negate its promise and hope but established them. It is this oversight that caused Feuerer and others to overlook Barth's refusal to abandon the church in favor of either quietism or political activism. Finally, the inaccessibility of the Göttingen dogmatic lectures on the church prevented critics from recognizing how quickly Barth shifted to a constructive ecclesiology (even if underdeveloped and one-sided) and away from a critical one (though Barth's view of the church was never purely critical, nor did he later abandon its critical element altogether).

What must also be noted is that Barth would reject every aspect of Feuerer's solution and see his either-or question as a false and dangerous dichotomy. Feuerer had stated that one either reject any concept of the visible church, or one accept the visible church, along with religion and dogma, not only as a necessary medium for revelation, but in fact as constitutive of revelation itself. Barth refused to follow the former path, stating that it was impossible to abandon the visible church, a position witnessed already in the *Romans* commentary. Yet on the other hand, Barth also rejected any equation of revelation with the visible church and its dogmas and repudiated any concept of a *potentia oboedientialis* and *gratia inhabitans* just as he would reject the *analogia entis*.[42] All were conceptions rooted in the same error: a

---

[42]That Barth rejected all of these conceptions and saw them as related is clearly witnessed in a lecture presented in 1929 and later published — see Barth, *The Holy Spirit and the Christian Life: The Theological Basis of Ethics*, trans. R. Birch Hoyle (Louisville: Westminster/John Knox Press, 1993), 3-6; also 13 (note 15); 14-15 (note 19). Notice that Barth finds the root of such difficulties not in Aquinas but in Augustine (3-5; 60-61). It should

confusion of revelation and history that ultimately undercut the freedom of God by making revelation a human possibility and the Holy Spirit a possession of the church. In effect, this confusion sacrificed the dialectical relation between God and the world and ultimately confused the church and its Lord. While Feuerer has pointed out real difficulties in Barth's early ecclesiology, his own solutions were ones Barth could not espouse, for such Catholic solutions were predicated upon a greatly different understanding of the relation between revelation and history, and between grace and nature, than Barth's own Reformed conception of these relations.

Barth's rejection of such solutions can be seen in his essay, 'Church and Theology,' written in response to Eric Peterson in 1925 and prefiguring his engagement with Catholicism in his Münster essays examined in the previous chapter.[43] Peterson had attacked the concept of dialectic in Barth's concept of revelation, seeing it as undermining revelation itself and dogma as well. In his reply, Barth stressed that while revelation itself was not dialectical, the relation between revelation and its historical medium is and remains so. Revelation never *becomes* history. In a parallel way, the church itself never ceases to be history; it does not become revelation but bears witness to it.[44] For Barth, this does not entail that the

---

not be overlooked that in this essay Barth attempts to speak of the place of human obedience while maintaining the freedom of the Spirit and the distinction between God and the world. Barth's understanding of the relation between 'The Holy Spirit and Christian Obedience' (32ff.) is but an ethical variation of a more general problematic of which another instance is the relation between the invisible and the visible church. That this is so can be readily seen when two quotations from Barth are compared. The first is taken from *The Holy Spirit and the Christian Life*: 'The *truth* of grace, which falls plumb down from above, is our judgment and our justification. But its *reality* — the reality of our sanctification — consists in this vertical line falling upon and cutting the horizontal line of our existence. At the point where our horizontal way becomes — nay, *is cut* in by — this vertical line (but this is really a mathematical point), there arises the problem of Christian obedience' (34). The second quotation echoes this passage in a different key, but in the same (geometrical) language: 'The Christology is like a vertical line meeting a horizontal. The doctrine of the sin of man is the horizontal line as such. The doctrine of justification is the intersection of the horizontal line by the vertical. *The remaining doctrine, that of the Church and of faith, is again the horizontal line, but this time seen as intersected by the vertical*' (Barth, *CD IV.1*, 643 [emphasis added]). The question of the church, of sanctification, and of ethics are thus interrelated.

[43]Barth's essay was written in response to Peterson's 1925 essay, 'Was ist Theologie?' in *Theologische Traktate* (Munich: Kösel Verlag, 1951), 9-44. Peterson's essay is reprinted in *Theologie als Wissenschaft: Aufsätze und Thesen*, ed. Gerhard Sauter (Munich: Kaiser Verlag, 1971), 132-151. For a general discussion of the debate, see McCormack, *Barth's Theology*, 367-371.

[44]Barth, 'Church and Theology,' 292-293.

church possesses no authority, but it does entail that this authority is not simply transferred from Christ to the church at the Ascension, for 'Christ's bestowal of his power on his Church cannot be reasonably understood to mean that he had partially relinquished his own power, that in relation to the Church he had ceased to be wholly God.'[45] The Ascension marked not the transference of Christ's glory and power to the church but rather signified a limitation and crisis of its authority, for the Head of the church lives now on high, yet his earthly body remains on earth. The church's authority as well as its dogmas are thus not infallible nor absolute, and it is best not to speak of a continuation or prolongation of revelation. The church and Christ remain eternally distinct, and the gift of the Spirit remains just that — a gift that never becomes a possession but must always be given anew.[46]

In the end, Barth argues, the need for dialectic in theology is itself rooted in Christology — the church must speak of both judgment and grace, of faith and obedience, and of the invisible and the visible church precisely because in relation to revelation in Jesus Christ we must speak of both God and man. As Barth writes: 'Only one who could say Jesus Christ, that is could say God become flesh, God and man, in *one* word, and that a true word, could pride himself on *not* being a "dialectical theologian."'[47] This is Barth's conclusive answer to Peterson.

Here Barth's rejection of a Catholic solution is clearly stated. What remains unclear is exactly how the invisible and the visible church are related, or how the authority of the church with its dogmas is exercised and what agency the church possesses. Barth's stress upon the church as event again overshadows its ongoing duration so that problems remain.[48] Nevertheless, his intention certainly was not to preclude such questions, but to take them up in an ordered and careful manner avoiding what he perceived to be mistaken notions in the Roman Catholic position (and the Neo-Protestant one), an intention evident in his later work. In 1938, while reflecting upon the previous decade, Barth would accept some of the responsibility for the criticisms that came his way, but he remained resolute that a theology of purely transcendent concerns that denied a role to human affairs was a mistaken caricature of his own:

---

[45]Ibid., 293.

[46]Ibid., 294-295.

[47]Ibid., 300-301.

[48]Barth's debate with Peterson has been critically assessed by Reinhard Hütter, 'The Church as Public: Dogma, Practice, and the Holy Spirit,' *Pro Ecclesia* 3 (1994): 334-361; also Hütter, *Suffering Divine Things: Theology as Church Practice*, trans. Doug Stott (Grand Rapids: Eerdmans, 2000), 95-115; cf. Hütter, 'Karl Barth's "Dialectical Catholicity,"' 137-157.

The abstract, transcendent God, who does not take care of the real man ('God is all, man is nothing!'), the abstract, eschatological awaiting, without significance for the present, and the just as abstract church, occupied only with this transcendent God, and separated from state and society by an abyss — all that existed, *not* in *my* head, but only in the heads of many of my readers and *especially* in the heads of those who have written reviews and even whole books about me. That I have not always succeeded, in former times and also today, in expressing myself in a manner comprehensible to all, is a part of the guilt which I certainly impute to myself when I see myself surrounded by so much anger and confusion.[49]

4. A Return to the Beginning

The central problem regarding the church during these early years of Barth's work was how to differentiate and not confuse the activity of the Holy Spirit (and, in another sense, that of Christ) and the activity of the church, while yet seeing their relation in a way that provides a positive place for the church as a visible entity in time. Barth wrestled with this problem in his lectures on Calvin in 1922.[50] What is the relationship between the invisible and visible church, or, as Barth stated, between the divine and human church, 'the church of God' [*Kirche Gottes*] and the 'church of men and women' [*Kirche der Menschen*]? This is the relationship between the 'vertical and horizontal, the above and below, eternity and time.' Such a problem was the relation between the divine and eternal and the human and historical, expressed in the time-eternity dialectic. It was in full view of the difficulty that Barth asked, 'Can we succeed in simultaneously saying the two things as one, that the church is God's work and yet that as such it is also a human reality?'[51]

Barth did not believe that Calvin himself succeeded in successfully joining these two realities, at times stressing the one side of the church over the other, the invisible or the visible. Yet Barth knew no easy solution was at hand: 'But if Calvin's undertaking did not and could not succeed — *the person who has found the right word in this predicament has not yet been born* — his intention is plain and

---

[49]*Karl Barth: How I Changed My Mind* (Richmond: John Knox Press, 1966), 48.

[50]Barth, *Die Theologie Calvins 1922* (Zürich: Theologischer Verlag Zürich, 1993), 237-250. ET: *The Theology of John Calvin*, trans. Geoffrey W. Bromiley (Grand Rapids: Eerdmans, 1995), 177-186. See also Matthias Freudenberg, *Karl Barth und die reformierte Theologie: Die Auseinandersetzung mit Calvin, Zwingli und den reformierten Bekenntnisschriften während seiner Göttinger Lehrtätigkeit* (Neukircher-Vluyn: Neukirchener Verlag, 1997), 154-157.

[51]Ibid., 237; ET 177.

instructive enough.'[52] While the temptation for Calvin was to abandon the visible church in history by appealing to an invisible, spiritualized church grounded in predestination, he did not succumb to this temptation — he never gave up the visible church.[53] Calvin's aim was always to speak both of the invisible church of God's election and of the visible church in human history, composed of real believers, knowing full well the danger and ambiguity that his move toward a visible church would bring. Barth concluded:

> What he [Calvin] really wanted deep in his heart was a church that can honor God in the world, a church that has the advantages of a sect without the disadvantages, a church that knows what it wants and does not want, a church that knows its people, a church militant that could be compared to the Jesuit order in external power if not perhaps in inward organization because after all it is not an order or society but in spite of everything a church."[54]

This judgment reveals the ongoing tension between Barth's interpretative and constructive programs, a tension already seen in Barth's interpretation of Paul, Schleiermacher, and Roman Catholicism.[55] For this quotation not only casts light

---

[52]Ibid., 237-238; ET 178 (emphasis added).

[53]Ibid., 243; cf. 246; ET 181; cf. 184.

[54]Ibid., 249-250; ET 186.

[55]Barth was not unaware of the nature of this tension. Commenting on Luther as a theologian versus Luther as an objective interpreter of the positions of others, Barth wrote: 'W. Koehler ascribes this attitude to Luther in relation to Carlstadt, of which I know too little to judge, "He was not capable of a calm judgement of an opponent, still less of any real evaluation of him"....In my opinion, this statement involves only a very limited condemnation of Luther. In all periods, those who were incapable of really comprehending the thought of others have not made the worst theologians. Luther belonged, I believe, to such wholly independent thinkers. Theological achievement and historical objectivity are perhaps mutually exclusive charismatic gifts. But this is not to say that everyone who lacks the second has the first — on the contrary' ('Luther's Doctrine of the Eucharist,' in *Theology and Church*, 108). In regards to Barth, we have defended his reading of various thinkers in broad outline, but we have noted that Barth left open the door for serious objections to some of his interpretations. In other words, Barth possessed both of the 'charismatic gifts' — they were not mutually exclusive in his case, and the care and seriousness with which Barth approached his subjects and the light he cast upon them is often overlooked. Nevertheless, the first gift greatly outshone the second, and the second at times was not as engaged as it might have been (Barth certainly had difficulty at times separating personal and professional issues). Again we are led to conclude that this quotation by Barth indeed says much about Luther, but also something about Barth himself.

upon Calvin's work but also reveals much about Barth, providing an insight into the principles that would guide his own ecclesiological development. It is hoped that at the conclusion of this study this comment might be remembered as a fitting summary of what Barth himself believed about and hoped for the church.

We return at the end to where we began. Barth's path led him away from the ways he had earlier followed, not only from the individualism of Herrmann but also away from the religious socialism he had embraced during his early years in Safenwil.[56] Herrmann had stated that the family, culture, and the state were the most important areas of human activity, but the first World War and its aftermath brought about a remarkable shift in outlook. The family was now seen by many as too limited an arena for Christian service; the culture of the previous century had been destroyed in the war; and the status of the state was precarious. In place of these, many turned to a new point of reference for Christian activity: the concept of the *Volk*. As Scholder relates:

> Within it they found something which transcended an individualism of which they had long been weary, because this individualism seemed too narrow, small and unfeeling. What German Protestantism had treasured as virtues, namely the desire for community and solidarity, for dedication and sacrifice, now flowed directly into the concept of the Volk.[57]

Just as Barth rebelled against the previous cultural religion of liberalism with its individualism, so he rejected this new *volkisch* religion of nation and race. Barth did not embrace the *Volk* as the defining Christian sphere of activity, and as his colleagues turned toward this concept of the *Volk*, Barth turned increasingly toward

---

[56]The outbreak of WWI marked not only Barth's final break from liberalism but also from religious socialism, as Barth himself noted in an autobiographical sketch: 'A change came only with the outbreak of World War I. This brought concretely to light two aberrations: first in the teaching of my theological mentors in Germany, who seemed to me to be hopelessly compromised by their submission to the ideology of war; and second in socialism. I had credulously enough expected socialism, more than I had the Christian church, to avoid the ideology of war, but to my horror I saw it doing the very opposite in every land' (*Karl Barth - Rudolf Bultmann Letters 1922–1966*, ed. Bernd Jaspert, trans. & ed. Geoffrey W. Bromiley [Edinburgh: T & T Clark, 1982], 154). Barth maintained that his commitment to socialism was always based upon practical considerations, not upon an ideological commitment. See Barth, *Final Testimonies*, ed. Eberhard Busch, trans. Geoffrey W. Bromiley (Grand Rapids: Eerdmans, 1977), 39; see also Barth, *God in Action*, 125. There Barth states: 'Let me tell you this: Once I was a religious socialist. I discarded it because I believed I saw that religious socialism failed to take as serious and profound a view of man's misery, and of the help for him, as do the Holy Scriptures.'

[57]Scholder, *The Churches and the Third Reich*, Vol. 1, 99-100.

a new understanding of the church, implicitly evident in his newly titled *Church Dogmatics* and explicitly witnessed in the *Barmen Declaration*, the first officially-adopted reformulation of the Protestant doctrine of the church to go beyond the Augsburg Confession.[58] Such a turn to the church was rooted in his early years in battles against Protestant liberalism and Roman Catholicism, grew in his battles with nationalistic Protestantism and National Socialism, and came to maturity in his own dogmatic thinking and the fully developed ecclesiology of the *Church Dogmatics*. This ecclesiology was shaped by a Chalcedonian Christology whose logic provided the normative patterns for the three primary aspects of Barth's ecclesiology pertaining to the church's nature, order, and task. Each of these aspects will merit a chapter below, but before they are addressed, we must examine the underlying theological and Christological presuppositions that shaped Barth's mature ecclesiology. We now turn from outlining the historical background of Barth's mature ecclesiology to this systematic task by examining the doctrines of election and reconciliation within the *Church Dogmatics* and their formative influence upon Barth's doctrine of the church.

---

[58]Scholder, *The Churches and the Third Reich — Volume Two: The Year of Disillusionment: 1934 Barmen and Rome*, trans. John Bowden (Philadelphia: Fortress Press, 1988), 152. For the text of the Barmen Declaration, see Arthur C. Cochrane, *The Church's Confession Under Hitler* (Philadelphia: Westminster Press, 1962), 237-242. An insightful discussion of the ecclesiology of Barmen in relation to the earlier Augsbur g Confession is provided by Rolf Ahlers, *The Community of Freedom: Barth and Presuppositionless Theology* (New York: Peter Lang, 1989), 105-136.

Part Two

Barth's Mature Ecclesiology

We believe the Church as the place where the crown of humanity, namely, man's fellow-humanity, may become visible in Christocratic brotherhood. Moreover, we believe it as the place where God's glory wills to dwell upon earth, that is, where humanity — the humanity of God — wills to assume tangible form in time and here upon earth. Here we recognize the humanity of God. Here we delight in it. Here we celebrate and witness to it. Here we glory in the Immanuel, just as He did who, as He looked at the world, would not cast away the burden of the Church but rather chose to take it upon Himself and bear it in the name of all its members. 'If God is for us, who is against us?'

Karl Barth, 'The Humanity of God,' 1956

Chapter Four

The Election of Jesus Christ:
The Foundation of Ecclesiology

1. Introduction — Theology as *Church* Dogmatics

The centrality of the church in Barth's mature and definitive dogmatics is witnessed by its very title. The change from the name '*Christian*' to '*Church*' *Dogmatics*, Barth relates in the introduction to the first volume, is his attempt 'to set a good example of restraint in the lighthearted use of the great word "Christian,"' a designation he understands to be both over-used and abused (*CD I.1*, xiii).[1] In speaking of a *church* dogmatics, Barth demonstrates the conviction that dogmatics is not a free science, but is bound to the sphere of the church and serves the church and not a 'community of theological endeavor' (*CD I.1*, xiii; xv). Theology is quite simply reflection upon the proclamation and talk of the church about God, a self-critical exercise whereby the church examines itself in light of its norm and standard, the revelation of God in Jesus Christ (*CD I.1*, 4).[2] The church is thus the *context* in which theology as critical reflection arises and is undertaken, the source of the *content* of theology insofar as its proclamation and dogmas provide the material for dogmatics, and the ground of the *purpose* of theology in that service to the church is the goal for which theology aims. Dogmatics is a function of the church, and outside of the church 'there is no possibility of dogmatics' (*CD 1.1*, 17).

As might be expected, Barth's understanding of the church and the task of theology is presented in the *Church Dogmatics* as an attempt to avoid the twin errors

---

[1]See also Barth, *The Holy Spirit and the Christian Life*, 37-38.

[2]'Proclamation is human speech in and by which God Himself speaks like a king through the mouth of his herald, and which is meant to be heard and accepted as speech in and by which God Himself speaks, and therefore heard and accepted in faith as divine decision concerning life and death, as divine judgment and pardon, eternal Law and eternal Gospel both together' (*CD I.1*, 52). Such proclamation is comprised of both preaching and sacrament (*CD I.1*, 56). Barth's description of the relation between preaching and sacrament is carried out in conversation with Neo-Protestantism on one hand and Roman Catholicism on the other (*CD I.1*, 61-71).

of Neo-Protestantism (which Barth at times refers to as 'pietistic and rationalistic Modernism') and Roman Catholicism (*CD I.1*, 34).[3] Against both Barth writes:

> The only possibility of a conception of dogmatic knowledge remaining to us on the basis of Evangelical faith is to be marked off on the one hand by the rejection of an existential ontological possibility of the being of the Church [i.e., Neo-Protestantism] and on the other hand by the rejection of the presupposition of a constantly available absorption of the being of the Church into a creaturely form, into a 'There is' [i.e., Roman Catholicism]. On the one side we have to say that the being of the Church is *actus purus*, i.e., a divine action which is self-originating and which is to be understood only in terms of itself and not therefore in terms of a prior anthropology. And on the other side we have also to say that the being of the Church is *actus purus*, but with the accent now on *actus*, i.e., a free action and not a constantly available connexion, grace being the event of personal address and not a transmitted material condition. On both sides we can only ask how it may be otherwise if the being of the Church is identical with Jesus Christ. If this is true, then the place from which the way of dogmatic knowledge is to be seen and understood can be neither a prior anthropological possibility nor a subsequent ecclesiastical reality, but only the present moment of the speaking and hearing of Jesus Christ Himself, the divine creation of light in our hearts (*CD I.1*, 41).[4]

Barth's understanding of the church and of the theological endeavor of dogmatics is articulated in constant conversation with these two positions and bears witness to his earlier theological struggles and development. In the following chapters, the dialectical relations pertaining to the church's nature, form, and task will be examined. These dialectical relations are prominent in Barth's earlier theological work as previously investigated in the opening chapters, and such relations are fundamental to Barth's own distinct ecclesiology in the *Church Dogmatics*. In his understanding of these relations and in developing his own ecclesiological thought, Barth charts his own course in counsel with the Reformers and with a constant wary eye upon the Neo-Protestant and Roman Catholic alternatives. Barth's doctrine of the church stands, however, under the influence and determination of another doctrine, that of a Christologically-grounded election (or conversely, a Christology shaped by

---

[3]See also *CD I.1*, 38-44, 61-71; passim.

[4]That these false options refer to Neo-Protestantism and Roman Catholicism respectively is clear when this quotation is seen within the context of Barth's discussion of both (*CD I.1*, 38-41).

election). Therefore, before Barth's ecclesiology in the *Church Dogmatics* can be directly investigated, the doctrine of election and its correspondent Christology must be examined.

2. The *Election* of Jesus Christ: The Church and Predestination

While Barth's developed ecclesiology is presented within the doctrine of reconciliation in volume four of the *Church Dogmatics*, the initial and foundational discussion of the church as the Christian community is discussed in volume two under the rubric of the doctrine of election, which itself is placed by Barth within the doctrine of God. The church for Barth is established by an eternal decree, and its own election stands under the election of Jesus Christ while preceding the election of the individual believer. The church thus stands between Christ and the Christian.[5]

The doctrine of election, Barth contends, should not be understood to pertain to a *decretum absolutum* that lies hidden behind God's revelation in Jesus Christ. Like the doctrine of God of which it is a part, election must rather be articulated in light of God's revelation in Jesus Christ and must not be promulgated because it is rooted in tradition, utility, experience, or an abstract concept of God as infinite power and will (*CD II.2*, 35-51). To see election apart from the particular determination it has taken in Jesus Christ is to deal with it in an abstract manner, regardless of whether one begins with experience and thus posits an abstract doctrine of election in light of a general object of election, i.e., humanity as a whole, or whether one begins with an abstract notion of the subject of election, i.e., a general metaphysical conception of absolute and arbitrary power, and posits election as a general decree of providence in light of this general conception of God (*CD II.2*, 48; cf. 38-51).[6] Both attempts fail to examine election in light of its particular determination in Jesus Christ.

When election is viewed in light of God's revelation in Christ attested in the Biblical witness, Barth maintains, Jesus Christ is seen to be both the electing God and the elected human being, and election is thus the decision of God not only in choosing humanity for himself but first and foremost in determining himself for humanity, to be God not apart from, but only in fellowship with, the world. As such, election is the 'sum of the Gospel' and the 'beginning of all the ways and works of God,' for it is a determination first of God's own self before it is a determination of humanity for God

---

[5]Barth's doctrine of election is developed in *CD II.2*. Barth's reformulation of the doctrine of election was greatly influenced by Pierre Maury. See *CD II.2*, 154-155; 191-192; see also Douglas R. Sharp, *The Hermeneutics of Election: The Significance of the Doctrine in Barth's Church Dogmatics* (Lanham: University Press of America, 1990), 22-27; McCormack, *Barth's Theology*, 455-458.

[6]For Barth's aversion to 'abstract' thought and the relation between abstract and concrete thought, see George Hunsinger, *How To Read Karl Barth*, 32; 32-35; passim.

(*CD II.2*, 3; cf. 10; 13-14).[7] Election is the 'free decision of His love,' a free decision which God is not compelled to make, for it stands in relation to a partner that is not himself, a relation that is thus *ad extra* to God's own being. Yet it is also a loving decision in that God has chosen to bind himself to the objects of his election, first to Jesus Christ and then to the people of his covenant, and it is thus an irrevocable decision. The content and reality of this decision is that God is God for us in Jesus Christ (*CD II.2*, 6-7). Election is therefore the basis and guarantee that God's grace is prevenient, free, and undeserved, but it is also the ground and warrant that God's relation to us is gracious, loving, and merciful. Barth states:

> That we know God and have God only in Jesus Christ means that we can know Him and have Him only with the man Jesus of Nazareth and with the people which He represents. Apart from this man and apart from this people God would be a different, an alien God. According to the Christian perception He would not be God at all. According to the Christian perception the true God is what He is only in this movement, in the movement towards this man, and in Him and through Him towards other men in their unity as His people (*CD II.2*, 7).

The covenant of election therefore does not pertain to a relation between God and the world in general, but to a relation between God and the one man Jesus, and only then with others in him, for 'the general (the world or man) exists for the sake of the particular' (*CD II.2*, 8; cf. 53). This relationship takes the form of a history between God and the world in which God's entire purpose for humanity is realized and achieved through the specific relation between God and this one man, Jesus Christ, and his people with him, those who belong to him. This 'primal history,' the particular history of this one man, is thus the definitive history of God's covenant with humanity and the concrete form in time of God's eternal free and loving decision to be God for us (*CD II.2*, 8-9; cf. 53-54). Such a decision not only determines God for humanity, but also humanity for God. The doctrine of God thereby includes both the being and decision of God (i.e., election) as well as the proper response of humanity to the divine determination and command (i.e., ethics), for God 'wills and expects and demands something from His covenant partner' (*CD II.2*, 11).[8] As Barth concludes:

---

[7]For an examination of Barth's exegetical practice in relation to the doctrine of election, see Mary Kathleen Cunningham, *What is Theological Exegesis? Interpretation and Use of Scripture in Barth's Doctrine of Election* (Valley Forge: Trinity Press, 1995).

[8]Note that the two divisions of *CD II.2* are 'The Election of God' and 'The Command of God.' Barth's takes up the theme of the 'Command of God' in chapter eight of *CD II.2* following the present chapter on election.

'There is no grace without the lordship and claim of grace. There is no dogmatics which is not also and necessarily ethics' (*CD II.2*, 12).

Barth's doctrine of election is a radical departure from Augustine, Calvin, and Reformed orthodoxy, and even from Barth's own earlier formulations of the doctrine, yet it does retain Barth's conviction that election does not involve a division between set groups of individuals but rather addresses all persons as simultaneously rejected and elect. Barth had never embraced Calvin's understanding of election as pertaining to two groups of individuals, one elect and one reprobate, the members of each determined in an irrevocable pretemporal decision — even in the *Römerbrief* and in the *Göttingen Dogmatics* Barth had never held such a position. Barth's new conception of election in the *Church Dogmatics*, however, while continuing to deny that election relates to two separate groups of individuals, now was drastically reformulated. Instead of an actualistic account of election grounded in God's action in the present reception of revelation, election now is Christologically grounded (though still actualistic) in that Christ is understood to be both the electing God and the elect human being. Christ, and not persons in general, is now the primary object of election (as he is also its Subject), and furthermore, Christ is the locus of both God's election and reprobation, both fulfilled in one person (*CD II.2*, 3ff.).[9] God's 'Yes' and God's 'No' are thus not two equal and balancing realities, but God's 'Yes' is preeminent and final whereas God's 'No' serves God's 'Yes' and is only penultimate to the ultimate gracious purposes of God, as the judgment that God chooses for himself in Christ serves God's intention of salvation for the world (*CD II.2*, 12-13).[10]

The conviction that God's judgment serves God's mercy, that rejection and election do not stand on equal footing but that the former serves the latter, is also not a new development but a faithful reiteration of what Barth had already said in the *Romans* commentary and the *Göttingen Dogmatics*. What is new is that election is now Christologically-determined in that it pertains not to a hidden inscrutable will of God actualized in the present, but to the realization and revelation of God's purposes in Jesus Christ. As such, it is a decision that precedes all others, but a decision that does not first pertain to the determination of the fate of individuals but to God's own disposition and determination of himself in relation to the world, a determination that takes the form of a person, Jesus Christ, who is both the elected and the rejected at once. 'What takes place in this election,' Barth states, 'is always that God is for us' (*CD II.2*, 25-26). In a memorable and striking passage Barth summarizes both his

---

[9]See also McCormack, *Barth's Theology*, 453-463.

[10]Barth can go so far as to say that the doctrine of predestination is originally and finally not dialectical but non-dialectical (*CD II.2*, 13).

difficulties with the traditional formulations of election and also what he believes must be said of predestination in light of the Biblical witness:

> Whatever may be the inner link in God's election between that giving of His only-begotten Son and the faith in Him by which the intended salvation is effected, this much is certain, that in this election...God loved the world. It is certain that this election is a work in which God meets the world neither in indifference nor in enmity, but in which at the very highest and lowest levels (in the giving of His only-begotten Son) He is for this man Jesus, and in Him for the whole race, and therefore for the world (*CD II.2*, 26).

The doctrine of election is thus coterminous with the doctrine of grace, in that election preserves God's freedom, sovereignty, and prevenience, the divine decision that precedes all creaturely choices, and yet such a decision does not demonstrate an arbitrary freedom between rival alternatives but is a free decision of love (*CD II.2*, 19; cf. 27-28). To speak of election is to speak of the Gospel, Barth notes (*CD II.2*, 26). God's love for the world comes not in a general form of love, but in the particular and specific form of Jesus Christ, yet it is an election that is neither owed to the creature nor necessary for God. It is a loving decision that is uncompelled, preserving the freedom, mystery, and righteousness of God (*CD II.2*, 29; cf. 27-34). Barth writes:

> According to Scripture, the divine election of grace is an activity of God which has a definite goal and limit. Its direct and proper object is not individuals generally, but one individual — and only in Him the people called and united by Him, and only in that people individuals in general in their private relationships with God. It is only in that one man that a human determination corresponds to the divine determining. In the strict sense only He can be understood and described as 'elected' (and 'rejected'). All others are so in Him, and not as individuals (*CD II.2*, 43-44; cf. 54; 58-59).

For Barth, election is first and definitively the election of Jesus Christ, and then the election of the community, and only finally the election of the individual.

If election is the beginning of the ways and works of God, the 'sum of the Gospel' first pertaining to God's own determination of himself for humanity before it pertains to a determination of humanity for God, it should then come as no surprise that Barth places the doctrine of election not within the discussions of God's relation to the world in creation, reconciliation, or redemption, but within the doctrine of God itself, for election precedes, grounds, and shapes these other correspondent relations (*CD II.2*, 76-77). This original move is justified by Barth on the grounds that God is none other than the God who has eternally decided through Christ to be God only in relation to humanity, or conversely, God has eternally chosen not to be God apart from the world. Barth writes:

> There can be no tenet of Christian doctrine which if it is to be a Christian tenet does not necessarily reflect both in form and content this divine electing — the eternal electing in which and in virtue of which God does not will to be God, and is not God, apart from those who are His, apart from His people. Because this is the case, the doctrine of election occupies a place at the head of all other Christian dogmas. And it belongs to the doctrine of God Himself because God Himself does not will to be God, and is not God, except as the One who elects. There is no height or depth in which God can be God in any other way. We have not perceived or understood aright the Subject of all Christian doctrine if in our doctrine of God there is lacking the moment which is the specific content of the doctrine of election (*CD II.2*, 77).

Barth's unique reconceptualization of election has a direct affect upon ecclesiology, for if the existence of the church is grounded in election and thus in an eternal decision (even though its historical reality is actualized in the history of reconciliation), then the church is not only discussed under the rubric of the doctrine of God, as election itself falls within this doctrine, but the church itself is viewed as part of God's eternal covenantal intention. The church is explicitly rooted in God's free decision of grace as it first takes the form of Jesus Christ and then of those who are in him, and it can never then be understood simply as a corporate collection of individuals who have chosen to assemble themselves based upon a shared religious experience. Consequently, the church must first be understood theologically before it is understood sociologically, for the ground of its existence is an eternal divine decision rather than human choice effected in history.[11] The church is not simply a contingent reality that exists within God's redemption of a post-fallen world, but is in fact a divinely-established reality that displays God's eternal purposes for humanity, though in a provisional form.[12]

It should be noted that a real problem arises when the church is understood as Barth has now construed it. Has Barth made the church a necessary aspect of God's existence? This question is simply a variation of the broader question of whether

---

[11]If, in fact, the church is to be understood sociologically at all. Whether Barth himself has a place for a sociological understanding of the church in history is a question that will have to be addressed at a later point.

[12]It should be noted here that the election of this community includes not only the church, but also Israel, as these together form the one community of God, a fact that will merit further examination below.

Barth has fallen into a Hegelian pantheism by making the world in general (and Christ's created humanity in particular) a necessary element of God's own being by speaking of their existence as due to an eternal decision whereby God exists only with and for the world. Such a position would be a serious problem if Barth truly held it. While it may at times appear that this is indeed the case, Barth's emphasis upon the dialectical nature of the decision itself must always be kept in view, which is to say that while the decision is an *eternal* decision, it is also an eternal *decision*, and as such it is free. Barth is adamant that while God determines himself to be God only for and with the world in Jesus Christ, God in no way sacrifices his freedom in making this decision, for God remains God over and apart from the world and is not mutually-conditioned by the created order and the historical process, even though once the eternal decision of grace has been made, God's identity is defined in relation to this covenant. Barth writes:

> Jesus Christ is the decision of God in favour of this attitude or relation. He is Himself the relation. It is a relation *ad extra*, undoubtedly; for both the man and the people represented in Him are creatures and not God. But it is a relation which is irrevocable, so that once God has willed to enter into it, and has in fact entered into it, He could not be God without it. It is a relation in which God is self-determined, so that the determination belongs no less to Him than all that He is in and for Himself (*CD II.2*, 7).

This position can perhaps best be explained by noting that while Barth refuses to separate God *from* his actions, and in fact sees such actions as defining God's own being, he nevertheless refuses to subsume God *into* his actions. The actions of God *ad intra* thus define his being and look forward in anticipation to their historical actualization *ad extra*.[13] God's actions *ad intra* and those *ad extra* are thereby inseparably related though the former cannot simply be subsumed into the latter. In other words, the immanent Trinity and the economic Trinity are identical in reality yet still distinguishable, for Barth refuses either to separate them or to subsume the immanent Trinity into the economic one. It is therefore accurate to say that while God's being is God's act *ad intra*, God's being is not simply equated with God's act *ad extra*, though the first is the anticipation of the second and thus the second follows

---

[13] I am borrowing the concept of 'anticipation' pertaining to the relation between the immanent and economic Trinity from Bruce McCormack, 'Grace and being: The role of God's gracious election in Karl Barth's theological ontology,' in *The Cambridge Companion to Karl Barth*, ed. John Webster (Cambridge: Cambridge University Press, 2000), 100. McCormack states that 'God is already in pre-temporal reality — *by way of anticipation* — that which he would become in time....History is significant for the being of God in eternity; but it is significant only because God freely chooses that it should be so.'

inseparably from the first. God's being is God's act, but God's act remains a *personal* act.[14]   While Barth posits the priority of God's act over God's being in describing God's existence, he continues to retain a dialectical tension between them, evident when he writes:

> When we ask questions about God's being, we cannot in fact leave the sphere of His action and working as it is revealed to us in His Word. God is who He is in His works. He is the same even in Himself, even before and after and over His works, and without them. They are bound to Him, but He is not bound to them. They are nothing without Him. But He is who He is without them. He is not, therefore, who He is only in His works. Yet in Himself He is not another than He is in His works. In the light of what He is in His works it is no longer an open question what He is in Himself. In Himself He cannot, perhaps, be someone or something quite other, or perhaps nothing at all. But in His works He is Himself revealed as the One He is. It is, therefore, right that in the development and explanation of the statement that God is we have always to keep exclusively to His works (as they come to pass, or become visible as such in the act of revelation) — not only because we cannot elsewhere understand God and who God is, but also because, even if we could understand Him elsewhere, we should understand Him only as the One He is in His works, because He is this One and no other. We can and must ask about the being of God because as the Subject of His works God is so decisively characteristic for their nature and understanding that without this Subject they would be something quite different from what they are in accordance with God's Word, and on the basis of the Word of God we can necessarily recognise and understand them only together with this their Subject (*CD II.1*, 260; cf. 257-272).[15]

---

[14]John Colwell, *Actuality and Provisionality: Eternity and Election in the Theology of Karl Barth* (Edinburgh: Rutherford House, 1989), 190.

[15]Barth's understanding of the relation between God's act and God's being (as well as the similar relation between God's freedom and constancy) is a complex one, further investigation of which would take us well beyond the scope of this study. For the relation between God's act and God's being in regard to the doctrine of election, see Bruce McCormack, 'Grace and being,' 92-110; John Colwell, *Actuality and Provisionality,* esp. 183-230; Colin Gunton, 'Karl Barth's Doctrine of Election as Part of His Doctrine of God,' *Journal of Theological Studies* 25 (1974): 381-392; and Jüngel, *God's Being Is in Becoming.* For the relation between them in regard to Barth's conception of eternity, see Colwell, *Actuality and Provisionality,* esp. 13-78; and George Hunsinger, '*Mysterium Trinitatis*: Karl Barth's Conception of Eternity,' in *Disruptive Grace: Studies in the Theology of Karl Barth* (Grand Rapids: Eerdmans, 2000), 186-209. Hunsinger's article is an important response to the more critical evaluation of

It is therefore the doctrine of election that both establishes God's particular identity as grounded in his decision and act to be God for the world, and also retains at the same time the differentiation between God and the world by maintaining that this decision is free and uncoerced. In sum, election serves as the safeguard against pantheism and as the guarantee that God's relation to the world is determined by grace and not necessity. For this reason, God remains free and Lord of the church even though the existence of the church rests upon an eternal decision.

Barth's conception of the church as rooted in the election of God entails other important ramifications that, though implicit in Barth's discussion of the Christian community in the doctrine of election, will become explicit in his discussion of the church within the doctrine of reconciliation. First, if the church is established in the free decision of God's grace, then its essential nature and historically-actualized and ongoing existence must be defined in relation to the work of the Spirit of God who remains free even as the church remains constantly dependent upon the Holy Spirit for its reality and life. Against the conception of Neo-Protestantism, the church is not in essence a voluntary society of religious persons, or in other words, self-elected, but it is rather called by God through the Spirit as the historical actualization of an eternal decision. In addition, against some Roman Catholic conceptions, the church is not in possession of the Holy Spirit but is in constant need of the Spirit, for the Spirit remains the free Lord that calls the church into existence as it remains dependent upon God's grace in the form of a free decision that becomes actualized in time. In continuity with Barth's earlier theology, the church exists fundamentally as event rather than as institution.[16]

Second, if the church is elect only as it is elect in Christ, then Christ can never be a projection of the church's religious consciousness, nor can the church take the place of Christ — put differently, Christ's person and work are not substitutable. For Barth, the first view is a mistaken one of Neo-Protestantism, the second, of Roman Catholicism. The church lives only as it lives in Christ, so that Christ precedes the church not only chronologically but logically and ontologically. The church cannot give rise to Christ as a postulate of its existence, nor can the authority of Christ be directly transferred to the church upon earth. Christ remains Lord, as the church must remain servant, for the church's election is a reality only as it partakes in the prior election of Jesus Christ who is both the electing God and the elect human being. There is thus an irreversible order between Christ and his people, the community of

Barth's position by R. H. Roberts, 'Barth's Doctrine of Time: Its Nature and Implications,' in *Karl Barth: Studies of his Theological Method*, ed. S. W. Sykes (Oxford: Clarendon Press, 1979), 88-146. For Barth's own rejection of Hegel's understanding of this relation, see Barth, *Protestant Theology*, 420-421.

[16]Whether Barth has an adequate conception of the church as an institution in time will be addressed in the following chapter.

the church, and Christ then provides the basis for the church's own organization and law.

Finally, if the church is established by God's original free and loving decision for the world insofar as the church is included within God's election of Jesus Christ, then the relation of the church to God cannot be one of direct contradiction (for the church is included in God's eternal redemptive purposes), nor can it be one of unqualified cooperation (for God's election is a free and uncompelled decision — the church does not exist on a par with God as an equal partner). The church, rather, must live a life of correspondence to God in that, while remaining within and part of the sinful world and thereby living in the contradiction of sin, it nevertheless displays the eschatological sign of corresponding obedience to its Lord, Jesus Christ. The church and its order are therefore distinct from and prototypical for the world and its law, as the vertical relation between God and the church determines the horizontal relation between the church and the world. The vertical relation respects the infinite qualitative difference between the Creator and the creature, but at the same time allows for the required correspondence of the creature to the Creator so that the relation between them is not one of opposition but obedience. This obedience is neither perfect nor peripheral, but exists as a sign within the contradiction of the church's sanctification and sinfulness, as these remain in dialectical tension. The horizontal relation between the church and the world is therefore determined in such a way that the church serves as a normative and exemplary witness both for the world at large and for the state in particular.

The doctrine of the church, like all doctrines, must therefore display in form and content its determination by the doctrine of election, for election stands at the beginning of all the ways of God and the knowledge of God (*CD II.2*, 77). Election exists within the doctrine of God and grounds the reality of the church — election should not, Barth maintains, be rooted in the doctrine of the church itself. This must be so because before there is an elect people there is an electing God:

> If, in our later treatment of the doctrine of the Church, we are to stand on the firm ground which is none other than the Church's eternal divine election....then we must begin our consideration of the divine election at a much earlier point, in the doctrine of God Himself as the Lord and foundation of the Church (*CD II.2*, 84; cf. 81-84).

Election therefore stands prior to and as the foundation of all of God's relations to the world, in creation, reconciliation, and redemption, and for this reason the doctrine of election is placed strategically before them in dogmatic theology, placed, in fact, within the doctrine of God (*CD II.2*, 88-89). As Barth writes:

> It is in virtue of this self-determination that God wills to be God solely in Jesus Christ. And it is as such that He is the Lord of Israel and the Church,

and as such, and not otherwise, that He is the Creator, Reconciler and Redeemer of the universe and man. But it is with this primal decision of God that the doctrine of election deals (*CD II.2*, 91).

3. The Election of *Jesus Christ*: The Church and Christology

The doctrine of election holds a central place within Barth's dogmatics, and one might even argue that it is the central doctrine of Barth's theology.[17] Election is not a self-standing doctrine, however, for as we have seen, it is not abstractly but concretely constituted in that it provides not only the basis for, but is itself reciprocally determined by, Christology.[18] Election takes the form of Jesus Christ, as Jesus Christ gives ontic shape and noetic insight to the doctrine of election.[19] The doctrine of election is not a 'material principle' for Barth if this is taken to mean a principle from which all other dogmas are deductively formulated. Such a principle could be considered to serve as a hermeneutical key through which Scripture is read, a key that is itself not derived and tested by the revelation witnessed in Scripture. Barth himself was more inclined to speak of election as the 'sum of the Gospel,' as we have seen above, rather than of election as a 'material principle.'[20] Election itself must be understood in light of the revelation of Christ attested in Scripture, and therefore

---

[17]As does Von Balthasar, *The Theology of Karl Barth*, 145.

[18]The relation between these doctrines is one of dialectical mutual conditioning, for Christology is the content of election even as election is the foundation of Christology. It is therefore puzzling when Sharp states that 'the christological determination of the doctrine of election in particular is not an influence brought to bear upon the idea of election' (*The Hermeneutics of Election*, 2). Sharp is right to see that election precedes Christology logically, but what also must be said is that election does not exist apart from its content, the person of Jesus Christ and therefore Christology. These two elements cannot be separated, even if they can be distinguished, and therefore one is warranted to say that election and Christology are mutually conditioned. It is certainly not the case that the direction of influence flows only from the first to the second. Rather, each conditions and gives shape to the other.

[19]See McCormack, 'Grace and being,' 92-93. The following account of Barth's understanding of election draws upon Bruce McCormack, 'The Sum of the Gospel: The Doctrine of Election in the Theologies of Alexander Schweizer and Karl Barth,' in *Toward the Future of Reformed Theology: Tasks, Topics, Traditions*, ed. David Willis and Michael Welker (Grand Rapids: Eerdmans, 1999), 470-493. See also Walter Kreck, *Grundentscheidungen in Karl Barths Dogmatik: Zur Diskussion seines Verständnisses von Offenbarung und Erwählung* (Neukirchen-Vluyn: Neukirchener Verlag, 1978), 188-283.

[20]See McCormack, 'Sum of the Gospel,' 476-478. According to McCormack, the *intention* of the doctrine of election is to witness to the unconditionality of grace, and it was this intention that Barth attempted to preserve even while changing the *form* of the doctrine (a dualism between elect and reprobate), which Barth saw as secondary (479).

election must be Christologically determined even while it also casts light upon Christology.[21] This reciprocal relation between election and Christology has been noted by McCormack:

> Is the doctrine of election, then, *the* central doctrine of Barth's theology? Is it the one doctrine which, more than any other, is the determinative center of Barth's theology? Our answer must be a cautious one. Barth's doctrine of election was, after all, christologically grounded — which means that the doctrine of election and Christology reciprocally condition each other at every point in a rather complex, dialectical way. It would be more accurate to say that if Barth's theology had a 'center' on the level of doctrinal expression, that center was an ellipse with two foci: election and Christology.[22]

Election, while not a deductive material principle, is nevertheless a central doctrine in the sense that it exerts an influence upon all other dogmas and shapes both their form and content.[23] Nevertheless, it would be a mistake to claim that election

---

[21]Ibid., 476.

[22]Ibid., 492-493.

[23]Ibid., 491-492. Our use of the term 'central doctrine' must be carefully qualified. We use it to refer to a doctrine that shapes the form and content of other doctrines, a use in line with that defined in McCormack's article. This use of the term should not be seen to contradict S. W. Sykes when he argues that for Barth there is 'no central doctrine, concept, or idea' (S. W. Sykes, 'Barth on the Centre of Theology,' in *Karl Barth: Studies of his Theological Method*, 25; see 17-54. Cf. Stephen Sykes, *The Identity of Christianity* [Philadelphia: Fortress Press, 1984], 174-208). Sykes uses the term 'central doctrine' in the sense of a 'material principle' as described above and rightly argues that Barth's refusal to find such a center for theology stems from his break from the 'hundred-year-long tradition of relating the writing of dogmatic theology to a definition of the "essence of Christianity"' ('Barth on the Centre,' 25). Barth's rejection of this reductionist tendency to define the essence of Christianity reacted against both its orthodox and liberal forms, i.e., a rejection of the attempt to find the essence in the fundamental doctrines (*fundamentum dogmaticum*) of orthodox scholasticism or in the religious experience or simple Gospel of Neo-Protestantism (ibid., 33-35; cf. *CD I.2*, 863-866). Barth perceived that such a reduction of Christianity and theology to an essence could leave theology open to the criticisms of Feuerbach, and he eschewed such a center as a threat to the freedom of the Word. Sykes correctly notes that Barth objected to any such theological system 'dominated by an *a priori* principle of interpretation' (ibid., 35; cf. *CD I.2*, 861-862). Sykes himself, however, does find in Christology a 'center' in Barth's theology (ibid., 40-44; 51). This point may be granted, but what must be said is that this Christology: 1) is not a center if this is taken to mean a 'material [deductive] principle,' and; 2) is from *CD II.2* onward a Christology explicitly shaped by election.

is the central doctrine if this would entail that it be seen as independent of Christology, which itself must be understood as a central doctrine in the aforementioned sense. The centrality of Christology for Barth's theology may be demonstrated from a consideration of two facts.

First, from a formal standpoint, Barth maintains that Christology must determine theological method and thus the shape and procedure of the dogmatic enterprise as well as its constitutive individual doctrines. Barth writes:

> A church dogmatics must, of course, be christologically determined as a whole and in all its parts, as surely as the revealed Word of God, attested by Holy Scripture and proclaimed by the Church, is its one and only criterion, and as surely as this revealed Word is identical with Jesus Christ. If dogmatics cannot regard itself and cause itself to be regarded as fundamentally Christology, it has assuredly succumbed to some alien sway and is already on the verge of losing its character as church dogmatics (*CD I.2*, 123; cf. also 883).[24]

Statements concerning the church and humanity are therefore true only if determined by Christology (*CD II.1*, 148-149).

Second, from a material standpoint, it is of interest to note that when Barth chooses to speak of a 'center' of theology he speaks not, interestingly, of election but of reconciliation,[25] as he does in his opening paragraph of his discussion of that doctrine:

> We enter that sphere of Christian knowledge in which we have to do with the heart of the message received by and laid upon the Christian community and therefore with the heart of the Church's dogmatics: that is to say, with the heart of its subject-matter, origin, and content. It has a circumference, the doctrine of creation and the doctrine of the last things, the redemption and consummation. But the covenant fulfilled in the atonement is its centre. From this point we can and must see a circumference. But we can see it only from this point. A mistaken or

---

[24]Cited also in Sykes, 'Barth on the Centre,' 40. For a discussion of the place of Christology in Barth's *Church Dogmatics*, see John Thompson, *Christ in Perspective: Christological Perspectives in the Theology of Karl Barth* (Edinburgh: Saint Andrew Press, 1978), 1-3.

[25]Nor, as we have seen, does he speak of the fundamental doctrines of orthodoxy or of the religious experience or simple Gospel of liberalism (Sykes, 'Barth on the Centre,' 33-35).

deficient perception here would mean error or deficiency everywhere (Barth, *CD IV.1*, 3).[26]

If it is remembered that the 'covenant fulfilled in the atonement' ['*Der im Werk der Versöhnung erfüllte Bund*'] is nothing other than the historical realization of God's eternal election to be for us in Jesus Christ, it is clear that Christology (in the form of both Christ's person and work in atonement, inseparably intertwined) is a central doctrine in the sense of one that exerts influence upon the remainder of the dogmatic corpus.[27]

The assertion that the atonement is the 'center' of Barth's theology, once again, should not be taken to mean that Christology serves as a material principle.[28] Sykes states:

> Barth strives to make clear a distinction between the idea of a real or actual centre of dogmatics, and a systematic centre. A systematic centre would be an idea or a principle, which would then govern the presentation of the whole, in the sense that all other parts would be related to it as either presuppositions or consequences. But such systematization is, he holds, illegitimate. By contrast the Atonement must be said to be the actual or real centre, in the sense that it is a report about the act, and hence the being, of God.[29]

---

[26]Cited in Sykes, 'Barth on the Centre,' 39.

[27]As Thompson rightly notes: 'Again, it should be clear what this does and does not mean. It does not mean that there is no theology except Christology, that all other theology is absorbed into it....It means rather that all aspects of theology and dogmatics must be dynamically related to this living and concrete centre and be determined throughout by it' (*Christ in Perspective*, 2). Barth states that Christology is related to the other doctrines in that it 'thereby describes as it were an inner circle surrounded by a host of other concentric circles in each of which it is repeated, and in which its truth and recognition must be maintained and expounded' (*CD I.2*, 133; cf. Thompson, *Christ in Perspective*, 2-3).

[28]To speak of the atonement is to speak, of course, of Christology. Christology for Barth includes not only a discussion of Christ's person but also of his work, and these in fact are inseparable, for as God's being is defined by his activity, so correspondingly is Christ's person defined by his work, a conviction expressed throughout Barth's doctrine of reconciliation. Both Barth's Trinitarian and Christological thought are thus actualistic rather than primarily based upon an ontology of substance or natures. For Barth's actualism in relation to Christology, see *CD IV.2*, 105-113; cf. *CD I.2*, 170-171. See also Thompson, *Christ in Perspective*, 15-16.

[29]Sykes, 'Barth on the Centre,' 40.

As Sykes notes, Barth was reticent to speak of a doctrine (Christology) rather than divine act (the reconciliation effected by God in Christ) as the 'center' of theology.[30] This reticence was due to his adamancy to protect the object of theology from control by the theologian.[31] Barth's genuine concern must be understood and not brushed aside, for Barth is surely correct in maintaining that the true foundation of dogmatics must reside in a divine event rather than human ratiocination. Nevertheless, from a *dogmatic* standpoint, that is to say, from the view of theological doctrinal formulation, it is entirely justifiable to examine the structure that Barth gave to his dogmatic presentation with an eye towards determining its center. It is in this sense undeniable that in spite of Barth's protestations against a center in theology, Christology does serve as such a center, though Barth would rather conceive this as God's own act rather than as a doctrine,[32] as this center itself must be determined by revelation.

To summarize this discussion we might say that in truth the center of theology for Barth is properly the Word of God, Jesus Christ himself. In a secondary sense, however, and in relation to doctrinal reflection and dogmatic structure, we might concur with McCormack in saying that the center is an ellipse with two foci, election and Christology, but only if this is further qualified and clarified by maintaining that: 1) election is not construed as a deductive principle but the beginning of all of God's ways and works with humanity, and thus the fulcrum of other doctrines; 2) Christology is seen not only as concerning Christ's person but also his work, so that one can say that the center is ontologically construed as the person of Christ but also narratively construed as the action of God in fulfilling this atonement in Christ, and that these are in fact inseparable and mutually determinative, and; 3) these two foci are themselves placed in a Trinitarian framework. The doctrines of the Trinity, of Christ, and of election are thus inter-twined.

In addition, it should be noted that other doctrines are not deduced from election and Christology but are influenced by them in that their content and the relation between the divine and human elements that they describe are shaped by the unity, distinctiveness, and asymmetrical and irreversible relation that one finds in the ultimate and paradigmatic unity of God and man in Jesus Christ, established in an

---

[30]Sykes states: 'The centrality of the Atonement is thus not the centrality of a doctrine of the Atonement, but the centrality of the act of Atonement in which God is God' (ibid., 40; cf. *CD IV.1*, 7).

[31]Ibid., 50-51.

[32]Ibid., 41-44. This point is put another way when Barth states that the 'centre and foundation of dogmatics and of church proclamation' is the Word of God (*CD I.2*, 869). In this way, the Word of God, or Jesus Christ, is never replaced by a doctrine of the person of Christ, or Christology.

eternal decision of grace.[33] Election and Christology are two sides of one reality, and they are thus mutually determined, in that for Barth a Christology of incarnation shapes the understanding of election, but election provides a foundation for such an incarnational Christology. We might even say that Barth's newly formulated doctrine of election provides the grounding for a conviction that Barth already held, namely, that the name 'Jesus Christ' denotes the incarnation of God and not the highest pinnacle of human religious consciousness or moral attainment.[34] It provides this basis in that the incarnation is now grounded in an eternal decision of God to be God for us in Jesus Christ, a decision of the Father, the Son, and the Holy Spirit (*CD II.2*, 101-102; 107; 110; 158).

If Christology determines election even as election determines Christology, then not only the doctrine of election but also Christology will influence the specific shape that the doctrine of the church takes in both its form and content. This not only means that the church finds its election only as it participates in the election of Christ, though this is true as seen in the previous section. It also entails that the relation between divine and human agency in the church, God's action in and through the church, will be patterned upon the paradigmatic reality of the Christological relation between the Word and flesh of Christ, the hypostatic union. The Chalcedonian pattern is thus not incidental but integral to the fact that God has chosen to predicate all of his relations with humanity upon the unique and irreplaceable relation between God and humanity in the person of Jesus Christ.

That this relation in Christ is unique and unsubstitutable, however, also grounds the irrevocable fact that the church can never be a second incarnation. The relation between the Word and flesh in Christ is a once-for-all and unique event. Nevertheless, the fact that the church exists only through the divine will entails that the relation between God and the church be patterned upon and correspond to the Christological definition. This must be understood if Barth's language of the church as Christ's 'earthly-historical form of existence' [*'irdisch-geschichtliche*

---

[33]Barth thus avoids speaking of both a 'material principle' for dogmatics (McCormack) as well as of an 'essence of Christianity' (Sykes) but replaces these with what he calls 'the sum of the Gospel' (election) and with the 'heart' and 'centre' of dogmatics ('the covenant fulfilled in the atonement,' i.e., Christology [*CD IV.1*, 3]).

[34]The difference between these two viewpoints may be described as the essence of the debate over Christology between Barth and Harnack in 1923. See Sykes, 'Barth on the Centre,' 28-29. Construed in terms of method, Barth emphasizes that the content of theology determines the method employed, whereas he held that this was the opposite for Harnack and the liberal tradition (ibid., 29). For an examination of the issues involved in the exchange between Barth and Harnack, see H. Martin Rumscheidt, *Revelation and Theology: An analysis of the Barth-Harnack correspondence of 1923* (Cambridge: Cambridge University Press, 1972); cf. George Hunsinger, 'The Harnack/Barth Correspondence: A Paraphrase with Comments,' in *Thomist* 50 (1986): 599-622; also included in *Disruptive Grace*, 319-337.

Existenzform'] is to be rendered intelligible (*CD IV.1*, 643; passim). The church does not replace Christ nor does it stand as a second incarnation. Yet its existence does stand in qualified correspondence to the divine and human relation that exists in the person of Jesus Christ.

To understand the shape of this Christology itself, we might begin by looking at Barth's understanding of the election of Jesus Christ as this is articulated in *CD II.2*. The opening thesis of § 33, 'The Election of Jesus Christ,' states:

> The election of grace is the eternal beginning of all the ways and works of God in Jesus Christ. In Jesus Christ God in His free grace determines Himself for sinful man and sinful man for Himself. He therefore takes upon Himself the rejection of man with all its consequences, and elects man to participation in His own glory' (*CD II.2*, 94).

This quotation implies that Jesus Christ is the basis of the relation between God and all that is not himself (*CD II.2*, 94-95). Put differently, election is the eternal foundation of God's free grace and Jesus Christ the historical expression of that loving will, as election preserves God's freedom, so that God is not 'objectified in history.'[35] God's works in time are thus grounded in the eternal decision of election whereby God's freedom and aseity are preserved, a decision which gives to 'the world and time and all that is in them their origin, their direction and their destiny' (*CD II.2*, 99-100). This is, of course, another way of saying that whereas history might be a predicate of revelation, revelation is never a predicate of history. Here election becomes, once again, the basis for a conviction that Barth had long held, as evidenced in his earlier polemics against liberalism and his debates with Catholicism.

Central to Barth's Christological thought is the understanding that what took place in Jesus Christ was not a historical contingency but was rather the fulfillment in time of the eternal decision of God in election: 'For what took place in Jesus Christ...was not merely a temporal event, but the eternal will of God temporally actualised and revealed in that event' (*CD II.2*, 179). Correspondingly, election itself is not a static concept, a pretemporal decision to which God is imprisoned, but a free divine decision. This God determines himself for humanity, but in so doing remains the living God, so that while God's action remains ever true to his character, it remains the action of a *living* God, and is thus dynamic, including 'developments and alterations' ['*Wendungen und Veränderungen*'] which do not undermine the unchangeability of election but in fact are its true expression. It is precisely because of the dynamic, rather than static, nature of election (contrary to a 'lifeless and timeless rule for temporal life' of the *decretum absolutum* [*CD II.2*, 187]) that

---

[35]D. F. Ford, 'Barth's Interpretation of the Bible,' in *Karl Barth: Studies of his Theological Method*, 62; cf. 69-70.

Christology also cannot simply be the description of static 'natures' undergirded by a metaphysical ontology of substance. It must be, rather, the description of a dynamic movement, or more accurately, movements, first from God to man, and then from man to God, best described within an actualistic, or historic, ontology.[36] These two movements are the description of a single history between God and the world in Jesus Christ, the historical actualization of the covenant, and they are best depicted in terms of a juxtaposition of narratives rather than as an explanation of a metaphysics of natures and substances, the narrative of the humiliation of God and that of the exaltation of humanity.[37] Barth relates this point: 'Who and what Jesus Christ is, is something which can only be told, not a system which can be considered and

---

[36]See *CD II.1*, 257-272; cf. *CD IV.1*, 6-8. For a discussion of Barth's actualistic ontology see McCormack, 'Grace and being,' 92-110; and George Hunsinger, *How To Read Karl Barth*, 4; 30-32; passim. We would add that this actualistic ontology is a historic (and thus narratively construed) one as well. It is so because God's being is not only determined by God's acts, but these acts are themselves consistent and coherent with one another. God does not act arbitrarily and without purpose — a purely event-oriented ontology could be nothing less than capriciousness (demonstrated in the ontology of existentialism and its [notorious] exemplification in Sartre's *Nausea*). This is certainly not the ontology embraced by Barth. What gives coherence to God's acts is the unified purpose behind them which arises from their basis in God's eternal gracious election and the consistency of God's character. Such actions are thus teleologically ordered and can be related in terms of a coherent history, or narrative (cf. McCormack, *Karl Barth*, 459-460). Nigel Biggar nicely summarizes this point in regard to the divine and human encounter as God's command in Barth's theology: 'The fact that each singular event of encounter between the commanding God and sinful human being is a moment in a history which is ordered by this definite intention of God gives to each historically contingent divine command its *ratio* and raises it above the status of one element in a chaos of individual conflicting intimations to individual human beings in individual situations' (Biggar, *The Hastening That Waits: Karl Barth's Ethics* [Oxford: Clarendon Press, 1993], 28). Such an approach is too often overlooked in understanding Barth's ontology and leads to a reading of Barth that denies a consistency to divine and human action. A narrative approach to Barth's ontology is witnessed from a theological standpoint in Hans Frei's *The Identity of Jesus Christ* (Philadelphia: Fortress Press, 1975) and is not unlike the philosophical standpoint presented in Alasdair MacIntyre's *After Virtue*, 2nd ed. (Notre Dame: University of Notre Dame Press, 1984). Barth's historic/narrative ontology is closely tied to his own reading strategy of Scripture. See Ford, 'Barth's Interpretation of the Bible,' 55-87; cf. also Ford, *Barth and God's Story: Biblical Narrative and the Theological Method of Karl Barth in the* 'Church Dogmatics' (Frankfurt am Main: Verlag Peter Lang, 1981).

[37]The concept of a 'juxtaposition' of narratives is borrowed from Hunsinger, 'Karl Barth's Christology: Its Basic Chalcedonian Character,' in *Disruptive Grace*, 135-137.

described' (*CD II.2*, 188). As George Hunsinger has stated, Barth's Christological thought here is closer to narratology than to metaphysics.[38]

Election is, on this account, the decision in which Jesus Christ lives with God and is thus an election of grace, in which God has determined himself to be for the world in Jesus Christ, and in doing so to be gracious to the world. Jesus is the personal realization in time of God's eternal gracious covenant with the world (*CD II.2*, 100-102). Yet even though the eternal election of Jesus Christ is a gracious one, this does not entail that only election and not reprobation remains. Election is still of a two-fold form, though now Christ himself is both the elect and the reprobate, even as he is both the electing God and the elected human being in one. In regard to the former relation of Christ as elect and reprobate, Barth contends that Christ's suffering and death signify that in the incarnation God has taken upon himself 'all the consequences of man's action — his rejection and his death' (*CD II.2*, 124). In Christ, God has both elected humanity for fellowship with himself and taken up humanity's own reprobation:

> If we would know what it was that God elected for Himself when He elected fellowship with man, then we can answer only that He elected our rejection. He made it His own. He bore it and suffered it with all its most bitter consequences. For the sake of this choice and for the sake of man He hazarded Himself wholly and utterly. He elected our suffering...He elected it as His own suffering. This is the extent to which His election is an election of grace, an election of love, an election to give Himself, an election to empty and abase Himself for the sake of the elect (*CD II.2*, 164-165).

That Christ is both the elect and the rejected is grounded in the fact that he is first both the electing God and the elected human being. In regard to the relation of Christ as both the divine Elector and the human elect, Barth writes:

> In its simplest and most comprehensive form the dogma of predestination consists, then, in the assertion that the divine predestination is the election of Jesus Christ. But the concept of election has a double reference — to the elector and to the elected. And so, too, the name of Jesus Christ has within itself the double reference: the One called by this name is both very God and very man. Thus the simplest form of the dogma may be divided at once into the two assertions that Jesus Christ is the electing God, and that he is also elected man (*CD II.2*, 103).

---

[38]Hunsinger, 'Karl Barth's Christology,' 137. Hunsinger rightly notes that Barth's Christology is Chalcedonian in that it takes up both Alexandrian and Antiochene concerns.

Not only does Christ embody God's election and rejection in one person, but Christ also is both the active Subject of election as God (with the Father and the Spirit) and the passive object of election as man (*CD II.2*, 103-106; also 115-117). For Barth it is crucial that Jesus Christ be not only the object but also the Subject of election, for if Christ is not God incarnate, we have no true knowledge of God, for God can be revealed only by himself. If then we ourselves are elect, it is only insofar as we are included in and with the election of Christ. It is in the election of Christ that we ourselves are elect and thus the inheritors of the covenant and children of God (*CD II.2*, 105-106).

Barth states that Jesus is the electing God, the Subject of the eternal election of grace, and that Jesus Christ is the elect human, the object of eternal election: 'Strictly speaking, the whole dogma of predestination is contained in these two statements' (*CD II.2*, 145). These statements cannot be separated, and we might even say that it is these two statements that now come to express Barth's Chalcedonian Christology, for Christ is both the electing God and the elected human person, the Elector and the Elect, both in an inseparable yet unconfused unity. In this Christologically-determined doctrine of predestination, Barth parts company with earlier formulations wherein the Subject of predestination is God and the object is humanity — for Barth, this leads to an unknown and abstract conception of God and humanity (*CD II.2*, 146). The difference from this and Barth's conception hinges, Barth states, upon the question of Christology, for Christ is the epistemological key to the doctrine of predestination just as he provides its ontological content (*CD II.2*, 149; 152-153).[39]

We now can see that Barth's reconception of the Reformed doctrine of double predestination refers to two polarities: 1) the electing act of God and the election of humanity, in that Jesus Christ is both the electing God and the elected human being, and; 2) the election of humanity in Christ and the rejection of sin taken up by Christ — God thus elects us for salvation and elects himself to take our rejection so that Jesus Christ is both the elected and rejected one. There is thus a gain for humanity, but a great cost for God (*CD II.2*, 161-165).

Barth's conception of Christ in the light of this new understanding of election (and of election in this new understanding of Christ) demonstrates an enrichment of

---

[39]'The will of God is Jesus Christ, and this will is known to us in the revelation of Jesus Christ. If we acknowledge this, if we seriously accept Jesus Christ as the content of this will, then we cannot seek any other will of God, either in heaven or earth, either in time or eternity' (*CD II.2*, 157). Barth had earlier expressed this point in his Gifford lectures: 'God's eternal decree and man's election and thus the whole of what is called the doctrine of Predestination cannot but be misunderstood unless it is understood in its connection with the truth of the divine-human nature of Jesus Christ' (Barth, *The Knowledge of God and the Service of God According to the Teaching of the Reformation* [London: Hodder and Stoughton, 1938/1949], 77; cf. 77-79).

his Christological thought, seen in a number of aspects. First, Christology is given a basis in an eternal decision, yet Christology, as the description of the historically actualized reality of this eternal decision, is now itself historically narrated or construed. Barth writes: 'Because it is identical with the election of Jesus Christ, the eternal will of God is a divine activity in the form of the history, encounter and decision between God and man' (*CD II.2*, 175).[40] God's works in the world *ad extra* are grounded in an eternal and free decision *ad intra*. The form that this divine activity in the world takes is Jesus Christ, and the person of Christ must be described in terms of his acts which themselves are united in a history. Barth's actualistic ontology thereby pertains not only to God's being as triune but also to Christ's own person, in that Christ's person cannot be described apart from his work. This description takes the form of a Christological narrative, and this is in fact what we find in Barth's Christology proper in the doctrine of reconciliation, though its basis is laid here in the doctrine of election.

Second, in election, God's freedom and sovereignty are preserved in that God's action precedes and human action follows. It is not that God and man simply cooperate:

> It is not that God and man begin to have dealings with each other, but that God begins to have dealings with man. Without any qualification the precedence is with God. There can be no question of any activity on man's part except upon the basis of the prior activity of God, and in the obvious form of a human response to this prior activity (*CD II.2*, 176).

Barth reiterates this point in the doctrine of reconciliation when he states: 'In this movement from a narrower to a wider usage the statement 'God with us' is the centre of the Christian message — and always in such a way that it is primarily a statement about God and only then and for that reason a statement about us men' (*CD IV.1*, 5).

This conception of election preserves the anti-adoptionist and anhypostatic-enhypostatic logic of his earlier Christology, in that Christ's humanity exists only insofar as it is established by a prior divine decision upon which it is forever dependent. This demonstrates the asymmetrical relation between Christ's divinity and humanity, the latter always dependent upon the former, for Christ's election as man

---

[40]This position is carefully developed here in the doctrine of election, but it is hinted at already in *CD I.2* where Barth asserts that to say that the 'Word became flesh' also means that the 'Word became time' (50; cf. 45-50). Here the basis is laid for a descriptive Christology that takes the form of a narration of Christ's action from two juxtaposed standpoints or descriptions within one history, rather than a metaphysical discussion of Christ's two natures within one person. Roberts neatly summarizes this point when he states that 'for Barth, time is a surrogate for substance in general' ('Karl Barth's Doctrine of Time,' 89).

is always dependent and established by the fact that Christ is first the electing God. At the same time, however, while Christ's humanity does not have an independent existence, there is a real sense in which the integrity and freedom of the creature is established precisely in and by the freedom of God's election, so that Barth can now speak also of man reciprocally electing God: 'There is, then, a simple but comprehensive autonomy of the creature which is constituted originally by the act of eternal divine election and which has in this act its ultimate reality' (*CD II.2*, 177; cf. 180). It should be obvious that such a statement would have been impossible in Barth's earlier theology, especially in the *Romans* commentary, and marks a real development in his thought.

In this newly formulated understanding, while Barth continues to stress the divine freedom and sovereignty, the divine prevenience and initiative in this relation between God and humanity, he also contends that God has given the creature a distinct place beside himself, though not an *independent* autonomy (*CD II.2*, 178). Barth's newly developed election-Christology provides a place for the human response and obedience of Christ (and therefore, through analogy, a place for an obedient response in all divine and human relationships) which, while preserving Barth's adamant prioritizing of the divine freedom and initiative consistently maintained throughout his earlier theology, has provided a real though qualified place for human freedom and agency, an agency that reflects but does not replace or replicate God's own activity. Human actions therefore exist in analogy to God's own activity, rather than in simple contradiction to it. This is the foundation for Barth's developed notion of correspondence in the *Church Dogmatics*.

Barth speaks of this relation of divine and human freedom as grounded in the Christological relation between Christ as both the electing God and the elected human being. He does so not in terms of nature but in terms of 'history, encounter and decision' (*CD II.2*, 175; 177). This is a history of freedom, for God's sovereignty is the sovereignty of his love:

> ....which did not will to exercise mechanical force, to move the immobile from without, to rule over puppets or slaves, but willed rather to triumph in faithful servants and friends, not in their overthrow, but in their obedience, in their own free decision for Him. This purpose and meaning of the eternal divine election of grace consists in the fact that the one who is elected from all eternity can and does elect God in return (*CD II.2*, 178).

The man Jesus, therefore, is not a marionette manipulated by God, but one who prays, speaks, and acts, and in his election he is free to obey (*CD II.2*, 178-179). This conception of Christology explicates a richer understanding of Christ's humanity than Barth's earlier Christological thought. No longer is Jesus's humanity spoken of primarily in simple formal terms, such as a 'veil of flesh,' through which revelation is mediated, a central theme of Barth's theology not only in the *Göttingen Dogmatics* but also in the first volume of the *Church Dogmatics* (*CD I.2*, 147-171). Now Jesus as a man is not simply an instrument or veil of the Word, or of divinity, but is a real person who is seen in a three-dimensional rather than a two-dimensional perspective, as he is described not only in the language of natures and substances but in the narrative of the obedient Son of Man who is exalted (*CD IV.2*, 3ff.). Jesus is really and fully divine and really and fully human, these realities being united yet distinct, with the latter established only by the former. Election thus becomes the basis for the incarnation and for a Chalcedonian Christology that is both traditional and innovative, as God in Christ chooses to be God for man, but also chooses as man for God.

The claim that Barth's reformulation of the doctrine of election in *CD II.2* marks a real advance for his Christology must be clearly explained lest it be misunderstood. A mistake is made when the development of Barth's Christological thought is either overlooked as negligible or seen as purely revolutionary. As previously noted, developments in Barth's theology always display at the same time both real innovation and true continuity, and Barth's Christology developed in the doctrine of election is no exception. The doctrine of election modifies the material content of Barth's Christology, as he moves from speaking primarily in terms of an incarnate Word in the veil of flesh and of divine and human natures, to speaking of two histories, the electing God choosing humanity and the elected human choosing God, these actions and histories and decisions taking place in the one person of Jesus Christ, both God and man. This narratively-construed Christology enriches Barth's earlier more metaphysically-oriented thought, in that Christ's humanity is given a more complete and developed formulation than before. Barth now can speak of the Son of God and the Son of Man in terms that give a richer value to the latter in that each can be narratively expounded from the vantage point either of the humiliation of the Son of God or of the exaltation of the Son of Man[41] — no longer does Barth speak of human 'nature,' or 'flesh' as the primary means of referring to Christ's historical human life.

This does *not* imply, however, that Barth's earlier Christology was not Chalcedonian, nor that it was intended to side solely with Alexandrian over Antiochene concerns in a docetic manner. Barth always affirmed the full humanity of Christ (*CD I.2*, 147-171). Barth's earlier Christology, from the *Göttingen Dogmatics* onward, is thoroughly Chalcedonian and wedded to a Reformed

---

[41]*CD IV.1* & *IV.2*, respectively. Barth himself recognized a development (though not a reversal) in his theological and Christological thought, and this development is outlined in the essay 'The Humanity of God' in Barth, *The Humanity of God*; 37-65. The significance of this essay for corroborating the present argument should not be underestimated.

anhypostatic-enhypostatic interpretation,[42] even though Barth's Chalcedonian Christology displays not only faithfulness to the tradition but also real innovation.[43]

Barth's development in Christology does entail that Barth's newly formulated election-Christology, as it came to be narratively construed, was now capable of giving a richer treatment to Jesus' historical life (and a more positive place to human freedom and agency), seen now as a history that could be narrated through an actualistic and historic/narrative ontology rather than simply as a 'veil of flesh' or as a human 'nature' to be explained in terms of an essentialist metaphysics.

Again, while this marks real progression, there is also important and overriding continuity in Barth's Christological thought throughout the *Church Dogmatics*. The formal Chalcedonian patterns articulated by Barth remain, for Barth does not leave these patterns behind.[44] Barth continues to speak in terms of a Chalcedonian Christology shaped by a Reformed anhypostatic-enhypostatic interpretation so that there is thus a unity, a distinction, and an asymmetrical relation between the divine and the human in Christ. These patterns serve Christology constitutively and bear upon all other divine and human relations regulatively, and they are deeply enmeshed in all of Barth's theology and are never abandoned. These patterns remain the same whether Barth is speaking in terms of Christ's divine and human natures, or of the humiliation of the Son of God and the exaltation of the Son of Man. Neither does Barth relinquish the insights of God's sovereignty and freedom as the Subject of the incarnation in his later theology.[45]

Materially, however, Barth now speaks of the humanity of Christ not simply in formal terms, but in richer and more developed ways. This redefinition of Christology was grounded in a new doctrine of election that itself gave rise to a more coherent actualistic and historic/narrative ontology, as was developed and can be demonstrated in Barth's Christological thought in the doctrine of reconciliation, where Barth can speak of two histories, or movements, the humiliation of the Son of God and the exaltation of the Son of Man, inseparably united in the one person of the God-Man, but irreducibly distinct in their description of his person. Again, this is not to say that such an ontology was wholly absent in Barth's earlier thought. It certainly

---

[42]For Barth's articulation of the anhypostatic-enhypostatic doctrine in the *Church Dogmatics*, see *CD I.2*, 163-165; also *CD IV.2*, 49-51; 90-91. See also Thompson, *Christ in Perspective*, 27-29. We have discussed this logic in the previous chapter.

[43]See Thompson, *Christ in Perspective*, 18-19. That Barth's Christology is best described as 'Chalcedonian' rather than as 'Alexandrian' (or 'Antiochene') is soundly argued by Hunsinger ('Karl Barth's Christology,' 131-147).

[44]Thompson, *Christ in Perspective*, 144, note 1.

[45]These themes are outlined in *CD I.2*, 132-146; see also Thompson, *Christ in Perspective*, 24-27.

exists there in nascent form.[46] Nevertheless, it is Barth's newly-formulated doctrine of election which views Jesus Christ as both the electing God and the elected human being that allows such a historic/narrative ontology to be fully utilized and Christ's humanity to be taken seriously in its own terms.

Barth's Christology thus takes up both Alexandrian and Antiochene concerns and can be described as a Christology 'from above' that incorporates a Christology 'from below.'[47] No longer are God and the world, revelation and history, viewed primarily from the vantage point of contradiction, as in the *Römerbrief* (though they were not viewed solely in this way even there). Now they are viewed primarily through their reconciliation in Jesus Christ (though the dialectical and asymmetrical relation between revelation and history, the Word and the flesh of Christ, is never abandoned, nor are God and the creature confused). Barth now sees Christ as both the revelation of the true God *and* as the revelation of the true human person, the humble Son of God and the exalted Son of Man. Both true God *and* true humanity are revealed in Christ, and this provides Barth's theology with a greater appreciation for human obedience through the notion of correspondence. Again, it is important to emphasize that Barth never retracted his emphasis, so clearly proclaimed in the *Römerbrief*, of the *deity* of God. But Barth now could also speak with equal force of the *humanity* of God. And Barth himself saw this as a true progression in his own thought.[48]

What remains to be seen is whether this advance in Christology, with its greater appreciation for the human response of corresponding obedience, is reflected in Barth's mature ecclesiology. This question will concern us in the following chapters. In concluding this section, we might note that this examination of the doctrines of election and Christology helps clarify Barth's evaluation of his own work. Whereas

---

[46]Barth could state already in *CD I.1*: 'When the Bible speaks of revelation, it does so in the form of the record of a history [*Geschichte*] or a series of histories [*Geschichten*],' 315. In the first English translation of *CD I.1*, G. T. Thomson rendered this sentence thus: 'When the Bible speaks of revelation it does so in the form of narrating a story or a series of stories' (*CD I.1*, trans. G. T. Thomson [Edinburgh: T & T Clark, 1936], 362). See also Ford, *Barth and God's Story*, 16-32.

[47]See Thompson, *Christ in Perspective*, 16-17.

[48]See Barth, 'The Humanity of God,' 37-65. Barth notes: 'I should indeed have been somewhat embarrassed if one had invited me to speak on the humanity of God — say in the year 1920, the year in which I stood up in this hall against my great teacher, Adolf von Harnack. We should have suspected evil implications in this topic. In any case we were not occupied with it. That it is our subject for today and that I could not refuse to say something on it is a symptom of the fact that that earlier change of direction was not the last word' (ibid., 38; cf. 43-46). See also Barth, *Gespräche 1964-1968* (Zürich: Theologisher Verlag Zürich, 1997), 11-12; 159-166.

Barth himself held *CD II* to be his greatest achievement, many others have considered his signal achievement to be found in *CD IV*.[49] What can be incontestably maintained, however, is that the revolution and foundation of the doctrine of reconciliation in *CD IV* lies within the doctrine of election in *CD II* and is made possible by this earlier work, whereas the pinnacle of the development and fulfillment of the themes outlined in *CD II* is to be found in *CD IV*. Election is indeed the foundation, and Barth's doctrine of reconciliation is indeed the capstone, of Barth's mature theology.

4. The Church in Light of the Election of Jesus Christ

The eternal election of grace, as the election of Jesus Christ, includes within it the election of the community of God. The term 'community' [*Gemeinde*] is chosen, Barth explains, because it can include both Israel and the church (*CD II.2*, 196). This one community, composed of both Israel and the church, attests Jesus Christ to the world and calls for faith in him. In the form of Israel the community is a representation of the divine judgment, whereas in the form of the church it is a representation of the divine mercy. The first hears the promise, the second believes it in faith. The first is the passing form, the second the coming form, of the community (*CD II.2*, 195). The two realties of Israel and the church thus reflect in their distinction the two-fold rejection and election that Jesus Christ embodies. As one united community, its election stands within, and not apart from, the election of Jesus Christ. There is thus a 'de-centering' of the individual in Barth's doctrine of election, in that election concerns first not individuals, but rather the one person of Jesus Christ, then the community that serves to proclaim and witness to him, and only then specific individuals. In chapter thirty-four, Barth addresses the election of the community, which includes discussion of both Israel and the church as the one community of God.

The election of the community, standing between the election of Jesus Christ and the individual believer, serves as a 'mediate and mediating election' (*CD II.2*, 196). The election of the community is the election not of individual persons in particular, but of a people in fellowship, a community eternally elect in Christ and appointed for a particular service of witness and equipped to fulfill this task. The election of the individual believer can only be understood in light of the prior election of the community, as both can be understood only in light of the election of Jesus Christ. Barth describes this community as follows:

---

[49]'Most people regard Volume IV as the high point of the *Church Dogmatics*, although Barth himself agreed that the high point had been reached in Volume II. Nevertheless *CD* IV surely constitutes the most powerful work on the doctrine of atoning reconciliation ever written, in which Patristic and Reformation insights are interwoven into a single fabric' (Torrance, *Karl Barth, Biblical and Evangelical Theologian*, 133).

The community is the human fellowship which in a particular way provisionally forms the natural and historical environment of the man Jesus Christ. Its particularity consists in the fact that by its existence it has to witness faith in Him. Its provisional character consists in the fact that in virtue of this office and commission it points beyond itself to the fellowship of all men in face of which it is a witness and herald. The community which has to be described in this way forms so to speak the inner circle of the 'other' election which has taken place (and takes place) in and with the election of Jesus Christ. In so far as on the one hand it forms this special environment of the man Jesus, this inner circle, but on the other hand it is itself of the world or chosen from the world and composed of individual men, its election is to be described as mediate and mediating in respect of its mission and function. It is *mediate*, that is, in so far as it is the middle point between the election of Jesus Christ and (included in this) the election of those who have believed, and do and will believe, in Him. It is *mediating* in so far as the relation between the election of Jesus Christ and that of all believers (and *vice versa*) is mediated and conditioned by it (*CD II.2*, 196; cf. 205-206).

The community thus serves as the natural and historical environment of the man Jesus Christ in such a way that it exists as the outer context of Christ as Christ exists as the inner reality of the community, a pattern that will be reflected in Barth's understanding of the relation between covenant and creation.[50] Barth can also speak of the community as the 'inner circle' that exists for the sake of the 'outer circle', i.e., the world:

> But this outer circle, too, is in its turn nothing without the inner one; all the election that has taken place and takes place in Jesus Christ is mediated, conditioned and bounded by the election of the community. It mirrors in its mediate and mediating character the existence of the one Mediator, Jesus Christ, Himself (*CD II.2*, 197).

The community is both mediate and mediating, and thus is the provisional reality and witness to what all persons are in Christ.

The community on this account has no independent election, but is elect only in Jesus Christ, and its own election is thus an election not of honor but of service and witness. It provides only the environment for Christ and the witness to him, and if it attempts to be an end in itself, it has 'forgotten and forfeited its election' (*CD II.2*, 196). It exists not for its own sake but for the world, to testify to Christ and call

---

[50]See *CD III.1*, ch. 41.

others to faith in him even as the community itself is founded by Jesus Christ (*CD II.2*, 196; 205-206). Yet even though the election of the community has no independent nature, existing only in the election of Christ and solely for the election of the world, it nevertheless has a real mediatorial function, in that persons only come to faith in Christ through its mediating witness. For this reason Barth can state that outside of the church there is no salvation (*CD II.2*, 197).[51] It should be apparent that for Barth the church's task is not one of cooperation in salvation but witness, that its election is not independent but grounded in Christ, that its standing is not permanent but provisional, and that nevertheless it has a real value and service that cannot be negated or ignored.

Barth states that just as the electing God is one and the elected man is one, so also the community as the 'primary object of the election which has taken place and takes place in Jesus Christ is one.' This unity exists even though the community is comprised of both Israel and the church. Jesus Christ is both the 'promised son of Abraham and David, the Messiah of Israel. And He is simultaneously the Head and Lord of the Church, called and gathered from Jews and Gentiles. In both of these characters He is indissolubly one. And as the One He is ineffaceably both.' Jesus Christ is the Lord of the church as Israel's Messiah, and he is Israel's Messiah as Lord of the church. As the Messiah he is a witness to God's judgment and the original hearer of the divine promise, and as the Lord of the church he is the witness to God's mercy and the 'original pattern of the believer' (*CD II.2*, 197-198).

The community thus exists in a two-fold form, as Israel and as the church, even as Christ exists as both Messiah of Israel and Lord of the church. For Barth, Israel is the Jewish people who resist their election: 'It is the community of God in so far as this community has to exhibit also the unwillingness, incapacity and unworthiness of man with respect to the love of God directed to him' (*CD II.2*, 198; cf. 206-210). By delivering Jesus unto death, Israel attests to 'the justice of the divine judgment on man borne by God Himself.' Israel hears but does not believe the divine promise, and this hearing is the service it performs within the one community of God (*CD II.2*, 233; 233-237). God's intention is for Israel to become obedient to its election, to believe the promise, and thus take its place as a witness within the church, though God's purpose for Israel is not frustrated by its unbelief. For this reason, whether in obedience or disobedience, faith or unbelief, the Jews cannot help but serve as a witness to God's election (*CD II.2*, 207-210). Nevertheless, Israel is the form of the community that is passing away, representing the passing form in the 'passing, the death, the setting aside of the old man, of the man who resists his election and therefore God' (*CD II.2*, 260; cf. 259-264). Israel serves this task. Even in its conversion to faith, Israel witnesses to the passing away of the one who resists God, performing this function even when brought into the church.

---

[51]Barth could of course speak this way already in the *Göttingen Dogmatics*, as seen above.

Over against unbelieving Israel stands the church. As Christ shows himself in the resurrection to be the Lord of the church, so the church attests to the mercy of God upon humanity. It is a community of faith and obedience. 'Israel is the people of the Jews which resists its election; the Church is the gathering of Jews and Gentiles called on the ground of election' (*CD II.2*, 199; cf. 210-213). The church not only hears the divine promise but believes and places its faith within this promise, and it is this belief which is the distinctive service of the church (*CD II.2*, 237-240).[52]   The church demonstrates God's mercy, what God chooses for humanity in election. It includes within itself the witness of Israel, and it is the final form of service as it proclaims both the judgment of God and the mercy of God. The church is thus inclusive of Israel's witness as an 'auxiliary service' (*CD II.2*, 210). It serves as a witness willingly whereas Israel does so unwillingly. Barth writes:

> The Church form of the community reveals what God chooses for man when He elects him for communion with Himself in His eternal election of grace. He chooses for man His whole selflessly self-giving love....The Church is the perfect form of the elected community of God....The church form of the community stands in the same relation to its Israelite form as the resurrection of Jesus to His crucifixion, as God's mercy to God's judgement (*CD II.2*, 210-211).

This entails, however, that the church is older than Pentecost, having lived in a hidden form in Israel. The church represents the coming form of God's kingdom. The church, as the 'perfect form of the one community of God consists in attesting, by faith in the Word heard, by laying hold of the divine mercy, the coming kingdom of God as the end of all human need, the coming new man and his eternal life' (*CD II.2*, 264; 264-267). The church thus completes the purposes of Israel and fulfills Israel's mission as it proclaims Israel's message: 'The Church of the Gospel is in fact the first and final determination of Israel' (*CD II.2*, 266).

This does not mean, however, that Israel is rejected and the church elect, even though one might be tempted to conclude that this is the case in light of what has been said. Barth denies such a judgment: 'We cannot, therefore, call the Jews the 'rejected' and the Church the 'elected' community. The object of election is neither Israel for itself nor the Church for itself, but both together in their unity' (*CD II.2*, 199). What is elected in Christ as his 'body' is thus the one community in its two-fold form as Israel and church. So while Israel corresponds to a human rejection of election, and the church to a believing response to election, both Israel and the church are the object of divine election as comprising the two forms of the one elect

---

[52]The church does remain dependent upon Israel, however, in that the promise must first be heard before it can be believed (*CD II.2*, 240).

community of God, for 'the bow of the one covenant arches over both' (*CD II.2*, 200). The rejection that Israel attests is in fact the rejection and judgment that God has taken upon himself.

Here again, God's judgment and mercy do not stand as two equal and symmetrical realities, as in a *decretum absolutum*. Rather, the former serves the latter in an irreversible relationship. Here too there is a Christological pattern, in that the 'No' of election exists only insofar as it is established by and for the divine 'Yes.' 'God is wrathful and judges and punishes as He shows mercy, and indeed for His mercy's sake, because without this He would not be really and effectively merciful' (*CD II.2*, 227; cf. 224-227). There are not two purposes of God, one to show mercy and one to show judgment. Rather, there is one purpose, to show mercy, and judgment is a penultimate goal to this ultimate aim.

The election of Israel, even though it represents rejection, is then possible because God's judgment for Barth is always subordinate to God's mercy. The judgment that falls upon Israel serves in the end to accomplish God's mercy, so that Israel as well as the church belongs to God's divine election. A distinction between rejection and election does exist, but these realities are two sides of one coin, so that it is impossible to simply equate Israel with rejection and the church with election, for while they are distinct in their attestation to each, they are united in sharing in election and thus rejection (*CD II.2*, 199-200). Here Barth displays once again, though in relation to rejection and election, a Chalcedonian pattern in that the two forms of the one community are both distinct and yet united. Where such a Chalcedonian pattern breaks down, however, is that here each form of the community shares in the qualities of the other, and this certainly does not reflect Barth's usual and strictly Reformed understanding of the *communicatio idiomatum*.[53]

The 'unity of the elect community' is 'knowable and actually known', though, only in the community of faith, i.e., the church (*CD II.2*, 200). The church is thus the epistemological necessity for seeing the unity of the covenant that spans both Israel and church and unites them as one community. This unity cannot be apprehended from a neutral standpoint, nor can Israel as an unbelieving people understand their own place in election with the church. Israel can see this only as it joins itself in the faith of the church (*CD II.2*, 200-201). It is thus only the church that knows the true identity of Israel, and the elect believer who understands the identity of the rejected. As judgment is subordinate to mercy and will pass away into it, so also Barth seems to hint that Israel will be subsumed into the church, as the rejected unbeliever will become an elect believer. This does not entail the disappearance of Israel, however, for Barth stresses that the church cannot exist without Israel. Israel and the church thus remain differentiated yet united. It is thus clear that these two forms are based on a pattern of unity and differentiation.

---

[53]See *CD IV.2*, 73f.

One can therefore speak with justification of a sense in which the church is the completion of Israel, yet what must also be recognized is that the church is forever bound to Israel so that Israel cannot pass away (*CD II.2*, 201). Barth is careful to say that Christ does not 'belong' to Israel, or to the church, but that both belong as one community to him (*CD II.2*, 204). But Jesus does come from the Jews, and here exists a particularity that cannot be denied. Barth thus dialectically balances the necessity of Israel and the church for salvation, while maintaining that this is a relative necessity in that Christ is not a possession of Israel or the church but is their Lord.

Barth's conception of Israel and the church as comprising the one community of God raises a number of difficult questions, and his doctrine of Israel merits a more in-depth examination than can be given here.[54] Yet, brief comment must be made. One way to begin to address this issue is to note that Barth's doctrine of Israel, as well as his understanding of the relation between Israel and the church, is at once both staunchly traditional and radically innovative, causing Stephen Haynes to describe it as 'radical traditionalism.'[55] As such, it is what we might have come to expect in Barth's treatment of dogmatic themes. It is traditional in its supercessionist elements, such as the claim that Israel only finds its completion by entering the church, as well as the emphasis upon Israel's disobedience and rejection of its own election. It is innovative in Barth's stress upon Israel's eternal election, its ongoing place in salvation history, and its service within the one elect community.[56]

Perhaps a nuanced and fair assessment of Barth's complex and paradoxical position regarding Israel is that of Katherine Sonderegger, who notes that Barth's

---

[54]Important studies of Barth's doctrine of Israel include: Katherine Sonderegger, *That Jesus Christ Was Born A Jew: Karl Barth's 'Doctrine of Israel'* (University Park: Pennsylvania State University Press, 1992); Bertold Klappert, *Israel und die Kirche: Erwägungen zur Israellehre Karl Barths* (Munich: Christian Kaiser Verlag, 1980); Stephen R. Haynes, *Prospects for Post-Holocaust Theology* (Atlanta: Scholars Press, 1991); also idem, *Reluctant Witnesses: Jews and the Christian Imagination* (Louisville: Westminster John Knox Press, 1995), 64-89; Friedrich Marquardt, *Die Entdeckung des Judentums für die christliche Theologie: Israel im Denken Karl Barths* (Munich: Christian Kaiser Verlag, 1967); Manuel Goldmann, *'Die große ökumenische Frage...': Zur Strukturverschiedenheit christlicher und jüdischer Tradition und ihrer Relevanz für die Begegnung der Kirche mit Israel* (Neukirchen-Vluyn: Neukirchener Verlag, 1997), 23-127; and Eberhard Busch, *Unter dem Bogen des einen Bundes: Karl Barth und die Juden 1933-1945* (Neukirchen-Vluyn: Neukirchener Verlag, 1996).

[55]Haynes, *Prospects*, 47ff.; 64-65. Haynes states: 'In what we have begun to see is typical Barthian fashion, the relationship between church and Israel described here is complementary and symbiotic, but it is also typological and integrationist' (ibid., 64). Elsewhere Haynes writes: 'In paradoxical fashion, the church-Israel relationship Barth elaborates in CD II:2 is simultaneously affirming of Jews and triumphalist' (*Reluctant Witnesses*, 72). See also Klappert, *Israel und die Kirche*, 47-52.

[56]Haynes, *Prospects*, 65; cf. Haynes, *Reluctant Witnesses*, 64-65; 78-79.

understanding is marked 'by the controlling ambivalence of deep hostility and deep, unshakable attachment.'[57] As such, the doctrine of Israel found in the *Church Dogmatics* is anti-Judaic, though not anti-Semitic.[58] It is this paradoxical understanding of Israel that gives rise to reactions that focus both on the revolutionary and traditional, the positive and negative, aspects of Barth's position, and that creates a split between Barth's (critical) admirers and (admiring) critics. Given the centrality of Jesus Christ for Barth's theology, it is understandable that Barth sides with a Christological reading of the Biblical canon that leads to a conflict with Jewish interpretation and thus with differing conceptions of Jewish and Christian identity. This understanding of Christ and its corresponding Christological hermeneutics is the basis for Barth's anti-Judaic position. Nevertheless, in the end, there remains a deep and unresolved tension in Barth's thought between seeing Israel as the 'passing form' of the community whose future lies in being subsumed into the church, and the necessity of Israel's ongoing existence as an enduring partner of the one covenant between God and the community as both Israel and church.

5. Summary

The doctrine of election in the *Church Dogmatics* is a significant achievement and a milestone in Barth's ecclesiological thought, continuing along the trajectory of Barth's positive assessment of the church witnessed in the *Göttingen Dogmatics*.[59] No longer is the historical church simply interchangeable with unbelieving Israel as in the *Römerbrief.* Now the church is seen in a more positive light, in that it is no

---

[57]Sonderegger, *That Jesus Christ Was Born A Jew*, 3.

[58]Ibid., 173-174.

[59]Barth's turn from liberalism was now far behind him, but shadows of Herrmann can be perceived in Barth's description of the community in the doctrine of election, though they should not be given undue weight. A first shadow is glimpsed in Barth's emphasis upon the community's task as one of *mediation* (though conceived significantly differently than Herrmann), so that the obedience of the church for Barth seems at times limited to its acceptance of the Gospel (understood primarily in cognitive terms) and to its proclamation of this Gospel in the world. The second shadow, and a related one, is a latent *individualism* that, while subdued and suppressed, has not been entirely stamped out, seen in Barth's statement that the election of the community is the means that serves the end of the election of individuals (see *CD II.2*, 310-311; 313-314). Barth can write: 'The community is [election's] necessary medium. But its object...is individual men' (*CD II.2*, 313; cited in: Scott Bader-Saye, *Church and Israel After Christendom: The Politics of Election* [Boulder: Westview Press, 1999], 76; see also 73-77). What is largely absent is the more nuanced dialectical understanding of the relation between the community and the individual that Barth would later expound (see *CD IV.3.2*, 681-682; cf. *CD III.3*, 190-191).

longer viewed as the height of humanity's religious *hubris*, the pinnacle of humanity's sinful ambition to reach God, but is instead seen as grounded in God's own eternal election. Where earlier the church could be substituted for unbelieving Israel, now the church is the complement to Israel, representing election, faith, and obedience, as Israel represents rejection, unbelief, and disobedience. Yet, both Israel and the church are united in one elect community, and it is the overcoming of rejection by election and their asymmetrical relation that remains constant throughout Barth's thought and that gives hope not only to the church but also to Israel.

By effectively grounding the reality of the church in the doctrine of election, Barth preserves and emphasizes the divine initiative as well as the theological character of the church. This emphasis is reinforced and complemented by a Chalcedonian and anhypostatic-enhypostatic Christology that preserves the divine freedom in terms of revelation and which itself is mirrored in ecclesiology. The reality of the church is thus the product of divine will rather than human desire, and for Barth the church must be described theologically as a divinely established community in relation to Christ before it is described sociologically as a historical society.

Yet what is missing in Barth's discussion of the community in the doctrine of election is precisely this latter type of concrete description. Barth's doctrine of Israel has been criticized for presenting an abstract notion of Israel,[60] but this critique could with reason be leveled against his understanding of the church in *CD II.2*. While Barth has provided a solid framework for the church in the doctrine of election, the church itself is dealt with more as a formal concept than as a concrete community. The church is not here seen as corresponding to Christ's humanity in all of its richness — in other words, the historical and social life of the church is not described in particular terms and concrete practices that express and correspond to the new humanity revealed in Christ and which mark it off from the world. In essence, while Barth's doctrine of election and its accompanying Christology provide for a greater emphasis upon human freedom and integrity in response to divine grace through a richer narrative description of Christ's humanity, this concrete description is itself not present in Barth's discussion of the community in the doctrine of election. The church is therefore primarily described as a formal and provisional conduit for the Gospel rather than itself a reflection of the Gospel's embodiment in a particular and concrete communal life.

It is therefore telling that while Barth speaks of a history of Christ, he refuses here to speak of a history of the community: 'The history of Israel is not continued after the crucifixion of Christ, while the Church has no history in the strict sense, but

---

[60]Haynes, *Reluctant Witnesses*, 81. Haynes' criticisms of Barth on this score, however, are at points overdrawn — at the very least, they should be balanced with Sonderegger's nuanced critique.

only (in the time that has still to be patiently endured until the revelation of the already consummated end of all time) a status of continual self-renewal' (*CD II.2*, 342). Such a statement seems to undercut any coherent notion of the church's enduring existence through time, thus threatening to spiritualize the church in a manner that relativizes its specific historical and communal form and its temporal actions within the world. That Barth later re-examined this issue will be witnessed in the next chapter.

It might be rejoined at this point that Barth's purpose in this section is simply to present the election-rejection distinction within the community as comprised of Israel and the church and not to provide a whole-scale ecclesiology. Such must be admitted, of course. Barth only developed his Christology proper in the doctrine of reconciliation, though as we have seen, its foundation is laid in the doctrine of election. So also Barth's fully developed ecclesiology is only found in the doctrine of reconciliation, though its basis too is found in the doctrine of election. On account of this fact, the criticisms here made must be held in abeyance until Barth's fully developed ecclesiology is examined. We now turn to the context of this ecclesiology within the doctrine of reconciliation and the specific presuppositions that shape it, especially with regard to Barth's conceptions of history and human agency.

Chapter Five

Reconciliation as the Context of Ecclesiology

1. Introduction — Jesus Christ and the History of the Covenant

With the doctrine of reconciliation in the *Church Dogmatics* we come to the most mature and complete expression of Barth's theology and the summit of his dogmatic achievement. Yet while the doctrine of reconciliation contains some of Barth's most original and creative work, the questions there addressed are shaped by Barth's ever-constant diligence to mold a theological position that avoids erroneous positions of the left and the right, a concern present from his earliest theological writings. Barth himself states in the prefaces to the volumes on reconciliation that his own dogmatic presentation is carried out in dialogue with Rudolf Bultmann, whom Barth perceived to be the heir apparent of Protestant liberalism, and with Roman Catholicism (with specific regard to its Marian dogma).[1] To understand Barth's theology aright, these discussions, though sometimes subdued and muted, must be taken into account, for they bear upon Barth's theology in general and upon his ecclesiology in particular.

The doctrine of reconciliation itself is the context for Barth's developed ecclesiology and is described by Barth as the heart of dogmatics and of the Christian faith: 'In this movement from a narrower to a wider usage the statement "God with us" is the centre of the Christian message — and always in such a way that it is primarily a statement about God and only then and for that reason a statement about us men' (*CD IV.1*, 5). Reconciliation is the fulfillment and the re-establishment of the original relationship between God and humanity, the covenant of grace instituted by God (*CD IV.1*, 22; cf. 36).[2] That this covenant is a covenant of grace entails that God

---

[1] *CD IV.1*, ix; and *CD IV.2*, ix, respectively.

[2] Barth elsewhere states: '"Reconciliation" in the Christian sense of the word — the reconciliation of which we have the attestation in the Holy Scriptures of the Old and New Testament, and in the recognition and proclamation of which the Christian community has its existence — is the history in which God concludes and confirms His covenant with man, maintaining and carrying it to its goal in spite of every threat' (*CD IV.3.1*, 3). This covenant includes within it the particular covenant with Israel, but according to Barth this covenant itself was provisional and pointed toward an inclusive covenant between God and all people (*CD IV.1*, 28; 31-32; 34).

is not compelled to establish it but grants it as a free gift to humanity, a gift that calls forth our gratitude and thankfulness (*CD IV.1*, 39-43).

The atonement, as God's supreme act of reconciliation in Jesus Christ, is comprised of two elements, or movements, the obedience of the Son of God, and the exaltation of the Son of Man, unified in the history of one person, Jesus Christ.[3] Materially, these two movements comprise the doctrine of reconciliation, though from a formal standpoint a third element must be added, the revelation of the reality and unity of the history of the atonement of Jesus Christ in its two movements. This third element does not add to the content of the first two, but it does merit its own consideration as the revelation of their reality and unity. For this reason, revelation and reconciliation are intrinsically related, for reconciliation entails its own revelation. So while the first movement is characterized in terms of Christ's priestly office and the second in terms of his kingly office, thereby together comprising the subject matter of the doctrine of reconciliation, this third element is characterized in terms of Christ's prophetic office and is as such the revelation of the material content of the doctrine.[4] Jesus is the Subject of the one history that unites and integrates these two movements within himself in such a way that his history, the history of salvation, is thus at one and the same time the history of revelation. Reconciliation is therefore revelation (*CD IV.3.1*, 38-39; 46).

These two movements, described as the obedience (or humiliation) of the Son of God and the exaltation of the Son of Man, are inseparable yet distinct. They are not on the same plane, however, for the first precedes the latter in an irreversible relationship, as God remains the Subject of this history, and not humanity. Barth states: 'Hence the movement from below to above which takes place originally in this man does not compete with the movement of God from above to below. It takes place because and as the latter takes place. It takes place as the response of gratitude to the

---

[3] 'The atonement is, noetically, the history about Jesus Christ, and ontically, Jesus Christ's own history' (*CD IV.1*, 158). Barth also can state that: 'The atonement as it took place in Jesus Christ is the one inclusive event of this going out of the Son of God and coming in of the Son of Man' (*CD IV.2*, 21).

[4] See *CD IV.3.1*, 6-11. Barth writes: 'Reconciliation is indeed revelation. But revelation in itself and as such, if we can conceive of such a thing, could not be reconciliation. It takes place as reconciliation takes place; as it has in it its origin, content and subject; as reconciliation is revealed and reveals itself in it' (ibid., 8-9).

grace of God' (*CD IV.2*, 47; cf. 70-72).[5] The movement from below to above thus corresponds analogically to that from above to below. As Barth writes:

> This grace of His [Christ's] origin does not involve or effect any alteration in His human essence as such. It does not result in any change, diminution or increase. His essence is that of a man like ourselves, the individual soul of an individual body, knowing and willing and feeling as a man, active and passive in the time allotted, responsible to God and tied to its fellows. What the grace of his origin does involve and effect, with supreme necessity and power, is the exaltation of His human essence. Exaltation to what? To that harmony with the divine will, that service of the divine act, that correspondence to the divine grace, that state of thankfulness, which is the only possibility in view of the fact that this man is determined by this divine will and act and grace alone, and by them brought in His existence into not merely indirect but direct and indestructible confrontation with the divine essence. We may indeed say that the grace of the origin of Jesus Christ means the basic exaltation of His human freedom to its truth, i.e., to the obedience in whose exercise it is not superhuman but true human freedom (*CD IV.2*, 91-92).

The relation between these movements in one history is thus predicated upon a Chalcedonian pattern and the logic of the hypostatic union and an anhypostatic-enhypostatic Christology complemented by a notion of correspondence.[6] One might say that Barth has 'historicized' the traditional concept of 'nature' in relation to Christ in order to speak of two movements within one history. The movements are thus

---

[5]'What we have here is a real history. It takes place both from above to below and also from below to above. But it takes place from above to below first, and only then from below to above. In it it is the self-humiliated Son of God who is also exalted man. He Himself is always the Subject of this history. It is not merely because they are different by definition, but because they have a different relationship to this Subject, that the divine and human essence bear a different character in their mutual participation' (*CD IV.2*, 71). This quotation readily evidences to: 1) a Chalcedonian pattern of unity and differentiation of movements; 2) an anhypostatic-enhypostatic logic that preserves the asymmetrical relationship between the movements, predicating the second upon the first and making the second entirely dependent upon the first so that it has no existence apart from it, while it is granted a true existence as established by the first; and 3) the reality of the hypostatic union, in that the divine and human movements, or natures, are united by the will of a single divine Subject who assumes human nature.

[6]The logic of Barth's understanding of the hypostatic union and anhypostatic-enhypostatic Christology, retained from his earlier theology, is developed within the discussion of the incarnation in the doctrine of reconciliation (*CD IV.2*, 36-116; see esp. 49-50; 91-92).

indivisibly united, yet differentiated, and related in an asymmetrical and irreversible relationship, the latter movement existing only as it is established by the first. Put differently, the Son of God did become human, but the Son of Man did not become God (*CD IV.2*, 71; 100). The incarnation is thus not the culmination or actualization of a capacity intrinsic within the historical process, but a divine creative and singular act of self-impartation and revelation (*CD IV.2*, 37). It is for this reason a unique event, and is in fact the only true sacrament. Yet, this singular and unique act also is the paradigm upon which all divine and human relationships are predicated, including that between Christ and the church, even though the church is in no way a prolongation of the incarnation (*CD IV.2*, 55; 58).[7]

Reconciliation has to do entirely with Jesus Christ, fully God and fully human, in whom two movements of humiliation and exaltation remain dialectically related yet are united in one history, the history of Jesus Christ, 'in whom the two lines cross — in the sense that He Himself is the subject of what takes place on these two lines' (*CD IV.1*, 135-136).[8] He is a 'being in a history,' a history that itself is the atonement (*CD IV.1*, 125-128).[9] Christ's person and work are intrinsically related and mutually definitive. As Barth asserts: 'His being as this One is His history, and His history is this His being' (*CD IV.1*, 128).[10] For the doctrine of reconciliation, it is therefore the case that 'Christology is the key to the whole,' the standpoint from which all the other aspects of reconciliation are developed (*CD IV.1*, 138). So while the ecclesiology of the doctrine of reconciliation is specifically and materially a doctrine of the Holy Spirit, as a pneumatological doctrine it is itself set within a larger formal Christological framework.[11]

---

[7]'But in Jesus Christ Himself...we have to do with the eternal basis and temporal fulfilment of the covenant and therefore with the ground and basis of all the natural and historical relationships in which the covenant is reflected as the basic relationship between God and man, God and the world, and in which it has therefore its analogies' (*CD IV.2*, 58).

[8]See also *CD IV.2*, 3-6; 20-21; and *CD IV.3.1*, 3-5; 165-166.

[9]Barth can thus speak of Christ's human 'nature' in terms of historical existence: 'By the "human nature" in which He who is very God is also very man we have to understand the same historical life as our own, the same creaturely mode of existence as an individually distinct unity of soul and body in a fixed time between birth and death, in the same orientation to God and fellowman' (*CD IV.2*, 25).

[10]'To say "Jesus" is necessarily to say "history," His history, the history in which He is what He is and does what He does. In His history we know God, and we also know evil and their relationship the one to the other — but only from this source and in this way' (*CD IV.3.1*, 179; see also 181).

[11]Geoffrey Bromiley notes: 'Recognizing that strictly the church ought to come under pneumatology, Barth still regarded it as important to set his doctrine of the church in the context of reconciliation. In this way, while maintaining the tie to the Spirit, he could keep

This act of reconciliation by God in Christ is therefore a history, a history that itself presupposes the covenant just as it presupposes election (*CD IV.1*, 44).[12] Reconciliation is not conceived in static terms, but as an event: 'Our starting-point is that this "God with us" at the heart of the Christian message is the description of an act of God, or better, of God Himself in this act of His...It is not a state, but an event' (*CD IV.1*, 6). This event is a history between God and the world actualized in Jesus Christ:

> To put it in the simplest way, what unites God and us men is that He does not will to be God without us, that He creates us rather to share with us and therefore with our being and life and act His own incomparable being and life and act, that He does not allow His history to be His and ours ours, but causes them to take place as a common history. That is the special truth which the Christian message has to proclaim at its very heart (*CD IV.1*, 7).

This history possesses a number of unique characteristics that identify it. As has been seen, it is first of all a common history between God and humanity. Second, it is a specific history, pertaining not to a general relation between God and the world but to a unique one established in Christ:

> And if the 'God with us' at the heart of the Christian message speaks of the unifying factor between God and man, it speaks of a specific conjoining of the two, not always and everywhere but in a single and particular event which has a definite importance for all time and space but which takes place once and for all in a definite *hic et nunc* (*CD IV.1*, 8).

In addition to being a common history and a specific one, this history is thirdly a redemptive history, a restoration of the covenant between God and humanity. 'From

---

the church in the closest of relations to Christ, whether in terms of its being as the body of Christ, its edification and order, or its mission and ministry' ('The Abiding Significance of Karl Barth,' in *Theology Beyond Christendom*, ed. John Thompson, [Allison Park: Pickwick Publications, 1986], 348).

[12]More specifically, the atonement presupposes the covenant ontologically as the covenant presupposes the atonement epistemologically (*CD IV.1*, 44-45). In other terms, this is akin to saying, as was said in the previous chapter, that reconciliation presupposes election ontologically as election presupposes reconciliation epistemologically. Cf. *CD IV.2*, 31-32; also *CD IV.3.1*, 3. In a secondary sense reconciliation therefore also presupposes the work of the Spirit in the incarnation, which serves as the basis of Christ's existence and of knowledge of him, as both *ratio essendi* and *ratio cognoscendi* (*CD IV.2*, 36ff.)

the standpoint of its meaning the particularity of this event consists in the fact that it has to do with the salvation of man, that in it the general history which is common to God and man, to God and all creation, becomes at its very heart and end a redemptive history.' Fourth, it is a free history. As Barth writes: 'The ordaining of salvation for man and of man for salvation is the original and basic will of God, the ground and purpose of His will as Creator.' God is not bound to offer this salvation, and humanity has no claim upon it or the ability to bring it to pass. It is rather the result of a free decision of God's eternal will, his divine election (*CD IV.1*, 8-9).

This history of redemption does not move in a straight line, however, for it encounters human disobedience. It is thus a threatened history, threatened through humanity's sin, which stands between God's original decree and its fulfillment. This sin is revealed precisely in the salvation of humanity, not through 'independent reflection' or by an 'abstract law.' Yet God overcomes this sin, so that this history can also be described as a unique history of substitution, for in this event 'God has made Himself the One who fulfils His redemptive will.' God himself became a man to save humanity from its sin by taking humanity's place. For this reason, Barth states: 'We cannot fully understand the Christian "God with us" without the greatest astonishment at the glory of the divine grace and the greatest horror at our own plight' (*CD IV.1*, 13; 10-13).

Finally, this history entails a movement not only from God to humanity, from 'above to below,' but also from humanity to God, 'from below to above.' This is seen uniquely in Christ who is at once the humble Son of God and the exalted Son of Man. Yet, this movement from 'below to above' pertains not only to Christ but also to the relation between God and those who are in Christ. While Christ's history is the true history in which our own lives are included, a life that is lived in our stead, this does not entail that our own lives, and the obedience we render, have been made irrelevant. Barth writes: 'From all this it is surely obvious that the "God with us" carries with it in all seriousness a "We with God": the fact that we ourselves are there in our being, life, and activity' (*CD IV.1*, 14).[13] Here Barth addresses the question of how human action has any significance if salvation is completed in Christ, and whether our history has simply been subsumed without remainder into his so that we are left with no history of our own, with no responsibility, being reduced to 'mere objects....mere spectators' (*CD IV.1*, 14-17).

Barth's answer to this question is paradoxical, or better, dialectical, for he states that Christ's life is indeed lived in place of our own, but that his unique history does not render our own lives insignificant. Rather, by Christ's atonement we are called and enabled to become what we truly are divinely intended to be. In Christ our identity is not sacrificed but established, our true freedom not lost but gained, so that we live not as passive observers, but neither as self-actualizing agents. We live,

---

[13]See also *CD IV.2*, 3-6.

rather, as persons who have been saved by Christ. He has indeed taken our place, but in so doing he has established our true place and our freedom rather than annulled them (*CD IV.1*, 14-15; 20). This conception of the relation between divine and human agency is central to Barth's construal of the church's action, witness, and mission.

2. Reconciliation and Human Agency: The Action of the Church

It is clear that this last aspect of Barth's exposition of reconciliation reveals his desire to address not only the sovereignty and grace of God in the act of reconciliation, but also the freedom and obedience of humanity that responds to such grace. Barth's attempt to speak of this relation between divine sovereignty and human freedom, between faith and obedience, is undertaken in a way that cannot simply be characterized in terms of traditional Augustinian or Arminian positions or according to modernist or Catholic solutions. Reiterating a common rebuttal to charges of monism, heteronomy, and other misunderstandings of his theology, Barth writes:

> It is apparent at once that the formula 'God everything and man nothing' as a description of grace is not merely a 'shocking simplification' but complete nonsense....The meaning and purpose of the atonement made in Jesus Christ is that man should not cease to be a subject in relation to God but that he should be maintained as such, or rather — seeing that he has himself surrendered himself as such — that he should be newly created and grounded as such, from above....By the grace of God, therefore, man is not nothing. He is God's man. He is accepted by God. He is recognised as himself a free subject, a subject who has been made free once and for all by his restoration as the faithful covenant partner of God. This is something which we must not conceal. It is something which we must definitely proclaim in our Evangelical understanding of grace. We cannot say and demand and expect too much or too great things of man when we see him as He really is in virtue of the giving of the Son of God, of the fact that God has reconciled the world to Himself in Christ (*CD IV.1*, 89-90).

Barth's concern is to provide a 'thick description' of human action that sees it not in cooperation with God's own action in order to effect salvation, nor as insignificant and illusionary in the light of divine sovereignty, but as a free and true response to the complete and sufficient salvation of God effected in the history of the person of Jesus Christ. As such, it is established and enabled by that salvation. There is on this account a truly altered human situation, though one accomplished only by God, and this altered situation allows for an authentic and free answer to be given from the side of humanity. Barth maintains that it is precisely because of this altered situation that 'we cannot think or demand or expect too much or too high things of man' (*CD IV.1*, 91). Such a Protestant answer that seriously addresses the real questions of human agency and freedom is necessary, Barth contends, if Catholic objections are to be met.

Yet, it is significant in light of his earlier theology that Barth can now speak not only of God but of humanity as an agent in reconciliation, though this is limited in reference to the person of Jesus Christ: 'It is with reference to Him [Jesus Christ] that in spite of all appearances to the contrary the Christian message dares to address man too as an active subject [*handelndes Subjekt*] in the event of redemption, and to its content there belong the praise which we offer to the grace of God *e profundis*, man's own faith and love and hope' (*CD IV.1*, 20).[14] There is, nevertheless, an active agency also proper to the believer, though this is given only by grace and is not a completion of or cooperation in salvation but a mirroring of the salvation achieved in Christ's unique work. In short, the covenant of grace calls forth from the Christian a response of gratitude — χάρις calls forth εὐχαριστία (*CD IV.1*, 41).[15]

Indeed, Barth can go so far as to speak of humanity as the 'covenant partner' of God (*CD IV.1*, 41-42).[16] Yet, it must be reiterated that this partnership pertains not to a cooperation in salvation if this is taken to mean a completion of something that was lacking in Christ's work, but rather refers to the task that humanity fulfills in announcing this completed salvation to the world. On this account, this partnership falls under the aspect of 'vocation' (rather than under 'justification' or 'sanctification'), and therefore, Barth's position remains decidedly Protestant and Reformed in its orientation (*CD IV.1*, 113-114; cf. 118-120). This 'partnership' is a partnership of service, in which the Christian does not cooperate in salvation but 'responds' [*antworten*] and 'corresponds' [*entsprechen*] to what is 'simply the work of God for him' (*CD IV.1*, 113).[17] The action of the Christian thus has value and

---

[14]See also *CD IV.2*, 19-20.

[15]To put this in other terms, divine grace calls forth corresponding human obedience (see *CD IV.3.1*, 166). Dogmatics thus includes ethics within itself.

[16]See also *CD IV.3.1*, 228. The concept of the human person as a 'covenant partner' of God is prevalent within the *Church Dogmatics* as a central theme, though Barth was not always so open to speak of humanity as a 'partner' (see *CD I.2*, 207) For a discussion of this concept in Barth's theology, see Wolf Krötke, 'Gott und Mensch als "Partner": Zur Bedeutung einer zentralen Kategorie in Karl Barths *Kirchlicher Dogmatik*,' in *Theologie als Christologie: Zum Werk und Leben Karl Barths*, ed. Heidelore Köckert and Wolf Krötke (Berlin: Evangelische Verlagsanstalt, 1988), 106-120; also Krötke, 'The humanity of the human person in Karl Barth's anthropology,' in *The Cambridge Companion to Karl Barth*, 163-166.

[17]It is true that Barth does refer to a 'cooperation' in relation to humanity's role in the history of salvation, but he is clear that this pertains not to humanity's present service but to its future task within the kingdom of God. In the present, the form that humanity's task takes is one of

existence only as it is grounded in the prior work of Christ, and exists in correspondence to that complete and unique work.

This notion of correspondence [*Entsprechung*] lies at the heart of Barth's understanding of the relation between divine and human agency, a conception that seeks to preserve at one and the same time both the uniqueness and singularity of God's redemptive work and a real and significant place for human action. As such, it is Barth's answer to synergistic and monistic understandings of divine and human interaction, and his own mature position and response to charges of heteronomy and monism.[18] It is crucial to understand that the concept of correspondence is itself rooted in a Christological logic, in that, as the human nature of Christ corresponds to his divine nature and exists analogically in relation to it, and as Jesus Christ himself lives in correspondence to God, so also the believer lives in correspondence to Christ, neither confusing nor separating his or her own work with or from that of Christ. As John Webster has insightfully noted, Barth's understanding of correspondence is grounded in a Christological framework that attempts to hold in dialectical tension a substitutionary Christology, in which Christ lives and acts in our stead due to our own sinfulness, and an exemplarist Christology, in which Christ provides the pattern for our own real and obedient action.[19] The dialectical tension between these two positions is never resolved in Barth's thought but remains as an eschatological tension predicated upon a Christological pattern, a tension understood under the category of vocation.

'response and correspondence.' But in the future, humanity will indeed serve in a 'co-operation of service with God.' It is in fact humanity's service with and for God that comprises humanity's future glory, joy, and rest (*CD IV.1*, 113-114). Barth elsewhere can briefly speak of humanity as a 'co-operating subject' with God in the present economy, but it is clear from Barth's qualification of the term that his reference precludes all synergistic understandings of salvation as a shared work between God and humanity (for example, *CD III.3*, 92; 254). He also states that the term 'service' or 'ministry' is preferable to 'co-operation' for expressing humanity's role in the history of salvation (see *CD IV.3.2*, 599-601; also 603-610).

[18] For the concept of 'correspondence' in Barth's thought, see John Webster, *Barth's Ethics of Reconciliation* (Cambridge: Cambridge Univ. Press, 1995); also Webster, *Barth's Moral Theology: Human Action in Barth's Thought* (Grand Rapids: Eerdmans, 1998). I am indebted throughout this section to Webster's work. See also Gollwitzer, 'Kingdom of God,' 97-99.

[19] John Webster, 'The Christian in Revolt: Some Reflections on *The Christian Life*,' in *Reckoning With Barth: Essays in Commemoration of the Centenary of Karl Barth's Birth*, ed. Nigel Biggar (London & Oxford: A. R. Mowbray & Co., 1988), 119-144; esp. 125; 128-129; 130. See also Webster, *Barth's Ethics of Reconciliation*, esp. 78; 138; 184-186. For the dialectical relation between the vicarious and the exemplarist Christological conceptions in Barth in relation to the concept of correspondence, see *CD IV.3.2*, 541-544; also 594-595; 604-607.

This vocation of the Christian is tied to the mission of the Christian community, and it is expressed in the discipleship that is rendered to Christ, a discipleship that is not a slavish imitation of Christ and his unique work, but is rather a true obedience that corresponds to this singular work.[20] Already in the first volume of the *Church Dogmatics* Barth could assert that the aim of Christ's action is such that 'out of man's life there should come a repetition [*Wiederholung*], an analogy [*Analogie*], a parallel [*Parallele*] to His own being — that he should be conformable to Christ' (*CD I.2*, 277).

To reiterate, just as the person of Jesus Christ corresponds within his life to the nature of God,[21] so also the Christian community and the individual Christian correspond to Christ, living in a way that, once again, neither presumptiously imitates nor replaces Christ, but in a manner that nevertheless follows in discipleship the pattern that Christ laid down, even including the bearing of the cross and sharing in the affliction Christ suffered.[22] Barth is adamant that there be no confusion here between Christ and the church or the individual Christian because Christ's work is unique and his alone, as he alone is the Subject of redemption. The relationship is thus one of 'indissoluble differentiation and irreversible order' (*CD IV.3.2*, 594; also 599). Yet at the same time, it must be said that there is also a real correspondence, a reflection, within the life of the church and the individual Christian to this unique work. There is thus no direct identification of the church or the Christian with Christ, but neither is there a trivialization of the church's action, for there is an irreversible yet indivisible fellowship between Christ and the community in which the second reflects the former (*CD IV.3.2*, 538-539).[23] This relation itself is thus predicated upon

---

[20]See *CD IV.1*, 229-230; cf. also *CD IV.3.2*, 592-610.

[21]'The royal man of the New Testament tradition is created "after God"...This means that as a man He exists analogously to the mode of existence of God. In what He thinks and wills and does, in His attitude, there is a correspondence, a parallel in the creaturely world, to the plan and purpose and work and attitude of God' (*CD IV.2*, 166).

[22]See *CD IV.2*, 263-264; also *CD IV.3.2*, 618; 637-647. For Barth's understanding of the centrality of discipleship to the Christian life, see *CD IV.2*, 533-553; also *CD IV.3.2*, 535-537; as well as *CD I.2*, 277-278. In reference to the cross of the Christian, Barth writes that it 'is not the cross of Christ. This has been carried once and for all, and does not need to be carried again. There can be no question of identification with Him, of a repetition of His sufferings and death. But it is a matter of each Christian carrying his own individual cross, suffering his own affliction, bearing the definite limitation of death which in one form or another falls on his own existence, and therefore going after Christ as the man he is, following "in his steps" (I Pet. 2:21)' (*CD IV.2*, 264). Barth refers to this as the 'little cross' of the Christian (ibid., 264). This can be compared to Barth's downplaying of Christian suffering and martyrdom in *CD I.2*, 108-109.

[23]See again Gollwitzer, 'Kingdom of God,' 97-99.

a Chalcedonian pattern and the logic of the hypostatic union. As Barth notes, the relation of Christ to the Christian (and also, antecedently, of Christ to the Christian community) thus stands as an analogy to the 'mystery and miracle of Christmas,' i.e., the incarnation (*CD IV.3.2*, 542; 538-545).

This task of response and correspondence bears directly upon the issue of ecclesiology, for it is the church, the Christian community, which is called to live and serve in response to this altered situation achieved in reconciliation. The church lives in correspondence to the reconciliation completed in Christ and serves the role of witness to this event. This is its primary purpose and task.[24] Again, the church's service of mission does not supplement the work of Christ but makes it known, so that the church lives in obedience to its Lord and in correspondence to Christ's own prophetic work. This is the commission laid upon the community, its missionary duty (*CD IV.3.1*, 303-305). This duty is undertaken, however, in the midst of the unmitigated sinfulness of the community, a sinfulness that cannot be denied (*CD IV.3.1*, 321-322). There is thus a deep eschatological tension between the church's sinfulness and its sanctification that itself stands in correspondence to the tension between Barth's vicarious and exemplary Christologies, as the church lives neither in a triumphalistic cooperation with its Lord, nor in hopeless contradiction to him, but in correspondence to Christ in the eschatological tension between sin and obedience. As Barth states:

> According to the obvious tenor of the statements of the New Testament, the distinctive feature of the being of Christians as the children of God thus consists decisively and dominatingly in the fact that, as those whom Jesus Christ has called and calls to Himself in the work of His Spirit, they exist in particularly [sic] proximity to Him and therefore in analogy to what He is. He is originally — not merely in the counsel of God but in the eternal being of God, and then in time, in the flesh and within the world in virtue of the counsel of God — that which men become as they are called to be Christians. That is to say, He is originally the Son of God. And in analogy and correspondence, which means with real similarity for all the dissimilarity, they may become sons of God. Their new and distinctive being as Christians is their being in this real similarity, for all the dissimilarity, to His being as the Son of God. They may become and thus be what He is originally and does not have to become. They are secondarily, as those who are called by Him, as those whom He adopts as His brothers and sisters, as those who become such, the children of God (*CD IV.3.2*, 532-533).

---

[24]See *CD IV.1*, 149-153; cf. *CD IV.3.2*, 573-575.

The action of the community and the Christian in Christ thus takes place in correspondence to the history of Christ and thus within a history of salvation (*CD IV.3.2*, 597-598). As Barth writes: 'The embracing concept of vocation describes a history, namely, the history of the Christian in connexion with that of Jesus Christ Himself as engaged in His prophetic work.' (*CD IV.3.2*, 663). It is to this notion of history that we now turn.

3. Reconciliation and History: The Nature of the Church

The aforementioned description of human freedom and agency displays the distance Barth has traversed since the *Romans* commentary. Another such characteristic of the doctrine of reconciliation that does the same is Barth's willingness to speak of revelation as a history [*Geschichte*], and these developments are not unrelated.

Barth's ambivalent stance towards history and historical questions in relation to revelation and faith during his early years is well known, as Barth refused to subsume revelation into history or predicate faith upon the findings of critical historical science.[25] Indeed, Barth could himself write Thurneyssen in 1916 and report that he was indifferent concerning historical questions, stating: 'Of course, that is nothing new for me. Already under the influence of Herrmann, I always thought of historical criticism as merely a means of attaining freedom in relation to the tradition, not, however, as a constituting factor in a new liberal tradition.'[26] Yet in the doctrine of reconciliation of the *Church Dogmatics*, Barth speaks of the concept of history in (surprisingly) positive terms:

> The atonement is history. To know it, we must know it as such. To think of it, we must think of it as such. To speak of it, we must tell it as history. To try to grasp it as supra-historical or non-historical truth is not to grasp it at all. It is indeed truth, but truth actualised in a history and revealed in this history as such — revealed, therefore, as history (*CD IV.1*,157).[27]

---

[25]The most pertinent materials in this regard are the 'Preface' to the first, second, and third editions of the *Römerbrief* and the reviews of that work by critics such as Jülicher, Schlatter, and Bultmann, as well as the correspondence between Barth and Harnack over the place of the historical-critical method in relation to faith, originally appearing in *Die Christliche Welt* in 1923. These documents are included, in translation, in Robinson, *Beginnings of Dialectical Theology*, 61-130; 165-187. See also Rumscheidt, *Revelation and Theology*; Hunsinger, 'The Harnack/Barth Correspondence,' 319-337; and Jüngel, *Karl Barth: A Theological Legacy*, 70-82.

[26]Smart, *Revolutionary Theology*, 36.

[27]See *CD IV.1*, 157-158; cf. *CD IV.2*, 106. Barth can go so far as to state that the term 'dialectic' should be abandoned in favor of the term 'history' (*CD IV.3.1*, 195).

What allowed Barth now to speak of history as central to salvation and revelation? The key to answering this question (as in much of Barth's theology) is to see his adoption of history as a central category for faith and dogmatics not as a reversal of his former aversion to liberalism (for Barth never retracted his criticisms of liberalism's understanding of the relation between faith and history and its sole reliance upon a critical historical science), but as made possible by a re-definition of history through an *Aufhebung* of the concept of history itself.[28]

Barth's early adversarial stance towards liberalism's understanding of history and its historical-critical method stemmed from its positing of a general account of history with its own criteria of verifiability by which revelation and the Biblical story of redemption had to be judged, resulting in an equation of revelation with the findings of historical-critical science. In other words, the story of redemption was seen to be an instance within general history, and thus one member of a class, so to speak.

Barth could only object to such a procedure, whether made by a Biblical scholar such as Jülicher or a historian such as Harnack. Such a concept of history was abstract, in that it existed and was defined apart from God's specific revelation in Jesus Christ. Barth's rejection of such a position is consistently maintained throughout his career, clearly evidenced not only in his debate with Harnack in 1923 but also in the latter volumes of the *Church Dogmatics* when he states that 'the concept of a history of man and men and mankind apart from the will and Word and work of God, is itself the product of the perverted and sinful thinking of man, one of the manifestations of human pride' (*CD IV.1*, 505). Moreover, Barth contends that historical scholarship itself, which adheres to such a conception of history, is also a form of pride and disobedience (*CD IV.1*, 506). This is the history of the Fall. Barth opposed such an understanding of history along with its concomitant methods of historical criticism which attempted to find a history 'behind' the text, a 'true' history, rather than seeing the true history of God in Christ which required the text to be a witness to a living Lord of history.[29]

For Barth, the prevalent method of criticism unfortunately dealt with the positing of possibilities according to the canons of historical-critical science rather

---

[28]Barth's use of such a procedure of deconstruction for the purpose of reconstruction [*Aufhebung*] is identified by Hunsinger as a central pattern of Barth's thought. Hunsinger defines this as 'the Hegelian pattern of affirming, canceling, and then reconstituting something on a higher plane' (*How to Read Karl Barth*, 85-86; passim).

[29]See, for example, Barth's commentary on the composition of the Gospel narratives, (*CD IV.1*, 320). Barth could, however, speak of a positive preliminary and provisional function for historical critical science in relation to theological exegesis — see Barth, *Credo* (London: Hodder & Stoughton, 1936), 186-191. Barth alluded to this preliminary role already in the prefaces to the first and second editions of the *Romans* commentary.

than attending to the reality of God's revelation in Christ and thereby formulating its method according to the object under consideration. For Barth, the history of Christ, which includes his resurrection, therefore cannot be 'proved' according to the canons of modern historical science, but this does not entail that this history, including the resurrection event, did not occur in time and space. This situation speaks not of the impossibility of the resurrection, but of the inadequacy of the criteria of modern historical scholarship to accommodate this unique divinely-actualized event within its scientific framework.[30]

Instead of completely casting off history (and historical-criticism), however, Barth redefines history and the methods of historical examination from a theological standpoint. For Barth, history is not to be conceived as an autonomous sphere apart from God. Rather, God himself is understood as having his own history, the specific history that he has assumed in Jesus Christ.[31] One therefore does not seek God in history, but one finds history in God. Barth's position neither posits two realms to history (as in a so-called *Heilsgeschichte*), nor is it pantheistic, for God takes up history as a free act of grace, grounded in an eternal decision of election. In other words, God remains God apart from this history, but God in his grace has chosen to be God in unity with this history, the history of Jesus Christ. This history of Christ directly includes the history of others in him, i.e., the history of the church, or community, and indirectly includes the entire history of the world. As John Thompson rightly comments:

> This primal history, as it might be called, has a transcendent character but with a particular historical manifestation. Our history is the predicate of revelation and not vice-versa. Since God has taken man and his history into union with himself in this particular form and place it has special significance for all times, places and people whether they know it or not. It is a history which, moreover, changes the whole relationship between God, man and the world....
>   ....This history is not atemporal but, as Barth says, in the contemporaneity of past present and future, is highly temporal. Thus by his

---

[30]See *CD IV.1*, 332-338. With specific reference to the resurrection, Barth states: 'Even accounts which by the standards of modern scholarship have to be accounted saga or legend and not history — because their content cannot be grasped historically — may still speak of a happening which, though it cannot be grasped historically, is still actual and objective in time and space' (ibid., 336). Such an event is in but not of history.

[31]'According to the witness of Holy Scripture — in correspondence with His triune being, and as indicated by the biblical concept of eternity — God is historical even in Himself, and much more so in His relationship to the reality which is distinct from Himself' (*CD IV.1*, 112).

reconciliation at a particular point in time God embraces all our life and history and at the same time transcends it.[32]

Christ's history thus does not stand within general history as a particular phenomenon within a larger and more foundational framework, but the history of the world exists for the sake of the history of Christ and as the context for his own history.

In essence, it is the history of the resurrected Christ that is truly real, and against which all other history is to be judged, rather than the reverse. To say that this is counter-intuitive is of course a gross understatement. Barth's position has been insightfully grasped by Ingolf Dalferth:

> The eschatological reality of the resurrection which Christians confess in the Credo has ontological and criteriological priority over the experiential reality which we all share. The truth-claims of the Christian faith are the standards by which we are to judge what is real, not vice versa.[33]

The Scriptures themselves therefore must not be read as mythical accounts that hide 'true' history behind them, but as witnesses that must be read realistically.[34] No longer is the Bible judged by the standards of an 'objective' history ascertained through an 'unprejudiced' historical science, but general 'objective' history is now judged and absorbed by the Biblical text, read realistically according to central theological and Christological commitments.[35] Whereas Harnack, for example, reads biblical history through the lens of general history and as an instance within it, Barth reads general history though the lens of Biblical history and sees general history as simply the external basis of the Biblical one, which is now seen as fundamental.

---

[32]John Thompson, 'Christology and Reconciliation in the Theology of Karl Barth,' in *Christ In Our Place: The Humanity of God in Christ for the Reconciliation of the World*, ed. Trevor A. Hart and Daniel P. Thimell (Allison Park/Exeter: Pickwick Publications/Paternoster Press, 1989), 218-219.

[33]Ingolf U. Dalferth, 'Karl Barth's eschatological realism,' in *Karl Barth: Centenary Essays*, ed. S. W. Sykes (Cambridge: Cambridge University Press, 1989), 22. Dalferth's article is a brilliant articulation of Barth's position in relation to the problems here being addressed.

[34]Ibid., 25. Barth's conception of revelation as manifested in the history of Jesus Christ thus directly affects the narrative structure of theology's exposition and its understanding of ontology, especially in relation to Christology, and therefore the realistic reading strategy of Barth's hermeneutics and exegesis.

[35]See, for example, *CD IV.2*, 149-150. For a related description of reading general history through the lens of the specific narrative of Scripture, see George Lindbeck, *The Nature of Doctrine* (Philadelphia: Westminster Press, 1984). See also Hunsinger, 'Beyond Literalism and Expressivism: Karl Barth's Hermeneutical Realism,' in *Disruptive Grace*, 210-225.

General history viewed alone, Barth maintains, can only be an abstraction and distortion of the true history that exists between God and humanity, and it must therefore be re-conceived theologically, and specifically, Christologically.

General world history, therefore, exists only as it is taken up by the specific history of Christ, as his context and stage, for just as creation is the external basis of the covenant, so world history is the external basis of the history of Christ and secondarily of the church, which is united to Christ.[36] As Dalferth has perceptively noted, 'what "history" really means is shown by the one history of Jesus Christ which, when interpretatively applied to our common understanding of history, shows this to be, at best, a preliminary, abstract and inauthentic understanding of history.'[37]

As stated, the history that has been described should not be viewed abstractly, but in relation to a particular manifestation of God's revelation within the world. More specifically, this history *is* the person of Jesus Christ (*CD IV.1*, 16-17). Put in other terms, 'Jesus Christ is the atonement' [*Jesus Christus ist die Versöhnung*] (*CD IV.1*, 34). Barth writes:

> We must realise that the Christian message does not at its heart express a concept or an idea, nor does it recount an anonymous history to be taken as truth and reality only in concepts and ideas. Certainly the history is inclusive, i.e., it is one which includes in itself the whole event of the 'God

---

[36]This point pertaining to the question of time is articulated by Dalferth in relation to the corresponding question of reality: 'Taken by itself it [the world] is nothing but an abstraction of the only concrete reality there is: God's self-realisation in the life, death and resurrection of Christ, the foundation of all this in the eternal will of God and its consequences in and for our world. It does not follow from this that what we experience as real is not real or only seems to be so. Rather it is a preliminary, penultimate, abstract reality which as such is in permanent danger of relapsing into non-existence. In short, our world of common experience is an *enhypostatic reality* which exists only in so far as it is incorporated into the concrete reality of God's saving self-realisation in Christ. Taken by itself natural reality is an anhypostatic abstraction, unable to exist on its own and systematically at one remove from the texture of concrete reality' ('Karl Barth's eschatological realism,' 29). For our purposes, it should be noted that Dalferth's reference to reality could be substituted with the concept of time with no loss in meaning or application. Barth not only attempted to 'stand our common notion of reality on its head by reconstructing it in terms of classical Christology rather than the other way round' (ibid., 29), but he also did the same with our common notion of time and history. Once again, for Barth, to say that 'the Word assumed flesh' was to say that 'the Word assumed time.' All reality is thus understood Christologically, as for Barth, 'it is the eschatological history of Jesus Christ which provides us with the prototypical understanding of the "true God," the "real man," the "real reality," the "real time," the "true being," the "true history," etc.' (ibid., 38).

[37]Ibid., 38.

with us' and to that extent the history of all those to whom the 'God with us' applies. But it recounts this history and speaks of its inclusive power and significance in such a way that it declares a name, binding the history [*Geschichte*] strictly and indissolubly to this name and presenting it as the story [*Geschichte*] of the bearer of this name. This means that all the concepts and ideas used in this report (God, man, world, eternity, time, even salvation, grace, transgression, atonement and any others) can derive their significance only from the bearer of this name and from His history, and not the reverse. They cannot have any independent importance or role based on a quite different prior interpretation. They cannot say what has to be said with some meaning of their own or in some context of their own abstracted from this name. They can serve only to describe this name — the name of Jesus Christ (*CD IV.1*, 16-17).[38]

Yet, though the life of Jesus Christ is described as a history, this does not entail that his appearance is due to history itself, the result of forces and causation intrinsic to the historical process. Barth's position remains dialectical, sacrificing none of his earlier commitments, refusing to subsume revelation into history, or to see revelation as a predicate of history. The opposite, in fact, is the case, for while history may become a vehicle for revelation as it is taken up for divine purposes, revelation itself can never be a predicate of history. As Barth relates, Jesus 'is not a product — not even the most perfect — of the created world as such. He is in it. He belongs to it. He exists and works and reveals Himself in its history. But He does not derive from it: it derives from Him' (*CD IV.1*, 50).[39]

It should be obvious how Barth's Chalcedonian and anhypostatic-enhypostatic logic is contained within this statement, now rendered in terms of a unified history, rather than of a union of natures, though the former presupposes the latter. This logic, paradigmatic and constitutive for Christology, also pertains regulatively to the church, for the church too is conceived by Barth as in but not of history. Yet, it must

---

[38]Barth can thus redescribe the characteristics of the history of reconciliation outlined above in terms of the personal characteristics of Jesus Christ (*CD IV.1*, 18-20). This again demonstrates Barth's conviction that Christ's person and work are inseparable and mutually definitive, i.e., reconciliation and Christology are coextensive.

[39]While Christ thus appears within a historical series of events, thus fulfilling Old Testament prophecy, his appearance is a new and miraculous event (see *CD IV.2*, 37-38). This understanding of Christ's appearance marks Barth's position off from that of Schleiermacher. See Kimlyn J. Bender, 'Between Heaven and Earth: Schleiermacher's Christology in View of Intrasystematic Tensions and Relations within the "*Glaubenslehre*,"' in *Schleiermacher's 'To Cecilie' and Other Writings by and about Schleiermacher – Neues Athenaeum, V. 6*, ed. Ruth D. Richardson, (Lewiston, NY: Edwin Mellen Press, 2001), 179-195.

always be remembered that while Christ is the basis and paradigm for every relationship between God and humanity, he is also unique in this relation, the unsubstitutable unity of God and humanity in one person, the fulfillment of God's eternal will (*CD IV.1*, 53-54). The work of the church and of the Christian therefore does not add to that of Christ, but bears witness to it. It is an analogy, a correspondence, to Christ in discipleship, a true following after, rather than a slavish imitation that attempts to do what Christ alone could accomplish (*CD IV.1*, 229-230; 635-636). Just as Christ's human nature corresponds to his divine nature, so Jesus Christ corresponds to God (*CD IV.2*, 166ff.). Jesus Christ therefore lives in correspondence to God, and in an analogical manner, the church lives in correspondence to Christ.

A. The Question of Historical Distance: Christ and the Church

The topics of human agency and history may be seen as related in Barth's theology when one begins to examine Barth's claim that Jesus Christ, as the resurrected Lord, is not absent but present within the world. The problem of Christ's historical distance from us, the problem of spanning a temporal divide between Christ and ourselves, was classically expressed by Lessing, and this problem is taken up by Barth (*CD IV.1*, 287-295). Barth, however, regards the problem itself as an illegitimate one, or rather, as a problem that is posed to hide the fact that Christ truly is present here and now in the resurrection and therefore someone with whom we have to deal. In short, Christ does not have to be made present because he already *is* present.[40] The real problem is therefore not one of historical or spacial distance, but of our sin which separates us from Christ. Put differently, it is an ontological rather than a spacial or temporal divide that stands between Christ and ourselves, and more specifically still, a divide between righteousness and unrighteousness.[41] Barth concludes: 'In and with the overcoming of the real and spiritual problem of the relationship between Jesus Christ and us, the technical problem of the relationship between the then and there and the now and here is also soluble and has in fact been solved' (*CD IV.1*, 293).

---

[40]See CD IV.1, 287-295; 314-318; also *CD IV.2*, 107; 110-113.

[41]The language of an ontological rather than a spacial (or temporal) divide is borrowed from Colin Gunton, 'No Other Foundation: One Englishman's Reading of *Church Dogmatics* Chapter V,' in *Reckoning With Barth: Essays in Commemoration of the Centenary of Karl Barth's Birth*, ed. Nigel Biggar, 75-76; cf. also Gunton, 'Transcendence, Metaphor, and the Knowability of God,' *Journal of Theological Studies*, 31 (1980): 501-516. Gunton uses this language in reference to God's transcendence in relation to the world, but it can also be applied here, as I have done, to understand questions pertaining to Christ's transcendence over and presence within history.

Barth's understanding of Christ's presence has a direct effect upon ecclesiology. First, because Christ is present in the power of the Holy Spirit, the church does not stand as a surrogate for Christ upon earth.[42] Barth consistently rejects any conception of the church as a vicar for Christ in lieu of Christ's own presence. Nor is it the church's task to make Christ present, nor to mediate the salvific effects of his past atonement through some form of sacramental action. Barth can in fact assert that there is only one true sacrament, that of Christ upon the cross (*CD IV.1*, 296; cf. *CD IV.2*, 55). The church's task is thus one of witness, rather than of sacramental mediation.

In a related way, this understanding of Christ's presence has real ramifications for the understanding of the nature and mission of the church (*CD IV.1*, 353-354). The community is not called to assist in the work of God's salvation, but simply to bear witness to the salvation accomplished in Christ. To live under and witness to this divine verdict, God's salvation, is the community's 'particular gift and task.' Referring to the church and to Christians, Barth writes:

> They have not to assist or add to the being and work of their living Saviour who is the Lord of the world, let alone to replace it by their own work. The community is not a prolongation of His incarnation, His death and resurrection, the acts of God and their revelation. It has not to do these things. It has to witness to them. It is its consolation that it can do this. Its marching-orders are to do it (*CD IV.1*, 317-318).

This time between the resurrection/ascension and the parousia is the time of the community, Christ's presence in the Holy Spirit during this 'time between the times' of Christ's first and second appearance.[43] Barth can thus go so far as to say that the community is, 'as the reality of the people of God in world history, the company of those who are not only His but can know and confess themselves as His, and therefore Him as theirs, their Head. Where this community lives by the Holy Spirit, Jesus Christ Himself lives on earth, in the world and in history' (*CD IV.1*, 353). In light of our earlier examination, this quotation reveals a tension in Barth's thought between stressing the presence of Christ, thus relativizing and undermining any need for the church to mediate the benefits of Christ, and stressing the absence of Christ during this time between the resurrection and final return in which the community is the presence of Christ through the power of the Holy Spirit in the world. This tension, a tension between Christ's presence and absence paralleled by a corresponding

---

[42]See *CD IV.3.1*, 349-350. Barth is here obviously thinking of Roman Catholic understandings of vicarious offices and ministries.

[43]See *CD IV.1*, 318-320; 323; 353-354.

tension between the church's task as a witness and a mediator, will merit further examination in the following chapters.

What must be noted for the current discussion is that Barth does speak of the church in terms of its own history. In other words, the church is given its own place within the one history of Christ and is not simply subsumed into Christ, as in a related vein its mission is not subsumed into the atonement. To speak of Christ, Barth states, is to speak not only of the person of Christ but also of those who are his own, i.e., the community of those who live in him. They exist as the earthly body of which Christ is the head. Therefore, just as the human nature of Christ does not exist apart from, but yet truly exists in, the Word of God, so also the church does not exist apart from, yet truly exists in fellowship with, Christ. There is thus a correspondence, or analogy, between the relation of the Word and flesh in Christ, and the relation of the heavenly and earthly forms of his existence, or, the relation of Christ and the church (*CD IV.2*, 59-60). To clarify, as the Word is to the flesh of Christ, so correspondingly is Christ to the church. The latter of each pair has no existence apart from, but does have a real existence in, the former. Barth presents this understanding in a very significant yet often overlooked passage:

> This people, this community, is the form of His body in which Jesus Christ, its one heavenly Head, also exists and has therefore His earthly-historical form of existence. It is of human essence — for the Church is not of divine essence like its Head. But it does not exist in independence of Him. It is not itself the Head, nor does it become such. But it exists (ἀνυπόστατος and ἐνυπόστατος) in and in virtue of His existence. It lives because and as He lives, elected and awakened and called and gathered as a people by Him. It is His work, and it exists as His work takes place. Not for a single moment or in any respect can it be His body without Him, its Head. Indeed, it cannot be at all without Him. It does not exist apart from Him. It exists only as the body which serves Him the Head. For this reason — for otherwise it would have a separate and autonomous existence — it cannot even be His likeness or analogy. We cannot speak, then, of a repetition or extension of the incarnation taking place in it. But He, the one Jesus Christ Himself, exists as man. He exists not only in heavenly form, but also in earthly-historical form. To His heavenly form of existence as Son of God and Son of Man He has assumed this earthly-historical — the community as His one body which also has this form. He carries and maintains it in this unity with Himself as the people which not merely belongs to Him but is part of Himself. In God's eternal counsel, in His epiphany, and finally in His revelation at the end of the age, He was and is and will be this *totus Christus* — Christ and Christians. And these two elements of His one being are not merely related to one another *as* He Himself as Son of God is related to His

human nature. But, in this second form, His relationship to His body, the community, *is* the relationship of God and man as it takes place in this one being as Head and body. Thus the community of Jesus Christ can be that which the human nature of its Lord and Head is. It cannot and must not be more than this. There can, therefore, be no question of a reversal in which either the community or the individual Christian equates himself with Jesus Christ, becoming the subject where He is only the predicate. There can be no question of a divinisation of the Church or the individual Christian which Jesus Christ has only to serve as a vehicle or redemptive agency. All this is cut away at the root and made quite impossible by the fact that He Himself is the subject present and active and operative in His community. 'Christ liveth in me.' He Himself lives in this His earthly historical form of existence, in the community as this form of His body (*CD IV.2*, 59-60).[44]

It is thus the case that just as general world history exists only in relation to the history of Christ, and thus exists as the external context for its internal basis found in the atonement, so also, in a secondary sense, general world history exists only in relation to the history of the church, the history of the *totus Christus*, Christ and the community of Christians, that provides world history with its meaning. As Barth states:

> The insignificance and petty history of Christians, as capacitated and actualised by the Holy Spirit, is not merely one history among others — however much this may appear to be the case from the external and historical standpoint — but a kind of central history among all others. It is in order that it may occur that world history and time continue. To put it epigrammatically, it is itself the true world history, and everything else that bears this name is only the rather remarkable accompaniment (*CD IV.2*, 334).

The history of the church thus has significance in that it shares in the history of Christ, serving as the context and environment for his existence. Christ stands at the center of general world history, and the church, as joined to Christ, therefore also stands at the center of world history. The history of Christ, and the church with him, is therefore significant because it is within this history, the history of the *totus*

---

[44]This passage is the closest that Barth ever comes to crossing the line of speaking of the church as a second incarnation; he otherwise consistently rejects such a position.

Christus, that God is present and active in the world (*CD IV.2*, 335).[45] As Barth states: 'Salvation history is the history of the *totus Christus*, of the Head with the body and all the members' (*CD IV.3.1*, 216).

Barth's Christological and ecclesiological thought is, on this account, shown to be marked by a chain of correspondences: as the Word is to the flesh in Christ, so is Christ to the church, and so also is the church with Christ, the *totus Christus*, to the world (or, when spoken of in political terms, the state). The second term can never be confused with nor take the place of the first, for the first is the reality which gives the second term its existence. There is thus an analogy between Barth's ecclesiological and Christological formulations, as this is then followed by an analogy between Barth's ecclesiological and political thought. These complex relations may be expressed as concentric circles, with Christ as the center circle, or according to the following formulaic conception:

[Jesus Christ = Word~Flesh] ~
[*Totus Christus* = Christ~Church] ~
[Scope of Redemption = *Totus Christus* ~ World]

where '~' signifies 'is the basis for,' and where the second term is defined by an anhypostatic and enhypostatic relationship to the first, standing as the circumference to the center which gives it existence and living in correspondence to that center. Barth writes:

> In the glory of the Mediator as such there is included the fact that He is in process of glorifying Himself among and in and through us, and that we are ordained and liberated to take a receptive and active part in His glory. In this respect as in others, namely, in the glory of His mediatorial work, Jesus Christ is not without His own. He is who He is as He is among them, the saving and illuminating centre of which they form the circumference saved and illuminated by Him. Virtually, prospectively and *de iure* all men are His own. Actually, effectively, and *de facto* His own are those who believe in Him, who know Him, who serve Him and who

---

[45]This history of Christ includes within it not only the history of the church, but also the history of Israel, so that Barth can speak of the history of Israel as standing as the center and meaning of external history in a manner similar to that of the church. Barth states: 'In all these things the history of Israel is a paradigm or model for the history of all nations, and to the extent that it is prophecy, and is known as such, it is the key to the understanding of world history. Hence it is mediatorial history in the sense of exemplary and therefore representative history. It takes place among all other histories, but in such a way that it implies, comprehends, repeats and anticipates their origin, content and goal' (*CD IV.3.1*, 64).

are thus the interconnected members of His body, i.e., Christians....With those who in the wider or narrower sense, virtually or actually, are His own, He thus forms a unity and totality. There is, of course, strict and irreversible super- and subordination. There is a strict and indissoluble distinction of position and functions. The centre cannot become the circumference nor the circumference the centre. But in this order and distinction there is a totality. He can as little be separated from them as they from Him. We can only misunderstand the whole being and action in the christological sphere if even temporarily or partially we understand it as exclusive instead of inclusive or particular and not at once universal in its particularity. Hence all the required and necessary looking away from the world and all men, even from the Church and faith, in short from ourselves to Him, can only be with a view to seeing in Him the real world, the real man, the real Church and real faith, our real selves (*CD IV.3.1*, 278-279).

What must not be overlooked in light of this passage is that the relationship between the Word and the flesh of Christ is not quantitatively but qualitatively different and unique in regard to the other relations. The church is not a second incarnation, to reiterate a common theme. But as Christ is the basis for the history of reconciliation, so the community is its goal (*CD IV.2*, 336-337). So while Christ and the community must be distinguished and not confused, Barth can in places go so far as to see their reality and activity as indirectly identical in the most intimate of ways: 'Notwithstanding the real difference, Jesus Christ and His ἐκκλησία constitute an interrelated totality, so that He can represent His community and it can represent Him' (*CD IV.3.1*, 207). Having made this statement, however, Barth is again quick to point out that the relationship between Christ and the church is not reversible. Christ cannot be subsumed into nor replaced by the church, for Christ indeed remains the head, as the church remains his body. And this unity of Christ and the church is in fact effected through the power of the Holy Spirit that mediates between them (*CD IV.2*, 339).

B. The Question of Historical Duration: The Spirit and the Church

The issue of history does bear upon another aspect of the church's existence, namely, the ongoing perpetuity and historical continuity of the church in relation to the Spirit's calling the church into existence ever anew. This question is pneumatological, as the former one, pertaining to the church's relation to Christ and its distinctive task in light of Christ's resurrection, is specifically Christological, though these are of course related questions and cannot be sharply separated.[46] In sum, this question deals with the church's essence or nature, its invisible and visible reality, and the manner in which the church exists both as a divinely-established event created anew and as a historical and enduring institution existing in the midst of world history. In *CD II.2* Barth denied that the church itself has a history (*CD II.2*, 342). In *CD IV.1*, however, Barth's position is more nuanced. Barth now speaks of the community not only as an event, but as a reality that endures through time.[47] He writes:

> The Holy Spirit as the Spirit of Jesus Christ is the awakening power of the Word spoken by the Lord who became a servant and therefore of the divine sentence which judges and justifies sinful man. The work of the Holy Spirit as this awakening power is the historical reality of the community. When that verdict — that verdict of God which, we recall, repudiates and accepts, kills and makes alive — is heard by men, there is in their inner fellowship and there arises in their outward assembly a new humanity within the old. A new history begins within world-history. A new form of fellowship is quietly founded amongst other sociological forms: the apostolate, the disciples, the community, the Church. Its members are those who can believe and understand that sentence, and therefore regard as accomplished the justification of man in Jesus Christ (*CD IV.1*, 151).

Barth's openness to speak of the church in historical terms, however, does not cause him to abandon his position which sees the church as an event that must be constituted again and again through the work of the Holy Spirit, an event that can only be hoped for by the community: 'The community exists in this fruitful expectation which can never cease and never be unrealised' (*CD IV.1*, 151). The order of this relationship, between the church as event and as historical institution, cannot be

---

[46]See, for example, the close relationship between the being and work of Christ and the being and work of the Holy Spirit that Barth posits in relation to reconciliation (*CD IV.1*, 147-149). The question of the church, as well as that of the individual believer, Barth maintains, falls under the work of the Holy Spirit and refers to 'the relationship between the objective ascription and the subjective appropriation of salvation' (ibid., 149). Barth can also compare these as the relation between the Christological and the anthropological 'sphere' (ibid., 283-284). In essence, this is the relationship between the work of Christ and that of the Holy Spirit. Barth's understanding of this relation is not that the second supplements the first, but that the work of the Holy Spirit (in the subjective, anthropological sphere) is a witness to the complete and sufficient work of Christ (as the objective, christological basis) — see ibid., 285-286. It should be noted that Barth has Bultmann explicitly in mind as he formulates this material.

[47]See *CD IV.1*, 149-153; also *CD III.3*, 204-210.

reversed — the church exists as a historical institution only as it first exists as an event. But as a true event, it takes a specific historical form. Barth's mature ecclesiology therefore attempts to provide a more developed treatment of the church's historical existence even as his mature Christology attempts to give a more developed treatment of Christ as a human person. Here again there is a correspondence between maturation in Barth's Christological and ecclesiological thought, both dependent upon his ever-deepening reflection upon the humanity of God, itself based in election.[48]

But just as for Barth the existence of Christ as the exalted Son of Man is dependent upon the fact that he is first the obedient Son of God, the second movement from below to above dependent upon the first from above to below, so also the church's existence as a historical institution is dependent upon its grounding in a divinely-constituted event. Reflecting upon his early ecclesiological thought years later, Barth acknowledged the need for a more positive understanding of the church than that found within his own early theology, but he nevertheless contended that 'it certainly was and is no good undertaking to reverse the sequence whereby *event* precedes *institution*.'[49] There thus exists an ongoing tension in Barth's thought between perceiving the church as an event and as an institution, and this unresolved tension is in fact a dialectical relation in which the church exists as the unity of an invisible event and a visible historical manifestation, with the second dependent upon the first in an anhypostatic-enhypostatic relationship, in that the second exists only in dependence upon the first, though it does have a real and true, and therefore visible and historical, existence through the first. As he had done in the *Göttingen Dogmatics*, Barth here rejects a purely invisible and disembodied church, and thus any gnostic or docetic type of ecclesiology.

But what of church institutions that are devoid of this event, and thus of the Spirit? Could churches continue to exist as historical institutions apart from the Spirit? What can be said of church institutions that exist in time but that have fallen away from faith and obedience? Barth addresses these questions in his essay, 'The Church — The Living Congregation of the Living Lord Jesus Christ.'[50] There Barth

---

[48]See Barth, 'The Humanity of God,' 37-65; esp. 62-65.

[49]Ibid., 63.

[50]This essay exists in two forms. The first and longer form was written in 1947 and is found in translation in: *God Here and Now*, trans. Paul M. van Buren, (New York: Harper and Row, 1964), 61-85. This essay will be referenced as: 'Living Congregation — *GHN.*' The original German text for this essay may be found in *Theologische Existenz heute*, N.F. 9 (1947): 3-23; and in *Theologische Studien* 22 (1947): 21-44. A second and briefer form of this essay was given before the Amsterdam Assembly of 1948 where the World Council of Churches was established. This address may be found in translation in: *Man's Disorder and God's Design*, (New York: Harper and Brothers, 1948), 67-76. This essay will be referenced as: 'Living

asserts that the nature and reality of the church exists in its divine constitution through Christ and the Spirit as an ever-new event [*Ereignis*], and that the church's historical existence and continuity is dependent upon this constant gift of Christ through the Spirit. The church is thus both an event and a history.[51] The true church is a living church, and it lives as it is united to its living Lord, who is its subject.[52] As Barth explains, the church is the 'living congregation of the living Lord Jesus Christ,' and is as such a dynamic reality that exists within a history between God and humanity, a history that exists between Christ's resurrection and his final return, the time of the church.[53] The church is thus visible in time as a particular gathering of people (and as an institution), but it is truly perceived as the real church only with the eyes of faith, for it is faith alone which sees not only the church's visible and historical manifestation but the invisible power that grounds its reality. As the church remains dependent upon receiving the Word of God anew, and thus in openness to Christ through the Spirit, the church comes into existence and endures through time.[54]

There is a danger that threatens the church, however, for even though 'from above' its existence is secure in Christ its Head, 'from below' it may fall into sin, unbelief, and error in a number of ways.[55] As Barth states:

> The common element in all forms of this danger to the Church consists in the fact that the history, the movement, the action begun by the first subject, by Jesus Christ, is not continued in the other subject, in His congregation, but suffers from arrested development. The vital current passing and re-passing between the Lord and His congregation is blocked by man's sin. The life of the congregation ceases to be 'event'; the congregation ceases to be a *living* congregation. But this means that the Church has ceased to exist.[56]

If the unity of the church with her Lord ceases, if the church is no longer addressed by her Lord and renewed by his Spirit, then it may very well be the case that the outer,

---

Congregation — *MDGD*.' The original German text may be procured in: Zeugnis und Zeichen: Reden, Briefe, Dokumente, ed. Friedrich W. Kantzenbach, (München: Kaiser, 1964), 234-244. The following account draws upon both forms of this address.

[51]'Living Congregation — *MDGD*,' 69.

[52]Ibid., 67.

[53]'Living Congregation — *GHN*,' 62.

[54]Ibid., 62-63; 68.

[55]'Living Congregation — *MDGD*,' 69f.; cf. 'Living Congregation — *GHN*,' 67f.

[56]Ibid., 71.

visible, historical, and institutional form of the church may still exist, and may even flourish. But this 'church' is no longer the true church, but is instead a 'nominal church,' or 'apparent church' [*Scheinkirche*], an 'ecclesiastical shell from which the life has fled' [*Kirchenschein*].[57] As Barth comments:

> The place of the church that is no longer a church is not replaced by a vacuum. Instead we have the phenomenon of the nominal church [*Scheinkirche*], or the church which is merely an ecclesiastical shell [*Kirchenscheins*]: the ecclesiastical *quid pro quo*, endowed with all the qualities (but deprived of all their content) of the really living congregation.[58]

The sign of this loss of a living relationship with her Lord is the church's loss of unity, for a living and a dead congregation can have nothing in common.[59]

Such a dead, or nominal, church is not without hope, however, for Christ may renew such a nominal church in order to make it a true and living congregation once again, and this renewal is in fact the constitution of the unity of the church.[60] Barth states:

> If the Church is preserved, if in spite of all it has continuance in time, then that must mean that it experiences anew, again and again, the same thing which it experienced in coming into existence, an eternally new *reformation* which corresponds to its formation. If the Church is not caught up in reformation, then it has fallen into temptation, fallen headlong into being non-Church, and so fallen beyond rescue.[61]

A danger and a promise thus hangs over every church, a danger of unbelief that can lead to a loss of the church's relation to her Lord, and a promise of divine faithfulness which can restore this relation once again.[62]

This essay illustrates two central principles of Barth's mature ecclesiology. First, it demonstrates that for Barth the true church exists only as a unity of event and historical manifestation in dialectical relation — the historical and enduring existence

---

[57]Ibid., 67.

[58]Ibid., 71. Cf. 'Living Congregation — *GHN*,' 72-73.

[59]Ibid., 72. Cf. 'Living Congregation — *GHN*,' 73-75.

[60]Ibid., 72. Cf. 'Living Congregation — *GHN*,' 75f.

[61]'Living Congregation — *GHN*,' 75.

[62]'Living Congregation — *MDGD*,' 72ff.

of the church exists only insofar, paradoxically, as it is an ever-new event. The first without the second would be a platonic conception of an invisible church that is disembodied, and thus not incarnate, whereas the second without the first leads to a loss of the church's very essence and can only be seen as an empty shell, a visible though dead and false church. The Christological and anhypostatic-enhypostatic logic thus holds here too, though in ecclesiology, unlike in Christology, one can in fact speak of the existence of the institution apart from the event (whereas for Barth one cannot speak at all of Christ's flesh as existing apart from the Word). There is therefore a real analogy, but also a radical discontinuity, between the reality of Christ as the incarnate Word and the church as the historically-embodied event of the Spirit's constitution, for whereas Christ was sinless, and his human life lived in perfect obedience to God, the church may fall into sin and out of fellowship with its living Lord.

Second, what is also clear in Barth's essay is his conviction that ecumenical unity cannot be obtained simply by alliances of ecclesiastical bureaucracies, but must result from a renewal of the churches by Christ and the Spirit, making them living congregations subject to their living Lord. Without such a renewal, without the reconstitution of the church as an event, no amount of political effort will be successful, for unity is a matter of united confession under a living Lord, not of a united political or bureaucratic arrangement. We might say that an effort at ecumenical unity that strove simply for the latter was for Barth the ecclesiastical equivalent of a Christology that was based upon the 'historical Jesus' considered apart from the confession of Christ as the 'Word made flesh.' Both focused upon historical phenomena apart from their basis in divine action.

In the end, the renewal of the church is an act of her Lord through the Spirit. All that the church itself can do to foster this renewal is to adopt a polity that removes barriers between the Lord and the local congregation, and in Barth's estimation, a congregational polity does this better than papal, episcopal, consistorial, or presbyterian-synodal forms.[63] For Barth, the church is first and foremost an event that occurs in a specific location. The church is thus first and foremost a local congregation, and its polity should reflect this reality,[64] though Barth also speaks of the church as the unity of the individual local congregations, i.e., as the universal church.

Barth's conception of the church is thus predicated upon a Christological pattern: as Jesus Christ lives as the unity of the Word that has taken flesh, and as the flesh exists only in dependence upon the Word, so the true church exists only as the unity of the invisible church as event and the visible church as historical institution,

---

[63]Ibid., 75-76. Cf. 'Living Congregation — *GHN*,' 76; 82-85.

[64]Ibid., 73; also 'Living Congregation — *GHN*,' 78-79.

with the second dependent upon the first. The true church is thus both invisible and visible, both divinely-constituted and historically situated. A church that is not in living contact with her Lord may appear in history as a church, but is in reality only a shadow of what the church is to be, only an empty shell devoid of life. The true church, as the living congregation existing in a specific historical locality, is thus a reality that can be seen as such only with the eyes of faith.[65] Such a position was initially sketched in the *Göttingen Dogmatics* and has now reached maturity. We will examine this dialectical relationship between the Spirit and the church, and thus between the invisible and visible church, the church as event and institution, in more detail within the next chapter.

4. Summary

It may be asked why so much time has been spent upon the themes of correspondence and history within this chapter. Why not simply move to a direct discussion of Barth's doctrine of the church in the specifically ecclesiological sections of the doctrine of reconciliation, those sections that form the heart of Barth's mature ecclesiology? The answer is obvious when one considers prior readings of Barth's ecclesiology. Common criticisms of Barth's doctrine of the church in such studies, such as the accusation that Barth has entirely eliminated the need for ecclesial and human agency and action, subsuming all action under divine sovereignty in a form of heteronomy or monism; or the charge that Barth's Christocentrism renders any real place for the church moot by completely subsuming the church into Christ; or the indictment that for Barth the church possesses no true or enduring historical existence, and that Barth has no place for the visible church — all are common charges found throughout the literature. Yet in light of Barth's nuanced conceptions of correspondence and history as these bear upon the question of the church, all of these criticisms are shown to be at best one-sided and at worst grave distortions of Barth's thought.[66] The situation is more complex and requires greater nuance. Barth

---

[65]In his essay 'The Real Church,' an address originally delivered in 1948, Barth states: 'The real Church is truly not invisible but visible. But it is visible only where it is rendered visible by the action of God, by the witness of the Holy Spirit. This is the visibility in which the Church is seen by faith. What is seen in the same place without faith and without this revelation and witness is not the real Church at all...' in: *Against the Stream: Shorter Post-War Writings 1946-1952*, ed. Ronald Gregor Smith (New York: Philosophical Library, 1954), 63-64; cf. 65.

[66]Even as thorough and sympathetic a commentator as O'Grady here falls into the pattern of making such one-sided and unqualified criticisms. See *The Church in Catholic Theology*, 1-3; 11; 19-20; 66-70; 74-78; 107-108; 127-128; 171; 250; 260-262; 263-266; 336-340. O'Grady's contention that Barth's Christology and ecclesiology are marked by a

did *not* eliminate the need for human action and thus for ecclesial mission, but he *did* reject all synergistic accounts of salvation. Barth did *not* render the church insignificant in the face of Christ's work, but he *did* maintain that the church and Christ were not substitutable, and that their relation was irreversible. Barth did *not* deny that the church existed in historical duration, but he *did* refuse to make the Spirit a possession of the church that rendered constant renewal and revitalization unnecessary. In short, Barth rejected contemporary Neo-Protestant and Roman Catholic solutions to what were real problems and attempted to forge his own answers in such a manner that his initial insights and achievements were preserved while his early excesses were corrected. There is thus solid continuity and real development in his thought. This should be clear in light of our earlier chapters.

While Barth's early ecclesiology was itself (self-admittedly) one-sided, his mature conceptions of correspondence and history were meant to provide a real place for the historical, temporal, and sociological reality of the church, as well as a distinct place for its real agency and mission, without losing the dialectical relationship between eternity and time, revelation and history, and without making the Spirit a possession of the church or the church a substitute for Christ, or seeing the church in a triumphant cooperation with God in salvation. All of these, Barth believed, were errors on the left and on the right, errors either of Neo-Protestantism and/or of Roman Catholicism, and errors Barth set out consciously to avoid, all the while keeping a running dialogue with both sides that was marked by a growing appreciation for the latter opponent if not for the former (though here, too, Barth's final comments on Schleiermacher betray a deep respect and admiration).

---

monophysitism (and monoactualism, in which God alone is an agent in redemption) and Nestorianism (charges already prefigured in Feuerer, who termed them 'monism' and 'dualism,' as examined above) fails to do justice to the richness of Barth's Christology and ecclesiology in the doctrine of reconciliation and its attempt to address both traditionally Alexandrian and Antiochene concerns, as well as Barth's express denial that in reconciliation 'God is everything and humanity is nothing' (see ibid., 66-70; 127-128; 336-340). O'Grady states that one 'could express the difference between the Barthian and Catholic conception of the economy of salvation by saying that the former is *solely theistic* while the latter is *theandric*' (ibid., 338). But this judgment itself is deeply problematic and merits serious qualification in light of Barth's own statement that one must speak not only of theology but more properly of 'theanthropology' in reference to the 'commerce and communion between God and man' ('Evangelical Theology in the 19th Century,' in *The Humanity of God*, 11; see also Barth's essay 'The Humanity of God,' idem, 37-65). O'Grady is correct in seeing that differences between Barth's ecclesiology and that of Roman Catholicism are rooted in different understandings of Christology, but his solutions are not ones Barth could espouse, and his criticisms of Barth often wide of the mark. Nevertheless, O'Grady's accomplishment remains his demonstration of the irreducible and irrevocable dialectical nature of Barth's understanding of Christology and the church.

Barth's own ecclesiology can thus be described in terms of its Christological logic that takes form within various relationships. In regard to the Christological logic itself, Barth's Christology took initial shape in the *Göttingen Dogmatics* and found its most mature expression in the doctrine of reconciliation within the *Church Dogmatics*. Barth's Christology in the doctrine of reconciliation preserves both his classical Patristic and Chalcedonian commitments while also setting them within a dynamic and historically-grounded framework. This Christology is simultaneously traditional and radical, displaying both the deep continuity and ongoing development in Barth's thought. It respectfully adheres to the classic Christology of the creeds, yet it also criticizes Chalcedonian Christology for its emphasis upon 'being' rather than upon the 'work' of Christ and its proclivity toward abstraction when shorn from Christ's history and activity (*CD IV.1*, 127-128).

Barth's achievement is to integrate Christ's person and work in such a way that both preserves the Patristic and classic creedal Christological logic while formulating a Christology that integrates a more dynamic, actualistic, and narratively-construed ontology. In so doing, Barth's traditionalism and innovation are both evident. It is this relationship between God and humanity in the incarnation that then becomes the basis and paradigm for all other relationships between God and the world — they exist in analogy to this reality, displaying both real similarity and radical difference.

Ecclesiology, while itself a pneumatological doctrine, is thus grounded in this Christology and shares its inherent logic and patterns. Barth's mature ecclesiology therefore presupposes his mature Christology, for as Christ's person and work cannot be separated, so also can ecclesiology not be separated from Christology and takes shape in light of its Christological norm (*CD IV.1*, 124).

In regard to the ecclesiological relations that exist as shaped by this Christological logic, these can be designated as follows: 1) the relationship between the Spirit and the church pertaining to the church's *origin*, or *nature*, and specifically regarding the Spirit and the church's essence as event in historical existence, i.e., as the invisible and the visible church; 2) the relationship between Christ and the church pertaining to the church's *order*, or *form*, specifically regarding Christ's singular office and task and the church's own rule and law, as well as its role and commission; and, 3) the relationship between the church and the world, specifically regarding the church's *ordination*, or *mission*, and thus its witness defined in relation to the eschatological tension between its own sinfulness and obedience in the time between Christ's first and second advent.

The questions of human agency and history addressed in this chapter have shed light upon these relations and the presuppositions that lie behind Barth's understanding of them. These relations will now be examined in more detail in the coming chapters which will address the sections in the doctrine of reconciliation specifically devoted to ecclesiology.[67]

---

[67]*CD IV.1*, §62; *CD IV.2*, §67; and *CD IV.3.2*, §72, respectively.

Chapter Six

The Origin of the Church as the Fellowship of the Spirit

1. Introduction — The Holy Spirit and the Christian Community

The fourth volume of Barth's *Church Dogmatics* addressing the doctrine of reconciliation is the locus of Barth's most developed doctrine of the church. While Barth's mature ecclesiology is deeply influenced and shaped by Christology, the doctrine of the church itself falls under the subjective side of the work of atonement and therefore belongs to the third article of the creed as a doctrine of the Holy Spirit.[1] Barth states:

> The particular problem involved might be described as the subjective realisation of the atonement. The one reality of the atonement has both an objective and a subjective side in so far as — we cannot separate but we must not confuse the two — it is both a divine act and offer and also an active human participation in it: the unique history of Jesus Christ; but enclosed and exemplified in this the history of many other men of many other ages (*CD IV.1*, 643).

The Christological pattern governing this ecclesiology can be demonstrated in three relations: in the relation between the Spirit and the church as a divine fellowship, defining the church's *nature*; in the relation between Christ and the church as his body determining the community's *form*; and in the relation between the church as the people of God and the world prescribing the church's *mission*. This chapter will examine the first, the relationship between the Holy Spirit and the church.

In §62, 'The Holy Spirit and the Gathering of the Christian Community,' Barth takes up the question of the *nature* of the church.[2] He begins this section by situating the church within the subjective sphere of the atonement and does so by drawing upon the geometrical imagery that he gleaned from Luther and used so often:

---

[1]As Barth writes: 'All ecclesiology is grounded, critically limited, but also positively determined by Christology' (*CD IV.3.2*, 786).

[2]Barth elsewhere emphasizes that this nature of the church is not something the church intrinsically possesses but is itself a gift of grace (see *CD IV.3.2*, 729).

The Christology is like a vertical line meeting a horizontal. The doctrine of the sin of man is the horizontal line as such. The doctrine of justification is the intersection of the horizontal line by the vertical. The remaining doctrine, that of the Church and of faith, is again the horizontal line, but this time seen as intersected by the vertical. The vertical line is the atoning work of God in Jesus Christ. The horizontal is the object of that work; man and humanity (*CD IV.1*, 643).[3]

This geometrical language is significant and revealing in a number of respects. First, just as the incarnation of Christ exists as a vertical event that breaks into and exists within time, and thus within the horizontal plane of history, so also the church exists as the intersection of a divine act and a historical reality, the intersection of a vertical and (transformed) horizontal plane. The reality of the first (the incarnation — the objective side of the atonement) thus includes the reality of the second (the church and the individual Christian — the subjective side of the atonement) within itself, and the second exists analogously to the first. As Barth states: 'The history which we consider when we speak of the Christian community and Christian faith is enclosed and exemplified in the history of Jesus Christ' (*CD IV.1*, 644). Christ's history is therefore both the basis and pattern for the second reality, that of the church (and the Christian). The church and the Christian in time are seen not in simple opposition to the vertical eternal reality, but as transformed through the intersection of the horizontal by the vertical in justification.

In turning to the doctrine of the church, Barth is therefore turning from the objective to the subjective side of the atonement and thus from the second to the third article of the creed, from the doctrine of Christ to the doctrine of the Holy Spirit, even though the doctrine of the church is developed within the more general doctrine of reconciliation, and thus within the framework of the second article.[4] The doctrine of reconciliation, explicated under the second article, is thus an inclusive doctrine that takes up questions of both the objective and subjective atonement. Both the objective and subjective aspects, however, belong to the creed, and therefore both are matters not of direct historical perception but matters of faith and confession. This means that, like Christ, not only is the true nature and reality of the church perceived and understood solely by the work of the Holy Spirit, but also the reality of the church

---

[3]For other instances of this geometrical language, see Barth's *Römerbrief*, 5-6; ET: 29-30; also *The Holy Spirit and the Christian Life*, 32-34. That Barth there describes the intersection of the horizontal line by the vertical as pertaining to the issue of Christian obedience signals the deeply ethical nature of his theology in general and of his ecclesiology in particular.

[4]See *CD IV.1*, 643-644; 645. Barth is adamant that in turning from the second to the third article, from the objective to the subjective atonement, the issue of Christology is in no way left behind.

itself is grounded in the agency of the Holy Spirit, and not in the actualization of a human possibility. The Spirit is not the possession of the church and should not be confused with the church's own spirit, for 'neither the Christian community nor the individual Christian can subjugate or possess or control Him, directing and overruling His work,' words that bring to mind Barth's comments made years earlier regarding Schleiermacher (*CD IV.1*, 646).

The Holy Spirit is therefore not just any spirit, not even the spirit of the church or of the individual Christian, but 'the Spirit of the God who acts in Jesus Christ' (*CD IV.1*, 647).[5] The manner in which the Spirit works, i.e., the 'how' of the formation of the Christian community and the calling of a Christian, is not however something that we are given but something that remains a mystery.[6] The Holy Spirit's work remains inscrutable yet real, the basis of the existence of the Christian community in time and the revelation of the church's true identity. The true nature of the church is therefore that of a reality that exists in time though its origin and basis lie outside of history in the Spirit's call:

> In everything that we have to say concerning the Christian community and Christian faith we can move only within the circle that they are founded by the Holy Spirit and therefore that they must be continually refounded by Him, but that the necessary refounding by the Holy Spirit can consist only in a renewal of the founding which He has already accomplished. To put it in another way, the receiving of the Holy Spirit which makes the community a Christian community and a man a Christian will work itself out and show itself in the fact that only now will they really expect Him, only now will they want to receive Him; and where He is really expected, where there is a desire to receive Him, that is the work which He has already begun, the infallible sign of His presence (*CD IV.1*, 647).

This quotation reveals Barth's understanding of the church as both divinely established and historically constituted, but it seems to raise more questions than it answers. What is one to make of the paradoxical statement regarding the founding and re-founding of the church? In essence, it expresses Barth's dialectical thinking of the church as simultaneously an event and an institution, an event created ever anew and a historical entity that exists through time. On the one hand, Barth is

---

[5]There is thus a Trinitarian shape to Barth's ecclesiological thought as well as a Christological one, though the former is more implicit than the latter.

[6]Barth writes: 'It is strange but true that fundamentally and in general practice we cannot say more of the Holy Spirit and His work than that He is the power in which Jesus Christ attests Himself, attests Himself effectively, creating in man response and obedience. We describe Him as His awakening power' (*CD IV.1*, 648; cf. 648-649).

adamant that the church must be recreated ever anew in an event that is in fact the re-enactment of the original work of the Spirit that established the church in the first place. Such a statement by itself could lead one to conclude that Barth's ecclesiology fails to provide any place for the historical continuity of the church. Yet this judgment would be premature, for Barth goes on to say that it is precisely the community's recognition of this need for constant renewal that demonstrates the continuous presence and activity of the Spirit within the church and its ongoing existence. It is in fact only this constant presence of the Spirit that leads to the desire for this renewed reception.

This is a strikingly paradoxical and dialectical notion: the recognition by the church of the need for constant renewal and reception of the Spirit is the sign of the continuous and ongoing presence of the Spirit's activity within the church. Perhaps this notion might be clarified by a comparison with another element of Barth's thought. Many have criticized Barth for a failure to provide a place for the ongoing subjectivity and growth of the moral agent, seeing Barth's emphasis upon the unique and ever-new command of God as undermining such continuity.[7] Yet, here too the issue is more complex. For Barth, there is a continuity even in the midst of this discontinuity. This paradox has been grasped by Nigel Biggar who writes, in a passage cited earlier:

> The fact that each singular event of encounter between the commanding God and sinful human being is a moment in a history which is ordered by this definite intention of God gives to each historically contingent divine command its *ratio* and raises it above the status of one element in a chaos of individual conflicting intimations to individual human beings in individual situations.[8]

Therefore, just as the history of the relation between God and the world, grounded in an eternal decision, provides a teleological ordering to the individual commands and allows for moral deliberation and real development and maturation in the moral agent, so also the history of redemption between God and his community gives the individual act of renewal of the church by the Spirit the characteristic not of a random occurrence, but of a faithful, promised, and expected encounter within the framework of an ongoing history between God and his people. Biggar's observation in regard to the moral agent is perfectly applicable to Barth's view of the

---

[7]One of the most insightful and classic statements of this critique is made by Stanley Hauerwas, *Character and the Christian Life* (Notre Dame: University of Notre Dame Press, 1975/1994). For a response to Hauerwas's charge, see William Werpehowski, 'Command and History in the Ethics of Karl Barth,' *Journal of Religious Ethics* 9 (1981): 298-320.

[8]Biggar, *Hastening that Waits*, 28.

church as well: 'For us to start again does not at all mean that we should always return to the same place, but that in different places we should be careful to return to the same posture — specifically, to our knees. Indeed, to begin again is the precondition of our progress, and so of our having (in another sense) a history.'[9]

The only qualification that may be needed in order to apply this statement to Barth's ecclesiology is to note that whereas the individual moral agent begins with personal prayer, the community is reconstituted afresh by a renewed listening to its Lord in Scripture and proclamation through the power of the Spirit. This is the reconstitution of the church, yet a reconstitution that occurs within an ongoing history between God and the community. The church can never claim the Spirit as a possession acquired once and for all, just as the moral agent cannot rest content in previous obedience.[10] Yet the promise of the Spirit provides a continuity to the renewal of the church, and the community's very expectation and desire for the Spirit's presence is grounded in his ongoing activity. As Barth can cryptically say, the '*communio sanctorum* is an event and has its history in many events' (*CD IV.2*, 652). It is a failure to see the continuity of the history between God and the community, grounded in an eternal divine decision, that leads to the oft-mistaken notion that Barth's emphasis upon the church as an event precludes any true conception of the historical existence and duration of the church.[11]

Barth can in fact speak of the community in terms of a *history*, a history that itself is grounded in and inseparably joined to the history of Jesus Christ, as the history of Christ includes the history of the community within itself. Barth maintains that to consider the second (the subjective atonement) is not to leave the first (the objective atonement) behind, but it is to consider the entire act of the atonement in a different light: 'We are not now in a different sphere; we are simply looking at it from a different angle' (*CD IV.1*, 644).

This language is in fact Christological language. Just as Barth approaches the person and work of Christ from two different angles, that of the obedient Son of God and the exalted Son of Man, yet maintains that both angles are simply two necessary ways of viewing one single subject, so also within the one act of reconciliation, Barth holds that there is both an objective and subjective side. These can and must be

---

[9]Ibid., 139; see 138-139.

[10]See ibid., 138.

[11]This point is of course related to Barth's actualism and the relation between *act* and *being*. With reference to Barth's actualism, Herbert Hartwell can write: 'Barth's actualism does not mean — in spite of a sometimes unqualified language which may seem to justify the opposite view — that his theology leaves no room for the idea of a "state" of things. It only denotes that there can be no "state" which does not arise out of God's constant giving' (Hartwell, *The Theology of Karl Barth* [London: Gerald Duckworth & Co., 1964], 36).

distinguished and may be considered alone, but they cannot be separated.[12] Moreover, just as the first movement of reconciliation, as the obedience of the Son of God, is the basis for the second movement of the exaltation of the Son of Man, in that the second has no existence apart from the first, so too the first and objective side of the atonement (Christ) is the basis for the second and subjective side (the Church and the Christian), whereby the second has no existence apart from the first. These relations are predicated upon a Chalcedonian logic of unity and differentiation, as well as the asymmetrical relation of an anhypostatic-enhypostatic Christology whereby the second term has no independent existence apart from, but has a real existence in, the first term. Furthermore, the second term exists in a relation of correspondence to the first term, in that it cannot be confused with nor replace the first term, yet exists in an analogical manner to it.

There is in Barth's Christology a correspondence between the two movements, as the Servant as Lord corresponds to the Lord as Servant, and this Christological correspondence is complemented by an ecclesiological correspondence between the unity of these movements in Christ and the church, as the church corresponds to Christ.[13] Moreover, there is within the second reality of the church itself a correspondence to the differentiation within the first reality of Christ, in that the church is composed of the unity of two activities, divine and human, invisible and visible, as Christ is composed of the Word and flesh, and of a divine and human nature. We might graph this relationship this way:

[Jesus Christ = Word (movement from above) ~ flesh (movement from below)] ~
[Church = Invisible Work of Spirit (Event) ~ Visible Manifestation (Institution)]

where '~' = 'is the basis for and is joined with'

There is therefore both a correspondence *between* the subjects (Jesus Christ and the church) and *within* the subjects themselves (between the movement from above and below in Christ and between the church as invisible and visible, between the church as event and institution). This chapter focuses on the relationship *within* the church itself, i.e., the nature of the church itself as event and institution, as invisible and visible. The next chapter will focus on the relation *between* Christ and the church. The final chapter will focus on the relation between the church and the world, which is also predicated upon this logic, although in this final relation the church takes the place of the first, rather than the second, term in the relation.

---

[12]For the two Christological movements, see *CD IV.2*, 3-6; 20-21.

[13]For the asymmetrical relation of dependence and correspondence of the second Christological movement to the first, see *CD IV.2*, 47; 70-72; 91-92.

2. The Reality of the Church: The Church as Event and Institution

While Barth drew upon common geometrical imagery in discussing both the incarnation and the church in the *Church Dogmatics*, it should be noted that this language of a true and lasting intersection of the vertical and the horizontal plane is quite different from the geometrical language used in the *Romans* commentary, where Barth described the intersection of revelation and history in terms of a tangent touching a circle, touching, and yet not touching, it. Such a view, coupled with an emphasis upon the radical *diastasis* between time and eternity, made any true conception of an incarnation in time problematic if not impossible, and it likewise made a conception of a true church with historical duration problematic as well. In *Romans*, the church in space and time is portrayed almost exclusively in terms of sin and as an example of the highest form of human *hubris*, i.e., religion. The true church is therefore predominantly portrayed as invisible and ahistorical (though it is never absolutely separated from the institutional church). Here in the doctrine of reconciliation Barth's incarnational Christology, articulated in terms of a relationship and history between God and the world in Jesus Christ, is complemented by a truly incarnational ecclesiology, with the true church seen as existing within space and time, the union of an eternal divine activity and a historical and human society.

It would be a mistake, however, to see Barth's final perspective on the church as marked by the abandonment of the conception of the church as eternal event and its replacement by an understanding of the church as historical institution.[14] This would be a distortion of Barth's truly dialectical position. The divine reality of the church as event and the historical reality of the church as institution can never be separated nor divided, but also cannot be confused nor mixed. The church exists as event only in concert with its historical manifestation as an institution, as a real society composed of flesh and blood persons. The relationship between these cannot be reversed, however, for the church as an entity in time exists only as it is called into existence by the Holy Spirit. The pattern whereby the church can be understood as the indivisible unity of a divine event and a historical and human institution in irreducible and unconfused distinction is the Christological pattern of Chalcedon and the anhypostatic-enhypostatic logic, whereby the church is a single reality composed of a divine call and a human society in asymmetrical relation, the second entirely dependent upon the first.

A. The Noetic Basis of the Church: The Church as an Article of Faith

Because the church is not simply a reality on the historical plane, but is in fact the unity of a divine act and a historical manifestation, Barth states that the true identity

---

[14]Barth opposed any such reversal — see Barth, 'The Humanity of God,' 63.

and reality of the church cannot be grasped through historical investigation alone but requires *faith*. Faith is required precisely because the church is a *mystery*. Here again, this understanding of the church as a mystery is predicated upon and patterned after Christology. Just as the reality of Jesus Christ (as God's revelation in Christ) cannot simply be read off the face of the historical Jesus but must be made visible to the eyes of faith through the work of the Holy Spirit, the mystery of the incarnation existing as the unity of the invisible Word made visible flesh, so also the church is only truly known in faith, and not simply by examining and considering the church as a social entity within history. The church is thus itself a *mystery*, for it is the unity of a divine action and a human historical existence, and as such it can be perceived in its true nature only by faith, and not solely by historical and empirical investigation.[15]

That the church exists in analogy to the incarnation is evident, Barth states, in the fact that in the reality of the Christian community and the Christian, the 'mystery of creation and of the incarnation is now in a sense brought home to us' (*CD IV.1*, 645). But the mystery of the church is not in fact for Barth a second mystery alongside the first, but 'another dimension of the one mystery.' So Barth can write: 'It is not identical with creation and the incarnation. Conceptually it has to be kept apart. Yet it had been in view, it had been envisaged in the incarnation and even in creation. It is actual and comprehensible only as it derives from and is related to them. It cannot, therefore, be separated from them' (*CD IV.1*, 645). The doctrine of the church is therefore a distinct sphere of the doctrine of reconciliation, but exists in unity with Christ, a unity comprising the totality of this doctrine.

The church itself has a two-fold nature that comprises it as a single reality. On one hand, the church is the work of the Holy Spirit, and as such it is an object of faith. On the other hand, however, the church exists within history 'in the form of a human activity' (*CD IV.1*, 650). It exists only as it is gathered by the Holy Spirit, but it exists as such within a definite world occurrence, within a definite history, and thus as Christians join together. Its true being is therefore an act, a dynamic event, but one which takes shape within history and thus possesses a specific historical form. As Barth states: 'The Church *is* when it takes place, and it takes place in the form of a sequence and nexus of definite human activities' (*CD IV.1*, 652). Barth clearly grounds the church as an institution upon the prior reality of the church as event. It

---

[15]For the relation between Barth's understanding of mystery, faith, and historical perception, see *CD I.1*, 324-326; cf. 304-333. The ontic and noetic basis of both the incarnation and the church is thus the Holy Spirit, who is the acting agent for both the conception of Jesus Christ and the constitution of the church, the first being the paradigm (though itself unique and irreplaceable) for the second. The Holy Spirit is thus the basis for the body of Christ in both its union to the Word in the incarnation and in its form as the church, Christ's 'earthly-historical form of existence.'

is only as the church exists in a divinely constituted act that it takes shape as a historical society of persons sharing distinct practices, and thus as an institution.

It is precisely *because* the church exists as this nexus of human activities that the church can be perceived and investigated as one phenomenal reality among others and described in 'historical and psychological and sociological terms like any other' (*CD IV.1*, 652). The church can be studied as one society among others, with its own convictions, teachings, and practices, and with these in relation to other historical and cultural entities. As Barth notes, such studies have indeed been conducted by many. But just as an investigation of Jesus as a historical figure fails to come to grips with his ultimate identity as the incarnate Lord, so also Barth believes that a purely historical or sociological investigation of the church fails to perceive its true nature. The church is truly visible — but it is also truly invisible. The church is therefore rightly perceived in its true identity only by faith: 'It will be always in the revelation of God that the true Church is visible' (*CD IV.2*, 619). For this reason, the church is the subject of an article of faith and of the creed, a mystery to be believed and confessed.

B. The Ontic Basis of the Church: The Church as Invisible and Visible

The church consists as the unity of an invisible activity and reality and a visible manifestation and embodiment. This is necessarily so, according to Barth, for the work of the Holy Spirit, the invisible work of God, gives rise to a specific historical manifestation. Just as the incarnation as the work of the Holy Spirit was the 'awakening power of the Word made flesh, of the Son of God, who Himself entered the lowliness of an historical existence in this world,' so also the Holy Spirit is the awakening power of the church, calling it into historical and visible existence, though grounded in an invisible power. As Barth enigmatically avers: 'Like begets like.' There is thus a close parallel and analogy between the conception of Christ by the Holy Spirit and the constitution of the church by the Spirit. Each is a divine event that calls into existence a historical reality that can be directly perceived and observed within history yet only fully understood by faith, a faith that opens the eyes to perceiving the unity of its invisible and visible reality, its divine origin in historical form. The church must therefore be both invisible and visible.[16]

---

[16]See *CD IV.1*, 652-653; cf. *CD I.2*, 219-220. For the following discussion of the church as invisible and visible, see also *CD IV.3.2*, 722-730. Barth there writes: 'As surely as its Lord Jesus Christ was elected from all eternity, not as the λόγος ἄσαρκος, but as the *Verbum incarnandum*, in His concrete humanity and visibility as the man Jesus of Nazareth...so surely in the same Jesus Christ God has also elected His community in its very being *ad extra*, in its visibility and worldliness, in its likeness with other peoples' (*CD IV.3.1*, 724).

Furthermore, just as a failure to understand this relation of the divine and human in Christ leads one to fall off the tightrope of truth into heresies on the right and on the left, into either docetism or ebionitism, so also a failure to perceive the two-fold reality of the church leads one into corresponding docetic and ebionitic ecclesiological heresies. The docetic tendency is to describe the church as in truth an invisible reality and to attempt to flee from and escape the contingency and imperfection of its historical form and existence, or to tolerate this existence only as a necessary evil. Such an escape into the invisible church, a '*civitas platonica*,' as Barth describes it, is something that may be appealing but is heretical none the less: 'The Church never has been and never is absolutely invisible.' As Barth states: 'For the work of the Holy Spirit as the awakening power of Jesus Christ would not take place at all if the invisible did not become visible, if the Christian community did not take on and have an earthly-historical form' (*CD IV.1*, 653).[17] The church exists only as a real human and historical fellowship comprised of human persons who have been called and joined together into a visible and concrete society through the hearing of the Word through the invisible power of the Spirit. In other words: 'The Christian community, the true Church, arises and is only as the Holy Spirit works — the quickening power of the living Lord Jesus Christ' (*CD IV.2*, 617). The church is a true church only as it is so constituted by the Holy Spirit and is not guaranteed simply by the existence of the church's institutions, traditions, and reformations (*CD IV.2*, 618).

To maintain that the church is an article of faith is not to overlook the concrete form of the church. Rather, Barth contends that to confess the church as an article of faith requires that one see it as the work of the Spirit that indeed calls into existence such a concrete form, just as to confess the resurrection of the body is not to overlook that this event, though divinely actualized, gives rise to a 'physical' reality, i.e., the resurrection of a *body*. Barth emphasizes that the real church is not to be sought apart from, nor even behind, its historical manifestation, but only within its historical form. Only by looking at what is seen, the visible church even in the midst of its imperfection and sin, do we perceive (by faith!) that which cannot be seen, the invisible power of the church. As Barth describes it, to confess our faith in the church

---

[17]Barth can also write: 'It is not that according to its proper nature on the one side the Christian community is invisible, and according to its improper nature on the other side visible. Rather it is totally and properly both visible and invisible. The christological background should be remembered. Jesus Christ is not visibly but improperly true man and properly and invisibly true God. In the one being He is both visible as true man and invisible as true God, and both properly. Thus it is in the totally visible being of the community that the totally invisible lives and moves as its secret. And the totally invisible calls for manifestation and declaration in the totally visible. It is as this particular people that it is one among others. And it is as one among others that it is this particular people' (*CD IV.3.2*, 726).

is to confess our faith 'in the invisible aspect which is the secret of the visible' (*CD IV.1*, 654; cf. 653-654). To believe in the church thereby entails that we participate in its visible life and existence, not try to escape from it. To fail to take seriously the historical reality of the church may be a sign, Barth avers, of failing to take seriously the humanity of Christ as well:

> Faith in His community has this in common with faith in Him, that it, too, relates to a reality in time and space, and therefore to something which is at bottom generally visible. If, then, we believe in Him, we cannot refuse — however hesitantly or anxiously or contentiously — to believe in His community in its spatio-temporal existence, and therefore to be a member of it and personally a Christian (*CD IV.1*, 654).

But there is an opposite error to that of a docetic ecclesiology, of the attempt to escape and flee from the historical and visible church. This is the error of understanding the reality of the church only in historical terms, of believing that the church is an entity that can be purely and exhaustively understood and described in terms of time and space and as the product of historical forces and human decisions. This is the error of an ebionitic ecclesiology, a mistake as real and serious as considering the church to be a purely invisible reality. The church indeed exists as a phenomenon in time like any other, but 'what it is, the character, the truth of its existence in time and space, is not a matter of a general but a very special visibility' (*CD IV.1*, 654). A failure to perceive the church in this 'special visibility' leads to a reductive phenomenological, historical, and sociological understanding of the church.

What Barth is here attempting to describe is the *mystery* of the church. If taken to be an exclusively historical reality, the church is understood as only relatively, rather than qualitatively, different from other human societies and organizations (and, indeed, not necessarily as the best one). Yet to examine the church in this way is to describe it not theologically, but according to historical, psychological, or sociological categories, and this is what Barth means by dealing with it abstractly. For Barth, this is inadequate. What must rather be done is to perceive the church theologically, i.e., as the unity of a divine act of constitution and a historical manifestation arising from and living from such a divine act. This is to perceive the church according to faith, to know it concretely, to know it in what Barth describes as the 'third dimension' of the church's existence, its 'special visibility' (*CD IV.1*, 655).[18]

---

[18]This position is consistently maintained and reiterated throughout Barth's exposition of the church in the doctrine of reconciliation. For example, in *CD IV.2* Barth states: 'It is clear, however, that to see and understand that which is effected by God, the Church, in its true

To fail in this regard, to see the church as one society among others, will ultimately lead one to subsume the church into general history, seeing it as solely the product of historical forces and viewing it on a 'historical and psychological and sociological level,' but not on a theological one, and thus not according to the church's true character. And when the church considers *itself* this way, it may indeed visibly flourish and be respectable in the eyes of the world as a religious society, but its true identity is forgotten and its true power, precisely because this power is not its own but that of the Spirit, is lost. This was the mistake of Schleiermacher, according to Barth, and it is an ever-present temptation for the church.[19]

To consider the church only on the historical plane, Barth continues, would be to consider it not as the church of Jesus Christ at all but, in the striking language reminiscent of the *Romans* commentary, as the 'synagogue of the Antichrist.' In language reminiscent of the *Göttingen Dogmatics*, Barth states that this temptation of the church to consider itself only as a historical reality is the 'sword which always and everywhere hangs over the *ecclesia visibilis*' (*CD IV.1*, 657). Nevertheless, as Barth writes:

> But this is a temptation which comes to the Church from without, from its own humanity. From within it will never find itself tempted to try to exist only in two dimensions and therefore in an abstract visibility. From within, in the light of its awakening by the Holy Spirit, it will always have to see and understand and confess itself in three dimensions, whether this is understood from without or not (*CD IV.1*, 656).

In sum, to deal with the church on a purely historical level is to deal with the church abstractly, apart from its unity with the divine reality that provides and defines its true nature. We might say that, for Barth, just as considering Jesus only from the perspective of historical criticism produces an abstraction of his true character, so also the church is dealt with as an abstraction if conceived apart from the call of God through the Spirit of Christ which gives it its true existence (*CD IV.2*, 616-617).

---

reality, we have not to lose sight even momentarily or incidentally of the occurrence of the divine operation, and therefore concretely of the divine work of upbuilding the community by Jesus Christ. The Church is, of course, a human, earthly-historical construct, whose history involves from the very first, and always will involve, human action. But it is *this* human construct, the Christian Church, because and as God is at work in it by His Holy Spirit' (*CD IV.2*, 617). Barth reiterates that to fail to see the church in this way, i.e., to consider it apart from this divine activity, is to deal with the church in an abstract manner. Furthermore, insofar as the church exists apart from such divine activity, it is a mere semblance of the church [*Scheinkirche*], and not the true church itself (ibid., 616-617).

[19]See *CD IV.1*, 655-656; cf. *IV.3.2*, 722; 721-725.

Barth describes the reality of the church in terms of its 'character,' its character being its true nature as the unity of a divine call and historical form, neither considered in abstraction from the other such that the church is conceived in a purely invisible or purely visible manner. Barth refers to this character in different ways — as seeing the church in 'three dimensions;' or, according to its 'particular visibility,' (as opposed to its 'general visibility' as a historical entity); or, as a 'spiritual reality;' or furthermore, as seeing it with eyes of faith, and thus as a reality that must be *believed* by faith rather than simply observed by sight (*CD IV.1*, 656-658). In all these ways Barth refers to the *mystery* of the church as a divine and human reality in analogy and correspondence to the reality of the incarnation:

> The glory of Jesus Christ was hidden when He humbled Himself, when He took our flesh, when in our flesh He was obedient to God, when He destroyed our wrong, when He established our right. So, too, the glory of the humanity justified in Him is concealed. And this means that the glory of the community gathered together by Him within humanity is only a glory which is hidden from the eyes of the world until His final revelation, so that it can be only an object of faith (*CD IV.1*, 656-657).

Furthermore, just as the flesh of Christ exists only in a relationship of dependence upon the Word, and thus in a relation defined according to an anhypostatic-enhypostatic Christology, so also the church exists only in the Spirit, but also really and truly through the Spirit (*CD I.1*, 660). Barth's Christological logic permeates his understanding of the nature of the church, and the church in Barth's thought quite simply cannot be understood apart from this logic without grave distortion.

3. The Obedience of the Church: The Church as Sinful and Sanctified

The reality of the church as a mystery leads Barth to understand its historical existence from two paradoxical and dialectically-related perspectives. First, if viewed abstractly and thus apart from its inner reality, the church as a historical society and organization must be seen as sinful, as relative and contingent, marred by weakness and imperfection, belonging to the realm of the flesh and fallen humanity. As such, its history is a sinful history. Nevertheless, Barth can also say that the church's essence, 'its mystery, its spiritual character, is not without manifestations and analogies in its generally visible form,' even though no visible form can be unequivocally identified with its invisible reality. Even in its visible and historical life, Barth contends, the church 'can and should attest its invisible glory' (*CD IV.1*, 657).

This view of the church marks another aspect of Barth's highly dialectical ecclesiological thought and one distinct from the first previously described. Not only is there on one hand a dialectical relationship between the vertical and horizontal realities of the church such that the invisible divine action of the Spirit and its visible and historical form can be neither separated nor confused. There is also, on the other hand, a dialectical relationship within the historical sphere itself between the sinfulness and obedience of the church. The first dialectical relationship pertains to the inviolability of the Creator-creature distinction that is central to Barth's thought from his earliest theology onward. But this second relation pertains to the creature as both sinful and obedient and hinges upon Barth's eschatological understanding of the church and his ethical conception of correspondence. This relation comes to play an important role as Barth focuses not only on the *distinction* between the Creator and the creature, but also upon their *relationship*, seen preeminently in Christ and secondarily in all divine and human encounters, including God's relationship to the community.

Therefore, the historical church cannot simply be described in terms of the first dialectical relation. It must also be understood in terms of the second through the concept of correspondence. That is, one has not said all that must be said by drawing attention to the gulf that separates the Creator and the creature, God and the church. The church is indeed a creation of God, but there is no sin in being a creature. In other words, the creature should not try to be God, but it should be an *obedient* creature, and this is the church's task. Barth is thus concerned both with the church's vertical and horizontal life, its faith and faithfulness.

The dialectic of sin and obedience in Barth's thought is therefore a complement to the Creator-creature distinction. When viewed solely as a historical reality, the church is seen as marked by sin and weakness. Yet, from another perspective, when viewed as a mystery, even its visible form should and does bear analogies to the revelation that calls it into existence. For this reason, even though no dogma or practice of the church can directly be equated with divine revelation, such dogmas and practices should reflect the divine revelation of God in Christ. The relation between the community as a visible and historical created reality and God the Creator is therefore not one of simple contradiction and opposition, but should be one of correspondence and obedience. There is a real sense in which the judgment upon the church, in which no direct identification of the church and revelation can be made, is simply for Barth the first though necessary step on the road toward providing a real place for a true witness to revelation in the church's dogmas and practices, its confession in word and deed. The emphasis upon God's 'No' must therefore give way to an emphasis upon God's 'Yes,' though the judgment of God is not left behind, for this is a shift in emphasis, not a reversal or replacement of the first by the second.[20]

On this account, the visible form and practices of the church should not be summarily dismissed as irrelevant or facilely judged and disregarded as sinful, but rather should be ordered according to the church's inner reality. The historical form and shape of the church is not a matter of indifference, but should be structured according to its inner character as a work of God's revelation through the Spirit. For Barth, the fact that the church cannot be identified with the kingdom of God, nor its dogmas and practices identified with revelation, should in no way lead one to think of these as of no serious consequence. Moreover, the humility of the church, seen in its recognition of its constant dependence upon the Spirit and its own weakness and sin, should not lead to a disregard for its historical form and shape. As Barth writes in a significant and revealing passage:

> *Credo ecclesiam* then means that the Church can take itself seriously in the world of the earthly and visible, with all humility but also with all comfort, at once directed and established by its third dimension. According to its best knowledge and conscience, it can and should create the forms [*Formen*] which are indispensable to it as the human society which it essentially is, the forms which are best adapted to its edification and the discharge of its mission. In its great hours it has always rightly done this and will continue to do so. It must do it in faith and obedience. It has to remember that it is not itself God but is responsible to God, that it does not have the last word. But with this reservation in relation to itself, with a

---

[20]Once again, this entails that Barth did not move 'from' dialectic 'to' analogy, for Barth remained thoroughly dialectical in his thought, even as analogy was present if muted already in his early theology. Nonetheless, there was a shift from an accent upon God's judgment in the *Romans* commentary to an accent upon God's grace in his later theology, from an accent upon the distinction between God and the creature to an accent upon their relationship. The latter, however, was a shift in emphasis, not an abandonment of earlier themes — Barth never cast away the dialectical convictions achieved in *Romans*, just as *Romans* itself knew not only of judgment but also of grace. Perhaps the shift is best expressed by Barth's own sons. Looking back upon the life of his father, Marcus Barth wrote: 'If there was a decisive development in his thinking between 1921 and 1935 — a change from the "old" to the "new" Barth, as some have said — it came in the recognition that God, ultimately, says "Yes" to his creature' — in *How Karl Barth Changed My Mind*, ed. Donald K. McKim (Grand Rapids: Eerdmans, 1986), 4. In the same volume, Christoph Barth states: 'There was, according to his own confession in *How I Changed My Mind*, a gradual transition from a radically "negative" toward a mainly "positive" style and accent of this theology. This change was certainly brought about by new biblical insights. But I'm inclined to presume that experiences with the factual world — to which the church of course belongs — strongly promoted it...' (ibid., 8).

consciousness of the relativity of its decisions, their provisional nature, their need of constant reform, standing under and not over the Word it can go to work with quiet determination, accepting the risk, but with the courage and authority of faith and obedience, and therefore without the false affectation which in order not to do anything questionable will never do anything at all, which in every conditional assertion scents an attempt at the unconditional, which out of a simple fear of hardening, orthodoxy, authoritarianism and hierarchy can never get past the stage of questioning and protesting (as though in the last resort formlessness and therefore chaos is the condition which is best pleasing to God) (*CD IV.1*, 660).

Such a quotation reveals why the *Romans* commentary was both necessary and also why it could never be the final word that had to be spoken. The critical task must move to the constructive one (though the second can never leave the first completely behind). What this quotation further demonstrates is a very deep level of dialectical thinking in relation to the church as a visible and historical reality. On one hand, the church cannot be identified with God's kingdom, nor its dogmas and practices thought of as the instantiation of revelation and directly identified with God's truth and activity. This, for Barth, would violate the Creator-creature distinction. But on the other hand, neither can the visible form and order of the church, along with its human and historical dogmas and practices, simply be set over against revelation in such a way that they be considered matters of indifference or simply dismissed as sinful. If they cannot be directly equated with revelation, neither can they simply be discarded as mistaken and worthless human productions which at best are insignificant and at worse in direct opposition to God. In the light of God's work they exist, rather, in analogy to the revelation of God through the Spirit that calls the church into existence, and therefore they exist in a relation of correspondence. Here we must emphasize that a failure to understand the meaning and significance of Barth's conception of correspondence [*Entsprechung*] leads to errors of interpretation all along the line, such as the mistaken notion that Barth simply places God and the world in opposition, or that Barth has no positive place for the church and its agency in the historical realm, making 'God everything and humanity nothing.'

What must also be reiterated is that it is precisely in the church's humility, in its recognition that it lives only in constant dependence upon a divine power and its awareness of the provisionality of its own dogmas and practices, that the church can live with confidence even in the precariousness of its historical existence and commit itself to ordering its external life in correspondence to its inner reality. 'If it lives also and primarily in its third dimension, it can and should act confidently on the level of its phenomenal being' (*CD IV.1*, 660). Turning an earlier image around, Barth states that the sword of judgment that hangs over the church also exists as the sword of the church's election and calling, and thus as a sword of protection. The church lives only by the Spirit and even under its judgment, but in the Spirit the church also does have a real, true, and *obedient* existence granted in mercy. Paradoxically, the church that lives in humble recognition of its invisible nature and in dependence upon the Spirit will, in the end, be in fact the best church even in its historical and visible form (*CD IV.1*, 660; cf. *CD IV.2*, 619).

This dialectical relationship of correspondence is itself predicated upon a Christological conviction. Though the historical person of Jesus cannot be directly equated with the Word and revelation of God, Barth sees the human life of Jesus not in simple contradiction to God, but in correspondence to God.[21] Certainly it must be admitted that at times Barth could speak of Christ's humanity as no different from others and of God's revelation as coming in a form in contradiction to himself.[22] Yet this is not the whole story, for Barth was more and more inclined to see the relationship between the humanity of Jesus and the Word of revelation in Christ not as a relation of contradiction between infinite opposites, but as one of correspondence between infinitely different realities in a relationship of analogy, or partnership, the second reflecting in its own form the reality of the first. This of course did not entail that Barth sacrificed his dialectical understanding of the distinction between revelation and its historical medium. With the notion of correspondence Barth does not abandon his understanding of the infinite qualitative difference between God and the world, nor his Chalcedonian Christology. He does, however, go beyond them in providing not only a formal description of the relation between the divine and human natures of Christ, but a positive and material description of their relation as one of corresponding life and action.[23] And this notion of correspondence is grounded in the doctrine of election, in which Christ is both the electing God and the elected human being, though it comes to maturity in the doctrine of reconciliation.

Of course, there is a great *discontinuity* as well as an analogical continuity between Christology and ecclesiology in this regard, for whereas Jesus is sinless, living a human life of perfect correspondence and obedience to God, the perfect unity of God and humanity in one person, the church is sinful and is not the union of a divine Subject and human flesh, of a divine and human nature. It is rather the unity

---

[21]'The royal man of the New Testament tradition is created "after God" (κατὰ θεόν). This means that as a man He exists analogously to the mode of existence of God. In what He thinks and wills and does, in His attitude, there is a correspondence, a parallel in the creaturely world, to the plan and purpose and work and attitude of God' (*CD IV.2*, 166). See also *CD I.2*, 155-156.

[22]See *CD I.1*, 166; also *CD IV.1*, 178.

[23]The relationship between revelation and its historical medium in regard to Christology and with reference to the issue of correspondence has been insightfully examined by Trevor Hart, *Regarding Karl Barth: Toward a Reading of His Theology* (Downer's Grove: Intervarsity Press, 1999), 1-27, esp. 17-26. His analysis parallels and supports the argument here being made.

of a divine activity of the Spirit of Christ and a historical and earthly fellowship. The church is not a second incarnation, and its correspondence to God is imperfect. The relationship between Christology and ecclesiology is thus one of radical dissimilarity *and* real similarity. The relationship is therefore one of analogy and correspondence established as a divine gift.

In bringing this section to a close, we might note that there is a deep and unresolvable tension in Barth's thought between seeing the church as sinful and seeing it as obedient, and these positions are fascinatingly not depicted by Barth as mutually exclusive but are dialectically related and indeed unapologetically juxtaposed. The church is both sinful and obedient.[24] It is not so sinful that it stands only in contradiction to God and his work, simply an agent of sin and evil. It is, however, not so obedient as to work with God in unqualified cooperation, without sin and with no need of justification. Rather, the church lives in qualified correspondence to God insofar as its historical life bears (divinely-actualized) analogies to its invisible and spiritual reality. The reality of the church is thus hidden under the visible form of sin, yet as joined to its invisible mystery, even this visible form may reflect its divine reality, though no direct identity can be drawn between them.

Barth does maintain that the church's true obedience and correspondence to its divine origin can be sacrificed, however. This correspondence is lost precisely when the church fails to keep to the simple task of witnessing to its inner reality and to Christ. When the church seeks to be something more than a witness, it paradoxically does not become something more but something less (*CD IV.1*, 657). For Barth, the glory of the church exists precisely in giving God the glory, and the true and rightful glory of the church exists in its humble witness and service to its inner basis in the Spirit.

To attempt to become more than a witness to this divine call is to confuse the church's real and invisible power of the Spirit with its historical existence and its external orders, practices, sacramental action, and relative authority. Barth argues that the question of whether this has in fact occurred must be directed not only to the Roman Catholic church but to all churches (though Barth himself sees this error as evident within the Roman Catholic conception of the church). As Barth states: 'Where the Holy Ghost is at work the step to visibility is unavoidable, but it is always and everywhere surrounded by this temptation' (*CD IV.1*, 658; cf. 657-659). This temptation can be avoided only by remembering the church's ongoing need of the Spirit, and that the Spirit controls the church, not the church the Spirit. To fail to see

---

[24]This tension is an eschatological one, in that the church lives in strength in the light of Easter, but lives in weakness in that it still awaits the culmination of all things in Christ's second return. The church thus lives between the first and second advent of Jesus Christ (see *CD IV.1*, 725-739; cf. also *CD IV.2*, 620-623).

the inner mystery of the church and esteem the church only in terms of the realm of history was Schleiermacher's error, whereas to confuse its historical form with the invisible basis of its mystery itself is the error of Roman Catholicism, in Barth's estimation. In both cases the church is no longer an article of faith, it is no longer *believed*, for its invisible reality is equated with its visible existence (*CD IV.1*, 656-658). In other words, revelation and history are equated and confused. Barth writes:

> No concrete form of the community can in itself and as such be the object of faith. Even the man Jesus as such, the *caro Christi*, cannot be this, just as the individual Christian cannot believe in his faith as a work. The community can believe in itself only when it believes in its Lord and therefore in what it is, in what it really is in its concrete form. The work magnifies the master. The visible attests the invisible. The glory of the community consists in the fact that it can give God the glory, and does not cease to do so. Its glory can appear only where there appears the glory of Jesus Christ and the sinner justified by Him. But as long as time endures, until the final manifestation of God and man in the future of Jesus Christ, the place where this takes place is hidden in its concrete form, with which it is only indirectly and not directly identical. For that reason this occurrence must be believed in the concrete form of the history which is visible to all (*CD IV.1*, 658).

4. The Growth of the Church: Numerical and Spiritual Increase

A final dialectical relationship pertaining to the nature of the church that should be considered is Barth's understanding of the relation between the church's numerical and spiritual growth. In accordance with his dialectical ecclesiological thought, Barth refuses either to separate these or to identify them. Numerical growth certainly will mark the community, Barth maintains, but this growth is secondary and dependent upon its spiritual growth. The expansive and numerical growth of the community is growth on the horizontal plane that is dependent upon its prior spiritual growth, and thus growth on the vertical plane. This inner invisible growth and maturity of the community is the basis by which the other exists. To consider numerical increase for its own sake would be an abstraction, a consideration of visible growth apart from the invisible power that makes it possible. Worse, a church's numerical growth could display not the true strength of the community, but may rather point to its weakness. Such growth in itself could be devoid of the church's inner power, and therefore an abstraction of the true reality of the church. Numerical success alone, Barth maintains, is an insufficient guide to the health and vitality of the church. For this reason, numerical growth should not be sought for its own sake but follows concomitantly in the wake of the community's superior commitment to the proclamation of the kingdom of God. This alone, Barth states, is the true end of the community, not numerical growth.

Such is not a dismissal on Barth's part of the need for numerical growth, but a relativization and qualification of it so that it might find its appropriate place as a consequence of prior and primary spiritual growth (*CD IV.2*, 644-647). The true and primary growth of the community is therefore an increase in spiritual maturity, and numerical growth is dependent upon and secondary to such spiritual growth. As Barth writes: 'The true growth which is the secret of the upbuilding of the community is not extensive but intensive; its vertical growth in height and depth' (*CD IV.2*, 648).

The relationship between spiritual and numerical growth, or in other terms, between vertical and horizontal growth, is thus irreversible. Numerical growth follows from spiritual growth, but they can never be equated. Numerical growth should not be pursued for its own sake, but neither should spiritual growth be pursued simply to procure numerical growth. While real spiritual growth will manifest itself in numerical growth, it is not simply a means toward this end:

> We cannot, therefore strive for vertical renewal merely to produce greater horizontal extension and a wider audience. At some point and in some way, where it is really engaged in vertical renewal, it will always experience the arising of new Christians and therefore an increase in its constituency, but perhaps at a very different point and in a very different manner and compass from that expected. If it is used only as a means for extensive renewal, the internal will at once lose its meaning and power. It can be fulfilled only for its own sake, and then — unplanned and unarranged — it will bear its own fruits. As the communion of saints takes place, the dominant and effective force is always primarily and properly that of intensive, vertical and spiritual growth (*CD IV.2*, 648).

5. The Marks of the Church: One, Holy, Catholic, and Apostolic

Barth's dialectical understanding of the church as both an invisible and visible reality, an event of the Holy Spirit and a historical entity, leads naturally to his dialectical understanding of the marks of the church: the church as one, holy, catholic, and apostolic. Barth interprets these traditional characteristics along the lines of his distinctive understanding of the dual nature of the church and its Christological logic. With reference to these marks, he speaks of the church both as a single universal entity and in terms of the individual congregations that comprise it, though his fundamental understanding of the church remains that of a local congregation called into existence by the Holy Spirit at a specific time and place.

A. The Church Is One

For Barth, the unity of the church consists in the midst of the visible plurality of its members and the various individual churches and confessions that comprise it. As there is only one God, one Lord Jesus Christ who is the head of the church, and one Holy Spirit who bestows gifts upon the church, so is there only one church (*CD IV.1*, 668).

> For this reason...the visible and the invisible Church are not two Churches
> — an earthly-historical fellowship and above and behind this a supra-
> naturally spiritual fellowship. As we have already seen, the one is the
> form and the other the mystery of one and the self-same Church. The
> mystery is hidden in the form, but represented and to be sought in it. The
> visible lives wholly by the invisible. The invisible is only represented and
> to be sought out in the visible. But neither can be separated from the
> other. Both in their unity are the body, the earthly-historical form of
> existence of the one living Lord Jesus Christ (*CD IV.1*, 669).

The basis for the unity of the church as a local congregation, as well as the unity between these congregations making them one church, is not to be found in an overarching ecclesiastical authority, hierarchy, or political arrangement, but is rooted solely in the one Lord who calls the community into existence and joins the communities to one another. He is the one who 'has promised to be in the midst of every community gathered by Him and in His name. He rules the Church and therefore the Churches. He is the basis and guarantee of their unity' (*CD IV.1*, 674-675).

Barth is of course fully aware that from a historical and phenomenal point of view, the church is not one but divided into many communions. In face of this empirical reality, how are we to speak, as we must, of the unity of the church, of the *unam ecclesiam*? Barth maintains that there are two heresies tempting ecclesiology at this point and that these must be avoided with reference to speaking of the church's unity. The first is the heresy of docetism: 'One thing is certain — this *credo* [i.e., *credo unam ecclesiam*] cannot consist in a movement of escape up or on from the visibility of the divided Church to the unity of an invisible Church' (*CD IV.1*, 677). Such a temptation is a real one for the believer who looks in dismay at the disunity of the church in space and time, but it is a temptation nonetheless, for Barth contends that to abandon the 'distress' of the community is to abandon its 'hope' as well (in language reminiscent of the *Romans* commentary). To flee from the problems of the visible church is in fact to abandon God's chosen means of redemption.

There is an opposite temptation, however, not an escape into invisibility but an attempt to establish the unity of the church only in the realm of history, to try to realize the one church 'externally *in abstracto*' (*CD IV.1*, 678). This is an ebionitic heresy. Once again, Barth's condemnation of such a solution points to his refusal to deal with the church abstractly, i.e., apart from its unity with Jesus Christ and his Spirit. To view the church only from the perspective of history is to deal with it as such an abstraction by seeking to establish some type of unity on the historical plane apart from a renewal of the church's invisible reality, its relation to its one Spirit and Lord. For this reason, this visible disunity cannot be resolved simply by attempting to heal the disruption through some type of unified confessionalism that ignores doctrinal distinctives. The *visible* disunity is in fact the result of a greater *invisible* distress, the loss of a living relationship to the Lord of the church. As Barth writes:

> Where the Church is divided in the way which now concerns us, the division reaches right down to its invisible being, its relationship to God and Jesus Christ and the Holy Spirit, and it develops from this, the external division being the result of an internal disruption, so that neither individuals nor the whole Church can overcome it by a flight to the invisible, but only by a healing of both its visible and its invisible hurt (*CD IV.1*, 678).

Unity therefore cannot truly be realized, Barth contends, simply on the level of superficial confessional agreement, or practical cooperation, or mutual recognition, or through a facile setting aside of distinctives, or especially a lackadaisical approach of toleration. Such approaches can in fact signify indifference, but not unity. To see the church as united does not require a church that takes itself less seriously, but more seriously. 'What is demanded is the unity of the Church of Jesus Christ, not the externally satisfying co-existence and co-operation of different religious societies' (*CD IV.1*, 678). The problem of visible separation and division in fact lies much deeper than on the historical plane, much deeper than what can simply be observed as divisions within space and time. As Barth writes:

> ....the distress and scandal consists in the fact that in its visible and also in its invisible being, in its form and also in its essence, the one community of Jesus Christ is not one, and that neither the community itself in its divided and opposing communions nor the individual Christians united in them can simply evade this disunity or overcome it by any kind of passivity or activity, notwithstanding the fact that to overcome it is undoubtedly envisaged and demanded by the *credo unam ecclesiam* (*CD IV.1*, 679).

How then can the unity of the church be established? Not by an escape from the visible church, nor by an attempt to unite the visible communions. Barth rejects both of these options, portraying them as ecclesiological temptations analogous to Christological heresies. Rather, unity is achieved by beginning within the particular communion in which one finds oneself and only then reaching out from there to the one church. The unity of the church is thus recognized only by beginning, paradoxically, within one particular and distinctive confession, and in humble loyalty to it. A commitment to the unity of the church in fact does not necessarily entail abandonment of one's particular confession, though one must be careful that the particularity of one's confession should be predicated upon a commitment to what is central to truth and not upon an intractable resistance to change and stubborn commitment to self-preservation for its own sake (*CD IV.1*, 679-681).

In the end, if the unity of the church is to be achieved, this will only happen when the churches allow Jesus Christ, the living Lord, freely to speak and to rule through the Holy Spirit by the witness of Scripture. Where he is heard and obeyed, where he is recognized as Lord of the church, there unity will without doubt follow (just as numerical growth will follow spiritual growth, as we have seen). For if Christ's real presence is acknowledged and recognized, allowed to be a living event that is believed, there a renewal of the church's unity would no doubt occur, for then the question of the church's unity would be addressed not from without but from the church's invisible living reality. 'The unity of the Church — which is not under the power of any man because the living Lord Jesus Christ in His own power is Himself this unity — would then begin not only to be a reality but to be realised as such in the many Churches' (*CD IV.1*, 682).[25] The important thing is not to attempt unity itself, neither in peaceful cooperation and dialogue nor in polemical argument, but first to listen honestly and attentively to the one Lord who alone is the basis of the church's unity, and then to listen honestly and attentively to others (*CD IV.1*, 684).

What should now be apparent is that Barth sees unity as grounded in a proper recognition and attention to the church as a mystery, a visible manifestation of an invisible call of the Lord through the Spirit. Unity in the visible realm among the individual churches therefore exists in correspondence to the unified recognition of this mystery among the churches in listening to their one Lord, and as they do so they are one. Unity is not achieved by either abandoning the visible church for a conception of a unified invisible church, or by attempting to achieve visible unity through a simple historical and political alignment gained by disregarding confessional differences or by polemical argument. Visible unity exists simply as a witness and correspondence to the unity of the church's one Lord, and therefore comes into existence only as the churches focus not upon unity for its own sake but instead dedicate themselves to listening to their one Lord.[26] The unity of the church is thus grounded in its one Lord Jesus Christ, and the logic of the church's unity is

---

[25]Interestingly, Barth cites Zinzendorf as one who grasped this truth, and whose Christocentrism was thus the basis for his ecumenism (*CD IV.1*, 683).

[26]This is a constant theme in Barth's writings concerning ecumenical relations. See Barth, *The Church and the Churches* (Grand Rapids: Eerdmans, 1936), esp. 26-32.

thus a Christological logic, whereby the visible unity of the church is neither separated nor confused with its invisible unity, but exists as dependent upon and in correspondence to it.

B. The Church Is Holy

Like the unity of the church, the holiness of the church cannot be read off of the surface of history but must be perceived by faith and described dialectically. Barth reiterates that the church is not a natural and historical society among others, but has its 'own basis and goal.' It is grounded in a divine call and is not simply an institution on the historical plane, and thus membership in it is dependent upon faith, making it unique (*CD IV.1*, 685).

Nonetheless, even though its nature and existence derives from a divine call, in its visible form it is indeed a human society like other societies, with its own 'sphere of power and interests and influence.' As a human society among others it is composed of human persons, and therefore, in spite of its distinctive basis, it can in its form and practices be compared with other societies and institutions. And in this regard, its holiness is far from apparent. The church's holiness, like its unity, is a matter of revelation and faith, yet because the holiness of the church, like its unity, is grounded in Christ through the Spirit, it is just as inviolable, certain, and sure (*CD IV.1*, 685-686).

The holiness of the church is therefore its own, but it is also a reflection of the holiness of Jesus Christ as he is united to it by the Holy Spirit. Once again, considered abstractly, the church is not holy. From a purely empirical and historical point of view, the church is fallen and sinful, but as it is united to its head, Jesus Christ, it is holy. Moreover, whatever holiness the church *may* present in its historical existence is ultimately attributable to the fact that it is joined to Christ. It is only in the church that this holiness is truly revealed, for 'in so far as the knowledge and revelation of Jesus Christ and faith in Him and the ministry of the proclamation of His name constitutes the holiness of the Church: *extra ecclesiam nulla sanctitas*' (*CD IV.1*, 686-689).

Because the church's holiness rests upon the holiness of Christ, the church is therefore indestructible, or infallible (*CD IV.1*, 691).[27] This implies that the church's holiness cannot be lost, nor the church's identity as set apart from the world sacrificed. This does not mean that the church is not under attack from without and often corrupt within. It does mean, however, that in spite of external threat and

---

[27]See also *CD IV.2*, 672-676. There Barth states that the indestructibility of the church is rooted in Scripture and, more specifically, in the living Lord who through Scripture is present to speak and act in the church.

internal weakness, the church endures and remains holy. The church's existence and holiness thereby rest upon a divine promise and foundation:

> What saves it and makes it indestructible is not that it does not basically forsake Him — who can say how deeply and basically it has often enough forsaken Him and still does? — nor is it this or that good that it may be or do, but the fact that he does not forsake it, any more than Yahweh would forsake His people Israel in all His judgments (*CD IV.1*, 691).

The holiness of the church resides in its internal and invisible relationship to its living Lord, united to him through the Spirit. For this reason, Barth warns, as he already did in the *Göttingen Dogmatics*, that one must be careful in criticizing the church so that he or she does not in fact criticize Christ (*CD IV.1*, 691-692).

But what, then, must be said regarding its historical form, and how does it relate to this inner holiness? Is it to be thought of as irrelevant? Barth states that the church's separation from the world does not in fact necessarily entail that the church in its outward form and activities is in every respect substantially different from the world and other human societies, nor that its holiness is automatically guaranteed by the fact that people unite themselves together to form a church. For this reason, the church should use the adjective 'Christian' with care (remember that Barth himself gave up this title for his dogmatics). This reality does not imply, however, that there are not distinctively Christian activities that correspond to its inner life (such as preaching, worship, ordinances, and theology), but these are witnesses to the inner life and cannot be confused with it (*CD IV.1*, 693-695). As Barth writes:

> There are human acts and attitudes which are holy as such, i.e., which have the character of real witness to the One whose earthly historical existence the Church is allowed to be. But that they have this character is always dependent upon the answering witness of the One whom they aim and profess to attest. It is a matter of His special care, of His free grace which he has promised to address to His community without committing it into the hands of His community (*CD IV.1*, 693-694).

What we should notice from this description of the church's holiness is the undeniable centrality of the notion of correspondence in Barth's thought, though here it is more implicitly rather than explicitly stated, along with Barth's resolute commitment neither to confuse nor absolutely separate divine and human holiness, or the holiness of Christ and that of the church. There is also a differentiation between the invisible holiness of the church and its outer form and practices such that these are never directly identified, yet the relationship between them is not only one of radical distinction but also of an analogical correspondence of the church's outer form and practices to its inner holiness. Barth's thought is permeated by the movement in which a concept is relativized and dismantled in order to be reconstituted in a relation of correspondence (through an *Aufhebung* of the concept itself). Pertaining to the marks of the church, there is never an identification of the inner reality of the mark with the historical form, but there is a reflection of the inner reality in the historical and empirical practices of the church.

Furthermore, the direction of the relation always moves from the first to the second term, so that Christ is and remains the Subject of the relation with the church, and the church's holiness remains bound to his own. The church cannot be holy apart from Christ and apart from the Holy Spirit, for as Barth insists, apart from Christ and the Spirit even the most 'Christian' of works are emptied of their divine power and thus profane: preaching becomes instruction; sacraments become religious rites; theology becomes philosophy; and mission becomes propaganda. So while these practices may be interesting from a historical, moral, or sociological viewpoint, they nevertheless are not holy. Their correspondence to Christ is the result of a divine actualization, not a permanent possibility or possession: 'The community is wholly in the hands of its Lord, and that means that it is thrown back on His having mercy upon it and making its unholy activity holy and acknowledging it as such' (*CD IV.1*, 694). The correspondence of its life and activities to those of Christ is therefore itself a divine gift as well as a task it undertakes.

There are on this account both docetic and ebionitic threats in relation to the church's holiness just as in relation to the church's unity. A particular ebionitic error is the attempt to escape into visibility by equating the church and its holiness with those who have been baptized, and this, coupled with the practice of infant baptism, leads to a view where Christ's gathering of the church is evaded in favor of an *ex opere operato*. Christ's divine call is also evaded where the visible holiness of the members is seen as the defining mark of the community. This second error is moral in nature as the former is sacramental, and Barth comments that sacramentalism is the natural reaction against moralism as moralism is the reaction against sacramentalism. In opposition to both positions, Barth states that true members of the church are the people 'assembled in it who are thereto elected by the Lord, called by His Word, and constituted by His Spirit: just so many, no more and no less, these men and no others. It is He who knew them and willed them and created them as such. It is He who knows and preserves them as His saints' (*CD IV.1*, 695-696). For this reason, the ultimate judgment as to who does or does not belong in the church is his, not ours (*CD IV.1*, 696-698).

Yet an opposite docetic error exists as well. The church cannot simply set aside its visible holiness, rushing into the opposite direction, into a solely invisible holiness. The holiness of the church, though invisible apart from faith, and not simply a predicate of its historical existence apart from reference to its Lord, is nevertheless witnessed even in the visible life and practice of the church. As the church is confronted by its Lord and his activity, 'it is continually asked whether and to what extent it corresponds in its visible existence to the fact that it is His body, His earthly-historical form of existence' (*CD IV.1*, 700-701).

So while the church cannot create its own holiness, it also cannot live in indifference to visible holiness, ignoring the holiness of Christ as 'the imperative and standard of its own human activity,' and 'without being summoned to a very definite expectation and movement' (*CD IV.1*, 701). Christ's holiness is thus not an excuse for its own lack of visible holiness, but a exhortation to prayer and obedience conforming to Christ's life. Christ's holiness is not only the basis of its own holiness, but also its norm and pattern, calling the church not to passivity nor indifference, but to obedience. The dialectic of the church's sinfulness and obedience is thus evident in Barth's understanding of the church's holiness, for while Barth does not deny and indeed insists that the church is marred by sin, he nevertheless ties sanctification not only to its invisible nature but also to its visible life.

C. The Church Is Catholic

The word 'catholic' denotes, Barth relates, something general and comprehensive, speaking of 'an identity, a continuity, a universality, which is maintained in all the differences. Applied to the Church it means that it has a character in virtue of which it is always and everywhere the same and always and everywhere recognisable in this sameness, to the preservation of which it is committed' (*CD IV.1*, 701). It is in this sameness that it shows itself to be the real and true church. Where this sameness is disregarded, i.e., where it is not the catholic church, it is not the true church of Jesus Christ. To speak of the church being catholic is to speak of its identical essence in all of its varied and changing forms. It therefore refers to the difference between the true church and the false, or heretical, church. Whether heretical or apostate, such a church is a schismatic church, breaking the true unity of the church at large. The word 'catholic' thus refers to what makes the church a true church and divides it off from the false church (*CD IV.1*, 701-702).

To confess that the church is catholic is to confess, by faith, 'the existence of a community which in the essence which makes it a Christian community is unalterable in spite of all its changes of form, which in this essence never has altered and never can or will alter' (*CD IV.1*, 702). The catholicity of the church thus refers to that which is the same in the church and which does not change in the midst of the very different forms that the church takes in various times and places. The church therefore exists within specific and particular cultures but is not dependent upon any one of them. It exists in continuity in the midst of the changing history and diversity over time of its many forms, and while it is itself a history, its essence remains the same through historical change (*CD IV.1*, 703-704).

Here too Barth distinguishes what he takes to be the true understanding of catholicity from what he perceives to be the erroneous positions of Roman Catholicism on one side and Protestant Liberalism on the other. The first equates the true church with the oldest church established through a legal succession of bishops or with a primitiveness of form. The second equates the true church with the exact opposite — the true church is the modern church. For Barth, neither points to the true essence of the church: 'Therefore neither flirtation with the old nor flirtation with the new makes the Church the true Church, but a calm consideration of that which as its abiding possession is superior to every yesterday and to-day and is therefore the criterion of its catholicity' (*CD IV.1*, 704-705).

What does it mean to confess that the church is catholic? Barth's answers in this way:

> I believe that the Christian community is one and the same in essence in all places, in all ages, within all societies, and in relation to all its members. I believe that it can be the Christian community only in this identity, and therefore that it is its task to maintain itself in this identity, and therefore in this identity to will to be, and continually to become and to remain, the Christian community, and nothing else, and therefore the true Church in all these dimensions (*CD IV.1*, 707-708).

Once again, Barth's answer is a matter of revelation and faith and is construed dialectically, for from an empirical and phenomenal point of view, the church appears not as a haven of pure truth but as a mixture of truth and error in constant battle. The church is not visible as the true church, but the church universal and every individual congregation is in battle to preserve its true essence and to refrain from falling into error. 'Just as without faith we cannot see its unity or holiness, so without faith we cannot see its catholicity.' And the opposite is also true, for where the church attempts to make its catholicity visible apart from faith, there it is marked by an arrogance that demonstrates that it has lost its true catholicity. A true church as a specific community recognizes the battle which it wages between truth and falsehood, and that it like all other Christian communities is threatened. 'A true Church is humbly content to be thrown back entirely upon faith in respect of its truth, and confidently to exist in this faith as the true community of Jesus Christ' (*CD IV.1*, 708).

So the truth of the church's catholicity thus resides in its divine call and inner reality. Here again, Barth's notion is one of dialectical unity and distinction, so that the church's catholicity is neither divorced from its visible existence nor simply equated with a visible catholic unity. The church's catholicity is therefore grounded in its relationship to Christ:

> But that means that objectively it is exactly the same with the catholicity and therefore the truth of the Christianity of a Church as it is with its unity and holiness: the Church has no control over it. Its being as *ecclesia catholica*, the fact that everywhere and at all times and in relation to all

other societies and to all its individual members it is one and the same, is actual in the fact that it is the body, the earthly-historical form of the existence of Jesus Christ. Therefore catholicity as its own actuality is grounded in Him as its Head (*CD IV.1*, 710).

Yet, even though the church is catholic only in relation to its head, Jesus Christ, who speaks and acts in the community, and who himself is the basis of its unchanging essence, there still exists an imperative for the community, i.e., that the church not fall into apathy or passivity in relation to its truth, its catholicity, but is called to renewed obedience and active faith. This obedience is rendered so that the church even in its visible form and practice may reflect the truth of its Lord, because though it is a spiritual society, it lives as a definite historical and physical society in the world. This is the paradox, for while the church truly exists only in dependence upon its Lord who makes it catholic, yet it is the very recognition by the church of its own weakness that demonstrates its catholicity and therefore its strength. Its very dependence upon its Lord and recognition of its constant need once again is said by Barth to demonstrate the ongoing continuity of the true church and the present work of the Spirit in it (*CD IV.1*, 710-711). The church will be catholic when it keeps its limit firmly in view, resting content in its Lord and serving and witnessing to him: 'And therefore faith in Him, which can never cease to be a busy faith, is the only effective and not really passive but supremely active realisation of the *credo catholicam ecclesiam*' (*CD IV.1*, 712).

Barth's understanding of the catholicity of the church is, like his understanding of the church's unity and holiness, highly dialectical. Barth refuses simply to speak of catholicity as pertaining to an invisible church, but he also refuses to equate the church's catholicity with its visible political unity. The first option betrays a mistaken docetic position, whereby the second demonstrates an ebionitic one. In contradistinction to these options, Barth speaks of a juxtaposed unity and differentiation between the inner mystery and outer form of the church's catholicity along a Christological pattern, in which the second is established by and remains dependent upon the first, and this conception is supplemented by his central notion of correspondence, whereby the church's visible form reflects and bears witness to its inner catholicity.

D. The Church Is Apostolic

As the church is one, holy, and catholic, so also is it apostolic, and Barth maintains that this final term summarizes and provides the spiritual criterion for judging whether the previous three are present. Barth notes that the term 'apostolic' is, however, a concrete term, in contrast to the other three. What this means is that while for the other three appeal was made to Jesus Christ as the foundation of the church's unity, holiness, and catholicity, 'apostolic' is a term that gives us a concrete criterion for finding the true church, though it too is also a spiritual criterion. As Barth writes: 'Apostolic means in the discipleship, in the school, under the normative authority, instruction and direction of the apostles, in agreement with them, because listening to them and accepting their message' (*CD IV.1*, 714). The church is the true church as it is apostolic in this sense — it stands under the concrete authority of Scripture. This predicate describes the church as an event, though this event itself takes place within a history between the apostles and the church today. Apostolicity can only be recognized from within, by one who actively participates within the community itself. So apostolicity, while tied to the concrete criterion of Scripture, is also a work of the Holy Spirit and perceived by faith (*CD IV.1*, 713-715).

It is therefore a mistake, Barth contends, to seek apostolicity on 'historical or juridical grounds.' The temptation in this respect is to equate apostolicity with the notion of apostolic succession. Such a view is to mistake a spiritual reality with a historical proof, to confuse revelation and history, and to subsume and enslave the former to the latter, making it a possession of the church. It is to affirm a spiritual reality by historical-critical methods. As Barth states: 'It is obvious that neither the Holy Spirit nor faith is necessary for this purpose, but only an uncritical or critical archaeological knowledge of the lists [of succeeding bishops]' (*CD IV.1*, 715). As such, this view of the church ceases to be a confession of faith. The Holy Spirit is no longer a free Lord but the possession of the community, and God's free grace is lost (*CD IV.1*, 716-717). Barth writes:

> Of course, the practical powers and legal authority of a bishop can be transferred institutionally and ritually from one man to another, like the staff and mitre and ring which symbolise them. But how can apostolic authority and power and mission, how can the Holy Spirit be transferred, when obviously apostolicity is His work and gift? — as though the Holy Spirit were a legal or technical or symbolical It, a property in the hands of one or many exalted members of the community which, without further ado, can be transferred by them into the power of others — simply because it has been institutionally arranged in this way, and simply because it takes place with due legality and ritual....
>
> No, just as Jesus Christ is a free subject when it takes place that the apostles become apostles, it is again an event in which Jesus Christ is a free subject and his Spirit moves where He wills when the apostolic community comes into being and exists as such, when there is an apostolic succession in the true sense in which this overburdened expression can be understood (*CD IV.1*, 717-718).

The apostolicity of the church thus takes rise by the Spirit's work and consists in the church's attentiveness and submission to its Lord as he speaks through the witness of the apostles in Scripture, the normative witness to Jesus Christ. The witness of the apostles is thus the medium of Christ's presence in the community and the medium by which the Spirit constitutes the church and calls it into existence. This witness is thus the earthly and historical corresponding reality to the glory of Christ and medium for the awakening power of the Holy Spirit. 'Thus the existence of His community is always its history in its encounter with this witness — the history in which it is faithful or unfaithful to it in its exposition and application. True apostolic succession thus pertains to the church's vigilance in listening to this witness' (*CD IV.1*, 718-719). But this succession can never be an attempt to possess the Spirit through a type of institutional succession, to control the mystery of his work. The only true succession is rather a succession of service and obedience. As Barth states, 'There can be no supposed human control over the Holy Spirit' (*CD IV.1*, 719-720).

The church is therefore apostolic where it listens to this mediate authority, the authority of the witness of the apostles, i.e., Scripture, which bears witness to the ultimate authority of Christ. The institution of the church thus must be renewed by the history of the event which takes place between Christ and his apostles, and then between the apostles and the church:

> What we have learned to know as apostolicity and therefore as the mark of the true Church is quite naturally identical in substance with the term which in a very different dogmatic context has been used to describe the authority of the Bible as the source and norm of the existence and doctrine and order of the Church — the 'Scripture-principle' (*CD IV.1*, 721).

The apostolic church is the church that reads and listens to and obeys Scripture as the witness to its one living Lord who speaks through it by the Spirit. As Barth writes: 'Thus the apostolic community means concretely the community which hears the apostolic witness of the New Testament, which implies that of the Old, and recognises and puts this witness into effect as the source and norm of its existence' (*CD IV.1*, 722).[28]

6. Summary

Barth's understanding of the nature of the church is predicated upon a highly dialectical notion of the church as a *mystery*, the union of an invisible event and a visible institution, an inner spiritual reality and a historical social form. In this union the two aspects of the single reality of the church are neither separated nor confused, with the latter existing in dependence upon and correspondence to the former. There is therefore a Chalcedonian pattern to Barth's understanding of the nature of the

---

[28]For the relation between the church's authority and freedom as it stands under the authority of Scripture, see *CD I.2*, 538-740.

church as event and institution, as invisible and visible, along with an asymmetrical relation between them rooted in an anhypostatic-enhypostatic Christological paradigm and wedded to a unique conception of correspondence of the latter to the former.

The mystery of the church as both a spiritual and physical reality is therefore grounded in the ultimate relationship between the Spirit and the church, the former calling the latter into existence and providing its ongoing character as a true church. The church cannot possess the Spirit, but the church does remain in constant dependence upon the Spirit for its life and identity. When the church forgets this dependence, it loses its character as the true church. This does not entail that the 'real' church for Barth is spiritual and invisible while the 'false' church is historical and visible. This would betray a docetic ecclesiology that Barth disavows. But it does protect against an opposite assumption, namely, that the church is simply one human society among others, a society of shared religious feeling or conviction. This view would betray an ebionitic error Barth equally rejects. The church is rather the union of an inner spiritual reality grounded in the Holy Spirit and a visible human society, the first giving rise to the latter in a manner analogous to the incarnation itself. Barth's understanding of the church's nature as an invisible and visible reality and of the relation between the Spirit and the church is thus patterned after the unique and irreplaceable union of the mystery and miracle of Christmas.

Chapter Seven

The Order of the Church as the Body of Christ

1. Introduction — Christ and the Christian Community

The twofold nature of the church can be described by Barth in terms of a relation between event and institution, or, of that between the invisible and the visible church, and these relations are defined by and included within the more general framework of the relationship between the Holy Spirit and the Christian community. We now take up the question of the form and order of the Christian community, itself determined by the relationship between Christ and the church, a relationship governed, determined, and shaped by a Christological logic.

In drawing this distinction and in moving to this second topic, however, one must in no way overlook the great overlap between these relationships in Barth's thought, precisely because the Holy Spirit is the Spirit of Christ. The Spirit calls the community into existence as his fellowship, thus defining its nature, yet it is also Christ who constitutes the church as his body through the Spirit, giving it a definite order and form, and it is the Father who ordains the community of Christ and the Spirit for a definite mission in the world. For Barth, speaking of the Holy Spirit who gathers, upbuilds, and sends the community thus entails speaking of Jesus Christ who does the same, and of the Father whose purpose wills that this should be so.

Along the same lines, it should again be noted that while Barth places his explication of the church under the third article of the creed, the doctrine of the church also falls within the more inclusive doctrine of reconciliation, itself defined according to the second article. Ecclesiology is thus shaped both by pneumatology and by Christology. So Barth in speaking of the church in the second volume of the doctrine of reconciliation can write:

> In the thesis at the head of the section we have spoken of the Holy Spirit as the quickening power by which Christianity is built up as the true Church in the world. But as we made it clear it is Jesus the Lord who is at work in this quickening power of the Holy Spirit. And we must now take up again that which we have already said, and maintain that according to the normative view of the New Testament the Holy Spirit is the authentic and effective self-attestation of the risen and living Lord Jesus; His self-attestation as the Resurrected, the living One, the Lord, the exalted Son of Man, in whom there has already been attained the

sanctification of all men, but also the particular, factual sanctification of Christians — their union with him and therefore with one another (*CD IV.2*, 651).[1]

What this quotation makes evident is that, in relation to the question of the church, the Spirit and Christ are understood by Barth to be joined in the most integral of ways.

2. Christ, the Spirit, and the Community

The manner in which Barth construes the relationship between the Holy Spirit and Christ with particular reference to the church is related to his answer to the problem of speaking of both the presence and absence of Christ during the time between Christ's ascension and return. As surveyed in our earlier discussion of Christ and the question of historical distance, Barth is reticent to speak of Christ as absent during this intervening time, for this might imply that the community needs to make him present through some form of sacramental mediation, a position Barth rejects.[2] Christ is present, not absent, Barth insists, and therefore he has no need of vicars or representatives upon the earth. Nor can he be subsumed into the church's proclamation, faith, or community, or be replaced by them (*CD IV.3.1*, 349-350). Yet, Christ is of course not physically present in the world today, having ascended and now delaying his second advent, and therefore the question of his absence cannot be ignored.

Barth's solution to this conundrum is to speak of Christ as present through the Holy Spirit in a manner that closely joins and nearly identifies the Spirit and Christ, and in a way that sees Christ to be present in the community which is his 'earthly-historical form of his existence.' The time between Christ's first advent and his second one is therefore not a period marked by Christ's absence, requiring the church to act as a mediator or vicar upon the earth, but as the time of Christ's presence precisely through the power of the Spirit in the community, the time of Christ's second form of existence. It is thus another form of the parousia of Jesus Christ. The Holy Spirit on this account is nearly identified with Christ himself, and Barth can even

---

[1]Barth can even go so far in places as to define the Holy Spirit as 'Jesus Christ Himself in the power of His resurrection' (*CD IV.3.1*, 352). He can also state that 'the only content of the Holy Spirit is Jesus' (*CD IV.2*, 654). Here the complaint is often raised that Barth has subsumed the Spirit into Christ, a charge that will be addressed below.

[2]See the earlier discussion of Christ and historical distance in chapter five above.

go so far as to assert that the Holy Spirit is 'Jesus Christ Himself in the power of His resurrection.'[3]

With this solution Barth can on one hand deal realistically with the absence of Christ as the eschatological problem in this time between the first and second advents, while on the other hand he can speak of a real presence of Christ during this time, though it is a presence mediated by the Spirit (*CD IV.2*, 652).[4] Barth writes: 'Where the man Jesus attests Himself in the power of the Spirit of God, He makes Himself present; and those whom He approaches in His self-attestation are able also to approach Him and to be near Him' (*CD IV.2*, 654).

This close identification of Christ and the Spirit solves a dilemma for Barth, namely, the problem of Christ's seeming absence and the need for ecclesiastical mediation in the present in light of this absence. His solution, however, raises some oft-noted difficulties. While Barth is not far from Calvin on this question of Christ's presence through the mediation of the spirit, at points Barth comes very close to identifying Christ with the Spirit and subsuming the Spirit into Christ. In the passages within the *Church Dogmatics* where Barth specifically addresses the question of the Trinity, there can be no doubt as to the integrity and distinctiveness of all three persons, or, as Barth prefers, 'modes of being' [*Seinsweisen*]. Yet in Barth's ecclesiological thought, Barth seems to be in danger of subsuming the person and work of the Spirit into Christ's person and work in a modalist fashion, making the Spirit simply the manifestation of Christ's presence in the community today. This would leave Barth not with a Trinity but a Binity, and although without doubt this is not Barth's intention, it is a question that hangs over his seeming identification of the Spirit as 'Jesus Christ Himself in the power of His resurrection' and equation of the person and work of the Spirit with Christ's own 'spiritual being and work.'[5] Here some ask whether Barth's pneumatology has been unduly influenced by his fear of

---

[3]See *CD IV.3.1*, 352; also 353; cf. 350-353. Elsewhere Barth writes: 'It is crucial that the Holy Spirit should not in any sense be understood as a relatively or absolutely independent and independently operative force intervening between Jesus Christ and the man who is called by Him, but as His Spirit, as the power of His presence, work and Word, as the shining of the life of which He is the fulness,' and 'The presence and action of the Holy Spirit are the *parousia* of Jesus Christ in the time between Easter and His final revelation' (*CD IV.3.2*, 503).

[4]Barth speaks of the time between the first and second advent as the time of the community, the time in which the church lives as a provisional representation, and thus as a real and true, though imperfect and incomplete, reflection of the sanctification of humanity in Christ (*CD IV.2*, 649; also *CD IV.1*, 725-739).

[5]See *CD IV.3.1*, 352-353; also *CD IV.1*, 147.

ecclesiastical and sacramental mediation, and whether the Holy Spirit has received short shrift in Barth's ecclesiology.[6]

Nevertheless, Barth's close union, if not identification, of Christ and the Spirit was driven by a legitimate concern, namely, that the Spirit could be divorced from Christ in a form of mysticism or existentialism so that the objectivity of Christ is sacrificed and replaced by an anthropologically-construed present experience of salvation. Barth himself glimpsed the former in Schleiermacher and the latter in Bultmann, and for Barth this subjective turn was the hallmark of Protestant liberalism past and present. Barth's solution may seem to be a pendulum swing too far in the other direction, the direction of a hard objectivism — he himself noted late in life that a legitimate theology of the third article could be written, but that this remained for others to achieve.[7] Yet Barth's own Christological concentration was an attempt to change the course of a long tradition, and it should not be surprising that such course corrections can lead to overcompensation and one-sidedness. Yet Barth himself held that a 'theology worthy of respect is always one-sided.'[8]

Finally, Barth's doctrines of election and Christology (in which reconciliation and redemption are united in Christ) no doubt impinge upon his pneumatology and disallow any strong distinctions between the work of Christ and the Spirit. As John Webster has noted, perhaps in regard to pneumatology Barth may be 'not so much deficient as different, less committed to a pluralist trinitarian theology, less anxious to identify the demarcations between the actions of Christ and the Spirit in the

---

[6]See Robert Jenson, 'You Wonder Where the Spirit Went,' in *Pro Ecclesia* 2 (1993): 296-304; see esp. 302-304. For a defense of Barth on this score, see George Hunsinger, 'The Mediator of Communion: Karl Barth's Doctrine of the Holy Spirit,' in *Disruptive Grace*, 148-185. For a critical introduction to Barth's pneumatology as it bears upon other doctrines within his theology, see Daniel Migliore, 'Vinculum Pacis: Barth's Theology of the Holy Spirit,' unpublished English manuscript, 2000. Published in German translation as: 'Vinculum Pacis – Karl Barths Theologie des Heiligen Geistes,' in *Evangelische Theologie* 6 (2000): 131-152.

[7]See Barth, *Theology of Schleiermacher*, 277-279. It should also be noted that Barth's doctrine of redemption, the proposed volume five of the *Church Dogmatics*, was never completed. This would no doubt have contained a more developed and detailed account of pneumatology, following Barth's Trinitarian structure of the doctrines of creation (*CD III*), reconciliation (*CD IV*), and redemption (the unfinished *CD V*). There Barth may well have spoken of the Holy Spirit more as an agent in his own right (see Hunsinger, 'Mediator,' 161). This would address Jenson's concern that in the doctrine of reconciliation the Spirit disappears whenever 'he would appear as someone rather than as something' (Jenson, 'You Wonder,' 304).

[8]Barth, 'Wilhelm Herrmann,' 268.

world.'[9] One thing is certain: questions regarding Barth's pneumatology will continue to be raised.

3. The Form of the Community

A. The Church as the Body of Christ

Barth speaks of the church in relation to Christ by means of a central image or concept, that of the church as the 'earthly-historical form of existence [*irdisch-geschichtliche Existenzform*] of Jesus Christ Himself,' the body of Christ that is 'created and continually renewed by the awakening power of the Holy Spirit' (*CD IV.1*, 661). According to Barth, Jesus Christ lives in two forms of existence: in a 'heavenly-historical form of existence,' i.e., as the incarnate Son of God, but also as joined with an 'earthly-historical form of existence,' i.e., his body, the church. Christ thus exists both as the incarnate Lord possessing a heavenly body, but also as the Lord united with an earthly body, which is the community itself: 'This particular element of human history, this earthly-historical form of existence of Jesus Christ, is the Christian community' (*CD IV.1*, 661). Christ lives as the head of the church, and the Christian community lives as his body, existing only because and as Christ himself exists. This community is the provisional representation of the salvation that Christ has accomplished for all, the community that acknowledges, recognizes, and confesses its Lord and what God has done for them, and for all, in Christ. There is on this account revealed to the community by faith what will be revealed to all by sight on the last day, the day of Christ's return (*CD IV.1*, 661-662).

The question must now be raised as to the precise nature of the relationship between Christ and the community. Barth is adamant on the one hand that Christ is superior to the community, that he remains transcendent and free in relation to it, and that the relationship between Christ and the community is irreversible. In other words, the community has no existence apart from Jesus Christ and cannot take his place. The church is not a religious society, Barth reiterates, but is tied to its Lord as 'an anticipation, a provisional representation, of the sanctification of all men as it has taken place in Him, of the new humanity reconciled with God' (*CD IV.2*, 654).

Barth is, however, equally adamant that Christ is not a captive to his own transcendence, separated and removed from his community — Christ is immanent within the community as well as transcendent to it. For this reason, Christ has both a 'heavenly-historical' and an 'earthly-historical' form of existence. The first is his own person, the incarnate Lord, the union of the Word made flesh. The second is the unity of Christ himself with the community, his earthly body. Existing as the first form, Christ remains transcendent and separate from his community. In the second

---

[9]John Webster, *Karl Barth* (London: Continuum, 2000), 138-139.

form, however, Christ is the Head of his earthly body, the community, in such a way that he is inseparably joined to it. Barth concludes: 'And in both cases, and either way, we speak of the one man Jesus Christ. It is He who is both there and here. It is He who is both the Head and the body' (*CD IV.2*, 652-653).

How are we to understand Barth's twofold conception of Christ's existence? To reach an answer, we must begin by examining the two forms of Christ's existence individually. The first form is that of the incarnation. In the incarnation, the Word took flesh, as the Son of God became man. This is the perfect unity of divinity and humanity, understood by Barth along Chalcedonian lines, so that there is a unity of natures, a distinction between them, and an asymmetrical relation whereby the second exists only in dependence upon the first. In sum, in the incarnation the Word remains the subject of the (hypostatic) union. As we have seen, Barth describes this asymmetrical relation of the Word to the flesh and of the divine to the human nature in terms of an anhypostatic-enhypostatic Christology. This first form of the incarnation is that which we usually think of when we make reference to Christ's existence.

The second form of Christ's existence for Barth is the unity of Christ, who is himself the union of God and man, with the community, a unity portrayed according to the Biblical image of Christ as the Head and the church as his body. What is important to note is that the Christological logic that orders the relationship of the first form of existence, i.e., of the Word and flesh in Christ, as well as the relationship between the divine and human natures, is analogously predicated of this second form of Christ's existence, in that Christ and the community are inseparably united, yet irreducibly distinct, and exist in an asymmetrical and irreversible relationship. The Chalcedonian logic, coupled with an anhypostatic-enhypostatic Christology, thereby also orders and determines this second form.

We might say that the first form and the second exist as concentric circles, the innermost circle of the Word being the basis for the surrounding circle of the flesh of Christ, and the unity of these circles as Jesus Christ providing the basis for the outer circle of the community. In other words, the Word is the inner basis of Christ's humanity, giving it existence and reality, and Christ (as the union of the Word made flesh) is the inner basis of the community, creating its existence and life. In terms of a formal relationship, the Word is to the flesh of Christ as Christ is to the community. The first relationship, though unique and irreplaceable, serves as the paradigm for the second, and the second exists in correspondence and analogy to the first, being governed by the same theological principles. These principles are defined by and constitutive for Christology, but they are also reflected by and regulative for all other divine human relations, and preeminently, for that between Christ and the church. Hence Barth understands the reality of the church as analogous to the incarnation: the relationship between Christ and the community is, Barth maintains, 'indirectly identical to the relationship between Himself as the eternal Son of God and His being as man' (*CD IV.2*, 59).

For this reason, the relationship between Christ's first and second forms of existence, i.e., between the incarnation and Christ's presence in the community as his body, is not one of contradiction but is itself one of correspondence, the first and second forms being marked by a unity, distinction, and irreversible relation between their first and second terms (i.e., between the Word and flesh in the first form, and between Christ and the community in the second). Barth's designation of the first form, the unity of God and man in the incarnation, is of course the name 'Jesus Christ.' Barth's designation for the second form is that of the '*totus Christus*,' the unity of Christ and his community, of Christ the Head and the church his earthly body (*CD IV.2*, 658; 659).

It is only when we understand this integral relationship between the first and second forms of Christ's existence that we can then begin to understand Barth's somewhat shocking assertion that 'Jesus Christ is the community' (*CD IV.2*, 655). Two things must be noted about this statement. First, Barth maintains that it is primarily and properly a Christological statement and only as such and secondarily an ecclesiological one. That is, it speaks of Christ's ability to create and indwell the community, not of the community's ability to take the place of Christ. Second, and following upon this, the relationship between Christ and the community is strictly ordered and asymmetrical. In other words, the relationship itself and the statement expressing it cannot be reversed, i.e., the community is not Jesus Christ, and while the statement, 'Jesus Christ is the community' is a valid one, a reversal of this statement, i.e., 'The community is Jesus Christ,' would be invalid (*CD IV.2*, 655).

It should be clear that Barth's understanding of the proposition, 'Jesus Christ is the community,' is entirely dictated by the logic of the proposition, 'The Word became flesh.' This proposition is also irreversible, and speaks of a divine action and actualization and not of a human potentiality or divinization. As such, it is a theological statement and only thereafter an anthropological one. Barth's understanding of the relationship between Christ and the community is thus entirely predicated upon and analogous to the prior relationship between the Word and flesh in Christ, or, in Barth's later and more common historicized terminology, between the obedience of the Son of God and the exaltation of the Son of Man. Barth can also see this relation as entailing a kind of ecclesiological *extra Calvinisticum* that protects the divine freedom of Christ, in that the being of Christ is not exhausted by the being of the community but rather transcends it. In a passage that both presents this point and summarizes the preceding discussion, Barth writes:

> There can be no thought of the being of Jesus Christ enclosed in that of His community, or exhausted by it, as though it were a kind of predicate of this being. The truth is the very opposite. The being of the community is exhausted and enclosed in His. It is a being which is taken up and hidden in His, and absolutely determined and governed by it. The being of the community is a predicate of his being. As it exists on earth and in

time in virtue of the mighty work of the Holy Ghost, it is His body; and He, its heavenly Head, the incarnate Word, the incomparable Holy One, has in it His own earthly-historical form of existence; He Himself, who is not yet directly and universally and definitively revealed to the world and it, is already present and at work in it. The community is not Jesus Christ. But He — and in reality only He, but He in supreme reality — is the community. He does not live because and as it lives. But it lives, and may and can live, only because and as He lives ... The sequence and order are all-important. But in this sequence and order it may and must be affirmed that Jesus Christ is the community (*CD IV.2*, 655).

Barth's statement that 'Jesus Christ is the community' is complemented by another equally surprising statement when first encountered. Because Jesus is the embodiment of the kingdom of God, Barth maintains that 'the kingdom of God is the community' (*CD IV.2*, 656).[10]

Does this assertion witness a reversal of his former opposition to some Catholic conceptions of this relationship? Though this may appear at first glance to be the case, the answer in the end must be negative when the following factors are taken into account. First, it must be understood that in speaking of the kingdom Barth speaks not of the final revelation of God's purposes and culmination of his salvific action, but of the new humanity in the time between Christ's first and second advent. This fact in itself greatly qualifies the statement. Second, and more significant still, for Barth it is the *order* of the statement that is all important, i.e., its irreversibility. Just as the statement, 'Jesus Christ is the community,' is irreversible, so for Barth the statement, 'the kingdom of God is the community,' is irreversible.[11] One *cannot* say that the church is the kingdom of God. So while the proposition, 'The kingdom of God is the community,' is valid, the proposition 'The community is the kingdom of God,' is, for Barth, invalid.

Echoing Barth's terminology, we might say that the statement, 'The kingdom of God is the community,' is properly and primarily an eschatological statement, and

---

[10]Barth writes: 'In sum, there is a real identity, not present *in abstracto*, but given by God and enacted in the mighty work of the Holy Spirit, between the Holy One, the kingdom of God as perfectly established in Him, and the communion of Saints on earth, which as such is also a communion of sinners. Thus the power of this Holy One, of Jesus Christ as the heavenly Head, in whom God's rule is perfectly established, is also the indwelling power of life and growth which is immanent in the community on earth' (*CD IV.2*, 656-657).

[11]The issue of the irreversibility of the relationship between Christ and the church (and between the kingdom and the church) is central to that which divides Barth from some of his early Roman Catholic critics. See Wendell S. Dietrich, *Christ and the Church, according to Barth and some of his Roman Catholic critics.*

only secondarily an ecclesiological one. The eschatological kingdom does take for itself the form of the community in history, creating an entity in time that corresponds to itself, but it is not exhausted by the community, nor can the community be equated with the kingdom of God. Barth thus maintains the Reformed understanding of the *extra Calvinisticum* and the *communicatio idiomatum* not only in his Christological thought, but also, and analogously, in his ecclesiological thought as well. This logic hinges upon the issue of the irreversibility of the relationship between Christ and the community and that between the kingdom of God and the community. As previously noted, this logic arises from and is constitutive for Christology, and it is reflected by and regulative for ecclesiology. The kingdom therefore gives rise to the community, but the community cannot be equated with the kingdom. The relation between them is, again, irreversible, asymmetrical, and based upon an anhypostatic-enhypostatic logic, wherein the second term in the relationship (i.e., the community) exists only because of the first (Christ and the kingdom).

B. *The* Totus Christus

Barth's manner of speaking of the relationship between Christ and the community is to speak of Christ (the Head of the community), and the church (as the earthly-historical form of Jesus Christ), as together comprising the *totus Christus*, Christ with his community in a differentiated, yet inseparable, unity. *Totus Christus* is thus the designation Barth uses to speak of the unity of Christ and his community and the unity of his history with theirs, the united history of salvation. Though the history of Christ and of the community are differentiated and should not be confused, the latter is inseparably joined to the first, and together they comprise salvation history. 'Salvation history is the history of the *totus Christus*, of the Head with the body and all the members. This *totus Christus* is *Christus victor*' (*CD IV.3.1*, 216). As now apparent, this relationship between Christ and the community is predicated upon the logic of Barth's Christology, evidenced in a number of respects.

First, the relationship between Christ and the community parallels that between the Word and flesh in Christ. Like the incarnate Word, the *totus Christus* exists as the inseparable unity of Christ and his earthly body, the church, yet even as these are inseparably united (for, as Barth states, Christ only exists with those who are his own), they can also never be confused but remain distinguished.

Second, and related to the discussion above, the relationship between Christ and the church is irreversible — Christ is the source of the community, but the community is not the source of Christ. The community has its existence only because of Christ's calling it into existence, though it has a true existence and task established through this call. Barth states: 'Because He is, it is; it is, because He is. That is its secret, its being in the third dimension, which is visible only to faith' (*CD IV.1*, 661). Christ and the community are related in the most intimate of ways, for as Barth elsewhere notes, the community can represent Christ as he can represent the community, seen in

Christ's confrontation of Paul on the way to Damascus, where Paul's persecution of the community is equated with a persecution of Christ himself (*CD IV.3.1*, 206-207). Nevertheless, Christ is always the subject and never the object of this relationship, for the direction of influence flows from Christ to the community and not vice versa. Christ therefore is the center, while the community is the circumference, and, in Barth's terms: 'The centre cannot become the circumference nor the circumference the centre' (*CD IV.3.1*, 278-279). Nor can there be a reversal or confusion of their position and functions. Barth refuses to see the community as continuing or completing Christ's office and work. Nevertheless, for Barth, Christ and the community are indivisibly united, and this unity is grounded in an eternal election. The community is eternally elected precisely because it is elect in Christ, who is the eternal electing God and the eternally elected human person in one. Christology is, therefore, not exclusive but inclusive, in that the election of Christ includes within it the election of humanity (*CD IV.3.1*, 278-279).[12]

Furthermore, just as the anhypostatic-enhypostatic logic preserves the gracious initiative of the Word in relation to the flesh of Christ, and of Christ's divine nature in relation to his human nature, so also, by analogy, does it preserve the gracious initiative and sovereignty of Christ in relation to the church (*CD I.2*, 216). The church has no independent existence apart from its living Head, and in Christ it is established and truly exists as the 'living congregation of the living Lord Jesus Christ.'

Finally, this asymmetrical relationship between Christ and the community is characterized as a relationship of correspondence as well as contradiction. Barth

---

[12]The relationship between Christ and the individual Christian is for Barth based upon the same patterns as that between Christ and the community. Barth refers to the union of Christ and the community as the *totus Christus*; he refers to the union of Christ and the believer as a *unio cum Christo*, a union with Christ. Both relationships are marked by a unity and differentiation of the partners in an irreversible and asymmetrical relation in which Christ is the true Subject who gives existence to the second, while the second lives in obedient correspondence or analogy to Christ as a true and free partner, yet never taking the place of Christ or his work. Barth sees the relationship between Christ and the Christian, like that between Christ and the community, as predicated upon the unique relationship between the Word and flesh of Christ, the 'mystery and miracle of Christmas,' but he disavows speaking of either relationship as an extension of the incarnation. The community and the Christian do not take the place of Christ — Christ 'gives, commands and precedes,' whereas the Christian (and the community) 'receives, obeys and follows' as a witness to him. And this witness marks the reciprocality of the relationship as one of correspondence. As Barth states, 'A justifiable concern for the unconditional predominance of the freedom, grace and decision of Jesus Christ which establish the relationship should not mislead us into suppressing or minimising the fact that His action has its correspondence in an action of the Christian.' See *CD IV.3.2*, 543-544; also 538-545; 594-595; 597-607.

consistently maintains that revelation comes in a form other than itself, and thus in a contradictory form. Yet, as we have seen, Barth also emphasizes in the doctrine of reconciliation that this form exists in a relationship of correspondence to the reality it reveals. This is paradigmatically the case with Christ, whose human life corresponds to God.[13] But this relationship of correspondence also holds for the relationship between Christ and the community. For while the community is never to be confused with Christ, nor could it take his place, it does live in correspondence to its Lord in its actions and deeds. This is the basis of the church's obedience, an obedience analogous though not identical to that of Christ.

In sum, this Christological logic of unity, differentiation, asymmetry, and correspondence is evident throughout Barth's presentation of the relationship between Christ and the church in their unity as the *totus Christus*.[14] The constituent elements of this logic are correspondingly the fundamental motifs of Barth's understanding of the church as the body of Christ. A failure to perceive and delineate these motifs results in a failure to understand Barth's ecclesiology in its most basic form.

There is, however, one further thing that must be said in drawing this section to a close, which is that with reference to the *totus Christus* the Christological logic is complemented by a Trinitarian one, and one that provides a pneumatological complement to Barth's Christological emphasis.[15] Barth states that as the Holy Spirit binds the Father and the Son in the Trinitarian life, so the Holy Spirit binds Christ and the community, and Barth sees in the latter relationship an analogy in time to the first, eternal relationship. The unity of Christ and the community in the fellowship of the Spirit is thus predicated upon the Trinitarian relations, and for Barth it itself serves as a *vestigium trinitatis*, though an indirect one. The Holy Spirit is the one who binds Christ to the community and is, as Barth says, the 'living transition from the one to the other' (*CD IV.2*, 336; 339). The Holy Spirit therefore joins both the Father and the Son and unites Christ and the community, the latter relationship a repetition within history of God's dynamic being in eternity (*CD IV.2*, 341). The relations of God in the eternal inner-Trinitarian life are therefore reflected in the relationship between Christ and the community in time, for, as Barth argues, God does not choose to be alone, but to exist with the world, though he lacks nothing in himself, and grants existence to the world purely as a gracious act (*CD IV.2*, 336-337; 345-346).

---

[13]As put so well by Trevor Hart: 'When God speaks his Word into the realm of flesh...it results not in an echo, but precisely in a reply, a response from the side of the creature to the Creator's call. In other words, attention must be granted here in christology to the enhypostatic as well as the anhypostasic aspect of the incarnation' (Hart, 'Was God in Christ?,' 22; see also 17-26).

[14]All of these elements are readily evidenced in a central passage of the *Church Dogmatics* previously quoted in chapter five above (see *CD IV.2*, 59-60).

[15]For the following exposition, see *CD IV.2*, 336-348.

Furthermore, though this is more implicit than explicit in Barth, as the Holy Spirit conceives and brings into existence the body of Christ in the incarnation, so also the Spirit calls and brings into existence the earthly-historical body of Christ as the community which is joined to its heavenly head. The Spirit is therefore the basis not only for the first form of Christ's existence as the incarnate Word, in that the person of Jesus Christ is 'conceived by the Holy Spirit,' the Spirit uniting Word and flesh,[16] but the Spirit is also the basis for the second form of Christ's existence, in that the community as the 'earthly-historical' body of Christ is likewise brought into existence and joined to Christ by the agency of the Holy Spirit in an analogical and related action.

There is, then, not only a direct Christological analogy between Christ and the community, but an indirect Trinitarian and pneumatological one, in that, as the Spirit binds together the Father and the Son (in the Trinity); and as the Spirit binds together the Word and flesh of Christ (in the incarnation); so also the Holy Spirit binds together Christ and the community. The theme of the Spirit as the 'bond of love' (*vinculum caritatis*) and the 'bond of peace' (*vinculum pacis*) therefore runs throughout Barth's Trinitarian, Christological, and ecclesiological thought, and indeed throughout his entire theology.[17] Barth's doctrine of the church is pre-eminently Christological in shape, but it contains Trinitarian and pneumatological aspects as well, aspects that should not be overlooked or ignored.

4. The Order of the Community

A. The Correspondence of the Life of the Community to Christ

As Christ's earthly life corresponds to the will and character of God, so also the community in its historical life corresponds to the life of Christ. It is important to note that this correspondence is analogical, therefore implying both real similarity and real dissimilarity between the life, existence, and activity of Christ and that of the community. The concept of correspondence does signify a reflection of Christ's life and activity by the community, but it does not imply that the community takes the place of Christ or supplements his unique work and sacrifice. As Barth states, there is a 'correspondence but no parity, let alone identity,' between Christ and the community (*CD IV.3.2*, 729). Barth insists that the church even as a mystery, as an invisible and visible reality, is not Christ or a second Christ, nor an extension of his

---

[16]See *CD I.2*, 196-202.

[17]This has been demonstrated by Daniel Migliore (in '*Vinculum Pacis*: Barth's Theology of the Holy Spirit'). I am indebted to this essay for the current discussion. Migliore insightfully states that the doctrine of the Holy Spirit as the *vinculum caritatis* is 'Barth's Nicene pneumatological complement to his regulative Chalcedonian Christology' (ibid., 5).

being. Nor is it a representative for Christ upon the earth or a co-redeemer in salvation, for as Barth strongly asserts: 'Thus to speak of a continuation or extension of the incarnation in the Church is not only out of place but even blasphemous.' All that can be said is that it is his body: 'It is indeed in the flesh, but it is not, as He is, the Word of God in the flesh, the incarnate Son of God' (*CD IV.3.2*, 729). The church's life therefore reflects Christ as a mirror reflects an object — it is the object that determines the image, rather than the image producing the object.

One of the primary ways in which the community reflects the life and activity of Christ is in its *order*. In speaking of the church as the *communio sanctorum*, Barth is adamant that the question of the form of the community logically entails the question of its order.[18] The upbuilding of the community takes a definite shape and exists in a very definite form, and therefore according to a definite order and law, a law that opposes lawlessness and chaos. Barth can therefore state that 'the christologico-ecclesiological concept of the community is such that by its very nature it speaks of law and order, thus impelling and summoning us to take up this question' (*CD IV.2*, 680). Such order pertains where 'definite relationships [*Verhältnisse*] and connexions [*Beziehungen*]' exist and are required by the matter in question (*CD IV.2*, 676-677).

This order and law of the community touches upon every sphere of activity within the community as it exists as a 'provisional representation of the sanctification of man as it has taken place in Jesus Christ' (*CD IV.2*, 677-678). The most concrete instantiation of this representation is public worship, though it goes beyond this to include the entire range of the community's life and activity:

> It is a matter of the order of the particular event in which the existence of the community finds not merely its most concrete manifestation but also its central point, namely, public worship. It is also a matter of the determination and distribution of the various inter-related responsibilities, obligations and functions to be discharged by individual Christians within the general activity of the community. It is also a question how the community is to maintain its common cause, and the majesty of this cause, in relationship to its individual members; how it is to exercise discipline and oversight and rule among its members in respect of the particular functions entrusted to them and their Christian life in general. It is also a matter of the relationship of individual Christian congregations to other congregations both near and distant; of the preservation and exercise of the unity of all congregations; of the achievement of reciprocity in action and

---

[18]We might say that the *form* of the community pertains especially to the Chalcedonian pattern and the asymmetrical relation between Christ and the community, whereas the question of the community's *order* pertains especially to the correspondence of the community to Christ.

therefore of mutual understanding; of a comprehensive direction which will co-ordinate their existence and action. It is a matter of the regulation — so far as this is possible and necessary — of the relationships of the community to other social forms, and especially to the most outstanding and comprehensive; of the order of its relationship to the existing and authoritative state and its laws, organs, and measures (*CD IV.2*,678).

Barth states that the details of these relationships and their regulation cannot be spelled out by dogmatics but belong to the realm of canon law. Yet, dogmatics must nevertheless address 'the standpoints normative for canon law' (*CD IV.2*, 678). Dogmatics thus provides the general criteria and presuppositions that govern and regulate the specific aspects of these various relationships as they are treated by canon law.

At the outset, it is essential to note that central to the question of order and law is Barth's conviction that this law is predicated upon Christology and is so for a number of reasons. First, in addressing the question of the community, and thereby the question of its law, one is necessarily speaking of two subjects, Christ as the Head and the church as his earthly body, though the relationship between these must not be reversed. The very fact that to speak of the community is to speak of Christ as the primary acting subject within it and the human society of believers as the secondary subject entails for Barth that when we speak of the community, we must therefore necessarily speak of law and order. The basic law and order of the community is therefore grounded in the relationship between Christ and the community, between the Lord on one side and the obedient community on the other. The basic law of the community *is* this relationship. This does not imply that all the specific details of the church's life and action are automatically answered by acknowledging this relation, but it does mean that such questions can be answered only with reference to it, and for this reason the question of church law cannot be ignored or relegated to a secondary role (*CD IV.2*, 678-680).

Second, because the community is determined by this unique relationship, the order and law that this community lives under cannot be based upon a general conception of order and law found within other human societies but must be derived from Christology. This is necessitated by the first principle itself, in that the relationship between Christ and the community cannot be reversed, so that not only the existence but also the form and order of the community must be Christologically grounded rather than independently derived and formulated. So just as the community has no existence apart from Christ, neither does it have an independent order and law and basis for action that is not derived from him:

If it is the case that in the concept 'community' Jesus Christ as the Head of His body is the primary acting Subject, compared with whom the acting human communion of saints can be regarded only as secondary, then in relation to the order of the community this fact must not only remain inviolate, i.e., it must not only be respected as theological truth, as a statement of Christian faith and its confession, but it must be given its proper place and expression in relation to the order of the community and in the solution of all the problems of order involved. In the Church, law is that which is right by the norm of this relationship. Everything else is wrong. This is the axiom which dogmatics has to proclaim to all existing or projected canon law, by which even its most detailed provisions must be measured, and to the acknowledgment of which it is invited or recalled (*CD IV.2*, 678-679).

That the law of the community must be based upon and analogous to Christ is central to Barth's ecclesiological thought. Barth goes so far as to say that it would be 'folly to try to derive canon law from any but a christologico-ecclesiological concept of the community' (*CD IV.2*, 679). It is only when this Christological basis of the community is recognized that both the specific form and unique order of the community can be understood.

B. The Dialectical Nature of Church Law

Barth's commitment to and discussion of church order points again to the deeply dialectical nature of his ecclesiological thought and its Christological foundation and regulative patterns. Regarding the question of church law itself, Barth's position stands over against both an ecclesiastical antinomianism on the left, as well as a staid and rigid ecclesiastical jurisprudence on the right, opposing both license and legalism. Barth insists that the church requires order, and even law and right.[19] While the

---

[19]In this, Barth opposes the formless ecclesiologies that he sees in Sohm and Brunner. Barth attributes the shortfall of Sohm and Brunner specifically to their failure to consider the Christological basis and nature of the question of the church, therefore substituting abstract notions such as 'spirit' or 'love' in place of Christ and therefore falling into an antinomian position that ignores the necessity of true church order and law. They therefore sacrifice structure to preserve spirit, rather than seeing these in dialectical relation. In addition, according to Barth, Sohm and Brunner make Christ a predicate of the community, rather than the community a predicate of Christ. They therefore not only fail to see the Christological basis of the church, but also fail to preserve the irreversibility of the relationship between Christ and the church as well. In the end, such antinomian mistakes reflect a deeper error, the error of embracing a purely invisible view of the church coupled with an indifference to questions of visible order and church law, betraying a docetic ecclesiology. See *CD IV.2*, 679-680; also 680-681; 682; 683-688. In contrast to Brunner and Sohm, Barth is much closer by his own admission to Erik Wolf, who has designated the community as a 'brotherly Christocracy' and 'christocratic brotherhood,' and its law as a 'confessing law.' See *ibid.*, 677;

church must oppose calcified forms of church order, 'juridification and bureaucratisation,' it should do so not by abandoning church order and law altogether, but by asserting the true church order and law of the community, derived from the 'christologico-ecclesiological concept of the community' (*CD IV.2*, 681).

Barth's conception of church law therefore mirrors his understanding of church dogma. Both are dialectically understood. Church law, like church doctrine, is neither to be seen as opposed to revelation and thus unnecessary and expendable, nor as identical with revelation and thus unchangeable and static.[20] For Barth, to cast off church law as unnecessary leads to an antinomianism that reflects a docetic ecclesiology. To equate church law with revelation itself in a dogmatic fashion leads to a rigid legalism that reflects an ebionitic or Eutychian ecclesiology. Barth rejected both positions in favor of a particular dialectical understanding that preserves church law as necessary for the life of the church, yet refuses to see any one type of law as infallible and divinely inspired.

We mentioned above that the reason that church law is Christological is, first, because of the very existence and form of the community as the body of Christ, and, second, because its specific order and law are derived from Christ and are unique and particular, and therefore not derived from general criteria (*CD IV.2*, 681).[21] We now take up this second point, examining the Christological basis for church order and law.

C. The Christological Basis of Church Law

For Barth, the order and law of the church must be grounded in and derived from Christ. Barth writes: 'The basic form which characterises the Christian community necessarily demands that the whole structure of its life whould [sic] be unique. There can be no question of its subjection to the rules which are valid, either generally or on certain historical assumptions, for the constitution and action of other human societies' (*CD IV.2*, 681-682). It is therefore not a general conception of law, but Christ, 'the Lord and Head, the primary acting Subject,' who orders the community: 'It is He who gives them, not only their faith and confession and prayer and proclamation, but also the form of their life, the law and order of all that they do' (*CD IV.2*, 682). Christ is therefore himself the 'living law' of the community, and the

---

680-681; 682.

[20] Both dogma and law are therefore to be seen as necessary replies to revelation rather than as revelation itself.

[21] As Barth writes, 'on a christologico-ecclesiological view of the community law and order are distinguished as Christian and ecclesiastical law and order from every other form, and are visible and effective in this distinctive form' (*CD IV.2*, 681).

question of its law will therefore always be the question of the community's corresponding obedience to the ordering and commanding of Christ. This is what makes the law of the church unique and concrete as the 'spiritual law' of the community of Christ. Barth writes:

> As such, all valid and projected Church law, if it is true Church law, will be clearly and sharply differentiated from every other kind of 'law.' In great things and small, in all things, true Church law arises from adhering to the voice of Jesus Christ. Neither formally nor materially does it arise elsewhere. To seek and find and establish and administer this law is an integral part of the action with which the community is charged in and in relation to the world. For this reason, too, we cannot eliminate the question of true Church law, or treat it as a question of minor importance (*CD IV.2*, 682).

This normative law of the community is presented in Scripture, the authoritative witness to Christ, through which Christ himself speaks to the community today. To hear Christ's voice in the community is to hear it as it speaks in Scripture. Here again, Barth's thought remains highly dialectical, rejecting options of the left and right. Barth is adamant that obedience to Christ requires obedience to Scripture, the medium through which he speaks to the church. The community therefore must 'receive direction from the Bible.' The command of God does not lack form and substance, and Barth opposes all spiritualistic and antinomian tendencies. Yet at the same time, obedience to Christ does not entail slavish imitation of the forms and order presented in the Bible. The church lives in obedience to Christ and the Scripture, but it does not simply adopt and slavishly imitate the form of life found in Israel or even in the first century Christian community. The community today therefore does not obey a form, even the Biblical one, but Christ: 'There can be no question of its obeying any given form of the body of Jesus Christ — not even the biblical — but only Jesus Christ Himself as the Head of His body' (*CD IV.2*, 683). Barth once again does not separate revelation and its form, but also does not univocally equate them.

There is for this reason a difference between slavish imitation of a past form on one hand and a correspondence to Christ on the other. The latter lives in both obedience to and freedom from past forms, including the Biblical ones. For Barth, obedience to Christ requires both a careful listening to Scripture and a freedom to develop forms that are not simply copies of Biblical models but are suited for obedience in the present day. For this reason, Barth can subscribe to a real and broad diversity and plurality in the form, order, and practices that a church may take, based upon the geographical location and time in which a particular church exists. Faithful obedience as correspondence therefore eschews both an orderless chaos on the left and a legalistic order on the right. The norm for the church's order, law, and specific practices in the present is therefore the living voice of Christ in Scripture, though not the specific order, law, and regulations of Scripture itself.

5. Dogmatic Presuppositions of Church Law

While Barth allows for real diversity in regard to the particular and specific form, order, and activities of a community based upon its geographical and temporal location, he also maintains that a 'christologico-ecclesiological view of the community' has certain basic presuppositions that are normative for every type of church law. Barth outlines four such presuppositions, and these are the regulating principles that are then to mold every individual law in the church. These presuppositions are the general principles that Barth elucidates as falling within the realm of dogmatics, while he leaves the application of each principle in the formulation of specific laws regarding particular cases to the area of canon law and to the various churches (divided by time and space) themselves (*CD IV.2*, 689-690).

A. Church Law as a Law of Service

The first presupposition is that church law is a law of service. The community is a society that serves Jesus Christ its Head, and as such its central task is defined by ministry first to its Lord and then to one another in the community. In this the community lives in correspondence to its Lord, who came not to be served but to serve, and who, in that very service, rules. The service of Christ is mirrored (not supplemented or replaced) in the service of the Christian community as the 'obedience of His community corresponding to his rule.' The law of service is thus predicated upon the service of Christ, and specifically, the service of Christ as presented in the Gospel narratives (*CD IV.2*, 690-691).

Furthermore, the service of the community reflects the humility of the Lord who became a servant. Barth's understanding of the church's service is conceived not primarily in terms of a meticulous imitation of Jesus' particular and historical acts of service and charity, but as a general orientation and conformity to the overarching narrative pattern of Christ's existence as one who humbled himself to take up the form and task of a servant.

Nevertheless, while Barth does not construe the community's correspondence to Christ as service in terms of a literal imitation of Christ's earthly deeds and consistently maintains the distinction between the revelation of God and the historical medium through which this revelation comes to us (preeminently seen in the union and distinction of the Word and flesh of Christ), Barth's upholding of the service of Christ in his earthly ministry as the pattern for the church's own service points to a normative status of Christ's historical life. Jesus Christ in his human action provides the pattern for the church's own historical action, and his humanity (i.e., his human and historical life) is therefore not seen in purely formal terms. Even though the primary manner of conceiving the pattern for the church's service is the divine condescension of the incarnation, this does not eliminate a normative place for the service rendered in Christ's earthly human life. The person of Jesus Christ is the revelation of both true God and true humanity (as he is both the electing God and the elected human person). For this reason, Barth can write that the community 'can be faithful to Him only in exact and honest and sober correspondence to His coming in the flesh' (*CD IV.3.2*, 725).[22] Therefore, as Jesus Christ did not come to be served but to serve, so also the church is to serve, and church law is thus a law of service, a law where privileges and duties are not distinct but identical (*CD IV.2*, 690-691).

Barth states that this determination of the community to service is 'unequivocal, non-dialectical and irreversible' (*CD IV.2*, 691). What Barth means by this is that this law of service is not dialectically related to a counter and coordinate position, an 'accompanying law of rule.' A dialectical understanding of the church's service would see the humble service of the community as balanced by a dignified law of rule with accompanying privileges and honors. This may be the case for human societies, Barth avers, but for the community of God, its law is singularly and solely that of service, a service not dialectically related to a complementary law of lordship. 'Unequivocally, and unconfused by any speculative end, the freedom of the community and each of the Christians assembled within it is the freedom to serve' (*CD IV.2*, 691). Christ's rule is therefore one aspect of his existence which is singularly unique and *without* correspondence in the Christian community.[23]

The law of service is not only undialectical and unequivocal, but it is also total, in that it marks and characterizes all of the activity of the church (i.e., there are no spheres of activity that do not fall under this rule of service, and thus church administration, for example, is just as truly defined by this law of service as is the ministry of the Word). Moreover, it is universal, in that every member of the community is commissioned and charged to undertake this service (i.e., there is no person who is exempt from this service, or who is committed to serve only in a limited role, and so there can be no stark division between clergy and laity). Every aspect of the church's activity and every member of the community thus falls within this law of service (*CD IV.2*, 692-695). Such shared service extends even to the theological task, and Barth stresses the interdependence of the members of the community for the interpretation of Scripture and thus for the task of theology itself. Barth can assert: 'The statement: "I am a mere layman and not a theologian," is evidence not of

---

[22]Barth writes: 'Sheer gratitude is called for in face of the astonishing fact that in correspondence with the coming of the Son of God in the flesh, in His discipleship, there may be a people like others which precisely as such is His people and may exist in His service' (*CD IV.3.2*, 725).

[23]The only exception to this seems to be Barth's very brief and highly qualified discussion of the church's participation in the kingly aspect of Christ's office (see *CD III.3*, 287-288).

humility but of indolence' (*CD IV.3.2*, 871; cf. 870-871; 882). Barth therefore has no patience for hierarchical systems of government or learning within the church, though he does have a place for differentiated functions (which he is reticent to designate as 'offices'). In sum, service defines every activity of the church, and service is the commission laid upon every member.

B. Church Law as Liturgical Law

The law of service that the church renders is liturgical law. As such, the church is defined and indeed constituted by its worship. Once again, Barth states that this is the case precisely because of the 'christologico-ecclesiological' nature of the community as the body of Christ. Christ is one who has lived a particular life, and thus who possesses a unique and particular history, the history of the one who traveled from Bethlehem to Golgotha and was raised to eternal life. Barth states that it is this history of Christ, the Head of the church, which is to be 'actively and recognisably reflected and represented in its [the community's] life.' And this occurs preeminently in the church's worship.[24]

Here the conceptions of history and correspondence meld together in a particular Christological and ecclesiological relationship. The history of Christ which defines his person is to be reflected in the history of the community. But this history of the community is itself grounded in an event, the event of worship whereby the community is constituted. The church is therefore an event before and logically prior to being an institution. It is, rather, 'an earthly-historical event, and as such it is the earthly-historical form of His [Christ's] existence' (*CD IV.2*, 696).

In the church's life there is then a correspondence to the history of Christ, and this is where worship becomes central. For even though the church is a community in the world among others, a historical society among other societies, it is nevertheless set apart from others in its relationship to Christ. This relationship is actualized in its worship, and thus in worship its correspondence to its Lord is made real, for it is precisely in worship that the community is made to correspond to the particular history and life of its Head, Jesus Christ.

Worship is the inner reality that enlivens the church's outer historical form and activity, just as the community exists as the inner reality of the world providing its meaning. Worship and the 'everyday life of Christians' are related as two concentric circles, the first being the inner circle which 'gives to the outer its content and character' (*CD IV.2*, 640). This complex thought is expressed by Barth in this way: As the total event 'community' stands out from the world within the world, so divine service stands out from the total event 'community' within this event. And it is only

---

[24]See *CD IV.2*, 695-696; also 638-639. It is in worship that the church 'becomes a concrete event at a specific time and place' (ibid., 639).

as the community has its distinct centre in its worship that it can and will stand out clearly from the world.   Such is necessary if in its history there is to be a representation of the particular history of its Head, an attestation of Jesus Christ (*CD IV.2*, 697).

This relationship between worship and the church's other activity is also predicated upon a Christological pattern. As the Word gives life to the humanity of Christ and stands as the center of his human activity, the center from which the periphery exists, so also is worship the active center which gives meaning and substance to the other daily activities of the church, the center from which this periphery exists. So as the Word is to the flesh of Christ, and as Christ is to the community, so also is worship to the other activity of the church. The everyday life of the church therefore corresponds to its central activity of worship, and it is as the church exists not only in general activity but specifically in worship that it corresponds to its Head, Jesus Christ.

Worship thus stands at the center of the church's active life. As Barth states: 'From this centre of its life there can and must and may and will be also true Christian being and action on the circumference, in the Christian everyday. From it there can and must and may and will be general law and order' (*CD IV.2*, 698). Notice again the geometrical imagery: the worship of the church is the center which provides the rest of its activity, the circumference (or periphery), with its inner reality, existence, and meaning.

> It [i.e., worship] is shown to be its centre because here — and in this way only here — the community exists and acts in direct correspondence to its basic law, in a particular and not merely a general historicity. In divine service it becomes and is itself a witness to its own being, to its determination in the world, to the factuality of its existence. And in divine service it exists and acts prophetically in relation to the world to the extent that in divine service — and here alone directly — there is a serious discharge of its commission to be a provisional representation of humanity as it is sanctified in Jesus Christ (*CD IV.2*, 698).

Worship is thereby united with all other activity but is at the same time distinct from it: 'In divine service there takes place that which does not take place anywhere else in the community' (*CD IV.2*, 697). It is in worship that the church is constituted, the event that gives it existence and meaning, the event both in which it corresponds to and is joined with its Lord and in which it is also set apart from the world. It is in this event of worship that the invisible becomes visible, the community taking a concrete form (*CD IV.2*, 697-698). In terms of our previous chapter, it is in and for worship that the Spirit calls the community into existence, the place where the invisible event becomes a visible society.

All law of the church has its source in divine worship, for it is in its worship that the community is established as Christ becomes present through the Spirit where 'two or three are gathered together' in his name. Christ is himself the source and basis of the church's order and law. Christ, as he is attested in Scripture and thus made present in the worship of the Christian community, is the one who determines what is 'lawful and right in the church.' The law of the community is the law of Christ, and Christ himself is the law of the community. The worship of the community is the source of the law of the community precisely because in the divine service the Lord of the community is present and active through Scripture (*CD IV.2*, 706).

So even though Christians remain sinners, the presence of Christ in the midst of the community provides the basis for the command of Christ and the corresponding obedience of the community so that his law is established. This law takes the form of the community's public confession in response to the Word of God, mutual recognition of one another as brothers and sisters in baptism, preservation and strengthening in the Lord's Supper, and corporate prayer with and for one another (*CD IV.2*, 698-706; cf. 707-709). In each of these activities, the Christian community reflects and mirrors the life of its Lord.[25] The community is therefore constituted in its worship and in the specific acts that compose that worship: confession, baptism, the Lord's Supper, and prayer.[26]

In the end, however, the dialectical relation between Christ and community remains, for the practices of the community are performed by sinful persons, and therefore they are never in perfect correspondence to the Lord of the community. Barth stresses that this recognition of sin and imperfection should not lead to indifference, however. Church law is the commitment to reform and order the church's liturgy. This liturgy is neither unimportant nor inerrant. It is, rather, to reflect Christ and to fulfill the church's proper task and role. Here again Barth's position understands the activity of the church to be simultaneously relativized and dignified. The liturgy of the church is not inerrant or perfect, but neither is it to be seen as a matter of indifference and therefore neglected. It has its proper role when seen in its proper place, and that is in correspondence to Christ (*CD IV.2*, 709-710). Once again it is the conception of correspondence that forbids both an identification of revelation and church law, as well as an indifference to church law which evaluates it as insignificant at best or inherently sinful at worst.

---

[25]So Barth can write: 'It is to be noted how the event of His own life is reflected and repeated in the event of the Supper (as in that of confession and baptism)' (*CD IV.2*, 703).

[26]Barth succinctly notes: 'The community is constituted as it prays' (*CD IV.2*, 705).

C. Church Law as Living Law

Church law is a law of service, and it is liturgical law. It is also living law, for it arises from a living Lord. Christ is present in the community by the power of the Holy Spirit and through the medium of Scripture, and as such he 'rules and upholds and orders' the community (*CD IV.2*, 710). The law of the community, as the law received from a living Lord, must therefore be 'living and dynamic.' It is neither established by nor patterned upon law in the secular realm, but has its own unique character and form as it is established by the Holy Spirit. So Barth insists (in what must be judged an overstatement): 'No dynamic from below can or should have any influence on Church law.' It is established, rather, from above. To say this is to say that it should be Christologically determined (*CD IV.2*, 710-711).

Here again Barth presents his own position over against two false alternatives. The first is a failure or refusal to outline specific proposals and formulations of church law in an emphasis upon the living and dynamic nature of church law. Against such a position, Barth argues: 'The recognition that canon law can arise and continue only as living law must not deprive it of the courage and pleasure of finding specific answers to its investigation of this law' (*CD IV.2*, 711). While the dynamic character of church law must be respected, the answers that are given must be specific and definite, including the formulation of legal propositions. Church law should be specific enough to provide for particular and concrete commands and prohibitions, as well as delineating matters left to personal judgment. The dynamic nature of church law should never lead one to ignore this concrete task: 'Living law does not mean law which is formless, which is unexpressed, which exists only in instincts and emotions, which finds utterance in uncontrollable inspirations and intuitions, which escapes juridical statement and codification' (*CD IV.2*, 712).

Such vagueness of form and deliberate denigration of the task of producing definite law is a sign of an ecclesiological docetism. Barth refuses to separate the living source of law from its concrete manifestation in individual, definite, and specific juridical pronouncements, and he sees the formulation of such pronouncements as the church's proper obedience of service. 'Everything else that we have to say about the living quality of Church law is based on the seriousness of the concrete venture in which it has to be sought and established and practiced. Apart from this, it can be regarded only as unprofitable Liberalism' (*CD IV.2*, 712-713). Once again, Barth sets his position over against an opponent on the left which he explicitly identifies as liberalism.

But there is another false alternative on the right. If the dynamic character of church law does not preclude its concrete formulation in specific pronouncements (as its living source is united to a concrete visible manifestation), neither does it entail that such concrete formulations can be confused with the living source that gives rise to them, so that they are identified with revelation itself and thus seen as unalterable.

Such a position betrays an ebionitic, or perhaps even more specifically, a Eutychian, ecclesiology.

In this opponent on the right, which Barth does not specifically identify, but which is undoubtedly Roman Catholicism, Barth opposes an objectivism that would identify revelation and concrete church law, giving the latter an unbending and irreformable character. Barth strongly rejects such a position, emphasizing that church law 'can only be human law and not divine' (*CD IV.2*, 713). That is, it is to be seen as a human response of obedience to its living Lord, but it is not to be absolutized as unchangeable or confused with divine revelation itself. It must, rather, be always open to reform and improvement: 'Hence the community will refuse to regard as necessary to salvation, or to invest with divine authority, the work of its obedience, and therefore the ecclesiastical propositions which it discovered and enforced yesterday' (*CD IV.2*, 715).

This distinction between divinity and humanity with particular regard to the question of church law is safeguarded in the church, Barth maintains, precisely by the source of the law itself, namely, the distinction between Christ the Head and his earthly body, the church. Barth's Christological thought works itself out here on a number of levels. First, church law is neither to be vague and abstract, according to a docetic ecclesiology, nor is it to be seen as divine and irreformable, according to an ebionitic, or a Eutychian, ecclesiology. Rather, church law is to take a concrete form, yet it is never to be absolutized, so that the form becomes confused with the source of law in divine revelation. This distinction and dialectical relationship is rooted in the dialectical relationship between Christ and the community itself, and thus mirrors this relationship. As Barth states: 'In Church law, however, this danger [i.e., the danger of the absolutation and divinisation of the law] is averted by the very root and essence of this law, by the basic law of the community, by the lordship of Jesus Christ over His body' (*CD IV.2*, 713).[27]

What this position demonstrates is twofold. First, Barth's ecclesiological thought is dialectical at various levels, whether pertaining to the general question of the nature of the church itself, or in the particular questions such as an understanding

---

[27]Barth earlier formulated the dialectical distinction that safeguards against such an objectivism not in terms of the relation between Christ and the community, but between Scripture and every ecclesiastical formulation of law (though these are of course related, for Scripture mediates the presence of Christ to the community): 'Scripture as the proper organ of Church government will not destroy the immediacy of the relation between the Church and its Lord, and will not impose on the Church the rule of law, so long as the distinction between Scripture itself and all human conceptions of it is maintained and continually made, so long as by constant attention to Scripture, in the unbroken discipline of its reading and exegesis, we allow it to take continual precedence of all human theories in order to follow it faithfully, so long as its government and its being allowed to govern are really taken seriously in the Church' (*CD I.2*, 694).

of church law. Second, this dialectic is predicated upon and analogous to the paradigmatic dialectical relationship between the Word and flesh of Christ, and between his divine and human natures. Every ecclesiological dialectical relation is therefore patterned upon the unique and definitive Christological one, and Barth portrays mistaken positions in ecclesiology as reflections of, and in terms of, Christological heresies.

In sum, for Barth church law is both concrete and reformable, both necessary and qualified. It must be obeyed, but not with an absolute obedience, for Christ alone merits such obedience. For this reason, church law (like church dogma!) must be dynamic in that it is open to further reform in light of a better understanding of the mind of Christ. The attitude of the church faced with the task of formulating both its doctrine and its law is therefore one of obedient humility, always open to further instruction from the Word of God. The past formulations of church law (like past formulations of dogma) are therefore to be respectfully consulted and considered (for they are *real* authorities), but at the same time, they are to be reformed and even in some cases abandoned if need be in the light of a better understanding of Scripture through the Holy Spirit (for they are *relative* authorities).[28] The church is therefore both bound and free in relation to the past. For this reason, prior formulations of church law should be obeyed unless a new obedience is rendered necessary in light of further direction from the Holy Spirit. In this way, church law is neither ignored as a matter of indifference, nor absolutized as inerrant. Church law is neither peripheral nor sterile, the latter being the danger of all secular law:

> As it takes this courage for living law, it will be protected against fatal indifference and negligence in respect of the question of order and therefore against disorder. But it will also be protected against the fatal overestimation of any particular answer to this question; against petrifaction in a particular tradition and against the legalism of sacrosanct institutions (*CD IV.2*, 716).

Barth therefore sets his dialectical understanding of church law against what he believes are mistaken positions on the left and the right, mistaken precisely because

---

[28]Barth's dialectical understanding of church law thus parallels and corresponds to his own dialectical understanding of church dogma. Both are seen as *relative* (rather than *absolute*) authorities, the latter qualifier belonging to Christ's authority (and secondarily to that of Scripture) alone. Church dogma and church law are therefore seen as necessary yet relative, authoritative yet reformable, both the response of human obedience to divine revelation. For Barth's understanding of the church's relative authority in relation to its dogmas, doctrines, and confessions, see *CD I.2*, 585-660.

they sacrifice the dialectical relationship of church law to one side or the other (*CD IV.2*, 713-719).

D. Church Law as Exemplary Law

For Barth church law is unique, derived from its Lord as its sole source and as he is met in the community's public worship. As such, church law is neither based nor dependent upon secular law. Nevertheless, Barth argues that church law does not exist simply for its own sake and solely for the community's benefit. Church law is, rather, paradigmatic 'for the formation and administration of human law generally, and therefore of the law of other political, economic, cultural and other human societies' (*CD IV.2*, 719).

The law of the Christian community thus fulfills a two-sided responsibility. First and foremost, it is responsible to the Lord of the community and as such serves to regulate the church's own life and activity. Yet in a secondary though necessary sense, it is also responsible to the world, for the mission and task of the Christian community itself is to serve as a provisional representation of the final goal of reconciliation which has already been accomplished not only *de iure* but *de facto* in Jesus Christ, a representation of humanity justified and sanctified in Christ (*CD IV.2*, 620-621). Barth designates this provisional representation as the 'upbuilding of the Christian community' (*CD IV.2*, 626).[29] The task of the community is therefore one of service first to Christ and then to the world, and its law therefore serves not only to maintain and define its own identity, but also as a pattern for law in other human societies. As such, it is exemplary law (*CD IV.2*, 719-720).

Again, Barth's position is a dialectical one. On the one hand, church law cannot be directly applied to other human societies so that it is made the law of the state. Church law itself is not the law of the kingdom of God, but only a reflection of it. For the world to completely adopt the law of the church would entail that it recognize the Lordship of Christ, and therefore it would not remain the world but would itself become church: 'Directly to take over the law of the community even at a single point the world would have to abandon its own assumptions and become the community' (*CD IV.2*, 721).

---

[29]Barth speaks of architectural imagery when he speaks of the church in the imagery of building, but he can also draws upon organic imagery when he speaks of the growth of the community (see *CD IV.2*, 644). Both types of imagery are, of course, found within the New Testament. In regard to the upbuilding of the community itself, Barth contends that 'as its upbuilding is wholly and utterly the work of God or Christ, so it is wholly and utterly its own work' (ibid., 634). The work of upbuilding the community is therefore the unity of divine and human work, though these are distinct so that the second exists only in dependence upon the first.

Yet on the other hand, church law does have a true paradigmatic and archetypical function for the world, in that it is a necessary aspect of the church's witness of the Gospel presented to the world in the form of particular law. It is this witness of an exemplary form of law that is the greatest contribution the community can make to the 'upbuilding and work and maintenance' of the civil community, according to Barth. Church law may therefore be reflected and mirrored by the law of the secular community, for as the community's law reflects the rule of the kingdom of God, yet is not equated with it, so also the world may reflect in its form and order the law of the community, though it also is not equated with the community nor is its law directly the law of the church. Therefore, church law is in a sense united to secular law, in that the latter is to correspond to the former, and yet in another sense they are not to be confused. The church is a human society among others, but it is an exemplary society serving as a witness to others. Church law is in one respect provisional and imperfect, not the law of the kingdom itself but a reflection of it, and yet in another respect it is better and superior to the law of the world, and therefore paradigmatic for secular law, though its advantage over civil law is relative, not absolute. Moreover, because Christ is Lord of the world, and not only of the Christian community, the community itself should not be surprised to find 'corresponding effects' ['*Auswirkungen und Entsprechungen*'] even outside the walls of the church, i.e., in the world and its law (*CD IV.2*, 720-723).

So, while the world and its laws are evil, they are not totally evil, Barth contends. The Lordship of Christ over the world entails that we should not be surprised to find 'analogies or correspondences' to ecclesiastical law even in the law of the world (*CD IV.2*, 724-725).[30] Both are human and temporal law, and therefore they are not entirely unrelated. Both church law and civil law find their ultimate basis in Christ, though the former lives in correspondence to Christ, whereas the latter lives in rebellion to Christ and reflects his lordship only unknowingly, partially, and in a fragmented sense. Yet, it may even be the case that at certain points the Christian community can learn from the witness of the civil one. Though this may at times occur, the normative relation between the law of the church and the law of the civil community will be that of the witness of the former to the latter, though church law will serve not as the exemplification of a perfect law, but as a corrective to the law which the civil community already possesses (*CD IV.2*, 724-726).

---

[30]Barth writes: 'It is not the case, then, that the relatively higher and better and to that extent exemplary law of the Church is indispensable or always and everywhere new and strange to the world and its law. If it were the case that ecclesiastical and temporal law confronted one another in absolute antithesis and mutual exclusion, the witness which the former has to bear to the latter would be impossible and pointless' (*CD IV.2*, 724). One wonders how this statement mitigates or qualifies Barth's harsh 'No!' to Emil Brunner in 1933 and his condemnation of a 'point of contact.'

In his discussion of the exemplary nature of church law one senses that Barth's focus has slightly shifted from considering the community in the light of Christ, to considering the world, or state, in the light of the community. This relation, between the community and the world, will be the topic of our next chapter. In this and the previous chapter, the emphasis has been upon the community as the second term in a dialectical relationship, either that between the Spirit and the community defining the church's nature, or between Christ and the community defining the church's form and order. In these chapters, the emphasis has focused upon the dependence of the community upon Christ and the Spirit and its correspondence to Christ, with particular attention placed upon the questions of the church's nature, form, order, and law. In the next chapter, the emphasis will be upon the community's relationship to the world, and the world's (and the state's) correspondence to the community and its law in light of the community's correspondence to Christ. The formal patterns will remain the same, however, for the terms in the relationship are defined according to their unity and differentiation in an asymmetrical relationship, as it is the first term in the relation that provides the basis and meaning for the second, whereas the second exists in correspondence to the first. Just as Christ serves as the inner reality of the community, which corresponds to Christ, so also the community (as joined to Christ) serves as the inner reality of the world, which corresponds to the community. It is the similarity of these patterns of relation, like a pattern of concentric circles, that provides the striking coherence and systematic beauty of Barth's ecclesiological thought.

6. Summary

In this chapter we have examined the relationship between Christ and the community in Barth's thought, a relationship that is marked by unity and differentiation, irreversibility, and correspondence. The relationship between Christ and the church is therefore ruled by the logic of the Word made flesh. Barth speaks of this ecclesiological analogy to the incarnation in terms of the church as the body of Christ, his 'earthly-historical form of existence.'

Barth's conception of the church as the body of Christ is the central image and conception ruling Barth's ecclesiology. Barth's systematic development and construal of this image and theme expresses the beauty, power, and coherence of Barth's doctrine of the church, as well as both its striking originality and its Biblical and traditional mooring. Barth's formulation of the community as the body of Christ does present some difficulties, however, of which we will mention three.

First, Barth's refusal to consider this image to be a metaphor and his strict literal interpretation of it raises the question of whether he has adequately protected against viewing the church as a second incarnation. If there is only 'one Christ, and therefore there is only one body of Christ' in its heavenly and earthly forms, then it becomes difficult to see how Barth can consistently maintain that the church is not a second incarnation, or perhaps more accurately, an extension of the incarnation. Though Barth strongly and consistently asserts that this is not the case, his statement that the church is the body of Christ in the same manner as is Christ's physical body, coupled with his insistence that there is in fact only one body, not two, can admittedly lead to this criticism.[31] This is further complicated by Barth's description of the 'earthly-historical life of the Church and the children of God' as an 'annexe [*Annex*] to the human nature of Jesus Christ.'[32] Nevertheless, it must be said that Barth takes great pains to distinguish Christ and the church even while speaking of the unity of the one body of Christ in its heavenly and earthly forms.

A second and more serious issue arises from Barth's conviction that Christ has assumed general human nature *en toto*, rather than a particular human nature, in the incarnation, so that his humanity is inclusive of the human nature of all persons.[33] Though such an understanding of the incarnation does have theological precedent, Barth's unique conception of this position presents a dilemma for ecclesiology and soteriology.

While Barth in the vast majority of cases equates the 'body of Christ' with the Christian community comprising those joined together by the Spirit's call, he can on at least one occasion also speak of the 'body of Christ' as referring not only to the community but to humanity as a whole, so that the body of Christ includes not only the members of the community but all persons (even though Barth realizes that the New Testament never refers to the body of Christ in such an inclusive sense).[34] This position would seem to find its basis in Barth's conviction that Christ has joined himself to human nature in a general sense so that all persons are thus 'in Christ' by participating in human nature *in esse*. Barth asserts: 'If it [the community] has a right understanding of itself...then as the body of Christ it has to understand itself as a promise of the emergence of the unity in which not only Christians but all men are already comprehended in Jesus Christ' (*CD IV.1*, 665).

---

[31]See especially *CD IV.2*, 59-60; *CD IV.1*, 662-667, esp. 666; also *CD I.2*, 215. O'Grady has criticized Barth on this very point — see *The Church in Catholic Theology*, 74-78.

[32]See *CD I.2*, 348; cf. 576. Barth does, however, provide a distinction between the two forms of Christ's body by means of the medieval distinction between a *gratia adoptionis* and a *gratia unionis*, the former describing the relationship between Christ and the church, the latter the incarnation itself. See *CD II.1*, 485-486.

[33]Barth can write: 'As we have seen already, the human nature elected by Him and assumed into unity with His existence is implicitly that of all men. In His being as man God has implicitly assumed the human being of all men. In Him not only we all as *homines*, but our *humanitas* as such — for it is both His and ours — exist in and with God Himself' (*CD IV.2*, 59).

[34]See *CD IV.1*, 662-668. 'The New Testament never expressly uses the term body of humanity as a whole....It uses it only of the Christian community' (ibid., 665). See also *CD IV.3.1*, 278.

Moreover, Barth expressly asserts that this is so *not* because of the dynamic work of the Spirit, but because of an eternal decision of election in which all persons are comprehended in Christ. It is this eternal election of all in Christ, not the Spirit of Pentecost, that creates the body of Christ (*CD IV.1*, 667). Barth writes:

> There can be no doubt that the work of the Holy Spirit is merely to 'realise subjectively' the election of Jesus Christ and His work as done and proclaimed in time, to reveal and bring it to men and women. By the work of the Holy Spirit the body of Christ, as it is by God's decree from all eternity and as it has become in virtue of His act in time, acquires in all its hiddenness historical dimensions (*CD IV.1*, 667).

Here we must frankly ask whether the dynamic and actualistic understanding of God's being and activity in salvation that Barth so consistently maintains is in danger of giving way to a static and pretemporal conception of election that compromises the divine freedom, a static conception that Barth perceived in Calvin and now ironically seems in danger of espousing himself, though in a universalistic, rather than a dualistic, sense. At this point one might wonder if Barth has not slipped from a Christocentric interpretation into a Christomonistic one, one that threatens to overshadow the role of the Holy Spirit by making the election of Christ an eternal pretemporal decision that, if it does not preclude the work of the Spirit entirely, limits the Spirit to a 'merely' [*'nur'*] revelatory function of a timeless reality in which all persons are eternally elect in Christ. Such a view can lead to a static and metaphysical conception of salvation rather than a dynamic and Biblical one where the body of Christ is composed of those who believe and confess by the Spirit, not of all persons by way of a general ontological reality.

Barth is certainly justified in guarding against an exclusive ecclesiastical triumphalism that happily condemns the world and restricts salvation to the church, but the question might be raised as to whether he has protected against this by losing the community into the world, here coming precariously close to replacing theology with a general metaphysics. For should Barth equate the body of Christ with the world in such a way that the distinction between the church and the world becomes negligible, then Barth would in fact fuse the Logos with the world in a manner that would seem to be more Stoic and Hegelian than Christian. If this were the case, the particularity of the incarnation in Christ would be lost, and the relation between Christ, the church, and the world would become not one of correspondence between distinct realities, but one of ultimate identity.

The possibility for such a position is raised by the problematic discussion of the σῶμα Χριστοῦ in *CD IV.1*, where the body of Christ as Christ's historical life and the body of Christ as the church are not sufficiently distinguished (*CD IV.1*, 662-668). There the distinction between the church as the body of Christ and the world as the body of Christ is also placed in question, so that Barth's dialectical structure of indirect identity is in danger of giving way to an undialectical identity. This problem is exacerbated when Barth states that the community is not made Christ's body through the work of the Spirit at Pentecost but in an eternal election in which all are included in Christ (*CD IV.1*, 666-667). This seems to make the work of the Spirit purely noetic and the subjective aspect of salvation purely cognitive, and the difference between the Christian and the non-Christian solely one of knowledge.[35]

Barth's conception of the church as the body of Christ is brilliant in nearly every respect, and one should perhaps not make too much of a single problematic passage. For the most part, Barth deftly parries such criticisms with a highly dialectical notion of the relation between Christ and the church as his body. Nevertheless, it is undeniable that in his discussion of the σῶμα Χριστοῦ in *CD IV.1* his position appears more metaphysical than theological, more ontological than dialectical. Christ seems to be more of a cosmic principle than a real person, and Barth's conception of Christ as the inner reality joined to a universal humanity is more reminiscent of a Platonic or Stoic 'world soul' type of incarnation than the particular incarnation and the distinct dynamic reality of the church as the body of Christ in the New Testament, where individual members are joined to Christ's body by faith through the Spirit, not through participation in human nature as eternally assumed by the Logos.

Finally, Barth's conception of the church as the body of Christ not only overshadows but at times seems nearly to exclude other images for conceiving the church, even other Biblical images.[36] This is a parallel and accompanying difficulty to Barth's overshadowing of the third article with the second, the sign of an underdeveloped, if not neglected, pneumatology. One might argue that such concerns may well have been addressed had Barth completed volume five of the *Church Dogmatics*. Yet such an argument from silence should not be used to stifle legitimate questions based upon Barth's extent ecclesiology.

---

[35]For example, Barth writes: 'For by Christ we will never be anything else than just what we are in Christ. And when the Holy Spirit draws and takes us right into the reality of revelation by doing what we cannot do, by opening our eyes and ears and hearts, He does not tell us anything except that we are in Christ by Christ' (*CD I.2*, 240). See also *CD IV.2*, 327-330; 651; *CD IV.3.1*, 192-193; for a different emphasis, cf. 339-340; *CD IV.3.2*, 493-494; *CD IV.1*, 118-120; also *CD III.4*, 577-588. For a sympathetic yet critical treatment of Barth's soteriology that addresses the above concerns, see Colin Gunton, 'Salvation,' in *Cambridge Companion to Karl Barth*, 143-158.

[36]See Migliore, '*Vinculum Pacis*,' 19-20. For the inherent weaknesses of ecclesiologies that focus upon a single image of the church, see Nicholas M. Healy, *Church, World and the Christian Life: Practical–Prophetic Ecclesiology* (Cambridge: Cambridge University Press, 2000), 25-51.

Chapter Eight

The Ordination of the Church as the People of God in the World

1. Introduction — The Community of God in World-Occurrence

As the Christian community embodies a specific nature and essence, and as it exists with a definite order and form, so it is entrusted with a concrete mission and task. We have examined Barth's understanding of the nature of the community in the light of the relationship between the Spirit and the church, as well as the form and order of the community in view of the relationship between Christ and the church. But as the church is the fellowship of the Spirit, and as it is the body of Jesus Christ, so also it is 'the people of God in world-occurrence' (*CD IV.3.2*, 681; passim.). Its existence as a visible community in the world is dependent upon God's call and election, and it is charged by God with a specific task (*CD IV.3.2*, 727-728). To speak of the ordination of the church is thus to speak both of its basis in God's eternal election and of its divine commission for ministry to the world, for in Barth's thought these are inseparable.

The final aspect of Barth's doctrine of the church to be considered is therefore that of the church's mission, or vocation. In Barth's understanding, the vocation of the church is complemented by the vocation of the individual Christian: both the community and the Christian are commissioned and sent to bear witness to God's reconciliation of the world in Jesus Christ (*CD IV.3.2*, 681-683). This final aspect of the church is also marked by a concrete relationship that is shaped by a Christological logic, and this is the relationship between the church and the world.

This relationship, however, is both similar and different from the previous two examined, those of the Spirit and the church and Christ and the church. It is similar to the others in that it is also governed by the Christological logic of unity and differentiation, asymmetry, and correspondence that governs the others. It is different in a very important respect, however, for whereas in the first two relationships the church is placed as the second term of the relation, and thus in complete dependence upon the Spirit and Christ, in this third relationship the church takes the place of the first term of the relation, and the logical ordering of the relation is therefore analogical to the first two yet not as strictly ordered, for it allows for a reciprocal influence between the church and the world.

This statement entails the controversial claim that the world exists as the context for the church, the church providing its inner ground of existence and meaning. It must be immediately added that, for Barth, the church has this significance only because it is joined to Christ, who is the absolute and sovereign ground of both the church and the world, and who serves as the center (as well as the periphery) of both (*CD IV.3.1*, 122-123).[1] The church does not accomplish this role apart and in abstraction from Christ. The church joined to Christ as his body is therefore the inner center of a circle of which the periphery is the world, but it is the center only because Christ is the center of both the world and the church itself and is himself present in the periphery. Once again we are presented with the image of concentric circles, with Christ as the center, the community as the next circle surrounding this center circle, and the world as the final circle surrounding that of the community.[2] As Christ is the center of the community, providing its existence and meaning, so the community joined with Christ serves as the center of the world, providing its own basis and meaning, though not negating the wider world's own unique place in God's providential design. With reference to the community and its relation to the world Barth can therefore state:

> There co-exists with it as this people [i.e., the people of God in world-occurrence], and *vice versa*, the whole cosmos both in its wider sense as the cosmos of all the reality distinct from God and created and ruled by Him, and also in its narrower and concrete sense as the cosmos of men and humanity. Its history as it takes place is surrounded by the history of the cosmos, and everywhere affected and in part determined by it. Conversely, it is not without significance for the cosmos and its history that its own history takes place (*CD IV.3.2*, 684).

As this quotation makes clear, for Barth the relationship between the community and the world is not ordered as strictly as that between Christ and the church.

---

[1]While Christ is described most often as the center, Barth can also describe Christ as 'the centre and therefore the whole of the periphery' (see *CD IV.3.1*, 123).

[2]In speaking of the relation between the church and the state, and therefore of a specific relation between the church and the world, Barth writes that the 'civil community shares both a common origin and common centre with the Christian community,' and this center is Jesus Christ (Barth, 'The Christian Community and the Civil Community,' in Barth, *Community, State, and Church* [Gloucester: Peter Smith, 1968], 156; 159 — hereafter, 'Christian Community'). The Christian community is therefore the 'inner circle' and the civil community the 'wider circle' or 'outer circle,' the center of both being Christ (see ibid., 157-159). All members of the inner circle are thus necessarily members of the outer circle, though the reverse is of course not the case.

Whereas this latter relationship is consistently ordered so that there can be no confusion between Christ and the church, the relationship between them being strictly irreversible so that influence flows only in one direction, the relationship between the church and the world, though ordered along a similar pattern, is that between two creaturely realities. This reality allows for a mutual and reciprocal relation of influence between church and world, though the Christian community is the norm for the corresponding action of the world, and therefore an asymmetrical relation does exist.[3] Nevertheless, the church does not exist in a position of lordship over the world but exists for the world in service, and therefore one can say that the church exists for service to the world even as the world exists as the context for the church's own life and history.

For Barth, then, the church as the body of Christ provides the inner meaning, basis, and pattern of the world's existence and correspondence, so that the community and the world are united and yet distinct, the world corresponding to the community in an ordered relation. Yet as we have noted, the distinction between the church and the world for Barth is not as sharply drawn as that between Christ and the church, nor is the order of the relation strictly irreversible. In other words, the distinction between church and world is at times unclear in Barth's thought, and the demarcation between the church and the world, as that between the Christian and the non-Christian, quite fuzzy with borders overlapping.[4] Furthermore, the influence of the world on the church at times can overshadow the influence of the church upon the world. Nevertheless, for Barth, the community's history is clearly normative and ontologically prior to that of the world, the community's history being the key to the

---

[3]This is clearly evidenced in Barth's discussion of the exemplary character of the church and its law, as examined below.

[4]See, for example, *CD IV.3.2*, 809-812. This relation between Christ and culture, and that between church and world, has been explored along lines very similar to the present study by Paul Louis Metzger, *The Word of Christ and the World of Culture: Sacred and Secular through the Theology of Karl Barth* (Grand Rapids: Eerdmans, 2003). Metzger very insightfully delineates the Christological logic that governs the relation between Christ and the world in Barth's theology, but the aspect of 'correspondence' in Barth's thought is often overlooked. Metzger rightly states: 'Barth is not a *political theologian*, imposing on theology and religion a political agenda. But he does engage in the *theologizing of politics* in the light of his Christological focus, providing the basis for *diastasis* and *synthesis*, that is, constructive critique and critical construction' (ibid, 170). Yet what must be added to this is that for Barth such critique and construction is predicated upon the correspondence of the state's law to the law of the church. Church law is *exemplary* law. Such comments should not detract from Metzger's fine study.

world's history, a history the world cannot truly understand apart from the witness of the community.[5]

This claim itself may seem not only odd but mistaken. Yet it becomes evident when one considers Barth's understanding of the covenant as the inner basis of creation.[6] For as creation exists only by and as the context for the covenant, so also general history exists, as we have seen, only on the basis and as the context for the particular history of Jesus Christ. And as Jesus Christ's own history includes within it the history of the community, this entails that the history of the world exists so that this particular history of Christ and his community may exist, even as the community of Christ also exists only in service to the world and as the environment of Christ himself. It is the community and its history (as it arises from Christ's own history) that provides the key to understanding the world and in fact gives the world its meaning. The history of the world exists as the external basis of the history of Christ, and as Christ is joined to the community, the world exists as the external basis of Christ with his community, the 'living community of the living Lord Jesus Christ' (*CD IV.3.2*, 681). This is the case, however, only because the world itself exists solely on the basis of Christ and has its own place in God's design. So while the history of the world does impact the history of the community, the direction of influence is primarily and normatively from the community to the world: 'In theory, and above all in practice, we have to confess that Church history does actually have priority over all other history, that with all its insignificance and folly and confusion in history generally, it is still the central and decisive history to which all the rest is as it were only the background or accompaniment' (*CD III.3*, 207).

Once again we see that Barth refuses any type of abstract discussion of the world or of history itself, that is, any standpoint that considers general history and the world as abstracted from and independent of the history of Christ and his community. Eschewing such a view, Barth writes:

> Our only option is truly to see and understand world-occurrence as the environment of the people of God and its history, recognising that it cannot be understood or interpreted in terms of itself but only of the community, or more strictly of its vocation, or more strictly still of the Lord who calls it and of the prophetic witness which He has entrusted to it, but recognising also that when it is understood in this way it is seen for what it really is, in its truth and actuality (*CD IV.3.2*, 685).

---

[5] For the relationship between the history of the community and general world history, see *CD III.3*, 204-210, as well as chapter five above.

[6] See *CD III.1*.

The community is therefore the place where the true nature of the world is revealed to the world itself. Barth asserts:

> The world does not know itself. It does not know God, nor man, nor the relationship and covenant between God and man. Hence it does not know its own origin, state nor goal....The community of Jesus Christ exists for and is sent into the world in the first basic sense that it is given to it, in its knowledge of God and man and the covenant set up between them, to know the world as it is. We may well say that, itself belonging also to the world, it is the point in the world where its eyes are opened to itself and an end is put to its ignorance about itself (*CD IV.3.2*, 769).[7]

We might say that for Barth the world's knowledge of itself is *abstract* knowledge, in that it knows itself in a manner abstracted from its real relation to God and Christ. The community exists to know this relation and to reveal it to the world so that the world might know itself as the community knows it, i.e., in relation to Christ. To proclaim this relation between God and the world established by God in Christ is the church's ordained mission.

2. The World in the Light of Christ and the Community

We have spoken earlier of the analogical relation between the incarnation and the community. That is, as the Word is to the flesh of Christ, so also, in analogy, is Christ to the community. The first relation describes his heavenly body, in Barth's terms, while the latter describes Christ's 'earthly-historical form of existence' as present in the church. What we must now also say is that as Christ is to the community, so also by analogy is the community to the world, or, more accurately still, is Christ with the community to the world. For as Christ is the center of the community, which forms his periphery and circumference, so also is the community as joined to Christ the center of the world, which forms its periphery and circumference. The church therefore exists as the inner circle of the outer circle of world history, as Israel in the Old Testament existed as the inner circle of the outer circle of the history of the nations around it.[8]

---

[7]See *CD IV.3.2*, 769-773; also 801-812.

[8]For Barth's discussion of Israel in this regard, see *CD IV.3.2*, 688-693. Barth there comments: 'It seems as though world history is ordained always to be the framework for the history of this people' (ibid., 690). Furthermore: 'It is indeed the case, and cannot be otherwise, that it is only in co-existence with the people of God, and not as the subject of independent or neutral interest, that the nations appear on the canvas of the Old Testament' (ibid., 691). Yet, the history of the nations is not without significance, but, as joined to Israel,

Certainly what must be stressed is that these are *analogical* relations, relations that bear similarity in great dissimilarity. The relation between Christ and the community is analogous to that of the Word and flesh in Christ, the church being Christ's earthly body. But the church is in no way a second incarnation, as Barth consistently maintains.[9] In a related (and analogous) manner, the relationship between the community and the world bears similarities in its formal logic to that between Christ and the community, but the world is certainly not a mirror image of the church, nor does it obediently correspond to Christ. We might summarize the similar though weakening patterns in each successive relation in the following manner: 1. Christ alone is the instantiation of perfect correspondence of a human life to God, and the relation of God and humanity in Christ, as the incarnate Word, is both unique and yet normative and paradigmatic for the other relations; 2. the church lives in obedient though imperfect correspondence to Christ — it is not a second incarnation but is marked by an imperfect though real, cognizant, and exemplary obedience and correspondence to Christ; and 3. the world lives in contradiction and disobedience to its Lord and at best displays only a broken, unknowing, and exceptional correspondence to Christ and to the community (though a correspondence does exist nonetheless, for the world too is under Christ's Lordship).[10]

What we have said thus far should prevent us from concluding that the history of the community and that of the world can be equated. Barth is adamant that they cannot be. Yet, because Christ stands at the center not only of the history of the community but also of the world, the world itself is not without a witness to Christ (*CD IV.3.2*, 686). So while the history of the world, marred by great disobedience, can never be equated with the history of the community, yet it too as a creation of God must fall under the Lordship of Christ and therefore within the sphere of his influence. For this reason, the world itself will bear witness to Christ, though in broken form, and will exist at points in broken though real correspondence to the Christian community itself. This relation between Christ and the world will always

---

is determined for the praise of God (ibid., 692). This relation between Israel and the nations is paralleled by the relation between the Christian community and the world.

[9]Though, as we have seen, his position is at points susceptible to the criticism that he has not adequately protected against identifying Christ's first and second forms of existence.

[10]Barth explores this relationship of correspondence between the truth of Christ and the truth found in the world under the themes of the greater and lesser lights and of 'parables of the kingdom' — see *CD IV.3.1*, esp. 38-165. We will explore the correspondence of the world to the community below, with specific regard to the question of the relation between the church and the state. In relation to Christ and speech that witnesses to him as the truth, Hunsinger states that Scripture is his 'direct witness,' the church his 'indirect witness,' and the world his 'unwitting witness' (Hunsinger, *How to Read Karl Barth*, 247). See also Metzger, *The Word of Christ and the Word of Culture*, 125ff..

be a dynamic, rather than a static, one. Therefore, one cannot presuppose or predict where such correspondence may be found, so that culture itself cannot be uniformly affirmed or condemned. With reference to the world's history, Barth can thus write:

> What takes place cannot be a wholly and absolutely different history. The community would be guilty of a lack of faith and discernment if it were seriously to see and understand world history as secular or profane history. In so doing it would in fact concede to this history the right to see and understand itself as such, and therefore as a history which is an independent and very different history in relation to the history of salvation and the Church. If it is not to bear some of the responsibility for its corruption, it cannot possibly allow it any such independence. The thought of God's royal lordship and fatherly providence overruling even world-occurrence must be the first and decisive step of all Christian thinking about world-occurrence.... (*CD IV.3.2*, 687-688).

The history of the world is therefore both distinct yet inseparable from the history of the community (*CD IV.3.2*, 687).

The history of the world bears a further similarity to Christ and the community: it cannot be truly known apart from faith. The analogy of ontology is thus mirrored by an analogy of epistemology. Just as the true identity of Christ as the incarnate Word must be discerned by faith and cannot be read off of the face of the historical Jesus; and as the mystery of the community also cannot be read off of the visible church in time but must be perceived by faith; so also the reality of the world in its true nature cannot be determined through a general investigation of history, but only by seeing world history in its relationship to the community and, more specifically still, in relation to Christ. This is to see the world itself by faith. In other words, the world, like Christ and the community, must be understood *theologically* (as opposed to purely historically or philosophically).

The world, like Christ and the church, must therefore be seen from two aspects. Just as Christ is understood abstractly when considered only as a human person, and thus apart from the Word; and as the church in time, the visible church, is viewed abstractly if considered apart from its inner invisible reality in the Spirit; so also the world is viewed abstractly if examined apart from Christ and the community. Barth speaks of this as seeing the world as '*hominum confusio*,' and speaks of the other aspect as seeing the world as under the '*Dei providentia*' (*CD IV.3.2*, 693-695). Seen from below, the world is marked by random events and confusion. Yet, seen in the light of God's providence, the world is under the rulership and lordship of God, who orders all things for his divine purpose. Once again, these realities are distinct yet united, but they are also ordered, in that God's providence rules over the chaos of the world.[11] God's providential care thus gives rise to the existence and reality of the world. An analogy exists between this invisible providence and visible chaos in the world and the invisible and visible realities of the church, though here again one must carefully and clearly state that this analogy bears witness to similarity in great dissimilarity, for while the visible life of the church knowingly though imperfectly corresponds in obedience to its invisible essence, the world's chaos disobediently opposes the will of God and only unknowingly and indirectly is subjugated under the providence of God to fulfill God's purposes. Here one can rightly speak of a contradiction, rather than a correspondence, between the world and God, yet this contradiction itself is forced in the end to serve God's sovereign plan.

World history must on this account be seen in 'two different ways,' Barth maintains, as both the confusion of humanity and the providence of God. The world exists in the ambiguity of being at once God's good creation, giving glory to God, yet at the same time a creation marked by evil, nothingness, and humanity's confusion and sin. Humanity's sin does not destroy the goodness of creation, but neither does it affirm it. It therefore exists as confusion, a confusion reflected in the world (*CD IV.3.2*, 694-696; 701). Therefore, 'nothingness is given that precedence over the good creation of God,' for the goodness of creation and nothingness are antithetical, yet humanity attempts to bring them into coordination. Here the dialectic of obedience and sin primarily pertaining to the community once again emerges and is applied in a secondary manner to the world at large, for Barth maintains that the world is not so good and perfect that it is free from evil and confusion, but that it is not so evil and depraved that God is seen to be completely absent from the world. Barth writes: 'What is world history? Even in its obvious and dreadful confusion, it is also the ongoing history of the good creation of God which cannot be destroyed by any confusion of man. It is also the history of the supply given to man in the cosmos around him, and of man's ability to recognise and use it as such' (*CD IV.3.2*, 696-698). The history of the world is therefore a history of both God's good creation and of humanity's confusion and sin, though God's sovereignty and grace assure that the first takes precedence and gains victory over the second.

Barth opposes, however, any attempt to achieve a Hegelian synthesis of these viewpoints, so that God's providence and humanity's confusion are seen as taken up into a higher synthesis. For Barth, the Christian community is not to present a

---

[11]Summarizing his discussion of divine providence and human confusion, Barth writes: 'We had to begin, as was only proper, by recalling the royal and fatherly world governance of God. Then in this bracket and under this presupposition we had to consider the great human confusion in which world history unfolds and displays itself. Both standpoints were and are theologically imperative and necessary.... World history takes place in this strange co-operation of God and man, which is so clear when seen from above, so obscure when seen from below' (*CD IV.3.2*, 701).

synthesis of these two views, but is simply to speak a name, Jesus Christ, a person, not a concept. Like in the *Göttingen Dogmatics* lectures on the church, Barth here puts forward not a Christian philosophy of history, but a history of redemption which is Jesus Christ's own history. The task of the community is neither to proclaim God's providence nor man's sin, but this new thing in Jesus Christ (*CD IV.3.2*, 703-709). 'The new thing which the people of God perceives in world-occurrence is the new, unique person Jesus Christ. It is the grace of God addressed to the world in Him.' Furthermore, it is 'as it looks at Him that His community in the world can see and understand world history in relation to Him.' Jesus Christ is therefore the reality for which world history truly takes place and also the basis by which the true identity of world history is known. The antithesis between God's providence and the world's chaos is therefore not removed but relativized in Christ (*CD IV.3.2*, 710-712). As Barth writes:

> This does not mean that the twofold aspect of world-occurrence — *hominum confusione et Dei providentia* — is dissolved or dispersed. It does not mean that Jesus Christ has merged into world-occurrence and world-occurrence into Him, so that we can no longer speak of them as separate things. This would be Christomonism in the bad sense of that unlovely term. What it does mean is that according to the true insight of the people of God the twofold form of world history loses the appearance of autonomy and finality, the character of an irreconcilable contradiction and antithesis, which it always seems to have at a first glance. The twofold view loses its sting. It acquires a good and natural sense, being indissoluble and indestructible simply because God and man are still different even in their unity in Jesus Christ (*CD IV.3.2*, 713).[12]

---

[12]It is precisely because of quotations like this one that the concept of 'correspondence' must greatly qualify the concept of 'coinherence' in understanding Barth's ecclesiology. For Barth, 'coinherence' is a Trinitarian concept pertaining to the inner life between the divine persons, and therefore has as such only a very limited and narrow application, though a real one, to ecclesial and ethical life for the church and the individual Christian. 'Correspondence,' however, is a Christologically-rooted term pertaining to the relation between God and humanity in Christ and by analogy to all divine and human relationships. Its range of application is thus richer and more broadly applicable. This observation does not ignore Barth's use of 'coinherence' as an ecclesial category, but it does highlight that such a notion should never be seen to negate the strong distinction Barth always draws between Christ and the church, as well as between God and the world and between the Creator and the creature. The relation of Christ and the church is not that of a mutual indwelling of one in the other by equal partners, but that of a Lord to a servant in which the former is the ground and source of the latter, and the latter lives in obedient correspondence to the former. The union is thus predicated upon the free decision of Christ, not the church.

This reality can only be seen by faith and not by sight, for by sight we see only the antithesis of God's providence and humanity's confusion. It will only be revealed to sight in the coming kingdom. For now, it is known only in faith and only by the community, not by the world at large. It is known only on account of the appearance of Christ, for it is Christ that reveals God's sovereign design in the midst of human confusion (*CD IV.3.2*, 714-715).

The reconciliation of the church with the world will also only take place with the final consummation of the kingdom of Christ, wherein the enmity of the world with God will be overcome and faith will be replaced by sight, though this kingdom already has been made present with the first coming of Christ, existing now as a hidden reality (*CD IV.3.2*, 715). The church thus views the world in the light of Jesus Christ, thereby viewing the world differently than the world views itself. The community, however, can only perceive the world in this way through the lens of Jesus Christ. Apart from Christ, the church can only see the world as marked by a wide gulf between God's providence that rules over the world and the human confusion that rules in it. Yet in the light of Christ, this imperfect perception is passing away, to be replaced by a more perfect sight (*CD IV.3.2*, 721). We might say that Christ provides the key not only for understanding the community but the world as well (*CD IV.3.2*, 714-715).[13]

By now it should be quite evident that Barth's understanding of the world itself is dialectically constituted. That is to say, there is not only a dialectical relation *between* the community and the world, but *within* the world a dialectical relation holds between the invisible providence of God and the visible human chaos that comprises the world and its history. This dialectical constitution of the world parallels the dialectic of the Word and flesh in Christ and the invisible and visible nature of the church, and as an ontic reality is itself complemented by a noetic of faith. As the person of Christ can only be rightly understood by seeing him as the incarnate Word in flesh, and as the church can only be truly understood as both an invisible and visible reality, weak in its visible life but made alive by the invisible work of the Spirit, so the world to normal perception appears simply to be marked by random and evil events, yet it is ruled and guided by the invisible providence of God

---

[13]Barth writes: 'The resulting restriction is that the reconciliation of the world to God, the fulfilment of the covenant, the reconstituted order between God and man and therefore the new reality of world history, is known even to the community only in Jesus Christ and cannot therefore be known to the world which does not participate in the knowledge of Jesus Christ' (*CD IV.3.2*, 714). It is this knowledge which constitutes the division between the church and the world in Barth's thought: 'This knowledge of the new heaven and the new earth already given in relation to Him distinguishes it, for all the restriction of its vision, from the rest of humanity which does not yet participate in the knowledge of Jesus Christ and what has taken place in Him. And it is this distinction which capacitates it for witness to the world, and commits it to this witness' (ibid., 715).

that guides these events to fulfill a sovereign purpose. This perception is given only to faith.

In conclusion, God's providence does not eliminate the reality of this chaos, nor can the chaotic events themselves be equated with the actions of God's providence. God's providence and the world's events cannot be absolutely separated nor summarily equated. For this reason, the world, like Christ and the church, can therefore be perceived truly only by faith. This dialectical understanding runs throughout Barth's thought on the community and the world, and finds its pattern and norm in the Christological logic of the incarnation. What Barth provides in his final chapter on the church is therefore nothing less than a theological description of the identity and reality of the world itself in the light of Christ and the community.

3. The Church in the World: The Influence of the World upon the Church

Having considered the nature of world-occurrence itself, Barth turns to the question of how the church should understand itself as existing within the world.[14] To begin, Barth reiterates that the church must be understood theologically, rather than according to a general phenomenological or sociological understanding (*CD IV.3.2*, 722).[15] He again explains that the church exists both as a visible society in the world among others, yet is unique in that its source, basis, and norm lies outside of the world in the call of God through Christ and the Spirit. The church is therefore both visible and invisible (see *CD IV.3.2*, 721-730). This understanding of the church is based upon a Christological pattern:

> The existence of the Christian community thus corresponds to the existence of Jesus Christ to the extent that He first came in the flesh, so that in His human nature He is the eternal Son of God, and as such different from the world in spite of His solidarity with it, confronting world-occurrence unequivocally as its Lord even while He inconspicuously integrates Himself into it. His community follows Him as it must understand and therefore express its own being as one which is wholly worldly and yet also as a being in encounter with world-occurrence (*CD IV.3.2*, 728).

With this in view, we might examine the relation of the church and the world by first examining Barth's understanding of the influence of the world's thought and life upon

---

[14]Barth here defines the church as 'the people which exists in the divinely given knowledge of the new reality of world-occurrence concealed in Jesus Christ, and in the resultant and distinctive resoluteness of its confidence, decisions and hope' (*CD IV.3.2*, 721).

[15]Barth here again compares this position to Schleiermacher.

the church, and then turn to the question of the influence of the church's thought and life upon the world.

A. Freedom and Dependence

What then is the relationship between the Christian community and the world with specific regard to the world's influence upon the community? First, the relationship between the church and the world is marked by a dialectic of freedom and dependence. Barth states:

> The Christian community, as one people among others and yet also as this people, i.e., the people of God, exists in total dependence on its environment and yet also in total freedom in relation to it. Neither its dependence nor its freedom is partial; they are both total. For its visibility and invisibility, its likeness and distinction in world-occurrence, are the twofold determination of its one and total being, just as Jesus Christ, in whose discipleship it exists in this twofold determination of its one existence, is with the same totality both true man and true God, and as such the one Jesus Christ (*CD IV.3.2*, 734).

The freedom of the community is thus total, as is its dependence. It is dependent in that the community is unquestionably conditioned by the world, and yet it is free in that it is distinct over against the world, having its own law and will and power (*CD IV.3.2*, 735). This mutual freedom and dependence is witnessed in two primary areas.

First, while the community is free from the world in relation to the content of its message, in that it has its own unique message to proclaim, it does not have its own language but utilizes the language of the world and is required to adopt 'the modes of thought and speech of its spatial and temporal environment more near or distant, more ancient or modern.' Barth succinctly puts this point: 'The Christian community has its own message to impart, but it is dependent on the world around in the sense that it does not have its own language in which to impart it' (*CD IV.3.2*, 735). On one hand, the church can only use, and cannot escape using, secular language, the language of the world. Yet on the other hand, the church is free in that this language is remolded and reshaped in light of the divine Word that speaks through such language: 'The freedom of the Christian community in this sphere of speech has its origin in the free omnipotent Word of the grace of God which it is charged to attest' (*CD IV.3.2*, 736).

These words and thought-forms, which do not cease to be secular, are utilized by the church and are then appropriated to convey divine truth not on account of a general capacity that they possess, but as they are graciously claimed and equipped for this service by the Word of God.[16] Profane language is thus sanctified. The community is free to use, or not use, any human concepts in order to convey the truth of the Gospel (*CD IV.3.2*, 737-738). Once again we see the dialectical nature of Barth's thought, in that the divine Word and the human words cannot be simply identified yet are inseparable, as well as the concept of correspondence, in that human language is portrayed as corresponding to and adequately conveying the divine Word. Moreover, there is for Barth a further dialectic in that the message of the community is both living and constant — addressed anew to each generation, yet remaining true to its central grounding in Jesus Christ. The church errs if it ignores either the living and dynamic nature of the Word on the one hand, or its unity and constancy on the other. Barth argues that failure on the one side will always lead to a failure on the other, and the only solution is to listen attentively to its one living Lord. The proclamation of the church can neither become a 'dead letter' nor 'another Gospel' (see *CD IV.3.2*, 813-824).

There is a second way in which the church is both free and dependent in relation to its environment. Not only is the church both free and dependent in terms of its language, it is also free and dependent in terms of its social form, its 'sociological structure' (*CD IV.3.2*, 739). Like language, there is no completely distinctive social form that belongs to the church. It has throughout time drawn upon various social, political, and cultural models for its own form and polity. The church is of necessity shaped by the social, cultural, and political patterns of the world that surround it, even though at times it must oppose and criticize these patterns themselves. There has never been, Barth avers, an 'intrinsically sacred sociology,' just as there is no 'intrinsically sacred language' (*CD IV.3.2*, 739). In regard to social structure as well as language, the community is dependent upon raw materials gleaned from its environment.

Yet, like language, there is also a freedom of the community in relation to social forms. The community is freed by the Word of God to adopt them in an *ad hoc* and pragmatic manner, to instill them with new meaning, and to re-shape them for the distinctive needs of the community, so that while human forms must be utilized, the community is not bound to any one in particular and is free to use any appropriate for the context in which the church finds itself. The community is therefore both free and bound to these forms, so that 'as it can use the secular possibilities of human speech,

---

[16]Metzger aptly states: 'Just as hearts are lifted up (*sursum corda*) to partake in the [Lord's] Supper without the properties of the elements undergoing change, so too human words are elevated to bear witness to the Word in the event of the divine commandeering of language by the Word without undergoing transformation' (*The Word of Christ and the World of Culture*, 141). Metzger refers here to a divine commandeering of language in the world of culture, but the same holds true for the divine elevation of the church's speech in its proclamation of the Gospel, speech itself borrowed from its surrounding culture.

to establish this particular society it can use the secular possibilities of social structuring, not changing them essentially nor divesting them of their secularism, but giving to them as they are a new meaning and determination' (*CD IV.3.2*, 740).

Barth maintains that the community can exist in various social forms, 'none of which is better adapted for the purpose than others....' (*CD IV.3.2*, 741). For just as human language does not intrinsically possess the ability to convey divine truth, yet is granted such a capability by God, so also the social forms themselves are not intrinsically suited to give shape and order to the community, but can be enabled by God to serve to make the invisible visible in the community:

> Intrinsically unholy possibilities in the structuring of man's life in society are sanctified and made serviceable to the gathering and upbuilding of the people of God in the service of its commission and for the purpose of its election and calling. The free God gives to this human people...the freedom to adopt its own form, i.e., the form corresponding to its calling and commission, in the sphere of general human possibilities (*CD IV.3.2*, 741).

The community is thus dependent upon the world for types of social structures and practices, but it is entirely free in the manner in which it utilizes and shapes them, for the community has but one Lord. The community is free in relation to the world just as its Lord is free, and its members are thus bound to the community before they are bound to any other state, nation, or society (*CD IV.3.2*, 741).

What might be criticized in Barth's thought at this point is his conception that these social forms, as well as the systems of thought spoken of previously, can be used interchangeably by the community and are of equal or neutral value. Barth seems to imply that any system of thought or social structure is as good as any other, so that any could theoretically be used by the church in proclaiming divine truth and providing shape to its historical life. While it is true that no system of thought or political structure in itself possesses the ability to convey divine truth or give proper social expression to a form of life reflecting the kingdom of God, it is very questionable that all are of equal value for the church's proclamation, teaching, and social life.

Barth himself seems to have realized that one must not only draw an absolute distinction between the divine Word and human words and between the kingdom of God and human social structures, but that one must also make relative distinctions and judgments between them as to their appropriateness for expressing divine truth and for reflecting in a concrete polity the eschatological kingdom. So while Barth here in *CD IV.3.2* seems to imply that the church can be either a national church, a state church, or a free church, none being superior to another, with the adoption of any polity simply a matter of pragmatic benefit based upon context (*CD IV.3.2*, 742), in other writings of his later years he favors 'a free church in a free state,' for a free church can best render free obedience to a free Lord.[17] This indeed seems to be the trajectory of his later thought. Furthermore, Barth certainly did not consider all social and political options as equally valid for the community when concrete forms were in question. Barth favored a democratic form of government as best suited to correspond to the Gospel and opposed totalitarian forms of government, as we will see below.[18]

It should also be noted that Barth increasingly came to see the primary definition and understanding of the church as the concrete local assembly, so that while he would continue to stress that the church is an invisible and divinely constituted event, he also saw the church's fundamental and necessary visible form as the local congregation: 'The primary, normal, and visible form of this event is the *local congregation* meeting in a "parish" or "district" with clearly defined boundaries.'[19] It is the concrete, specific, and local congregation that grounds the church in history and is what staves off all notions of a docetic ecclesiology. In line with this emphasis upon the local congregation came a renewed examination upon the church's polity, and in later essays Barth clearly favors a congregational order for the church (rather than episcopal, monarchial or synodotal ones).[20]

What is of utmost importance to understand is that this decision on Barth's part to favor congregational polity and a democratically-conceived 'free church in a free state' was not simply the product of pragmatic considerations in light of the horrors of totalitarianism or his estimation that the time of the *corpus christianum* was at an

---

[17]See especially 'The Church — The Living Congregation of the Living Lord Jesus Christ.' For a discussion of this essay, see chapter five above. When asked during his visit to New York in 1962 as to his stand on the question of the church and state, Barth replied: 'I think that they should be separate. Especially for the Church, it is better not to be involved in political arrangements. My idea is a free church within a free state.' See Barth, *Gespräche 1959-1962* (Zürich: Theologischer Verlag Zürich, 1995), 492; 284. Cf. also *CD IV.2*, 689. There Barth states: 'What the state needs...is a free Church, which as such can remind it of its own limits and calling, thus warning it against falling either into anarchy on the one hand or tyranny on the other.' For a similar sentiment earlier expressed, see Barth, 'Für die Freiheit des Evangeliums,' in *Theologische Existenz heute* 2 (1933): 7. These statements must be compared, however, to Barth's reticence in 1936 to endorse a specific church polity in relation to the state, along with his more critical assessment of a free church paradigm due to a fear of its sectarian implications. See Barth, 'Volkskirche, Freikirche, Bekenntniskirche,' in *Evangelische Theologie* 3 (1936): 411-422. For a discussion of this essay, see Kurt Meier, 'Die zeitgeschichtliche Bedeutung volkskirchlicher Konzeptionen im deutschen Protestantismus zwischen 1918 und 1945,' in *Nordische und deutsche Kirchen im 20. Jahrhundert*, ed. Carsten Nicolaisen (Göttingen: Vandenhoeck & Ruprecht, 1982), 183-185.

[18]See Barth, 'Christian Community,' 181-182.

[19]'Living Congregation — *MDGD*,' 73; 'Living Congregation — *GHN*,' 78; 79.

[20]See 'Living Congregation — *MDGD*,', 73-76.

end.[21] Barth's conviction was grounded in the deeper theological question of *correspondence* — namely, which form of church order and polity best corresponds to the freedom of Christ and his Word? To answer this question, church polity must be determined *Christologically*: 'The Church's polity, no less than the preaching and confession of the Church, must be shaped root and branch in correspondence to the Word of God.'[22]

Therefore, in order to determine proper polity, one must judge them in light of the Word of God and with special reference to God's revelation in Jesus Christ. The superior order is that which removes barriers so that Christ can be readily heard. Barth writes:

> Church order, like the Church itself, is not an end in itself. It is man's attempt so to serve God's Word in obedience to it, that in face of the danger menacing the Church, the wisest, boldest and most effective steps are taken to ensure that the immediate meeting and communion of the living Lord Jesus Christ with His congregation shall take place anew. No human effort can ensure this divine encounter. But man *can* clear the obstacles out of the way; and *this* is the purpose of church order.[23]

When Barth examines the forms of church order available to him (episcopal, synodal, and congregationalist), he sides with the congregationalist.[24] So in relation to the question of the church's relation to the state, Barth consistently maintained in his later writings a commitment to a free church rather than a national one, and in relation to the question of the church's own polity, Barth argued, though guardedly and

---

[21]Though of course such considerations were not absent and played no small part in Barth's thinking. In light of the changing conditions regarding the church in Germany in 1935, Barth could indeed assert that 'Christendom in its form earlier known to us is at an end.' See Barth, 'Das Evangelium in der Gegenwart,' in *Theologische Existenz heute*, 25 (1935): 33. Cited in: Eberhard Busch, 'Die Kirche am Ende ihrer Welt-geltung: Zur Deutung der Ekklesiologie Karl Barths,' in *Das Wort, das in Erstaunen setzt, verpflichtet*, ed. Dieter Jeschke, Eckhard Langner, et al. (Wuppertal und Zürich: Brockhaus Verlag, 1994), 85.

[22]'Living Congregation — *GHN*,' 82.

[23]'Living Congregation — *MDGD*,' 75. Cf. 'Living Congregation — *GHN*,' 76.

[24]Ibid., 75-76. Barth writes: 'This paper is not a plea for the uncritical adoption of this particular system [i.e., congregationalism]. But the principle of Congregationalism— the free congregation of the free Word of God — is sound enough' (ibid., 75). See also 'Living Congregation— *GHN*,' 83-85. Barth had not always spoken so warmly of congregationalism, having seen it as a precursor of liberalism — see *CD I.1*, 38. Nevertheless, Barth's congregational leanings are readily apparent in his mature ecclesiology and remarks concerning the church.

critically, for a congregational form. Here we see a shift in emphasis, in that it is not the world that provides political and social options from which the community must choose (though there is this too, of course), but it is primarily the Christological determination of the church's own polity and life that provides the models and patterns for the world at large.[25] The influence of the church upon the world is therefore exemplary and normative, whereas the influence of the world upon the church is secondary and exceptional.

B. Weakness and Strength

For Barth, the influence of the world upon the church is also marked by a dialectic of weakness and strength, and Barth states that like freedom and dependence, both weakness and strength are total in relation to the community. These exist together, for the strength of the community is a strength that exists in weakness. In this way, the community reflects its Lord, who also was strong only in weakness. 'It is the glory of the community to follow Him in this too, and therefore to be totally strong only as it is totally weak, but to be really strong, of course, in its weakness' (*CD IV.3.2*, 742).

In its relation to the world, the church is weak in that its place in the world is neither self-evident nor assured. Unlike the state, work, or culture, it cannot be said to be a necessary element of 'human existence and therefore of world-occurrence' (*CD IV.3.2*, 742-743). It is marked out from the others in that its origin is not found in world-occurrence, nor is it sustained by the forces of creation. The existence of the community therefore belongs not to the order of creation but to the new work of reconciliation that God has effected in Christ (*CD IV.3.2*, 743).

Yet, even in this weakness there is strength, for the community is divinely sustained in its existence throughout time, enduring in both 'its Israelite and Christian forms' despite opposition, and posing a riddle to the world as to its continual existence. Barth writes: 'In the light of its visible history and present reality, it can hardly be denied that in the Christian community there dwells a hidden but uniquely effective power which enables it to persist in spite of all expectation' (*CD IV.3.2*, 744-746). This power is the power of its election and calling to which it witnesses, the strength that God provides. We should note that this is an invisible strength that works through visible weakness (i.e., the invisible and visible church).

The community is weak not only in regard to its place in the world, but also in respect to its work and activity. The weakness of the church is expressed in the fact

---

[25]Barth's most in-depth examinations of this type of correspondence or analogy are found in 'The Christian Community and the Civil Community,' as well as in his discussion of church law as exemplary law for the world in the *Church Dogmatics* (*CD IV.2*, 719-726). These texts will be investigated below in more detail.

that it has no 'instrument and weapon' apart from its witness, its ministering word. The church can therefore only speak in obedience but can impart no power to its word and witness. In addition, the weakness of the church is shown in its lack of visible success, the inability to quantify its achievement, and its insignificance in the face of other human endeavors and accomplishments (*CD IV.3.2*, 747-748).

Yet here, too, the invisible power of the community comes through visible weakness in a manner analogous to the work of Christ. The community is not only sustained, but its work made effective, through the divine gift and action even in the midst of its feebleness and vulnerability:

> Yet it is in the weakness of its efforts and achievements that there is concealed and active its strength, its superior ability to all other powers. The people of God need not be ashamed of its weakness. It can renounce all attempts to give itself the appearance of strength. It can count it an honour that in this respect, too, it may share the weakness of Jesus Christ, being unimpressive and unsuccessful in company with Him. It can thus be conscious of its hidden but very real power, and rejoice with a merriness of heart of which other peoples with their deployment of power can have no inkling (*CD IV.3.2*, 749).

The community's work, though hidden, is on this account more significant and determinative than that of any other human society, for it concerns itself with what has happened in Jesus Christ and with witnessing to him. It thereby concerns itself with

> the divine decision which has been taken in Jesus Christ in favour of all men and for their deliverance from sure and certain destruction....This decision and its revelation are that which inwardly holds the world together, whether it realises it or not. But with this decision and its revelation no other human work, however great or imposing its performance may seem, has anything whatever to do. The Christian community may do what it does in the service of this cause. If others refer to the periphery, it concerns the centre of human existence. This is its secret strength, and the strength of its work (*CD IV.3.2*, 749).

Here again we notice the geometrical language of center and periphery. Christ stands at the center, the ground and basis of the world and its history. The world stands at the periphery, living outside of the knowledge of its own reconciliation in Christ. Between them stands the church, commissioned to proclaim to the world the reconciliation accomplished in Christ, in which the church already knowingly shares. This proclamation is its mission and task. With this observation we turn from a discussion of the world's influence upon the church to a discussion of Barth's understanding of the church's mission for and influence upon the world.

4. The Church for the World: Its Task and Ministry

The community of Jesus Christ exists for the world. While the community itself lives within the world, it is also set apart from the world by God in order to carry out its divinely-appointed commission of witness to the world. It therefore exists for the world and also for God, to serve God's purposes and to serve the world's need (*CD IV.3.2*, 762).[26] The community is set apart from the world, and yet set apart for service to the world, called out of the nations in order to live for the nations (*CD IV.3.2*, 763-764). The church has no independent existence apart from this task and ministry entrusted to it by Christ (*CD IV.3.2*, 795-796; 830-831).

Barth's ecclesiology is on this account shaped considerably by a teleological, rather than purely ontological, concern: the church does not simply exist for itself, but exists to serve the world. Barth's ecclesiology attempts to define the church according to its missionary activity, and not simply in reference to its self-constituting practices, as does the Ausgburg Confession.[27] This latter definition is not wrong in what it affirms, Barth maintains, but in what it fails to articulate, namely, the essential missionary nature of the church. Barth faults the Reformation in both its Lutheran and Reformed branches for failing to restore the missionary activity of the church and to define the church according to this task (see *CD IV.3.2*, 764-767). He also interestingly sees that it was not the magisterial Reformers, but Anabaptism and Pietism, that perceived mission to be central to the church's very existence.[28] It must be said that this emphasis upon the missionary task of the church is one of the most central and distinguishing features of Barth's own ecclesiology. As Barth can state: 'The Church is either a missionary Church or it is no church at all' (*CD III.3*, 64).

Once again we witness Barth's actualistic ontology, though here with an ecclesiological spin: the church exists first where God acts to bring it into existence, and secondarily where it acts in witness to the world, in mission. The second activity

---

[26]'The community of Jesus Christ is the human creature whose existence as existence for God has the meaning and purpose of being, on behalf of God and in the service and discipleship of His existence, an existence for the world and men' (*CD IV.3.2*, 762). Barth can also write that the Christian community is 'both a ministry to God and a ministry to man: a ministry to God in which it may serve man; and a ministry to man in which it may serve God; and therefore a ministry to the God who speaks to man in His Word, and to the man who is already called and now summoned to hear, perceive and accept the Word of God' (ibid., 831).

[27]'The church exists where the Gospel is purely proclaimed and the sacraments rightly administered' (Augsburg Confession, Article 7).

[28]See Barth's discussion of the history of mission in *CD IV.3.1*, 11-38, esp. 25; 28.

of the church corresponds to the constitution of the church itself by Christ through the Spirit. The church as mission thus corresponds to the church as event. It also corresponds to God's action in Christ — the witness of the church is the appropriate human response to the prior and complete salvation brought in Jesus Christ. The relation of correspondence *between* Christ and the church is again evident, as is that *within* the church itself between its invisible and visible realities. The activity of Christ through the Spirit constituting the church and the activity of the church in mission therefore cannot be separated nor confused, the latter existing only on account of the former, yet also corresponding to it.

On this account, the church's central task is defined as witness: it proclaims to the world the reconciliation that God has accomplished in Christ. The church indeed stands between Christ and the world, proclaiming Christ to the world, and the community's ministry reflects that of Christ. For Barth, however, this statement must always be carefully qualified. Here we hearken back to the theme of the relationship between Christ and the community examined in the previous chapter and to convictions held consistently throughout Barth's theological career.

A. The Mission of the Church in the Light of Christ's Mission

The community is united with Christ, and both are sent for the sake of the world, yet their missions are distinct and cannot be confused: the church's mission is not a 'repetition, extension, or continuation' of Christ's own. The church does witness to Christ, and it must do so because God is God not only of the community but of the world.[29] Yet, its act of witness reflects but does not supplement or supplant the unique and irreplaceable work of Christ, for he remains the Subject of the community, and the community's confession can only bear witness to him and his own irreplaceable work. The church can do no more nor no less than witness to Christ (*CD IV.3.2*, 834-838).[30]

Furthermore, because the mission of the church corresponds to that of Christ but does not supplement or replace it, the community can never see itself as a representative, or vicar, of Christ to the world. It cannot assist Christ in the reconciliation of the world, nor take his place upon earth, mistakes that Catholicism

---

[29]See *CD IV.3.2*, 787-790; also *CD IV.3.1*, 303-305.

[30]Barth notes that the church's prophecy 'lives as true prophecy by the fact that it remains distinct from His, that it is subject to it, that it does not try to replace it, but that with supreme power and yet with the deepest humility it points to the work of God accomplished in Him and the Word of God spoken in Him, inviting to gratitude for this work and the hearing of this Word, but not pretending to be claimed for more than this indication and invitation, nor to be capable of anything more' (*CD IV.3.2*, 836).

and Eastern Orthodoxy make, according to Barth (*CD IV.3.2*, 729; 835-836).[31] The church's relationship to the world can never be equal to that of Christ with the world precisely because the church itself is ever a creature, not the Creator, and it is in no way a co-Redeemer with Christ.[32] The relationship between Christ and the community is only one of correspondence and discipleship, not of identity or replacement. It remains, therefore, a dialectical relationship from first to last. The church 'is indeed in the flesh, but it is not, as He is, the Word of God in the flesh, the incarnate Son of God' (*CD IV.3.2*, 729). Following from this, the relationship of the community and the world is therefore governed by this prior relationship between Christ and the community.[33] We might conclude that it is precisely because Christ is the Lord of the community, and is himself the one and only Lord, that the relation of the community to the world cannot be one of lordship but of witness and service. And it is precisely this special service of the community that marks it off from the world at large, not its spiritual or moral superiority.

The mission of Christ and that of the community are therefore not on the same plane, for the community's mission is

> simply ordered on its own lower level in relation to His, as is necessarily the case since He Himself gave it, but neither quantitatively nor qualitatively is it equal. He is sent to precede it on the way into the world. It is sent to follow Him on the same way. These are two things. But the two sendings are comparable because they have the same origin. The one

---

[31]Barth writes, 'In the sphere of Romanism and Eastern Orthodoxy we have examples of the transgression of this upper limit of the ministry of the community to the extent that in them the Church ascribes to itself, to its life and institutions and organs, particularly to its administration of the sacraments and the means of grace entrusted to it, and in Romanism to its government by the teaching office, certain functions in the exercise of which it is not only not subordinate to Jesus Christ but is ranked alongside and in practice even set above Him as His vicar in earthly history, its ministry of witness being left far behind as it shares with Him an existence and activity which are both human and divine, and human in divine reality and omnipotence' (*CD IV.3.2*, 836).

[32]Barth can therefore assert: '1. The world would be lost without Jesus Christ and His Word and work; 2. the world would not necessarily be lost if there were no Church; and 3. the Church would be lost if it had no counterpart in the world' (*CD IV.3.2*, 826). This should be contrasted with Barth's earlier positive discussions of the dictum '*Extra ecclesiam nulla salus*' (see *CD IV.2*, 620-622; cf. *CD IV.1*, 725-239; also *CD I.2*, 211; 215; 217; 220). These discussions themselves, however, should be compared to Barth's statement that the intention behind this dictum is better expressed by saying '*Extra Christum nulla salus*' (*CD IV.1*, 688).

[33]'In Jesus Christ the community and the rest of humanity constitute a differentiated, yet in this differentiation firmly integrated, whole' (*CD IV.3.2*, 826). The Chalcedonian pattern in this language is easily recognized.

God who sends Him as the Father also sends them through Him the Son. Again, they are comparable because they have the same goal. He and they are both sent into the world, which means very generally that they are directed to the world and exist for it (*CD IV.3.2*, 768).

Therefore we must note that not only the community's nature and existence, but also its mission and task, exist in a relation of correspondence to that of Christ and are molded along a Chalcedonian pattern. The mission of Christ and that of the community are united yet not confused, the latter dependent upon the former and existing only in service to it, yet existing in a relation of correspondence to it, rather than contradiction.

It must be stressed that Barth's qualification of the church's ministry is in no way meant to be seen as a denigration of it. Barth emphasizes that even though the church's ministry is limited and subordinate to that of Christ, it is also sustained and empowered by the Spirit of God and the Word of Christ himself (*CD IV.3.2*, 838-843). The ministry of the community can therefore bring about real change within the world, though Barth does not like to speak of a 'causal connexion' between them. Rather, the results in the world are 'signs' that point beyond themselves not to the church *per se* but to God's work through the agency of the church (*CD IV.3.2*, 841-842). This fits with Barth's emphasis upon the indirect identity between the inner power of revelation and the outer sign which manifests that power, in this case, the transformations within the world that result, though indirectly, from the witness of the community. For Barth, the ministry of the community is therefore definite and limited, yet it is also full of promise, for the power of the community that effects change in the world is not its own but that of the Spirit of God and the Word.

It is significant that in speaking of the ministry of the community Barth ties the constitution of the church to Christ's prophetic office. This explains his defining the church according to its mission, its task in the world, for as Christ proclaims himself in his prophetic office, so also does the community proclaim him as its prophetic and missionary task (*CD IV.3.2*, 790). The community fulfills this task not only as it proclaims Christ and the kingdom of God but as it is itself a 'likeness' [*Gleichnis*] or 'subsequent and provisional representation' [*nachträgliche und vorläufige Darstellung*] of the kingdom of God (*CD IV.3.2*, 792). The community can only reflect this reality; it can never be identified with it. Barth defines the kingdom as 'the establishment of the exclusive, all-penetrating, all-determinative lordship of God and His Word and Spirit in the whole sphere of His creation. Jesus Himself is this kingdom in all its perfection' (*CD IV.3.2*, 792). So if Jesus Christ is the kingdom, and the community is to reflect and correspond to this kingdom, then we might safely conclude that for Barth the community is to reflect and correspond to Christ. The church corresponds to Christ, and the church, as the provisional representation of the kingdom of God, is then the pattern, though provisional, of what the world is to be. The fact that its representation is provisional means that it is both incomplete and questionable on the one hand, and real and assured on the other. This is the eschatological tension (and dialectical tension) in which the church lives between Christ's ascension and return (*CD IV.2*, 620-621).[34]

B. The Mission of the Church as Solidarity with the World

With particular regard to the participation of the community in the world, Barth outlines a number of distinct features that characterize the mission of the community. The community is the place where the reconciliation achieved in Christ is proclaimed to the world, and it is also the place, as we have noted above, where the true nature and identity of the world is revealed, and where the world itself is shown its true identity (*CD IV.3.2*, 769-772). The church is more than this, however — it is also a place where there can be real solidarity, though not conformity, with the world. The community is for the world and therefore takes an active part within the world: 'The community which knows the world is necessarily the community which is committed to it' (*CD IV.3.2*, 773; 773-776). Barth thus opposes an ecclesiological sectarianism that would separate from the world and urges a true solidarity, although of course a critical and qualified one, in that the community must not conform to the world by adopting its modes of thought and life, especially if this means losing its distinctive message and fellowship. Nor does Barth overlook the real external danger and threat that the world poses for the church, opposing it with either an inpatient and passive disdain and dismissal or an open and aggressive opposition and persecution (*CD IV.2*, 661-665).

Barth thus has the church walk a tightrope between a sectarian opposition to the world and an accommodating acculturation to the world. These are the internal dangers, the temptations to which the church itself is prone. He rejects on one hand a 'self-glorification' and 'sacralization' of the church, in which the church views itself as superior to the world, as well as on the other hand an alienation and 'secularization' of the church, whereby the church becomes indistinguishable from

---

[34]Barth writes: 'As it beholds Him "with open face" (2 Cor. 3:18), it is changed, not into an *alter Christus*, but necessarily into an image of the unrepeatably one Christ. It receives from the Lord, who is the Spirit, a glory which, if it is not the same as His own, corresponds and is analogous and similar to it — the glory of His own image....The purpose of its existence is the subsequent and provisional representation of the calling of all humanity and all creatures to the service of God as it has gone forth in Jesus Christ. The origin and goal of the ways of God, which took place initially but perfectly in the resurrection of Jesus Christ, and which will take place definitively and no less perfectly in His final appearing, is the calling of every man and indeed of all creation to the service of God. The function of the community is to follow and yet at the same time to precede His universal call' (*CD IV.3.2*, 793; see also 794-795).

the world (*CD IV.2*, 667-671).[35] The church must neither neglect those in the world nor patronize them. To neglect the world is for the community to betray the very reason for its existence. To patronize the world is to use the world merely as a means for its own ends. Both errors fail to address the task that has been entrusted to the community, namely, to bear faithful witness to the world of the church's one Lord (*CD IV.3.2*, 824-830). The relationship of the church to the world is therefore neither one of passivity and 'neutral co-existence,' nor of 'dominion and control' (*CD IV.3.2*, 833).

Finally, the community is the place where people are made responsible for the world.[36] This does not mean that the community shares the responsibility that God has taken for the world, for the church itself is part of the world as a creature. But it does entail that the community reflect this responsibility in its own life and in active service to the God who has created and reconciled the world in Christ. Barth can put this in the strongest possible terms:

> Within the limits of its creaturely capacity and ability it is ordained and summoned to co-operate with Him in His work [...*zur Mitarbeitershaft an seinem Werk bestimmt und berufen*]. And since His work is on and in the world, in its own place and manner it, too, is pledged to the world and made responsible for what is to become of it. Different though its action may be from His, in its own definite function and within the appointed limits it, too, is summoned and freed and commissioned for action in and towards the world (*CD IV.3.2*, 777).

The church exists for service and witness to the world in such a way that even the 'No' which the church must at times assert to the world serves a larger 'Yes,' the good of the world as a whole (*CD IV.3.2*, 773; 797-798). The community is in short a witnessing community that exists for the world. Barth summarizes the above points this way:

> The true community of Jesus Christ is the society in which it is given to men to see and understand the world as it is, to accept solidarity with it, and to be pledged and committed to it. We have made these statements in development of the proposition that the Church as the true community exists essentially for the world and may thereby be known as the true Church (*CD IV.3.2*, 780).

---

[35]There can be little doubt that for Barth the first temptation describes Roman Catholicism, whereas the second describes Neo-Protestantism.

[36]'As they know it, and are united in solidarity with it, they are made jointly responsible for it, for its future, for what is to become of it' (*CD IV.3.2*, 776; cf. 776-780).

For Barth, the fact that the community exists for the world is as central to the Gospel as that God lives or that Jesus Christ is risen from the dead (*CD IV.3.2*, 786). Once again, the community's existence for the world is described in terms of a real and certain correspondence that is divinely established between God's own action for the world in Christ and the action and life of the community which parallels this divine being and activity. In other words, ecclesiology is patterned according to Christological concerns:

> As God exists for it [the world] in His divine way, and Jesus Christ in His divine-human, so the Christian community exists for it in its own purely human. All ecclesiology is grounded, critically limited, but also positively determined by Christology; and this applies in respect of the particular statement which here concerns us, namely, that the Church exists for the world. The community neither can nor should believe in itself. Even in this particular respect, there can be no *credo in ecclesiam*. Yet as it believes in God the Father, the Son and the Holy Ghost, it can and should believe and confess its own reality: *credo ecclesiam*, and therefore the reality rather than the mere ideal that it exists for the world (*CD IV.3.2*, 786).

The *nature* of the community influences its *form*, which then influences its *mission*. Yet one can reverse this line of reasoning as well, for its divinely-appointed mission gives rise to its existence and form. Barth can thus say of the church:

> Its true invisible being, and therefore its real distinction from and superiority to the world, is that it is elected and called to be a people alongside and with Jesus Christ and with a share in His self-declaration, that it is given to it to be appointed His witness, to be set in the service of the eternal Word of God spoken in Him, to be ordained to follow the Son of God incarnate in Him. This is its incomparable glory and dignity which it would be mad to surrender by grasping at anything higher. This is what makes it unique among all peoples. Its particular structure and situation do not make it this, for they might be similar to or like others. The crucial point is that it exists on the basis of the call and summons of Jesus Christ, that His commission and command are the meaning of its structure, that it belongs to Him and is His possession in this particular sense. These things cannot be said of any people or society which has come into being by natural or historical means. In virtue of them, it cannot be understood only in historical and sociological terms. In virtue of them, even though it participates at every point in it, it is also opposed to world-occurrence, and indeed opposed in a way which is teleologically meaningful, in fruitful

antithesis. It cannot possibly receive the particular grace freely addressed
by God to it, nor rejoice in nor boast of this grace, without being at once
aware of the prophetic task therewith implied, without taking up this task,
without giving itself wholly to it. To recall the starting-point of the
discussion, it can understand itself as the community of Jesus Christ only
as it ventures to exist with that resoluteness and therefore to bear the
witness entrusted to it (*CD IV.3.2*, 729-730).

What it is so important to note from this passage is that the church's mission not
only flows out from an understanding of its nature and order but in turn conditions
and defines them as well (see *CD IV.3.2*, 730-734).[37] That is, its invisible nature as
a unique society of the Spirit that is ordered according to its relationship to Christ
gives rise to its unique mission in and for the world, and its unique election for this
service is in turn the basis and ground of its existence and form. Its unique mission
is grounded in an eternal election that gives rise to its very existence, nature, and
form, including the nature of its ministry and the various practices that constitute it.
What is the nature of this ministry, and what are the specific practices that comprise
it, when we go beyond the general category of 'witness?'

C. The Nature of the Church's Ministry

Barth's discussion of the nature of the church's ministry hinges upon an investigation
of what remains the same in each of the church's particular and specific forms and
practices of ministry (*CD IV.3.2*, 843). Barth finds the answer in the three elements
of witness as 'declaration, exposition and address, or the proclamation, explication
and application of the Gospel as the Word of God' entrusted to the community (*CD
IV.3.2*, 843).
The nature of the church's ministry is defined according to these three enduring
elements that comprise its activity. The ministry and witness of the community is first
of all in all its forms 'the declaration of the Gospel.' Barth writes:

Whatever else the community may plan, undertake and do, whatever else
it may or may not accomplish, it has always to introduce into the sphere
of world-occurrence and to disclose to men a human historical fact which,
not itself the kingdom of God but indicating it as a likeness, corresponds
and points to the divine historical fact which constitutes the content of the
Gospel (*CD IV.3.2*, 844).

---

[37]The same holds true for Israel in the Old Testament, for both Israel and the church serve this
same witness in that their existence is the product of a divine election and calling. Both Israel
and the church are therefore the 'people of God.'

The community does not reproduce or replace this fact but does bears witness to it both in its proclamation and in its provisional representation of the kingdom within its historical life. This is the content of its witness to the world: 'The world needs the human historical fact of the declaration of the Gospel. It differs from the community in that the Gospel as news of the decisively important divine historical fact is still unknown to it' (*CD IV.3.2*, 844). The community cannot make the world believe this news, for this is the work of Jesus Christ himself and his Spirit, and it should focus on its faithfulness, not upon the success of its witness. This witness can be carried out in various forms of speech and action, but it must be carried out, for this is the primary and central task of the community (*CD IV.3.2*, 844-846).

The ministry of the community is also the 'explanation or explication of the Gospel' (*CD IV.3.2*, 846). The community thus presents and expounds the inner logic and intelligibility of the Gospel for the world:

> The Gospel gives itself to be understood, and wills to be understood. Hence the human historical fact which corresponds to its content, and which it is the task of the ministry of the community to introduce, consists not only in the declaration of the Gospel but also in its explanation. It has to follow the elucidation which constantly issues from the self-declaration of Jesus Christ, from the content of the Gospel itself. It has to copy with the human means at its disposal the work of the prophecy of the divine-human Mediator (*CD IV.3.2*, 847).[38]

Barth is surprisingly optimistic in regard to the possibility for the success of this explanation even from a natural point of view, though its explanation must derive from its own inner logic, and not be explained by 'alien principles,' whether metaphysical, anthropological, philosophical, or other.[39] This inner logic is tied to the narrative character of the Christian Gospel, and an explanation of this Gospel must thus pattern its method according to the nature and logic of this structure. Barth writes:

---

[38]'What else is the whole of Church history but a constant attempt on the part of the community not only to declare the Gospel to the world but to make it intelligible and therefore to explain it, to bring out the perspicuity of its content?' (*CD IV.3.2*, 848).

[39]Barth surprisingly writes: 'For it is surely possible for even the most obstinate of unbelievers, whether or not they can come to a knowledge of the truth, at least to appreciate the inner consistency and to that extent the meaning of the evangelical message....The Gospel is not generally knowable. But it is generally intelligible and explicable. For its content is rational and not irrational' (*CD IV.3.2*, 848-849).

To explain the Gospel is generally and very simply to narrate the history which God Himself has inaugurated, which He rules, in which He has taken the world and man to Himself, and in which man finds himself taken up into intercourse and fellowship with Him. And it means in detail to indicate all the individual elements, moments and aspects of the content of the evangelical message, not as a collection or mosaic of static Christian truths, nor as mere parts of a Christian or other system, but dynamically as elements, moments and aspects of that history, i.e., of the history of salvation and revelation....We have called it the divine historical fact in correspondence with which the community, turning to the world in which it lives, has to introduce the analogy of the human historical fact of its witness (*CD IV.3.2*, 849).[40]

We might say that, for Barth, the community provides a description and explication of the Gospel and its meaning first, in narrating its truth, and second, by existing as an analogy to its divine truth in the human and historical realm. This is the nature of the community's witness and correspondence to Christ.

Finally, the ministry and witness of the community is not only declaration and explication but also 'evangelical address, i.e., proclamation and explication in the form of application' (*CD IV.3.2*, 850). This address sets the truth of the Gospel before the world in such a way that invites decision and action. As such, it is an invitation for all people to the Gospel. So even though it is God alone who can awaken this knowledge and effect such a decision, the community is to 'encourage readiness for it and thus to set them on the way to the goal' (*CD IV.3.2*, 852). Though the community cannot produce in others the knowledge of the Gospel, for this is the work of the Spirit, it 'can and should not merely proclaim and explain the Gospel but summon men with all its power to make ready for this knowledge' (*CD IV.3.2*, 853). The proclamation and explanation of the Gospel therefore serve this end, i.e., that they be addressed to the world, a world for which Jesus Christ died and was raised to life. The declaration and explanation of the Gospel by the community therefore takes the form of an appeal to the world, calling the world to 'the rest and peace of God,

---

[40]Barth writes: 'To explain the Gospel is to expound, unfold and articulate its content, with no effacement of its unity and simplicity, but rather in enhancement of its unity and simplicity. It is to assert and honour it synoptically in all its richness, displaying the place and manner of each individual part. It is to make known the periphery in each section as that of the true centre, and the centre as in every respect that of the distinctive periphery. When the community is occupied with this explanation of the Gospel in every form of its ministry, there arises as its human work the likeness of the kingdom of God, to represent which is its modest but definite task and the meaning of its existence and ministry' (*CD IV.3.2*, 850).

inviting them to the feast which is prepared...and thus summoning them to joy' (*CD IV.3.2*, 851).

In sum, the community in its proclamation and life corresponds to Christ and presents to the world a witness that calls to it and appeals for a response and thus a similar correspondence to the one Lord of the church and the world, known by the one yet unknown by the other. This understanding of the church's ministry is predicated upon Barth's conviction that the church exists for the world and yet cannot be confused with the world, that the world exists as the context for the church even as the church exists for the sake of the world, presenting to the world a provisional representation of what all the world is one day to be. The church presents to the world a life in conformity to Christ, and the world is to conform to this reality itself. In all of this Barth neither glorifies the community as an incarnation of the kingdom, nor relativizes the church by including it within the world's rebellion, but rather sees the church both as implicated in the old order of sin while sharing in the new order of the resurrection. The church truly stands between the perfect obedience of Christ and the rebellion of the world, bearing witness to the former in its own life for the sake of the latter, and thus standing within the eschatological tension between Christ's ascension and his return.

D. The Forms of the Church's Ministry

The final and most extensive discussion by Barth pertaining to the church's mission in the *Church Dogmatics* concerns the various forms of ministry themselves (*CD IV.3.2*, 854). Barth begins by acknowledging that while the church's witness is concrete and unified, the witness may and does in fact take many different forms, being comprised of a multiplicity of practices:

> At every point and in all the functions of its life the Church is concerned to offer that great likeness of the kingdom of God. There can and should be no question of a cleavage in its activity. If it is ever concerned to do other than to offer that likeness and therefore to declare and preach the Gospel and appeal for faith and obedience, it neglects and denies and betrays its ministry. Nevertheless, its activity neither can nor should be uniform. If it is to be faithful in its ministry, it must be integrated and manifold. This inwardly necessary multiplicity of its activity carries with it the differentiation of human means which it uses to do what it is commissioned to do, and also the differentiation of aspects under which it presents itself externally to the world to which it is sent (*CD IV.3.2*, 854).

This multiplicity is not something of which the church should be ashamed. Rather, the multiplicity of the church's practices is essential to its single mission of witness, and Barth provides a Trinitarian reason for this multiplicity: as God is one yet exists in a differentiated unity as Father, Son, and Holy Spirit, so also the witness of the church is one but exists in a differentiated unity comprised of a multiplicity of forms and practices of ministry. The church therefore exists in *correspondence* to the life and being of God, 'as a living people gathered and continually upbuilt and set in the service of God by the special callings and endowments of individuals' (*CD IV.3.2*, 854-855).

The multiplicity and individuation of tasks does not undermine or threaten, but rather strengthens, the church's unity of witness, though Barth acknowledges that the legitimacy of this multiplicity can indeed be undermined and perverted, leading not to unity but to division within the community itself. As opposed to such division, the true multiplicity of forms of ministry is the gift of the Spirit of God: 'The Holy Spirit does not enforce a flat uniformity' (*CD IV.3.2*, 855).[41] The various forms of ministry are multiple gifts of the one gift of grace.

The multiple forms of ministry are described by Barth: 1. pneumatologically, in that they are gifts of the Spirit; 2. Christologically, in that the unity and multiplicity are to be understood according to the image of the body of Christ as one body comprised of many members, and; 3. in a Trinitarian way, in that the multiple gifts themselves are reflections of the unified mutiplicity of God's being as triune and as 'works of God, of Jesus Christ, of the Holy Spirit' (*CD IV.3.2*, 857). The community's multiple gifts that serve its unified witness thus exist by the power of the Spirit and in correspondence to Christ, who serves as 'the original of the relations of unity and multiplicity,' the community being his 'reflection and likeness' ['*Nachbild und Gleichnis*'] (*CD IV.3.2*, 859). The community exists in correspondence to the Trinity as well, for as God exists as one God yet in the differentiated unity of Father, Son, and Holy Spirit, so also the church exists as one in life and witness, yet in the differentiated unity of a multiplicity of members, gifts, and forms of ministry (*CD IV.3.2*, 854-855).[42]

To specify and distinguish the various forms of ministry, Barth begins by asking what forms exist in every time and context, though naturally in multiple variations (*CD IV.3.2*, 859-860). In other words, what are the constant and lasting forms of ministry, enduring throughout the necessary modifications that they undergo throughout the history of the church?

Barth attempts to answer this question by locating the source of these practices in the ministry of Jesus and 'the directions given to the disciples in the Gospels when

---

[41]Barth here understands the multiplicity according to Paul's image of the one body of Christ with many members (*CD IV.3.2*, 856-859).

[42]In this discussion of the forms of the church's ministry Barth's Christological logic is thus readily evident, but what is of perhaps equal significance is the manner in which a Trinitarian pattern is explicitly rather than implicitly delineated.

they were sent out by Jesus Himself' (*CD IV.3.2*, 860). What is significant and indeed fascinating regarding Barth's approach is that he grounds the concrete forms of the community's current practices in the concrete life of Jesus Christ as presented in Scripture. This would have been impossible in his early theology, but his Chalcedonian Christology as interpreted according to an understanding of the election of Christ as the true human person allows for the concept of correspondence rather than contradiction to rise to the fore. As the historical life of Christ corresponds to the divine will of the Father, so also the life of the community corresponds to Christ's own life. For Barth, Christ is therefore the revelation of God *and also* the revelation of true humanity, and Barth grounds the practices of the community in the divine authority that has been given to the person of Jesus Christ and thereby to his teaching. This is important, for the community now lives in correspondence to its heavenly Lord and to his earthly teachings as well.

What should also be noticed is that for Barth the unity of Christ's mission is paralleled by the unity of the church's ministry, which is witness. This is the one thing that underlies all the variation in forms. This was described in Barth's previous section pertaining to the nature of the church's ministry. Now, regarding the forms of ministry, the unity of Christ's ministry expressed in various forms of speech and action is paralleled in the multiplicity of the church's gifts that serve its single mission.[43] The multiplicity of its forms of ministry reflects the ministry of Christ himself, whose ministry can be seen as comprised of speech on the one hand and action on the other, though Barth emphasizes that the speech itself is a form of action, and the action a form of speech. Both together serve the one ministry of Christ, the declaration of his own person, his self-declaration, and they may be subdivided into specific types of speech and action (*CD IV.3.2*, 862).

This twofold ministry of Christ is reflected in the twofold witness of the community to Christ, in its speech and action. The community is to perform one ministry, a witness to Christ, but it does this in various practices that can be grouped together in a twofold manner, under the category of either speech or action. Barth insists that neither the community's speech nor its action can be neglected, for speech entails action, and action entails speech. Nevertheless, there is an ordered relation between the two, for speech is given precedence in this order, i.e., speech precedes action, and action follows speech, though higher value is not assigned to either. Though different, both serve a single goal: 'The burden of both the speech and the action of the community is that men are called to knowledge, yet not to empty but to active knowledge. Because it is a matter of knowledge, speech must come first. But

---

[43]See *CD IV.3.2*, 860. Notice that Barth appeals to the Great Commission in Matthew chapter twenty-eight as the basis for this unity as well. It is to this passage that Barth also appeals to demonstrate the authority given to Christ.

because it is a matter of active knowledge, the element of action must not be lacking' (*CD IV.3.2*, 862-863).

The manner in which Barth describes these again witnesses to an implicit Christological pattern. The priority of speech to action is described by Barth in terms of a 'unity and differentiation' and according to a relation that is 'irreversible,' speech inseparable yet distinct from action, while also preceding and giving rise to action. The relation between them seems to be that action corresponds to speech as its basis and pattern, though Barth elsewhere seems to provide for some flexibility in their order. As he later relates in regard to the community: 'The right order is that it should first speak. But with the same seriousness and emphasis it has also to act in correspondence with its word. In this unity and differentiation it represents what it is its task to represent to the world, namely, the likeness of the kingdom of God' (*CD IV.3.2*, 864).

This twofold ministry can then be further subdivided, as the community's speech is comprised of six practices, and its action of an additional six. The practices of the church's speech are: 1. the praise of God; 2. the proclamation of the Gospel (preaching); 3. instruction in Scripture and the faith; 4. evangelization to the surrounding culture; 5. mission to the nations; and 6. the discipline of theology.[44] It is in fact theology that examines the appropriateness not only of the other practices of the community's speech (i.e., praise, preaching, instruction, evangelization, and missions), but also of its action, and it is these actions to which Barth turns next.

The six practices, or 'forms of ministry,' that comprise the church's action are: 1. prayer; 2. the cure of souls (pastoral care); 3. the production of exemplars of Christian life; 4. the rendering of service (diaconal ministries that address physical needs and that include within them a place for Christian social criticism); 5. the prophetic action of the community based upon the discernment of current events, and; 6. the establishment of fellowship.[45]

Barth outlines each practice in detail. What is important for our purposes is to recognize that each practice serves two functions. First, the practice lends itself to serve the identity of the church; it serves as a defining characteristic of the community. But secondly, each practice serves not only the church itself but gives witness to the world. Each thus serves a primary function for the church, but one that cannot be separated from its secondary function to witness to the world — indeed, to lose the second is to lose the first. So, the praise of God that the community gives serves as a provisional representation of what will one day be the praise of all creation (*CD IV.3.2*, 865). Likewise, preaching is heard not only directly by the community, but also directly or indirectly by the world (*CD IV.3.2*, 867); its instruction is given

---

[44]See *CD IV.3.2*, 865-882.

[45]See *CD IV.3.2*, 882-901.

not only to the community but to the world at large (*CD IV.3.2*, 870); evangelization and mission are directly aimed to the world (*CD IV.3.2*, 872; 874); and theology is the critical account of the faith that the community gives not only itself but to the world (*CD IV.3.2*, 879). Theology is in fact the critical examination of the practices of the church that shape its identity and its mission, and therefore the critical task of theology is connected to the community's mission of witness (*CD IV.3.2*, 879).[46]

The church's action also serves not only to shape its identity and minister to its own members, but serves the world as well. Its prayer is needed by the world and, like its praise, serves to represent and intercede for the world (*CD IV.3.2*, 883-884); the cure of souls witnesses as a sign not only to those within but also to those without the church (*CD IV.3.2*, 885); its models and exemplars inspire not only the community but serve as shining lights to the world (*CD IV.3.2*, 889); its ministry to physical needs is undertaken not only for its own members but for those outside of the community (*CD IV.3.2*, 890); its prophetic action addresses and challenges the world (*CD IV.3.2*, 895-897); and its fellowship not only mirrors the fellowship of the divine Trinitarian life and of Christ with his community but represents the fellowship that God has established between himself and the whole world (*CD IV.3.2*, 898).

The church presents to the world a sign of God's kingdom, and thus challenges the world's own speech and action, calling it under judgment, yet doing so for the world's own ultimate benefit. The church presents to the world a sign of witness, calling for the world's conversion and providing a pattern that the world, even in its fallen state, at times is seen to emulate. The church addresses the problems of nationalism, racism, elitism, and economic stratification within itself, which in turn serves as a beacon to the world, as it establishes fellowship in baptism and the Lord's Supper between people of various nations, races, cultures, and classes, and thereby provides an alternate community of peace in contrast to the world's own strife and enmity (*CD IV.3.2*, 899-901).

5. The Church and the State

Nowhere is Barth's Christological logic more evident in regard to the relationship between the community and the world than in Barth's understanding of the particular form of this relationship between the church and the state, or, as Barth at times refers to them, as the Christian community and the civil community.[47] It is not our intention

---

[46]For Barth, this theological task includes the exegetical, historical, dogmatic, and practical disciplines of theology (*CD IV.3.2*, 879-880).

[47]Barth defines the Christian community (i.e., the church) as 'the commonalty of the people in one place, region, or country who are called apart and gathered together as "Christians" by reason of their knowledge of and belief in Jesus Christ.' He defines the civil community (i.e., the state) as 'the commonalty of all the people in one place, region, or country in so far as they

here to investigate comprehensively Barth's political thought, so our examination is limited to the particular manner in which Barth's Christological logic is evidenced in the specific relationship between the church and the state.[48]

First and foremost, it is important to remember that Barth's political positions are shaped and determined by theological convictions, even while recognizing the influence that political context has upon Barth's theology.[49] Specifically, Barth's mature political thought is shaped by Christological convictions, as Barth refuses to identify and define the state as an independent entity apart from Christ. In other words, Barth refuses to see the state (as the world at large) as an *abstraction* apart from Jesus Christ.[50] For this reason, Barth takes the unique position of including the state not under the order of creation, but under the order of reconciliation, addressing

---

belong together under a constitutional system of government that is equally valid for and binding on them all, and which is defended and maintained by force.' See Barth, 'Christian Community and Civil Community,' 150.

[48]For the following discussion, see especially: Barth, 'Church and State,' in *Community, State, and Church*, 101-148. (This essay was originally published in 1938. A better English title for this work might be 'Justification and Justice,' since the original German title is '*Rechtfertigung und Recht*'). See also Barth, 'The Christian Community and the Civil Community,' also in *Community, State, and Church*, 149-189 (originally published in 1946 as '*Christengemeinde und Bürgergemeinde*' — hereafter, 'Christian Community'); and *CD IV.2*, 719-726. For an examination of the development of Barth's political thought itself, see Frank Jehle, *Ever Against the Stream: The Politics of Karl Barth 1906-1968*, trans. Richard and Martha Burnett (Grand Rapids: Eerdmans, 2002).

[49]As Will Herberg states: 'No one can make any real sense of Barth's pronouncements on social and political questions without some understanding of his basic theological orientation' (Herberg, 'The Social Philosophy of Karl Barth,' in Barth, *Community, State, and Church*, 13). Similarly, Jüngel writes: 'Simply put, for Barth, the political is surely a predicate of theology, but theology is never a predicate of the political' (*Karl Barth: A Theological Legacy*, 104).

[50]Barth faults the Reformation at large, and Calvin in particular, for failing to provide a Christological foundation for the state and thus dealing with it independently of Christ and redemption. Barth claims that it was this failure that led eventually to the mistakes of a spiritualistic and quietistic pietism on the one hand and a natural law Enlightenment secularism on the other, and it would not be out of line to label these as rejected docetic and ebionitic options in Barth's thought. See Barth, 'Church and State,' 102-105. It is indeed justified to conclude that Barth's criticism of both Calvin's understanding of the state and his doctrine of election hinge upon the same point: for Barth, both doctrines are *abstract*, i.e., they are developed independently from a concrete Christological grounding in the revelation of Christ. Barth attempts to redefine both according to the second article of the creed rather than the first, and it should therefore not be surprising that the Christological logic in Barth's doctrine of election is carried into his doctrine of the state, defined not in terms of a general doctrine of providence and natural law but within the particular doctrine of reconciliation and redemption.

the state within the general framework of the second article of the creed, rather than the first, and thus in relation to the particular revelation in Christ rather than in relation to general revelation or natural law.[51] Barth therefore defines the state not only theologically but *Christologically*: 'When the New Testament speaks of the State, we are, fundamentally, in the *Christological* sphere; we are on a lower level than when it speaks of the Church, yet, in true accordance with its statements on the Church, we are in the same unique Christological sphere.'[52] As the church falls within the larger framework of the second article, so also the state, though an entity distinct from the church, stands as an element under the umbrella of the second article as well, its source lying not in history or nature but in God's ordination.

Barth's understanding of the church's relationship to the state is thoroughly defined according to his Christological logic, with the church standing as the first term of the relation and the state in the second. This logic can be readily outlined. First, the church and the state belong together within God's order of reconciliation, yet each must remain distinct, so that neither may be subsumed into the other. Both serve an important though singular role within the time of redemption between Christ's first and second advents, and Barth therefore sees a *positive* relationship between the church and the state rather than one of conflict.[53] He understands the state as an expression of God's grace in redemption, rather than simply as a restraint upon evil provided by God's law in creation and itself a fallen reality.[54] It is an authority, an 'angelic power,' created yet invisible and spiritual, which is established to serve God and Christ, though it may also be perverted and stands under the threat of 'demonization.'[55] The state therefore in itself is good, but it may be corrupted and become evil, though even in a perverted and fallen form it cannot help but be forced

---

[51]See Barth, 'Church and State,' 120; 114; also Barth, 'Christian Community,' 163-165. Barth placed the state within the order of reconciliation rather than within the order of creation already in his ethics lectures of 1928/1929, though he had of course not yet fully developed his Christological basis for the state. See Barth, *Ethics*, ed. Dietrich Braun, trans. Geoffrey Bromiley (New York: Seabury Press, 1981), 445-446; cf. 518. It is interesting that there Barth seems to make the *state* the inner circle within the larger circle of the *church*, whereas later Barth will reverse this order, so that the *church* is the inner circle of the wider circle of the *state* (see ibid., 441).

[52]See Barth, 'Church and State,' 101-102.

[53]As Barth avers: 'Clearly we need to know not only that the two are not in conflict, but, first and foremost, to what extent they are connected' (ibid., 102; cf. 107).

[54]Barth can therefore assert: 'However much human error and human tyranny may be involved in it, the State is not a product of sin but one of the constants of the divine Providence and government of the world in its action against human sin: it is therefore an instrument of divine grace' ('Christian Community', 156).

[55]Barth, 'Church and State,' 107; 115; also Barth, 'Christian Community,' 156-157.

to fulfill and serve God's sovereign purposes.[56] Such perverted powers will not in the end of time be annihilated but will be forced to return to their good state of service and will be 'restored to their original order.'[57] Even now in its rightful form the state serves Christ and the justification of the sinner through its administration of justice and its protection of the law. For Barth, a just state is one that performs this duty and grants the church the freedom to fulfill its own task.[58] As such, it has been granted its authority by Christ himself, and the church is readily to acknowledge this legitimate though indirect and qualified authority.[59]

This does not imply, however, that the church is blindly to follow and obey the state in whatever it demands. The subjection required of the church and of Christians is qualified, for the church renders obedience only as the state does not infringe upon its own freedom of the Gospel. Yet even in its criticism, the church may render its proper service and even subjugation to the state, for Barth maintains that its critical stance in certain circumstances may itself be the highest honor the church can render to the state.[60] So while the church may at times openly support the state and at other times openly resist it, what is not allowed is a position of neutrality or indifference towards the state, for this would in fact constitute a rebellion against a divinely established authority. The church therefore cannot fail to practice discernment in determining a just from an unjust state and to make relative judgments between forms of government.[61] In this regard, Barth himself sees the democratic state as most in line with the Gospel, but refuses to specify any form of government as uniquely Christian.[62]

---

[56]Barth, 'Church and State,' 111. For Barth this is seen nowhere as clearly as in Pilate's sentencing of Jesus to death (see ibid., 111-114).

[57]Ibid., 116-117. 'The destiny of the rebellious angelic powers which is made clear in Christ's resurrection and parousia is not that they will be annihilated, but that they will be forced into the service and the glorification of Christ, and, through Him, of God' (ibid., 116-117; 118-119).

[58]Ibid., 118-119.

[59]Ibid., 122.

[60]Ibid., 138-139; also Barth, 'Christian Community,' 159. Barth acknowledges that while the state may require oaths (though not totalitarian ones) and even military service, it may not require that its citizens adopt a specific world-view, an inward claim upon their conscience ('Church and State,' 142-143).

[61]Barth, 'Christian Community' 157; also 162.

[62]See Barth, 'Church and State,' 144-145; Barth, 'Christian Community,' 160-163; 181-182. Barth writes: 'When I consider the deepest and most central content of the New Testament exhortation, I should say that we are justified, from the point of view of exegesis, in regarding the "democratic conception of the State" as a justifiable expansion of the thought of the New

The church and the state are thus intricately united in the overall purpose of redemption, though they cannot be confused — neither can take the place of the other. Pertaining to the specific role of the state, Barth notes that in the New Testament we see that the state is viewed as uniting the church with the cosmos,[63] and we might say that for Barth it does so in a way that parallels the manner in which the church unites Christ and the state, or the world at large.   Barth therefore views the state in a secondary mediating role, complementing the primary mediating role of the church (though of course talk of the church's mediation itself requires qualification in light of Barth's reticence to use such language).   Neither the church nor the state are ends in themselves, but each serves the Gospel, the first by proclaiming it and the justification that God has effected, and the second by providing the space for such proclamation through the establishment of justice. The church therefore rightly prays for the state, so that justice, freedom, and peace might be established and that the Gospel might go forth.[64] The ministry of intercession is the primary service that the church owes the state, as its witness to Christ is the primary service it owes the world at large.[65]

We have mentioned Barth's conception of a rightful authority of the state that must be recognized by the church, and for Barth this authority is further substantiated by the fact that the coming kingdom of God is to be a *political* reality, a political order. Barth can even go so far as to assert that the future hope of the church does not reside 'in any heavenly image of its own existence but in the real heavenly *State*.'[66] The present state itself should bear witness to this future kingdom (though it most often does not), and on this account it is neither to be identified with that reality (the

---

Testament' ('Church and State,' 145). Barth certainly believed that relative judgments could be made between forms of state, and while reticent to identify one form as *the* Christian one, he certainly did not consider all forms to be equal: 'The assertion that all forms of government are equally compatible or incompatible with the Gospel is not only outworn but false.   It is true that man may go to hell in a democracy and achieve salvation under a mobocracy or a dictatorship. But it is not true that a Christian can endorse, desire, or seek after a mobocracy or a dictatorship as readily as a democracy' (ibid., 144-145, note 34). Barth can therefore conclude in his later essay: 'Taking everything into account, it must be said that the Christian view shows a stronger trend in this direction [i.e., democracy] than in any other. There certainly is an affinity between the Christian community and the civil communities of the free peoples' (Barth, 'Christian Community,' 182).

[63]Barth, 'Church and State,' 121.

[64]See ibid., 129.

[65]See ibid., 135-136. It is interesting in this regard that here Barth seems to speak of a 'priestly function' of the church, whereas he otherwise seems to insist that the church's role can only be prophetic, not kingly or priestly (ibid., 138).

[66]Ibid., 124.

mistake of deifying the state) nor is it to be seen only as opposed to it (the mistake of demonizing the state).[67] The role of the state in Barth's thought may then legitimately be described as a type of witness. The church recognizes this witness in 'the external, relative, and provisional sanctification of the unhallowed world which is brought about by the existence of political power and order.'[68] The state is therefore 'outside the Church but not outside the range of Christ's dominion — it is an exponent of His Kingdom.'[69] Neither the state nor the church can be identified with the kingdom of God, nor does the church expect the state to become the kingdom.[70] Nevertheless, both point to the kingdom as witnesses.

Barth thus refuses to either divinize or demonize the state. The church and the state cannot be confused, but they cannot be set in absolute conflict precisely because they share a common center. Barth writes:

> An equating of State and Church on the one hand and State and Kingdom of God on the other is therefore out of the question. On the other hand, however, since the State is based on a particular divine ordinance, since it belongs to the Kingdom of God, it has no autonomy, no independence over against the Church and the Kingdom of God. A simple and absolute heterogeneity between State and Church on the one hand and State and Kingdom of God on the other is therefore just as much out of the question as a simple and absolute equating. The only possibility that remains — and it suggests itself compellingly — is to regard the existence of the State as *an allegory, as a correspondence and an analogue* to the Kingdom of God which the Church preaches and believes in. Since the State forms the outer circle, within which the Church, with the mystery of its faith and gospel, is the inner circle, since it shares a common centre with the Church, it is inevitable that, although its presuppositions and its tasks are its own and different, it is nevertheless capable of *reflecting indirectly the truth and reality which constitute the Christian community.*[71]

Barth states that it indeed is the justification that the church proclaims that grounds the justice of the state, so that the state cannot take the place of the church. Yet the reverse is also true, in that the church should not set itself up as a state over against the earthly state, for the church is not to be viewed as itself a state within or

---

[67]Ibid., 124-125.

[68]Barth, 'Christian Community,' 157.

[69]Ibid., 156.

[70]Ibid., 167-168.

[71]Ibid., 168-169 (emphasis added).

above the earthly state. The church cannot become a state anymore than the state can become a church.[72] Nevertheless, the question of the state cannot be ignored by the church and must be answered from within the church itself. The church resembles a state, with its order and church law.[73] From the New Testament standpoint, Barth asserts, the state is never dealt with as an independent entity, but as an outer aspect of the Christian community itself, included within its own order, even as the church resides within the larger context of the world and its laws.[74] This raises the pointed question of the ranking of the church and the state in the order of redemption.

For Barth, while the relation between the church and the world is on the whole positive, and while each serves a necessary function, they do not in the end stand on the same plane. A strong case can be made that, for Barth, the church precedes the state both ontologically and epistemologically, the church providing the meaning of the state rather than vice versa. The relation between the church and the state, while to some degree reciprocal, is therefore on the whole predominantly an asymmetrical one. While this theme is hidden and underdeveloped in his essay 'Church and State,' it is clearly the logic of 'The Christian Community and the Civil Community' as well as his exposition of church law as exemplary law in the *Church Dogmatics*. Already in the earlier essay Barth could write:

> After all that we have seen as constituting the relation between the two realms, the answer must be given: that apart from the Church, nowhere is there any fundamental knowledge of the reasons which make the State legitimate and necessary. For everywhere else, save in the Church, the State, and every individual state, with its concern for human justice, may be called into question. From the point of view of the Church that preaches divine justification to all men this is impossible. For in the view of the Church, the authority of the State is included in the authority of their Lord Jesus Christ.[75]

In the later essay the priority of the church to the state becomes more pointed and explicit. Barth emphasizes that the state's task and goals are 'external, relative, and provisional,' and for this reason the state is marred by that which the church can do without, i.e., physical force as the guarantee of its authority.[76] Whereas in 'Church and State' each seemed to be on a level playing field and given equal rank and status,

---

[72]Barth, 'Church and State,' 126-127; 131.

[73]Ibid., 132.

[74]See ibid., 133-134.

[75]Ibid., 140.

[76]Barth, 'Christian Community,' 151; cf. 154-155.

in Barth's 1946 essay his thought seems to have slightly shifted. He there states: 'One cannot in fact compare the Church with the State without realising how much weaker, poorer, and more exposed to danger the human community is in the State than in the Church,' though Barth quickly adds that the church itself suffers from its own weaknesses and from every problem that plagues the state.[77]

Barth does continue to emphasize that the relationship between the two communities is a positive one, each requiring the other.[78] But Barth is now more open to claiming that the church itself is a political entity with its own 'definite authorities and offices, with patterns of community life and divisions of labour,' and that the existence of the church itself is a political existence, so that 'we are entitled and compelled to regard the existence of the Christian community as of ultimate and supremely political significance.'[79] The church's own task of the proclamation of the Gospel not only has political implications but is itself a political act, and this in such a way that the church's politics serve an exemplary function for the state.[80]

The relation between the church and the state is therefore not of two equal partners under the Lordship of Christ, though each requires the other, but is best portrayed in the imagery of concentric circles, as we have examined earlier. Christ is the center of both the church and the state, but of these two the church forms the inner circle and the state the outer one.[81] So while the church and the state both share a 'common origin and a common centre' in Christ who establishes them, standing in absolute dependence upon him, and while the state has a relation to the ordination of Christ that is not solely dependent upon the church's mediation, there is nonetheless a real though relative ordering of the church in relation to the state, in that the church takes precedence over the state in the order of redemption and provides the primary, normative, and intentional witness to Christ for the world, while the state bears a secondary, broken, and unknowing witness. Already in his ethic lectures of 1928/29 Barth could exclaim: 'Between church and state there is no equality, but superiority in the church's favor.'[82]

Some may question this interpretation of Barth, seeing more of an equal and reciprocal relationship between church and state. Does Barth not emphasize a relationship of mutual influence, maintaining that the church can itself learn from the

---

[77]Ibid., 152.

[78]Ibid., 153.

[79]Ibid., 153-154.

[80]Ibid., 184-185.

[81]See ibid., 155-157; 158-160.

[82]Barth, *Ethics*, 449; cf. 520.

world?[83] Such must indeed be admitted, yet what must be remembered is that while for Barth the church may be influenced and indeed learn from the world and its law, this is the *exception*, whereas the church's own law is *exemplary* for the world.[84] It is the church that is the model for what the state is to be, not the state which is to model what the church is to be. Barth writes: 'Perhaps the most important contribution the Church can make is to bear in mind in the shaping of its own life that, gathered as it is directly and consciously around the common centre, it has to represent the inner within the outer circle. The real Church must be the model and prototype of the real State.'[85] For this reason, the greatest service the church can perform for the state is for the church to be the church.[86] In doing so it provides a paradigm for what the state is to be.

So while it is true that both church law and civil law are human constructs that remain ultimately dependent upon their center in Christ, this does not relativize the real differences between them. Church law does not have an absolute priority over civil law, nor is it without defect, for church law itself is provisional. But it *is* 'different, corrected...and to that extent higher and better' than civil law.[87] Barth can therefore say of the church what he could not say of the state: 'The law of the Church is the result of its attempt to think and act in recognition and acknowledgment of the law of Jesus Christ — this human attempt which is so defective and provisional. On this basis and in this respect it has a relative — although not an absolute — advantage over all human law' (*CD IV.2*, 722).[88]

---

[83]See, for example, *CD IV.2*, 723; 724-725; cf. 721.

[84]See esp. *CD IV.2*, 719-726.

[85]Barth, 'Christian Community,' 186. As with its law, so also with its authority, the church is the exemplar for the state: 'Because there is revelation and the Church, there is also the family and the state, not *vice versa*. If the order of the family or the state wants to be and have genuine authority, it can do so only as an imitation of the authority of the Church' (*CD I.2*, 587).

[86]Barth, 'Church and State,' 146; also Barth, 'Christian Community,'186; *CD IV.2*, 721. Barth asserts: 'There can be no doubt however...that the decisive contribution which the Christian community can make to the upbuilding and work and maintenance of the civil consists in the witness which it has to give to it and to all human societies in the form of the order of its own upbuilding and constitution' (*CD IV.2*, 721). This can be compared to Barth's assertion that the primary task of the community for the world is one of intercession, seen above.

[87]See *CD IV.2*, 722; also 724.

[88]It is the recognition of the difference between absolute and relative distinctions that is largely missing in George Hunsinger's 'Karl Barth and the Politics of Sectarian Protestantism: A Dialogue with John Howard Yoder,' in *Disruptive Grace*, 114-128. While it is true that in (absolute) contrast to Christ and the kingdom all differences between the church and the state pale in comparison, it is not true than in relation to one another all differences are relativized.

The law of the church is normative and exemplary for the law of the state, though these cannot be simply interchanged. Church and state are united yet distinct, existing in an asymmetrical relationship in which the church takes the prior and normative position in their relation, and in which the state's existence is to correspond to the church's as the church itself is to bear witness to the law of the kingdom, though it does so indirectly. In other words, we might say that Barth's understanding of the relation between the church and the world was not unlike his view, following Calvin, of the relationship between God's means of grace within the church and outside of it (though by the doctrine of reconciliation, Barth was quite reticent to use the term 'means of grace' at all). While God *can and does* work outside of the walls of the church, the normal and established means of grace are in the Word and the sacraments of the church.[89] The external means are exceptional and hidden, the internal means exemplary and revealed.

In terms of the state's relation to the church, this is defined according to the notion of correspondence. Barth can speak not only of a relation of correspondence

---

The church joined with Christ is the *inner circle*, with the world as the *outer circle*, of redemption, so that church law is *exemplary* law, and therefore the norm and pattern for civil law, rather than the reverse. Hunsinger rightly perceives that for Barth both the Christian community and the civil community are derived from a common center in Christ (126). Nevertheless, it may be asked whether Hunsinger has not overstated the independence of the civil community over against the Christian community (124-125). While Hunsinger is right to insist that the church does not have an *absolute* priority over the state in God's plan, one may ask whether he has given adequate weight to the *relative* and real priority that the church does have (125). Hunsinger's statement that, for Barth, Christ and God's kingdom 'relativized all differences' (126) between the Christian and civil communities merits qualification — while it is true that Barth recognized a reciprocal influence between the church and the state, the differences between them were significant in Barth's estimation. These differences include the following:

1. The church knows Christ and patterns its law accordingly; the world does not know Christ and patterns its law after natural law. The law of the church is therefore Christologically-determined; the law of the state bears only broken correspondence to Christ. 2. The flow of influence of the world's law to the church, which, it must be admitted, truly exists, is nevertheless the exception; the influence of the Christologically-determined law of the church upon the world is the rule. 3. The meaning of history is found in Jesus Christ, and it is found in a secondary sense not in the world but specifically in the history of Israel among the nations and in the history of the church in the world. Christ's history includes that of the community, and therefore Christ and the community form the center of world-occurrence.

In this essay Hunsinger treats the church and the state too much like independent circles, rather than as concentric ones ordered according to a Christological logic. He himself provides a more nuanced description of the relationship of the church and the world in *Barth, Barmen, and the Confessing Church Today*, 289-293.

[89]See *CD I.2*, 224; 227-228; 236.

between the church and the state, but between divine justification and human justice, and between the church's 'divine service' in worship and its 'political service' in public life, thus forging an integral link between theology and ethics.[90] The latter term in each relation is to correspond to the former. Barth provides twelve examples of ways that the political life of the state can correspond to the truth of the Gospel as it is embodied in the church,[91] which Barth calls 'examples of analogies and corollaries of that Kingdom of God in which the Church believes and which it preaches, in the sphere of the external, relative, and provisional problems of the civil community.'[92] Barth acknowledges that these judgments may not be unique to Christianity, but he emphasizes that they are compatible with it.[93]

Once again, what must be noted is that it is the Christian community's presence and input that gives witness to what the state truly is to be. The state does not know the truth of its identity and therefore can only draw upon 'the porous wells of the so-called natural law,' and it requires 'the wholesomely disturbing presence, the activity that revolves directly around the common centre, the participation of the Christian community in the execution of political responsibility.'[94] And as the Christian community participates in the state and its life, choosing among the political possibilities of the time, 'it will choose those which most suggest a correspondence to, an analogy and a reflection of, the content of its own faith and gospel.'[95]

6. Summary

Barth's understanding of the relationship between the church and the world is characterized by a qualified form of the Christological logic that governed other relationships in Barth's thought, such as that between Christ and the community. The relationship between the church and the world is marked by the unity and distinction, asymmetry, and correspondence of Barth's Christological logic, but the application of this logic is qualified in a few significant respects. First, the relationship itself is on the horizontal plane, rather than on the vertical one, in that it is a relationship not between a divine and human partner but between two created realities. This in turn entails that the relationship is not strictly irreversible — while the church is the normative pattern for the world and its law, providing the inherent meaning of the

---

[90]See Barth, 'Church and State,' 101-102.

[91]See Barth, Christian Community,' 171-179. See also *CD IV.2*, 723-724.

[92]Ibid., 179.

[93]See ibid., 180-181.

[94]Ibid., 170.

[95]Ibid., 170. The church therefore naturally desires that the state reflect the kingdom of God in its earthly life (see ibid., 170-171).

world's history, the church itself is influenced by the world. The world is therefore not dependent upon the church for its existence, but both are dependent upon Christ. Nevertheless, the history of Christ includes the history of his community, and it is this history that provides the world with its meaning and reveals to the world its own identity. The world therefore corresponds to the community, but only as the community itself corresponds to Christ and the kingdom.

While the Christological patterns are weakened in this relationship precisely because of the nature of its members, this does not negate the fact that these patterns are nevertheless present. Though the particular relation between the Christian community and the civil community may not be strictly irreversible and marked by absolute contrasts, it is ordered in such a way that the church and its law take precedence and possess a relative superiority over the state and its law. The witness of the Christian community to Christ is normative and its law exemplary, whereas the witness of the state is broken and its law uneven.

If Barth's position on church-state relations has been criticized, it is most often in regard to Barth's attempt to determine specific Christological analogies within the state.[96] Barth's derivation of these analogies has often been judged to be arbitrary, governed not by Christology but by an attempt to shore up preconceived political convictions through Christological means.[97] Furthermore, the question has been raised as to what controls these analogies in the first place — they seem to lend themselves more to abstract than concrete ethical questions.[98]

Here a choice seems to be necessary. One may abandon Barth's attempt to ground ethics and politics in Christology as misguided and turn to a foundation in natural law or some other general criteria, or one can attempt to hone and correct Barth's method of analogy and correspondence in such a way that its arbitrariness and abstract character are remedied.[99] One must either abandon Barth's central

---

[96]See 'Christian Community,' 171-179.

[97]Herberg, for one, concludes: 'Is it possible to doubt that what Barth is really doing is adjusting his "Christological" arguments to conclusions *already* reached *on other grounds?* In other words, Barth takes the values of a pluralistic constitutional democracy as given, ingeniously discovers more or less plausible counterparts for them in the realm of Church and Gospel, and then proceeds to "derive" the former from the latter' ('The Social Philosophy of Karl Barth,' 35-36).

[98]See Stanley Hauerwas, 'On Learning Simplicity in an Ambiguous Age,' in *Barth, Barmen, and the Confessing Church Today*, 133. Hauerwas asserts that 'Barth's Christological justification of the State is so abstract that concrete application always tends to ideological distortions' (137).

[99]See George Hunsinger, 'To Hauerwas: On Learning Faithfulness in a Fallen World,' in *Barth, Barmen, and the Confessing Church Today*, 254. He writes: 'Although Barth's case for the analogies is not convincing, that does not in itself render the analogies, or even the

Christocentric tenet, or one must attempt to articulate it in a manner that corrects its inherent shortcomings. A third option does not seem to be forthcoming.

---

method of analogy, as being automatically false. Barth explicitly stated that the analogies were intended to be suggestive not definitive. As suggestive I think they succeed. What is needed, in my opinion, is more reflection on the method, not a scrapping of the method itself.'

Chapter Nine

Looking Back and Looking Ahead

Karl Barth's doctrine of the church is rich and complex, resisting facile analysis or simple classification. It weaves together multiple strands of thought into an elegant tapestry that, upon careful inspection, reveals deep Christological patterns that govern the whole, patterns that bear witness both to the consistency of Barth's central theological convictions across time, as well as to the remarkable innovation in his mature thought. The development and logic of these patterns disclose Barth's attempt to articulate a particular Chalcedonian ecclesiological solution to what he believed were mistaken positions on both the left and the right, against both docetic and ebionitic ecclesiologies, and against both synergistic and heteronomous understandings of ecclesial agency. Close examination of this tapestry reveals that many criticisms of it either present a distortion, or at best a one-sided presentation, of the fabric itself. Such misrepresentations are most often due to a failure to discern its controlling Christological logic. This logic provides the tight organization of the tapestry's weave, a weave that attempts to integrate both dogmatic and ethical threads, as well as what may appear at first sight to be mutually exclusive motifs. Barth's ecclesiology demonstrates a remarkable accomplishment, foremost for its careful and strict articulation of the *theological* character of the church, as well as for its preservation of the freedom, initiative, and Lordship of Christ and the Spirit over the church in an irreversible relationship. Furthermore, it does this while providing a real and true place for the church in the economy of salvation through the notions of witness and correspondence. This unique conception of the Lordship of Christ mirrored in the witness of the church is the enduring legacy of Barth's achievement. Yet, this real achievement does not entail that Barth's ecclesiology is immune from all criticism.[1] There are a few frayed areas.

---

[1]Recent examinations, while more careful, can also be quite critical. With particular relevance for the following discussion, see Nicholas M. Healy, 'The Logic of Karl Barth's Ecclesiology: Analysis, Assessment and Proposed Modifications,' *Modern Theology* 10 (1994): 253-270; Stanley Hauerwas, *With the Grain of the Universe: The Church's Witness and Natural Theology* (Grand Rapids: Brazos Press, 2001); Hütter, 'The Church as Public,' 334-361; idem, 'Karl Barth's "Dialectical Catholicity": *Sic Et Non*,' 137-157; idem, *Suffering Divine Things*, esp. 95-115; Joseph L. Mangina, 'Bearing the Marks of Jesus: The Church in the Economy of Salvation in Barth and Hauerwas,' *Scottish Journal of Theology* 52 (1999): 269-305; idem, 'The Stranger as Sacrament: Karl Barth and the Ethics of Ecclesial Practice,' *International Journal of Systematic Theology* 1 (1999): 322-339; and most recently, John Yocum, *Ecclesial Mediation in Karl Barth* (Hampshire/Burlington: Ashgate Publishing, 2004). In fairness to

Barth's ecclesiological thought is marked by coherence, consistency, and innovation, providing the basis for its impressive and compelling quality. Yet it is also characterized by deep and abiding (dialectical) tensions. First, there is an enduring tension between understanding the church as event and as institution, and, in a related manner, as both invisible and visible. For Barth, neither term of either relation can be excluded. To maintain that Barth has sacrificed the latter to the former term in either of the respective relations is not only to misunderstand Barth's intention, but to fail to discern his true accomplishment. It is patently false to maintain that Barth precludes historical continuity in his definition of the church's substance, as we have seen. Barth does not simply set an invisible, true church of event over against a visible, false institutional church. It is precisely such a dichotomy that Barth's ecclesiology attempts to overcome. While it is certainly true that Barth's early ecclesiology left itself open to such a charge (even if it was not always fairly assessed), Barth's mature ecclesiology cannot be accurately represented in this way. It was not the visible church that Barth opposed (for the *true* church was both invisible *and* visible).[2] What Barth opposed was a sociological understanding of the church that failed to discern its true theological character. So to state that Barth has a low ecclesiology, one that relativizes the visible, and to assert that for Barth the church 'is not a qualitatively distinct entity, for it has neither unique powers nor a distinctive ethos that would give its members the opportunity to engage in the most adequate way of life or response and witness to Jesus Christ,' is to put matters in a way that is quite difficult to defend.[3] For Barth, the church *is* a distinct entity, for it is called into existence by the power of the Holy Spirit, the church's 'sword of protection,' and it is this power that not only calls the visible church into existence but

---

Healy, it should be noted that he seems to have retracted his strong criticisms of Barth's ecclesiology upon further investigation. See Healy, 'Karl Barth's ecclesiology reconsidered,' *Scottish Journal of Theology* 57 (2004): 287-299. Nevertheless, while this point should be constantly kept in mind, the influence of Healy's earlier article upon later examinations of Barth's ecclesiology requires that it be assessed on its own terms. For a detailed examination of such discussions beyond what can here be provided, see Kimlyn J. Bender, 'Karl Barth's Doctrine of the Church in Contemporary Anglo-American Ecclesiological Conversation,' *Zeitschrift für dialektische Theologie* (forthcoming). See also James J. Buckley, 'Christian community, baptism, and Lord's Supper,' in *The Cambridge Companion to Karl Barth*, 195-211.

[2]Yocum writes that in the final volume of the *Church Dogmatics* (*CD IV*) there is 'an implied choice between distinctive, visible, concrete forms of the church as a social body and its invisible essence' (121). As should be evident by now, Barth simply refused such a choice.

[3]Healy, 'The Logic of Karl Barth's Ecclesiology,' 265.

also sets it apart from every other historical society. In short, the church is a *mystery* (in analogy to the supreme mystery and miracle of Christmas itself).

Furthermore, the church is distinct because it *does* have a unique way of life, a way that is the normative pattern for all other familial, social, and political forms of life, and normative precisely because it exists in correspondence to Christ's own life. Church law is exemplary law. It is thus not the case that for Barth the church's empirical distinctiveness is in effect relativized and its historical reality and embodiment of no importance.[4] To maintain that Barth has de-historicized the church so that its empirical and concrete practices are relativized is therefore not an accurate construal of Barth's position.[5] Barth certainly does not want to 'de-historicize' the church anymore than he wants to 'historicize' it. He firmly maintains that the visibility and temporality of the church are central to its identity and rejects any ecclesiological docetism, while equally rejecting a flight into visibility that simply reduces the church's essence to its historical and social existence.[6]

Now it must be granted that the matter is not always clear in Barth's actual exposition, due to another enduring tension in Barth's thought, that between the church's sinfulness and its obedience. The criticism that Barth has either undermined or relativized the history, order, and practices of the church due to its inherent sinfulness is misplaced, but the charge can be understood. It arises precisely by grasping upon singular statements read in an exclusive (and therefore non-dialectical) manner. Such a reading fails to take into account the intrinsically dialectical nature of Barth's ecclesiological thought. This dialectical understanding of the church is

---

[4]Many critics of Barth's ecclesiology not only overlook Barth's discussion of the ministry of the community and its specific forms of ministry (see *CD IV.3.2*, 864-901), but also neglect to discuss Barth's understanding of church law as exemplary law. It can of course only be exemplary if it is concrete and observable.

[5]As does Mangina, 'Bearing the Marks of Jesus,' 277-278. In his earlier article, Healy seems to lean toward this understanding as well, and tends to equate the visible church of witness with Barth's concept of the *Scheinkirche*, though these are of course not the same (see Healy, 259). It is not that the true church is invisible and the false church visible; the true church is the visible church as it is called and joined to its Head, and the false church is the church that no longer heeds the voice of its Lord. Healy thus sees a greater bifurcation in Barth's understanding of the church than is actually there. Hütter follows Healy on this point (see 'Karl Barth's "Dialectical Catholicity,"' 149).

[6]This refusal to equate and in fact reduce the reality of the church to its concrete embodiment and practices is what distinguishes Barth from many of his modern critics. For the charge that Barth fails to offer a 'concrete ecclesiology' in this regard, see Hütter, *Suffering Divine Things*, 133; idem., 'Karl Barth's "Dialectical Catholicity,"' 148; Mangina, 'Bearing the Marks of Jesus,' 301; Hauerwas, *With the Grain of the Universe*, 173-204, esp. 192-193; Healy, 'The Logic of Karl Barth's Ecclesiology,' 263-264. Again, whether Healy would maintain such a criticism is questionable in light of his later article.

predicated upon the conviction that the mystery of the church is incapable of being expressed by a single term or description. One must therefore incorporate seemingly contradictory statements, and this dialectic marks not only his early, but also his mature, ecclesiological thought.

Barth speaks of the church as corresponding even in its visibility to Christ. Yet, he can also speak of the church as sinful and contrary to Christ. He can speak of the unique and exemplary nature of the community even within its visibility. At other times, he can state that the community in history is no different in its social practices from other human societies, and may not even be the best one. In sum: Barth speaks on one hand of the superiority of the church to the world, of its obedience and belief, of its exemplary character, and of its unique correspondence to its Lord. On the other hand, Barth is adamant that the church is not equal to its Lord, that it remains sinful, and that it is not exempt from error, and therefore, from judgment. In his early theology, the emphasis is certainly upon the latter description (though the former one is not entirely absent – even in the *Romans* commentary Barth could speak of the church in terms of a parable of the Kingdom). In his mature thought, the former theme predominates (though the latter theme does not disappear). Critics of Barth grasp upon the latter theme and point to its inadequacy, while defenders point to the former one. The issue is indeed complex, even paradoxical, and such a paradox can only be made intelligible when the dialectical nature of Barth's ecclesiology is fully understood.

There is thus a deep and enduring tension between speaking of the church as in obedient correspondence to its Lord, and speaking of it as in sinful contradiction to him.[7] Barth does both. There is another path that could be followed, however, a path that would retain the critical element Barth's dialectic sought to preserve. This path would be to speak of imperfect and varying correspondence. To speak of imperfect correspondence would in fact be better than to speak of contradiction. It would still preserve Barth's critical dialectic that rightfully guards the distinction between divine and human action while shining a light upon the church's intractable sinfulness. Indeed, correspondence itself, like the analogy of faith, is an inherently dialectical concept. To speak of imperfect correspondence would therefore preserve both the vertical dialectic between the Creator and the creature, as well as the horizontal dialectic between the church's sin and obedience, recognizing that this relation of sin and obedience in fact varies within concrete circumstances. Nevertheless, Barth allows a place for talk of contradiction that is not always helpful or clear, and which too often tends toward abstraction from the actual historical variance between

---

[7]This tension is to some degree related to the tension between Barth's substitutionary and exemplarist Christologies. See Webster, 'The Christian in Revolt,' 119-144.

episodes of the church's concrete obedience and sin, and in the end threatens to relativize their differences.

In a related way, while Barth is masterful at protecting and delineating the *distinction* and *irreversibility* between ecclesiological strands, i.e., between the church as event and institution, between the invisible and visible church, and between theological and sociological descriptions of the church, he is often less adept at describing their *unity* and *relation*. This is not the same as stating that Barth sacrifices one strand for the other. Rather, this deficiency points to Barth's overriding concern that they not be confused. While he holds that the strands also cannot be separated, he is often less successful in describing their relation than their distinction.

We might take the relation between theological and sociological description of the church as an example. Barth is rightly concerned that the church not simply be described in sociological terms, or that such description be substituted for theological exposition itself. For Barth, this is a concomitant error to the mistake of subsuming revelation into history and thus confusing them, precisely the problem that Barth perceived in his early opponents. Nevertheless, at times Barth seems to set theological and sociological descriptions of the church against one another in competition and as mutually exclusive, rather than integrating the latter into the former.[8]

Furthermore, as John Webster has noted, in regard to the church Barth 'has a rather slender account of the moral processes of common life.'[9] That Barth leaves the ecclesial practices of moral formation and discernment largely unspecified is common knowledge. It might be said in response that Barth may well have addressed such matters in more detail in the ethics of reconciliation (left incomplete) and in the ethics of redemption (which was never written). Nevertheless, this incompleteness and lack of specificity lies at the root of the oft-stated criticism that Barth's ecclesiology lacks concreteness (and is in fact a more accurate way of identifying what is at issue). Yet any charge brought against Barth's ecclesiology on account of its lack of specificity must provide a place for the recognition of a number of facts that greatly qualify it.

First, if Barth's ecclesiology is criticized for its emphasis upon formal relations and sparse description of specific practices, such a criticism should only be made after a thorough examination of Barth's descriptions of precisely such practices in *CD IV.3.2* has been conducted.[10] There, Barth discusses twelve forms of ministry, and it is both strange and curious that some who charge Barth with a lack of ecclesial

---

[8]To integrate the latter, sociological description would of course require a reconstitution (*Aufhebung*) of it.

[9]Webster, *Karl Barth*, 161. Webster does not, however, see this lack of specificity necessarily to be a weakness.

[10]See *CD IV.3.2*, esp. 864-901.

concreteness fail to consider these quite specific and concrete practices.[11] Certainly Barth does not find the ultimate definition of the church in these practices. But to say that for Barth '*What* people do, as such, is not a constituent element of the church's identity' is too strong a statement.[12] Certainly Barth's ultimate criterion for the church's identity is theologically described in terms of God's action in Christ through the Spirit to call the Christian community into existence. Nevertheless, this divine action calls into existence a *particular* fellowship with *particular* forms of ministry, some of which Barth can even say are universal, demanded 'always, everywhere and in all circumstances' (*CD IV.3.2*, 864). Indeed, they are in this sense even constitutive, for they are required by the church's very nature and 'cannot indeed be lacking in so far as they are generally posited by God' (*CD IV.3.2*, 859).[13] Barth's discussion of these forms of ministry provides a very fruitful reflection upon the church's historical life, and, for this reason, these forms rightly merit attention.

Second, that Barth's descriptions at times appear markedly formal and abstract may be due to his insistence that all forms of ministry must arise from particular circumstances, and therefore the theologian cannot in fact prescribe a timeless system of such practices. Barth maintains that investigation of specific forms of ministry belongs to practical, rather than dogmatic, theology, the multiplicity of forms making a systematic presentation impossible:

> For even today the history of the community moves on from century to century. And under the influence of different traditions, but also of the different places and circumstances in which it exists, the community might well find itself inspired and summoned to new variations of the basic forms, and endowed for them. Our concern, then, is with the forms of

---

[11]It is interesting that Hütter's works (and Healy's early article) largely ignore these forms of ministry. Especially surprising is Hütter's appeal to the practices outlined by Luther as evidencing a 'concrete catholicity' that can correct Barth's 'dialectical catholicity,' for in fact many of the concrete examples given by Luther, along with the supplements by Hütter, can be found or at least roughly correlated with those in Barth's own list of twelve. See 'Karl Barth's "Dialectical Catholicity,"' 149-152; and 'The Church As Public,' 353-357. Mangina does examine these practices, making his critique of Barth more careful and nuanced ('Karl Barth and the Ethics of Ecclesial Practice,' 330-331).

[12]Healy, 'The Logic of Karl Barth's Ecclesiology,' 260; cf. also Mangina, who follows Healy in this interpretation ('Bearing the Marks of Jesus,' 278).

[13]The fact that Yocum overlooks these forms of ministry undermines his charge that, by lacking such social concrete practices by which to identify the church, Barth is in danger of the 'ecclesial Docetism' which he himself rejected (119). Such a charge is the latest example of a historic pedigree of misreadings and completely ignores Barth's discussion of church law and ministry.

differentiated ministry which persist in both past and present (*CD IV.3.2*, 859-860).

In light of charges of a lack of concreteness in his description of the church's historical life, we can imagine that Barth might respond that such critics themselves are not thinking concretely enough. It is precisely the variation of specific circumstances across time and space that make a complete description of church order and forms of ministry impossible. All that dogmatic theology can do is to outline the enduring and general principles of order and forms of ministry, for their concrete embodiment belongs to the individual Christian communities to determine in light of their own concrete circumstances, and these cannot be dictated by the theologian.

Third, there is room for reading Barth as not ruling out detailed sociological description, but simply ruling it out of the realm of *dogmatics*. As noted above, Barth holds that sociological description, as well as a complete investigation of the church's order and forms of ministry, belongs not to dogmatics but to practical theology and to canon law.[14] While this observation may not allay all criticism, it does provide a rationale for Barth's rather formal description of the church's concrete practices. This complements Barth's recognition that these practices cannot be given in detail in dogmatics because they will vary greatly over time and from one location to the next. A dogmatics that is too specific may therefore also be too provincial.

Finally, one must recognize that Barth's fears of sociological description were not unfounded. Reductive sociological understandings of the church were prevalent in the nineteenth and early twentieth centuries, and Barth justifiably reacted against them. Against sociological reductionism, Barth strongly maintained the irreducibly theological character of the church. He would no doubt be uncomfortable with recent descriptions of the identity of the church as coextensive with the particularity of its historical and sociological existence and forms of life. For Barth, the reality of the church is visible, but it is more than its visibility.

These observations mitigate and lessen the force of the criticism that Barth's ecclesiology lacks concrete historical description and fails adequately to outline detailed and explicit forms of order and ministry. They do not eliminate all concerns, however. Barth believes that dogmatics should be content with the description of general principles of church order and forms of ministry rather than with matters regarding specific application, and he is inclined to leave such questions to the realm

---

[14]See, for example, *CD IV.3.2*, 859-860; also *CD IV.2*, 678. Barth elsewhere makes a similar distinction between 'theological ethics' and 'Christian ethics,' the former concerning itself with the general ethical principles to be examined by dogmatics, and the latter addressing the concrete ethical application of these principles to actual human situations. See *CD II.2*, 542; related in Biggar, *Hastening*, 159. I thank Daniel Migliore for drawing my attention to this latter insight.

of practical theology and canon law. This tendency to exclude specific questions of definite church order and forms of ministry from the realm of dogmatics does raise the danger that such order and practices will in fact be determined and shaped not by the inner logic of the Gospel, but by alien and foreign principles and pragmatic considerations. Yet here, too, Barth may simply have more trust in practical theology to draw out the implications of the thick descriptions provided by dogmatic theology than others do. A lack of specificity in his descriptions therefore may be due more to his understanding of inter-disciplinary boundaries rather than to deficiencies of thought. Certainly Barth's sensitivity to concrete historical circumstances and respect for the self-determination of local congregations is both refreshing and commendable, demonstrating a trust in, rather than disdain for, the churches. Barth simply refuses to have the theologian dictate to the churches from on high regarding their embodied life. The service of theology therefore resides in its guidance, not its prescriptions, for the church.

Another frequent criticism of Barth's ecclesiology is that it does not provide an adequate place for ecclesial agency. This criticism itself involves a number of recurring themes.[15] First, Barth's ecclesiology is judged to be over-determined by Christology and correspondingly under-determined by pneumatology, thus denying the Holy Spirit any distinctive agency in the role of redemption and salvation history, and with it, any role to the church.[16] As has already been noted, Barth's theology does appear at times to give short shrift to the Holy Spirit, though a fair assessment of this would lead us far afield. This criticism is not new, and Barth himself was one of the first to make it.[17] With specific regard to the question of ecclesiology, certainly at the very least Barth did not develop other images for the church in the manner that

---

[15]Many of these themes, such as Barth's understanding of baptism and the Lord's Supper, go beyond the scope of this investigation and require studies of their own.

[16]Magina writes: 'Since Barth treats the cross as bringing history to a close, the Spirit's work is "short-circuited". The Spirit can only appear as a predicate of Christ's reconciling work, a *manifestation* of the latter rather than an *agency* of its own. Correspondingly, the church "shows" or signifies Christ but does not serve as the means through which believers begin to participate in the new life he brings. The result is an odd hiatus between the church (in the full theological sense) and the ordinary, empirical practices of the Christian community across time' ('Bearing the Marks of Jesus,' 270; see also 282).

[17]In response to a student's inquiry in the 1950s as to why the Holy Spirit was largely absent in Barth's section on the 'revealed Word,' Barth responded: 'You must remember the theological situation in 1932. At that time I wanted to place a strong emphasis on the objective side of revelation: Jesus Christ. If I had made much of the Holy Spirit, I am afraid it would have led back to subjectivism, which is what I wanted to overcome. Today I would speak more of the Holy Spirit. Perhaps I was too cautious. You students should not make that mistake in your polemical writings!' (*Karl Barth's Table Talk*, 27).

he developed the Christological ones, and this indeed could lead to an imbalance. For Barth, the church was almost exclusively described as the 'body of Christ,' and other biblical images (such as 'royal priesthood'), though not entirely neglected, are for the most part underdeveloped, while the image of the church as the 'bride of Christ' is almost entirely ignored.[18]

There is also indeed some truth in the charge that for Barth redemptive history is portrayed as coming to a close with the cross, so that the resurrection adds nothing more to Christ's death than to reveal its true character, and this in turn seems to undermine a significant role for the church and its activity in history.[19] Yet, it is mistaken to conclude that Barth leaves no place for ecclesial and human agency. This charge can only be made by overlooking Barth's rich notions of witness and correspondence.

It is indeed much more accurate to say that Barth excludes a certain *type* of human and ecclesial agency than that he excludes human agency altogether. The issue is not that Barth has provided a purely monistic account of agency, excluding the human for the sovereignty of the divine and relegating the church's activity to inconsequence in the face of the finality of Christ's all-sufficient sacrifice. As Barth himself constantly reiterated, the dictum that 'God is everything and humanity is nothing' is not only false but nonsense. The issue is, rather, that he describes human agency in general, and ecclesial agency in particular, in terms of correspondent witness rather than direct cooperation or mediation. This is the basis of the church's vocation.

Barth's understanding of ecclesial agency can only be understood by a serious examination of his notion of correspondence, an idea crucial to his thought. Barth strongly maintains that the work of Christ requires no supplementation, which is first

---

[18]See O'Grady, *The Church in Catholic Theology*, 278. Yocum faults Barth for precisely this deficiency, but his discussion itself is problematic. He writes: 'The term "body of Christ" is used twice in the New Testament in reference to the Church, while the motif of the bride is used directly of the church at least twice (2 Cor 11:2; Eph. 5:25ff.). It is used of the relation of Christ and the Church less directly four times (Rev. 19:7; 21:2; 21:9; 22:17) and possibly five (John 3:29)' (120). He goes on from here to argue for a greater place for the latter. Now there are a number of problems here, not least of which that the term 'body' in direct or indirect reference to the church (or to the church and Israel as one community) occurs many more than two times, even if not always specifically designated the 'body *of Christ*' (see Rom. 12:5; 1 Cor. 10:17; 12:12-27; Eph. 1:22-23; 2:16; 3:6; 4:4; 4:12; 4:16; 5:23; 5:29-30; Col. 1:18; 1:24; 3:15). The issue, however, is not only about counting texts. The more important issue is that no image for the church (and certainly not that of the bride) is as richly developed in the New Testament as is that of the church as a body, and specifically, the body of Christ. The only image developed in a comparable way is perhaps the architectural one employed in 1 Peter chapter two.

[19]See Mangina,'Bearing the Marks of Jesus,' 275-278; see also Webster, *Karl Barth*, 139.

and foremost the case because Christ's work encompasses both reconciliation and redemption, and because Christ is not absent, but present, and thus requires no mediation by the church to make him present. This assertion of Christ's presence does raise the question of the Spirit's distinctive role in the economy of salvation, and may also be read as a denial of ecclesial agency. Yet such a reading would be inaccurate, for Barth relativizes the work of the church in order to establish it, insofar as by ridding it of the untenable task of divine mediation, Barth believes it may be free for its true human vocation of witness.[20] Barth's concept of correspondence allows him to provide a place for concrete and material obedience by the church in its very visible and historical existence, giving his ecclesiology, as his theology as a whole, an essential ethical character.[21]

Furthermore, correspondence guards against seeing the church as irrelevant in light of a divine monergism and Christological monism, and as triumphant and independent in light of a human and ecclesial autonomy.[22] For this reason, Barth's articulation of the relationship between Christ and the church is not solely exhausted by moving 'between the poles of complete identity and complete non-identity,'[23] but in fact speaks of an analogical relation between them that is defined neither by identity nor contradiction, but by correspondence. In correspondence to Christ, the church receives its true task of witness and attestation to the reconciliation of the world accomplished solely by Christ.

Yet here again, such comments do not eliminate all criticisms. Barth's strength is preserving the distinction and irreversibility between divine and human agency, as well as that between the work of Christ and the church. He is less successful in describing their relation and inseparability. Especially in the final volumes of the

---

[20]As Webster states: 'The move Barth is making here at one and the same time relativizes and establishes the activity of Christian witness. "Relativizes", because it asserts the entire adequacy of Jesus' own self-declaration; "establishes", because the willed form of that self-declaration includes its echo in human declaration' (*Barth's Moral Theology*, 144). This relativization is thus a liberation for the church to fulfill its proper task without burdening it with the work of what God alone can accomplish, a fact Webster believes Hütter has underestimated (see ibid., 146; also 170).

[21]Webster, *Barth's Ethics of Reconciliation*; also idem, *Barth's Moral Theology*.

[22]Cf. Webster, *Barth's Ethics of Reconciliation*, 57. While Webster applies this description specifically to Barth's ethics, it is equally applicable, with only slight qualification, to Barth's ecclesiology. Barth can designate the church that exalts itself and claims for itself what can only belong to its Lord as the 'church in excess.' Likewise, the church that does not take itself seriously and therefore fails to take up its divinely-appointed task with courage is designated by Barth as the 'church in defect.' See Barth, *The Christian Life: Church Dogmatics IV, 4 Lecture Fragments*, trans. Geoffrey W. Bromiley (Grand Rapids: Eerdmans, 1981), 136-140.

[23]Mangina, 'Bearing the Marks of Christ,' 301-302.

Church Dogmatics, Barth often speaks of a parallelism of action, rather than an embodied action, so that divine and human activity are portrayed as in conjunction, rather than in terms of the divine acting in and through the human, Christ acting in and through the church.[24] The point might be illustrated by asking whether Christ comes to us *through* the proclamation of the church or *along side* of it.

Barth firmly rejects what might be called strong notions of ecclesial mediation, i.e., any that might imply that the church adds to or cooperates with Christ's unique and irreplaceable work as the mediator between God and humanity such that the atonement is ecclesially extended. Barth's doctrines of election and reconciliation (and redemption) disallow such positions. God's salvation of the world is complete in Christ and requires no further extension or supplementation. This is the basis for Barth's insistence in his later work that Christ is the only true sacrament. He is such, because he is the one true mediator. Any view of mediation that fails to reckon with the finality and perfection of Christ's work is one that Barth can only reject.

More problematic is Barth's late penchant for seemingly rejecting what might be termed even weak notions of ecclesial mediation, i.e., that the proclamation of this finished event of Christ's sacrifice comes to us through human agency as Christ takes up human words and actions (preaching, baptism, and Lord's Supper) for proclaiming this message and revealing himself to us. Barth comes close to stating that even the pronouncement of this finished work is carried out by Christ in an im-mediate, rather than mediated, way: 'All real acquaintance with Him rests on the fact that he makes Himself known. All adequate conception rests on the fact that he introduces Himself. No other can do this for Him. He does not need the help of any other' (*CD IV.3.1*, 46; see also *CD IV.3.2*, 514-516). The question remains, however, whether Christ, who truly needs no other for his Self-proclamation, nevertheless invites others to share in his Self-proclamation, not as equal partners, but as those through whom he graciously calls the world to faith and obedience. As Christ says, 'Whoever welcomes you welcomes me, and whoever welcomes me welcomes the one who sent me.'[25] Here some ask whether statements late in the *Church Dogmatics* concerning the immediacy of Christ's Self-proclamation do not undermine Barth's earlier discussions of secondary objectivity, namely, that God's revelation to us occurs through the

---

[24]I owe this insight to George Hunsinger.

[25]Matthew 10:40 NRSV. Elsewhere Paul can write: 'We also constantly give thanks to God for this, that when you received the word of God that you heard from us, you accepted it not as a human word but as what it really is, God's word, which is also at work in you believers' (1 Thessalonians 2:13 NRSV; cf. Romans 10:14-15; 1 Corinthians 15:1-2).

mediation of created things.[26]   Indeed, the very notion of witness itself seems to require some such position. Barth's recurring reticence in the final volumes of the *Church Dogmatics* to speak of ecclesial agency and witness in terms of mediation even of the most circumscribed and qualified kind is no doubt the reason that Barth's notions of correspondence seem to some to be strained and inadequate.

Here judgments must be careful and fair. Barth had good reason to fear the loss of Christ's objectivity in relation to the church, as well as an ecclesial sacramental manipulation of grace. Furthermore, he was understandably reticent to speak of the connection between Christ's work and that of the church in causal terms, eschewing 'secondary causes.'[27]   The activity of God and the activity of the church are distinct and are therefore to be carefully distinguished. In good Reformed manner Barth attempted to protect and clarify the distinction. His weakness is seen in his attempt to articulate how they are united and conjoined. What is largely missing is a satisfactory account of how the activity of the church is not only a response to the Gospel, but a means taken up by God for its proclamation and a community shaped by the Gospel itself.   For some, this deficiency points to the inadequacy of the concept of witness and correspondence to describe the church's task exhaustively.[28]

Yet once again such a judgment may point not so much to a deficiency in Barth as to a real difference from other notions of ecclesial mediation. In light of such

---

[26]Barth writes in *CD II.1*: 'God is objectively immediate to Himself, but to us he is objectively mediate. That is to say, He is not objective directly but indirectly, not in the naked sense but clothed under the sign and veil of other objects different from Himself' (16). If this is true, then one cannot abandon all talk of ecclesial mediation, for knowledge of God is mediated to us through human means such as the pastor who preaches and the (humanly-written) words of Scripture. Indeed, Barth can even talk of the church's election in terms of mediation: 'It is *mediate* [*mittlere*], that is, in so far as it is the middle point between the election of Jesus Christ and (included in this) the election of those who have believed, and do and will believe, in Him. It is *mediating* [*vermittelnde*] in so far as the relation between the election of Jesus Christ and that of all believers (and *vice versa*) is mediated and conditioned by it' (*CD II.2*, 196; quoted in Yocum, 57). I am indebted to Yocum for drawing my attention to this latter passage as well as for the current discussion on mediation. (See Yocum, 57; 65-66; et al.) Whether Yocum wants to retain not only weak, but also strong, notions of mediation is unclear.

[27]See *CD IV.3.2*, 841. Barth could use the language of primary and secondary causation in the third volume of the *Church Dogmatics* (III.3, 98ff.), but seems to abandon it in the fourth volume. One wonders if correspondence comes to serve as Barth's distinctive Reformed answer to the Catholic conception of *causae secundae*. Regardless of whether this is the case, by the final volumes of the *Dogmatics*, Barth refuses to bring divine and human (ecclesial) activity under the common concept of 'causation' (in a similar manner to his refusal to bring the Creator and the creature under the general notion of 'being').

[28]See Mangina, 'Karl Barth and the Ethics of Ecclesial Practice,' 332-333.

criticisms here mentioned, Barth might retort, 'What does it mean to say that witness is not enough?' For Barth, the church's attestation to Christ is in fact the church's true glory, so that the church does not become greater, but less, in trying to do more than this. Furthermore, Barth would be highly suspicious of speaking of the church's witness as a *necessary* one unless highly qualified, due to his firm commitment to the asymmetry and irreversibility of the relationship between Christ and the church. Barth's strict insistence upon the asymmetry in this relation is not predicated upon a faulty view of Christ's humanity, but rather upon Barth's recognition that God and humanity stand on different planes. In other words, asymmetry is not read into the Chalcedonian formula, but is simply the acknowledgment that Christ's divinity and humanity do not stand on equal footing.

To transpose this line of thinking into a different key, what Barth seems to have, and what so many of his critics seem to lack, is an ecclesiological *extra Calvinisticum*. In other words, Barth insists that while the church is necessary for us because God has freely chosen this and freely joined himself to it, it is not necessary for God, nor is God's salvific activity limited to the church by some type of necessity (*CD IV.3*, 790). For Barth, any position that denied this would betray God's freedom and undermine the sufficiency of Christ's salvific work itself. Yet the question of the relation of divine and human action, of Christ's activity *in and through* the life of the church, still remains in light of Barth's emphasis upon the parallel nature of their distinct activity. Is there a way out of this impasse?

Late in his life, and in light of recent developments in Roman Catholicism seen eminently in the Second Vatican Council, Karl Barth liked to speak of the church in comparison to a well-known Biblical character. Whereas the Catholic church likened the church to Mary, Jesus' mother, Barth's favorite exemplar for the church was the person of Joseph, the father of Jesus. It was Joseph, not Mary, Barth believed, that best served as a model for the church, a model not of active cooperation in redemption but of humble witness. The image of a quiet and attendant servant was for Barth a better representation for the church and its task than that of the bejeweled and crowned 'queen of heaven.'[29]

But could there not be a place for *both* Joseph and Mary? For Barth, the central task of the church is witness, pointing to the complete and perfect work of God to which the church adds nothing. As its representative, Joseph can simply point to Christ in the manger, just as John the Baptist points to Christ on the cross in Grünewald's depiction of the crucifixion, an image so beloved to Barth.[30]

---

[29]See Barth, *Ad Limina Apostolorum*, trans. Keith R. Crim (Richmond: John Knox Press, 1968), 72; also Barth, *Letters 1961-1968*, trans. Geoffrey W. Bromiley (Grand Rapids: Eerdmans, 1981), 75; 84; 94; 245; and John O'Brien, *Steps to Christian Unity* (Garden City: Doubleday & Co., 1964), 97.

[30]Matthais Grünewald, 'The Crucifixion of Christ,' a panel of the *Isenheim Altarpiece*.

Nevertheless, Mary's presence in the Christmas story points to another truth of God's salvation. This divine visitation, this perfect and complete work of singular and uncompromised grace, is an act that God chooses to bring about through a human partner. And this suggests a real, though radically chastened, form of mediation. In the end, it is questionable whether a choice can be made between such witness and mediation. Are not both needed to qualify each other and together point to a deeper and inexpressible reality, the one protecting against a synergistic understanding of grace, as the other protects against a monistic one? Both Joseph and Mary were present at the manger, and both testify to the mystery and miracle of Christmas.

Here is another way to address the issue. Barth once expressed a concession that the Reformed position on Christology needed its complement, and rival, in the Lutheran position, and vice versa. The Reformed position safeguarded the distinction of the natures within the union as well as the event-character of the Word made flesh, whereas the Lutheran position safeguarded the relation of the natures and the product of the union. Barth recognized that to those of the Lutheran camp, the Reformed position seemed to lead to Nestorianism, a separation of the natures in Christ. To the Reformed, the Lutheran position seemed to fall into Eutychianism, leading to an identification and confusion of the natures.[31] As Barth noted, one side viewed the incarnation as a *'completed* event,' the other side as a 'completed *event'* (*CD I.2,* 170).

Barth believed and maintained the Reformed position to be superior, and held that the Lutheran position was in danger of sacrificing the irreversible relation between God and humanity. Yet, upon reflection, he could at least on one occasion concede the necessity of both. Each pointed to a reality so rich that no single viewpoint alone could grasp it, but which required two (dialectically) related witnesses:

> Perhaps there can be no amicable compromise in Evangelical theology as regards the order of merit between these two views. Perhaps if it is to be Evangelical theology at all...there always has to be a static and a dynamic, an ontic and a noetic principle, not in nice equilibrium, but calling to each other and questioning each other. That is, there must be Lutherans and Reformed: not in the shadow of a unitary theology, but as a twofold theological school – for the sake of the truth about the reality of Jesus Christ, which does not admit of being grasped or conceived by any unitary theology, which will always be the object of all theology, and so perhaps inevitably of a twofold theology – object in the strictest sense of the

---

[31]See *CD I.2,* 161-162; 170-171. Cf. *CD IV.2,* 66-69; 82-83. In light of these comments, it should not be surprising that Barth's ecclesiology has often been criticized for being Nestorian in nature.

concept. It may even be that in the unity and variety of the two Evangelical theologies in the one Evangelical Church there is reflected no more and no less than the one mystery itself, with which both were once engrossed and will necessarily be engrossed always, the mystery that o λόγος σάρζ ἐγένετο (*CD I.2*, 171).[32]

Could there be an ecclesiological parallel to this description? If ecclesiology is patterned upon Christological norms, might there not need be two irreducible positions, two sides that respectively emphasize the church as '*event* as institution' and as 'event as *institution*,' two sides pointing to the one mystery that is the church, a mystery in correspondence to the 'mystery and miracle of Christmas?' Likewise, might there be a place for *both* descriptions of the task of the church as witness and for descriptions of it as mediation, the first ensuring that divine and human action are not confused or equated, the latter ensuring that this sovereign divine action is correctly perceived as graciously enacted through very imperfect 'earthen vessels?'

Barth certainly sides with the former viewpoint – and this accounts for the distinctive emphases, and in some cases one-sidedness, in his theology. Nevertheless, this one-sidedness is not corrected by abandoning his position, but by extending it into neglected areas. For to abandon it would be to forget its most important lesson, that the Lord remains Lord of the church, and in this fact comes not only its humiliation but ultimately its exaltation. The church thus exists by grace and grace alone, and therein lies its salvation. In the end, future ecclesiologies are wise not to go around, but to go through, Barth's doctrine of the church. They may find need to address deficiencies; they dare not ignore his lessons.

A further observation is in order. Future studies of Barth's ecclesiology may well need to address his critical yet undeniable retrieval of themes most generally associated with (though not in every case exclusive to) the free church tradition and shaped by his own Swiss Reformed context.[33] Tracing these particular strands in Barth's thought, much less assessing their significance, lies far beyond the scope of

---

[32]For similar sentiments pertaining to soteriology, see Barth, *The Theology of John Calvin*, 81-82; 90.

[33]For Barth's understanding of the Reformed tradition with special application to the question of ecclesiology, see especially 'Reformierte Lehre, ihr Wesen und ihre Aufgabe,' in *Das Wort Gottes und die Theologie*, 179-212; ET: 'The Doctrinal Task of the Reformed Churches,' in *The Word of God and the Word of Man*, 218-271; 'The Desirability and Possibility of a Universal Reformed Creed,' in *Theology and Church*, 112-135; and *The Theology of the Reformed Confessions*, trans. Darrell L. Guder and Judith J. Guder (Westminster/John Knox Press, 2002). Like Barth's other historical investigations previously witnessed, this one bears the marks of his own distinct questions, and points to his own distinct answers. The present discussion is best read in light of these texts.

the current study. Nevertheless, they are also a part of Barth's ecclesiological tapestry, and while often ignored, they are recognizable, widely attested, and deeply woven into the whole. A few prominent examples of such strands should suffice to illustrate this claim:

1. Barth's emphasis upon the *local community of believers* as the primary locus of God's activity is a central theme running throughout his theology. This theme is witnessed linguistically in his preference for the term *'Gemeinde'* rather than *'Kirche,'* and practically in his favoring of a 'bottom-up' rather than 'top-down' approach in addressing ecumenical questions.

2. Barth gives consistent articulation to *a non-hierarchical form of order* that not only rejects strong distinctions between clergy and laity and rigid definitions of 'offices,' but that also attempts to embody the priesthood of all believers not only in principle but in practice.

3. The church's mandate of *mission*, so central to Barth's very conception of the church and its task, is rediscovered by Barth not in magisterial Protestantism, but in the despised fringe groups of the Radical Reformation.[34]

4. In regard to *the relation of church and state*, Barth's mature motto, 'A free church in a free state,' can serve him in a pinch as an accurate and sufficient way to summarize his position on the question, a position that holds the Christian community and its order to be both distinct and exemplary.

5. Barth's rejection of infant baptism and espousal of *believer's baptism* may be the most famous of the strands, but only one among several, and interwoven with the others at that. For instance, this strand cannot be separated from Barth's emphasis upon *discipleship* as a central aspect of the Christian life (and a strand itself inseparable from the theme of correspondence, a fact often overlooked). Nor can it be separated from his distinct ecclesial moral ontology in which God's free call is echoed in humanity's free response, a response that does not deny the sociality of Christian faith but that recognizes the constituency of the people of God as comprised of confession rather than biology.[35]

6. To these might be added Barth's *typological reading of Scripture*, coupled with his *refusal to absolutize confessional standards* in a way that would insulate them from reform in response to a fresh hearing of the Word of God in Scripture. For Barth, no binding and irreformable creed could replace the need for the church's living confession, for the church was not an institution of staid orthodoxy but the 'living congregation of the living Lord Jesus Christ.'

---

[34]See *CD IV.3.1*, 28.

[35]Barth's rejection of infant baptism is thus not simply predicated upon a cultural critique of Constantinianism. Its roots lie deeper than often acknowledged — see Webster, *Barth's Ethics of Reconciliation*, 166-173. The phrase 'moral ontology' is borrowed from Webster.

7. Related to these strands, though not identical to their concerns, is the question of Barth's mature assessment of *congregationalism*. While Barth's early references to congregationalism were strongly negative, in later years he could speak of it in surprisingly positive terms, witnessed in his address to the Amsterdam Assembly of 1948.

These strands themselves form a secondary, though substantial, pattern in the tapestry. For some, they may seem superfluous and unnecessary. Yet to attempt to pull them out of the weave is not so easy. For instance, despite a commonly held misconception, Barth's commitment to a free church is *not* simply based upon a pragmatic democratic sensibility peripheral to his real theological concerns. The freedom of the church is, rather, as elemental to Barth's theology as the freedom of theology itself. The church must be a free society for the same reason that theology must be a free science. Theology and the church have the same Lord, and thus both must be free to render free obedience; neither can be ruled nor subject to a foreign power. This experiment could be repeated with the same outcome. Pull and tug – the individual strands do not seem to come out without damaging the tapestry as a whole.

In great irony, Barth's ecclesiology may in the end be rejected by many not because it lacks concreteness and does not provide a significant place for the church, but because it is too concrete and demands too much. For if ecclesiology stands in analogy to Christology, the concrete particularity of the incarnation is reflected in the particularity of ecclesial agency. And for Barth, the church capable of concrete action and ministry, the church capable to be the subject of true confession, is the particular congregation comprised of responsible confessors sharing a common life, each one taking up his or her unique task.[36] The concrete congregation is thus the primary and most significant ecclesial referent for the term 'church.'[37] Barth's ecclesiology presents us with a view of the church that has so radically cast off all remnants of the *corpus Christianum* it can only appear disorienting, unsettling, and strange, even while captivatingly fascinating. It turns ecumenicity on its head by seeking universality precisely through, rather than against, particularity, seeing the latter not as an embarrassment but intrinsic to the historic rootedness of the Gospel. For this reason, Barth's reflections on the unity of the church (and the churches) sound quite different from many dominant ecumenical discussions of the twentieth century and today.

---

[36]Here we recall again that Barth will not relegate even such an austere task as theology only to the theologians, but makes it the responsibility of every Christian, so that 'every Christian is responsible for it and has indeed to think of himself as a theologian' (*CD IV.3.2*, 882).

[37]As Barth states: 'When I say congregation, I am thinking primarily of the concrete form of the congregation in a particular place....*Credo ecclesiam* means that I believe that here, at this place, in this visible assembly, the work of the Holy Spirit takes place' (*Dogmatics in Outline*, trans. G. T. Thomson [New York: Harper & Row, 1959], 142-143).

For those who long for the stability of a past Christendom, or, if rejecting such a dream, substitute an ecclesial stability grounded in external objectivity, Barth's description of ecclesial life and practice can only appear unrealistic if not irresponsible. Barth's indifference to guarantees of the church's external stability and historic continuity is often seen as a detriment which must be corrected by a flight to irreformable dogma, an infallible church office or biblical text, an irrevocable ministry of historic apostolic succession, or a hierarchically-arranged ecumenical alliance.

Barth, quite simply, followed none of these paths in his life (indeed, he opposed them all), yet he feared neither subjectivism nor the loss of the church's relevance. We would do well to ask why. The answer seems to lie in his deep and firm conviction that not only is the Spirit free, the Spirit is also faithful. Upon the faithfulness of God the church could stand. Once Barth came to understand that, all attempts to ground ecclesial stability in unchanging external norms appeared to him to be rooted in a misunderstanding of the Spirit's freedom, judging it a curse, rather than a blessing, for the church. Yet it is a consideration of Barth's emphasis upon divine freedom without attention to his quiet yet unshakable confidence in the Spirit's faithfulness that may be the reason some regard Barth's theology in general, and ecclesiology in particular, as inherently unstable, or occasionalistic, or a-historical, ultimately incapable of providing truly viable guidance and direction for an embodied ecclesial life. Barth would in all likelihood look askance at his critics and wonder if their longing for stable objectivity might be a symptom of a deep anxiety regarding the church's self-preservation and a failure to trust the *living* voice of Christ. For Barth, any church committed to *ecclesia semper reformanda* is inherently unstable. And he does not see such instability as a bad thing.

In the end, Barth leaves us with a very different picture of the church than many to which we have become accustomed, a picture he knew might well leave him in 'theological and ecclesiastical isolation.'[38] Indeed, in his understanding of the Christian community, as in so many other areas, Barth continues to swim against the stream.

---

[38]This phase is Barth's own, with specific reference to his view of baptism (*CD IV.4*, xii).

Bibliography

Works by Karl Barth

Ad Limina Apostolorum. Translated by Keith R. Crim. Richmond: John Knox Press, 1968.
Against the Stream: Shorter Post-War Writings 1946-1952. Edited by Ronald Gregor Smith. New York: Philosophical Library, 1954.
'Biblische Fragen, Einsichten und Ausblicke.' Chapter in *Das Wort Gottes und die Theologie*, 70-98. ET: 'Biblical Questions, Insights and Vistas.' In *The Word of God and the Word of Man*, 51-96.
'Brechen und Bauen: Eine Diskussion.' Chapter in *Der Götze Wackelt*, 108-123.
'The Christian Community and the Civil Community.' Chapter in *Community, Church, and State*, 149-189.
The Christian Life: Church Dogmatics IV,4 Lecture Fragments. Translated by Geoffrey W. Bromiley. Grand Rapids: Eerdmans, 1981.
Die christliche Dogmatik im Entwurf. Vol. 1. Munich: Christian Kaiser Verlag, 1927.
'Church and Culture.' Chapter in *Theology and Church*, 334-354.
'Church and State.' Chapter in *Community, Church, and State*, 101-148.
The Church and the Churches. Grand Rapids: Eerdmans, 1936.
'Church and Theology.' Chapter in *Theology and Church*, 286-306.
Church Dogmatics I.1: The Doctrine of the Word of God. Translated by G. T. Thomson. Edinburgh: T & T Clark, 1936.
Church Dogmatics I.1: The Doctrine of the Word of God. 2nd ed. Edited by G. W. Bromiley and T. F. Torrance. Translated by G. W. Bromiley. Edinburgh: T & T Clark, 1975.
Church Dogmatics I.2: The Doctrine of the Word of God. Edited by G. W. Bromiley and T. F. Torrance. Translated by G. T. Thomson and Harold Knight. Edinburgh: T & T Clark, 1956.
Church Dogmatics II.1: The Doctrine of God. Edited by G. W. Bromiley and T. F. Torrance. Translated by T. H. L. Parker, W. B. Johnston, et al. Edinburgh: T & T Clark, 1957.
Church Dogmatics II.2: The Doctrine of God. Edited by G. W. Bromiley and T. F. Torrance. Translated by G. W. Bromiley, J. C. Campbell, et al. Edinburgh: T & T Clark, 1957.
Church Dogmatics III.1: The Doctrine of Creation. Edited by G. W. Bromiley and T. F. Torrance. Translated by J. W. Edwards, O. Bussey, et al. Edinburgh: T & T Clark, 1958.
Church Dogmatics III.2: The Doctrine of Creation. Edited by G. W. Bromiley and T. F. Torrance. Translated by H. Knight, G. W. Bromiley, et al. Edinburgh: T & T Clark, 1960.
Church Dogmatics III.3: The Doctrine of Creation. Edited by G. W. Bromiley and T. F. Torrance. Translated by G. W. Bromiley, R. J. Ehrlich, et al. Edinburgh: T & T Clark, 1960.
Church Dogmatics III.4: The Doctrine of Creation. Edited by G. W. Bromiley and T. F. Torrance. Translated by A. T. Mackay, T. H. L. Parker, et al. Edinburgh: T & T Clark, 1961.
Church Dogmatics IV.1: The Doctrine of Reconciliation. Edited by G. W. Bromiley and T. F. Torrance. Translated by G. W. Bromiley. Edinburgh: T & T Clark, 1956.

Church Dogmatics IV.2: The Doctrine of Reconciliation. Edited by G. W. Bromiley and T. F. Torrance. Translated by G. W. Bromiley. Edinburgh: T & T Clark, 1958.

Church Dogmatics IV.3.1: The Doctrine of Reconciliation. Edited by G. W. Bromiley and T. F. Torrance. Translated by G. W. Bromiley. Edinburgh: T & T Clark, 1961.

Church Dogmatics IV.3.2: The Doctrine of Reconciliation. Edited by G. W. Bromiley and T. F. Torrance. Translated by G. W. Bromiley. Edinburgh: T & T Clark, 1962.

Church Dogmatics IV.4: The Doctrine of Reconciliation. Edited by G. W. Bromiley and T. F. Torrance. Translated by G. W. Bromiley. Edinburgh: T & T Clark, 1969.

'The Church — The Living Congregation of the Living Lord Jesus Christ.' In *God Here and Now*, 61-85. German original in *Theologische Existenz heute*, N.F. 9 (1947): 3-23; and *Theologische Studien* 22 (1947): 21-44.

'The Church — The Living Congregation of the Living Lord Jesus Christ.' In *Man's Disorder and God's Design*. New York: Harper and Brothers, 67-76. German original in *Zeugnis und Zeichen: Reden, Briefe, Dokumente*, ed. Friedrich W. Kantzenbach, 234-244. München: Chr. Kaiser Verlag, 1964.

Community, State, and Church. With an Introduction by Will Herberg. Gloucester: Peter Smith, 1968.

'The Concept of the Church.' Chapter in *Theology and Church*, 272-285.

'Concluding Unscientific Postscript on Schleiermacher.' Translated by George Hunsinger. In *The Theology of Schleiermacher*, ed. Dietrich Ritschl, 261-279. Grand Rapids: Eerdmans, 1982.

Credo. London: Hodder & Stoughton, 1936.

'The Desirability and Possibility of a Universal Reformed Creed.' Chapter in *Theology and Church*, 112-135.

Dogmatics in Outline. Translated by G. T. Thompson. New York: Harper & Row, 1959.

Ethics. Edited by Dietrich Braun. Translated by Geoffrey Bromiley. New York: Seabury Press, 1981.

'Evangelical Theology in the 19th Century.' Chapter in *The Humanity of God*, 11-33.

Evangelical Theology: An Introduction. Translated by Grover Foley. New York: Holt, Rinehart and Winston, 1963.

'Das Evangelium in der Gegenwart.' *Theologische Existenz heute* 25 (Munich: Chr. Kaiser Verlag, 1935).

Final Testimonies. Edited by Eberhard Busch. Translated by Geoffrey W. Bromiley. Grand Rapids: Eerdmans, 1977.

'Für die Freiheit des Evangeliums.' *Theologische Existenz heute* 2 (Munich: Chr. Kaiser Verlag, 1933).

'Die Gerechtigkeit Gottes.' Chapter in *Das Wort Gottes und die Theologie*, 5-17. ET: 'The Righteousness of God.' In *The Word of God and the Word of Man*, 9-27.

Gespräche 1959-1962. Zürich: Theologischer Verlag Zürich, 1995.

Gespräche 1964-1968. Zürich: Theologischer Verlag Zürich, 1997.

God Here and Now. Translated by Paul M. van Buren. New York: Harper and Row, 1964.

God in Action: Theological Addresses. With an Introduction by Elmer G. Homrighausen. Translated by E. G. Homrighausen & Karl J. Ernst. New York: Roundtable Press, 1936.

Der Götze Wackelt. Edited by Karl Kupisch. Berlin: Käthe Vogt Verlag, 1961.

The Holy Spirit and the Christian Life: The Theological Basis of Ethics. Translated by R. Birch Hoyle. Louisville: Westminster John Knox Press, 1993.

How I Changed My Mind. Richmond: John Knox Press, 1966.

The Humanity of God. Translated by John N. Thomas and Thomas Wieser. N.C.: John Knox Press, 1960.

'The Humanity of God.' Chapter in *The Humanity of God*, 37-65.

Karl Barth's Table Talk. Recorded and edited by John D. Godsey. Edinburgh: Oliver and Boyd, 1963.

The Knowledge of God and the Service of God According to the Teaching of the Reformation. London: Hodder and Stoughton, 1938/1949.

'Luther's Doctrine of the Eucharist.' Chapter in *Theology and Church*, 74-111.

'Die Not der evangelischen Kirche.' Chapter in *Der Götze Wackelt*, 33-62.

'Not und Verheißung der christlichen Verkündigung.' Chapter in *Das Wort Gottes und die Theologie*, 99-124. ET: 'The Need and Promise of Christian Preaching.' In *The Word of God and the Word of Man*, 97-135.

'Offenbarung, Kirche, Theologie.' *Theologische Existenz heute* 9 (Munich: Chr. Kaiser Verlag, 1934). ET: 'The Church.' Chapter in *God in Action: Theological Addresses*, 20-38.

'The Principles of Dogmatics according to Wilhelm Herrmann.' Chapter in *Theology and Church*, 238-271.

Protestant Theology in the Nineteenth Century. Valley Forge: Judson Press, 1973.

'*Quoques Tandem. . .?*' Chapter in *Der Götze Wackelt*, 27-32.

'The Real Church.' Chapter in *Against the Stream*, 62-77.

'Reformierte Lehre, ihr Wesen und ihre Aufgabe.' Chapter in *Das Wort Gottes und die Theologie*, 179-212. ET: 'The Doctrinal Task of the Reformed Churches.' In *The Word of God and the Word of Man*, 218-271.

'Roman Catholicism: A Question to the Protestant Church.' Chapter in *Theology and Church*, 307-333.

Der Römerbrief [Erste Fassung] 1919. Edited by Hermann Schmidt. Zürich: Theologischer Verlag Zürich, 1985.

Der Römerbrief. 2nd ed. München: Chr. Kaiser Verlag, 1923. ET: *The Epistle to the Romans.* Translated by Edwyn C. Hoskyns. Oxford: Oxford University Press, 1968.

'Schleiermacher.' Chapter in *Theology and Church*, 159-199.

'Schleiermacher's *Celebration of Christmas*.' Chapter in *Theology and Church*, 136-158.

'Das Schriftprinzip der reformierten Kirche.' Chapter in *Vorträge und kleinere Arbeiten, 1922-1925*, 500-544.

Die Theologie Calvins 1922. Zürich: Theologischer Verlag Zürich, 1993. ET: *The Theology of John Calvin.* Translated by Geoffrey W. Bromiley. Grand Rapids: Eerdmans, 1995.

Theologische Fragen und Antworten. Zollikon: Evangelischer Verlag AG Zollikon, 1957.

The Theology of Schleiermacher: Lectures at Göttingen, Winter Semester of 1923/24. Edited by Dietrich Ritschl. Translated by Geoffrey W. Bromiley. Grand Rapids: Eerdmans, 1982.

The Theology of the Reformed Confessions. Translated by Darrell L. Guder and Judith J. Guder. Louisville: Westminster John Knox Press, 2002.

Unterricht in der christlichen Religion, I: Prolegomena, 1924. Edited by Hannelotte Reiffen. Zürich: Theologischer Verlag Zürich, 1985. ET: *The Göttingen Dogmatics: Instruction in the Christian Religion.* Vol. 1 Translated by Geoffrey W. Bromiley. Grand Rapids: Eerdmans, 1991.

Unterricht in der christlichen Religion, II: Die Lehre von Gott/Die Lehre vom Menschen, 1924/1925. Edited by Hinrich Stoevesandt. Zürich: Theologischer Verlag Zürich, 1990.

ET: *The Göttingen Dogmatics: Instruction in the Christian Religion*. Vol. 1. (contains the first third of German edition).

Unterricht in der christlichen Religion, III: Die Lehre von der Versöhnung/Die Lehre von der Erlösung, 1925/1926. Edited by Hinrich Stoevesandt. Zürich: Theologischer Verlag Zürich, 2003.

'Volkskirche, Freikirche, Bekenntniskirche.' *Evangelische Theologie* 3 (1936): 411-422.

Vorträge und kleinere Arbeiten, 1922-1925. Edited by Holger Finze. Zürich: Theologischer Verlag Zürich, 1990.

'The Word in Theology from Schleiermacher to Ritchl.' Chapter in *Theology and Church*, 200-216.

'Das Wort Gottes als Aufgabe der Theologie.' Chapter in *Das Wort Gottes und die Theologie*, 156-178. ET: 'The Word of God and the Task of the Ministry.' In *The Word of God and the Word of Man*, 183-217.

Das Wort Gottes und die Theologie. München: Chr. Kaiser Verlag, 1925. ET: *The Word of God and the Word of Man*. Translated by Douglas Horton. Gloucester: Peter Smith, 1978.

Other Primary Materials

Herrmann, Wilhelm. *The Communion of the Christian with God*. Edited by Robert T. Voelkel. Translated by J. S. Stanyon and R. W. Stewart. Philadelphia: Fortress Press, 1971.

_____. *Dogmatik*. Gotha/Stuttgart: Verlag Friedrich Andreas Perthes, 1925. ET: *Systematic Theology*. Translated by Nathaniel Micklem and Kenneth A. Saunders. New York: Macmillan, 1927.

_____. *Ethik*. 5th ed. Tübingen: J.C.B. Mohr, 1913.

Karl Barth: Letters 1961-1968. Edited by Jürgen Fangmeier and Hinrich Stoevesandt. Translated by Geoffrey W. Bromiley. Grand Rapids: Eerdmans., 1981.

Karl Barth – Rudolf Bultmann Letters 1922-1966. Edited by Bernd Jaspert. Translated and edited by Geoffrey W. Bromiley. Edinburgh: T & T Clark, 1982.

O'Brien, John. *Steps to Christian Unity*. Garden City: Doubleday & Co., 1964.

Peterson, Eric. 'Was ist Theologie?' Chapter in *Theologische Traktate*, 9-44.

_____. *Theologische Traktate*. Munich: Kösel Verlag, 1951.

_____. *Theologie als Wissenschaft: Aufsätze und Thesen*. Edited by Gerhard Sauter. Munich: Kaiser Verlag, 1971.

Revolutionary Theology in the Making: Barth-Thurneysen Correspondence, 1914-1925. [Edited by James D. Smart]. Translated by James D. Smart. Richmond: John Knox Press, 1964.

Robinson, James M., editor. *The Beginnings of Dialectic Theology*. Translated by Keith Crim and Louis DeGrazia. Richmond: John Knox Press, 1968.

Schleiermacher, Friedrich. *Der christliche Glaube*. Vol 2. Edited by Martin Redeker. Berlin: Walter de Gruyter, 1960. ET: *The Christian Faith*. Edited by H. R. Mackintosh and J. S. Stewart. Translated by J. S. Stewart, H. R. Macintosh, et al. Edinburgh: T & T Clark, 1989.

Tillich, Paul. *Systematic Theology: Vol. 2 — Existence and The Christ*. Chicago: University of Chicago Press, 1957.

Secondary Materials

Ahlers, Rolf. *The Community of Freedom: Barth and Presuppositionless Theology*. New York: Peter Lang, 1989.

Bader-Saye, Scott. *Church and Israel After Christendom: The Politics of Election*. Boulder: Westview Press, 1999.

Baier, Klaus A. *Unitas ex auditu: des Einheit der Kirche im Rahmen der Theologie Karl Barths*. Bern: Verlag Peter Lang, 1978.

Bäumler, Christof. 'Die Lehre von der Kirche in der Theologie Karl Barths.' *Theologische Existenz heute, Neue Folge*. 118 (1964): 1-60.

Bender, Kimlyn J. 'Between Heaven and Earth: Schleiermacher's Christology in View of Intrasystematic Tensions and Relations within the *Glaubenslehre*.' In *Schleiermacher's 'To Cecilie' and Other Writings by and about Schleiermacher – Neues Athenaeum, V. 6*. Edited by Ruth D. Richardson. Lewiston, NY: Edwin Mellen Press, 2001. 179-195.

____. 'Karl Barth's Doctrine of the Church in Contemporary Anglo-American Ecclesiological Conversation.' *Zeitschrift für dialektische Theologie* (forthcoming).

Berkhof, Hendrikus. *Two Hundred Years of Theology: Report of A Personal Journey*. Translated by John Vriend. Grand Rapids: Eerdmans, 1989.

Biggar, Nigel. *The Hastening That Waits: Karl Barth's Ethics*. Oxford: Clarendon Press, 1993.

____, editor. *Reckoning With Barth: Essays in Commemoration of the Centenary of Karl Barth's Birth*. London & Oxford: A. R. Mowbray & Co., 1988.

Bromiley, Geoffrey. 'The Abiding Significance of Karl Barth.' In *Theology Beyond Christendom*. Edited by John Thompson. Allison Park: Pickwick Publications, 1986. 331-350.

Busch, Eberhard. 'God is God: The Meaning of a Controversial Formula and the Fundamental Problem of Speaking About God.' *Princeton Seminary Bulletin*. N.S. 7 (1986): 101-113.

____. *Karl Barth: His Life from Letters and Autobiographical Texts*. Translated by John Bowden. Grand Rapids: Eerdmans, 1994.

____. 'Die Kirche am Ende ihrer Welt-geltung: Zur Deutung der Ekklesiologie Karl Barths.' In *Das Wort, das in Erstaunen setzt, verpflichtet*. Edited by Dieter Jeschke and Eckhard Langner, et al. Wuppertal and Zürich: Brockhaus Verlag, 1994. 83-97.

____. *Unter dem Bogen des einen Bundes: Karl Barth und die Juden 1933-1945*. Neukirchen-Vluyn: Neukirchener Verlag, 1996.

Cochrane, Arthur C. *The Church's Confession Under Hitler*. Philadelphia: Westminster Press, 1962.

Colwell, John. *Actuality and Provisionality: Eternity and Election in the Theology of Karl Barth*. Edinburgh: Rutherford House, 1989.

Cunningham, Mary Kathleen. *What is Theological Exegesis? Interpretation and Use of Scripture in Barth's Doctrine of Election*. Valley Forge: Trinity Press, 1995.

Dalferth, Ingolf U. 'Karl Barth's eschatological realism.' In *Karl Barth: Centenary Essays*. Edited by S. W. Sykes. Oxford: Clarendon Press, 1979. 14-45.

Dietrich, Wendell S. *Christ and the Church, According to Barth and Some of His Roman Catholic Critics.* Unpublished Ph.D. diss., Yale University, 1960/1987.

Dorrien, Gary. *The Barthian Revolt in Modern Theology: Theology Without Weapons.* Louisville: Westminster John Knox Press, 2000.

Duke, James O., and Robert F. Streetman, eds. *Barth and Schleiermacher: Beyond the Impasse?* Philadelphia: Fortress Press, 1988.

Fahlbusch, Erwin, and Jan M. Lochman, et al., editors. *The Encyclopedia of Christianity: Volume 1 A-D.* Translated and edited by Geoffrey W. Bromiley. Grand Rapids: Eerdmans; and Leiden: Brill, 1999. S.v. 'Church,' by Erwin Fahlbusch.

Feuerer, Georg. 'Der Kirchenbegriff der dialektischen Theologie.' *Freiburger Theologische Studien* 36 (1933): 1-133.

Foley, Grover. 'The Catholic Critics of Karl Barth: In Outline and Analysis.' *Scottish Journal of Theology* 14 (1961): 136-155.

Ford, D. F. *Barth and God's Story: Biblical Narrative and the Theological Method of Karl Barth in the* 'Church Dogmatics'. Frankfurt am Main: Verlag Peter Lang, 1981.

_____. 'Barth's Interpretation of the Bible.' In *Karl Barth: Studies of his Theological Method.* Edited by S. W. Sykes. Oxford: Clarendon Press, 1979. 55-87.

Frei, Hans. *The Identity of Jesus Christ.* Philadelphia: Fortress Press, 1975.

Freudenberg, Matthias. *Karl Barth und die reformierte Theologie: Die Auseinandersetzung mit Calvin, Zwingli und den reformierten Bekenntnisschriften während seiner Göttinger Lehrtätigkeit.* Neukircher-Vluyn: Neukirchener Verlag, 1997.

Fries, Heinrich. 'Kirche als Ereignis: Zu Karl Barths Lehre von der Kirche.' *Catholica* 11 (1956): 81-107.

Goldmann, Manuel. *'Die große ökumenische Frage. . .': Zur Strukturverschiedenheit christlicher und jüdischer Tradition und ihrer Relevanz für die Begegnung der Kirche mit Israel.* Neukirchen-Vluyn: Neukirchener Verlag, 1997.

Gollwitzer, Helmut. 'Kingdom of God and Socialism in the Theology of Karl Barth.' In *Karl Barth and Radical Politics.* Edited by George Hunsinger. Philadelphia: Westminster Press, 1976. 77-120.

Gorringe, Timothy. *Karl Barth: Against Hegemony.* Oxford: Oxford University Press, 1999.

Gunton, Colin. 'Karl Barth's Doctrine of Election as Part of His Doctrine of God.' *Journal of Theological Studies* 25 (1974): 381-392.

_____. 'No Other Foundation: One Englishman's Reading of *Church Dogmatics* Chapter V.' In *Reckoning With Barth.* Edited by Nigel Biggar. London & Oxford: A. R. Mowbray & Co., 1988. 61-79.

_____. 'Salvation.' In *The Cambridge Companion to Karl Barth.* Edited by John Webster. Cambridge: Cambridge University Press, 2000. 143-158.

_____. 'Transcendence, Metaphor, and the Knowability of God.' *Journal of Theological Studies* 31 (1980): 501-516.

Hamer, Jerome. *Karl Barth.* Translated Dominic M. Maruca. Westminster: Newman Press, 1961.

Hart, Trevor A. and Daniel P. Thimell, editors. *Christ In Our Place: The Humanity of God in Christ for the Reconciliation of the World.* Allison Park/Exeter: Pickwick Publications/Paternoster Press, 1989.

Hart, Trevor. *Regarding Karl Barth: Toward a Reading of His Theology.* Downer's Grove: Intervarsity Press, 1999.

Hartwell, Herbert. *The Theology of Karl Barth.* London: Gerald Duckworth & Co., 1964.

Hauerwas, Stanley. *Character and the Christian Life*. Notre Dame: University of Notre Dame Press, 1975/1994.

____. 'On Learning Simplicity in an Ambiguous Age.' In *Barth, Barmen, and the Confessing Church Today*. Edited by James Y. Holloway. Lewiston: Edwin Mellen Press, 1992/1995. 131-138.

____. *With the Grain of the Universe: The Church's Witness and Natural Theology*. Grand Rapids: Brazos Press, 2001.

Hauser, Martin, editor. *Unsichtbare oder sichtbare Kirche?: Beiträge zur Ekklesiologie*. Freiburg: Universitätsverlag, 1992.

Haynes, Stephen R. *Prospects for Post-Holocaust Theology*. Atlanta: Scholars Press, 1991.

____. *Reluctant Witnesses: Jews and the Christian Imagination*. Louisville: Westminster John Knox Press, 1995.

Healy, Nicholas M. *Church, World and the Christian Life: Practical-Prophetic Ecclesiology*. Cambridge: Cambridge University Press, 2000.

____. 'Karl Barth's ecclesiology reconsidered.' *Scottish Journal of Theology* 57 (2004): 287-299.

____. 'The Logic of Karl Barth's Ecclesiology: Analysis, Assessment and Proposed Modifications.' *Modern Theology* 10 (1994): 253-270.

Herberg, Will. 'The Social Philosophy of Karl Barth.' In Karl Barth, *Community, State, and Church*. Gloucester: Peter Smith, 1968. 11-67.

Holloway, James Y., editor. *Barth, Barmen, and the Confessing Church Today*. Lewiston: Edwin Mellen Press, 1992/1995.

Honecker, Martin. 'Kirche als Gestalt und Ereignis: Die sichtbare Gestalt der Kirche als dogmatisches Problem.' In: *Forschungen zur Geschichte und Lehre des Protestantismus*. Edited by Ernst Wolf. No. 10, v. 25 (München: Chr. Kaiser Verlag, 1963).

Hunsinger, George. 'Beyond Literalism and Expressivism: Karl Barth's Hermeneutical Realism.' Chapter in *Disruptive Grace*, 210-225.

____. *Disruptive Grace: Studies in the Theology of Karl Barth*. Grand Rapids: Eerdmans, 2000.

____. 'The Harnack/Barth Correspondence: A Paraphrase with Comments.' *Thomist* 50 (1986): 599-622. Also chapter in *Disruptive Grace*, 319-337.

____. *How To Read Karl Barth: The Shape of His Theology*. New York/Oxford: Oxford University Press, 1991.

____, editor. *Karl Barth and Radical Politics*. Philadelphia: Westminster Press, 1976.

____. 'Karl Barth and the Politics of Sectarian Protestantism: A Dialogue with John Howard Yoder.' Chapter in *Disruptive Grace*, 114-128.

____. 'Karl Barth's Christology: Its Basic Chalcedonian Character.' Chapter in *Disruptive Grace*, 131-147.

____. 'The Mediator of Communion: Karl Barth's Doctrine of the Holy Spirit.' Chapter in *Disruptive Grace*, 148-185.

____. '*Mysterium Trinitatis*: Karl Barth's Conception of Eternity.' Chapter in *Disruptive Grace*, 186-209.

____. 'To Hauerwas: On Learning Faithfulness in a Fallen World.' In *Barth, Barmen, and the Confessing Church Today*. Edited by James Y. Holloway. Lewiston: Edwin Mellen Press, 1992/1995. 252-256.

Hütter, Reinhard. 'The Church as Public: Dogma, Practice, and the Holy Spirit.' Pro Ecclesia 3 (1994): 334-361.

____. *Evangelische Ethik als kirchliches Zeugnis: Interpretationen zu Schlüsselfragen theologischer Ethik in der Gegenwart.* Neukirchen-Vluyn: Neukirchener Verlag, 1993.

____. 'Karl Barth's "Dialectical Catholicity": *Sic et Non.*' *Modern Theology* 16 (2000): 137-157.

____. *Suffering Divine Things: Theology as Church Practice.* Translated by Doug Stott. Grand Rapids: Eerdmans, 2000.

Jehle, Frank. *Ever Against the Stream: The Politics of Karl Barth, 1906-1968.* Translated by Richard and Marth Burnett. Grand Rapids: Eerdmans, 2002.

Jenson, Robert. *God after God: The God of the Past and the God of the Future, Seen in the Work of Karl Barth.* Indianapolis: Bobbs-Merrill Co., 1969.

____. 'You Wonder Where the Spirit Went.' *Pro Ecclesia* 2 (1993): 296-304.

Jeschke, Dieter, and Eckhard Langner, et al., editors. *Das Wort, das in Erstaunen setzt, verpflichtet.* Wuppertal and Zürich: Brockhaus Verlag, 1994.

Journet, Charles. *L'Église du Verbe Incarné: V.2: Sa Structure Interne et son Unité Catholique.* Desclée de Brower, 1951.

Jüngel, Eberhard. *God's Being Is in Becoming: The Trinitarian Being of God in the Theology of Karl Barth.* Translated by John Webster. Grand Rapids: Eerdmans, 2001.

____. *Karl Barth: A Theological Legacy.* Translated by Garrett E. Paul. Philadelphia: Westminster Press, 1986.

Klappert, Bertold. *Israel und die Kirche: Erwägungen zur Israellehre Karl Barths.* Munich: Chr. Kaiser Verlag, 1980.

Köckert, Heidelore, and Wolf Krötke, editors. *Theologie als Christologie: Zum Werk und Leben Karl Barths.* Berlin: Evangelische Verlagsanstalt, 1988.

Kreck, Walter. *Grundentscheidungen in Karl Barths Dogmatik: Zur Diskussion seines Verständnisses von Offenbarung und Erwählung.* Neukirchen-Vluyn: Neukirchener Verlag, 1978.

Krötke, Wolf. 'Gott und Mensch als "Partner": Zur Bedeutung einer zentralen Kategorie in Karl Barths *Kirchlicher Dogmatik.*' In *Theologie als Christologie.* Edited by Heidelore Köckert and Wolf Krötke. Berlin: Evangelische Verlagsanstalt, 1988. 106-120.

____. 'The humanity of the human person in Karl Barth's anthropology.' In: *The Cambridge Companion to Karl Barth.* Edited by John Webster. Cambridge: Cambridge University Press, 2000. 159-176.

Lang, U. M. 'Anhypostatos-Enhypostatos: Church Fathers, Protestant Orthodoxy, and Karl Barth.' *Journal of Theological Studies* 49 (1998): 630-657.

Lamirande, Emilien. 'The Impact of Karl Barth on the Catholic Church in the Last Half Century.' In *Footnotes to a Theology.* Edited by H. Martin Rumscheidt. Corporation for the Publication of Academic Studies in Religion in Canada, 1974. 112-141.

____. 'Roman Catholic Reactions to Karl Barth's Ecclesiology.' *Canadian Journal of Theology* 14 (1968): 28-42.

Leuba, Jean-Louis. 'Die Ekklesiologie Karl Barths.' In *Unsichtbare oder sichtbare Kirche?.* Edited by Martin Hauser. Freiburg: Universitätsverlag, 1992. 59-82.

____. 'Le Problème de L'Église chez M. Karl Barth.' *Verbum Caro* 1 (1947): 4-24.

Lindbeck, George. *The Nature of Doctrine.* Philadelphia: Westminster, 1984.

MacIntyre, Alasdair. *After Virtue.* 2nd ed. Notre Dame: University of Notre Dame Press, 1984.

Mangina, Joseph L. 'Bearing the Marks of Jesus: The Church in the Economy of Salvation in Barth and Hauerwas.' *Scottish Journal of Theology* 52 (1999): 269-305.

____. 'The Stranger as Sacrament: Karl Barth and the Ethics of Ecclesial Practice.' *International Journal of Systematic Theology* 1 (1999): 322-339.

Marquardt, Friedrich. *Die Entdeckung des Judentums für die christliche Theologie: Israel im Denken Karl Barths.* Munich: Chr. Kaiser Verlag, 1967.

McCormack, Bruce. 'Grace and being: The role of God's gracious election in Karl Barth's theological ontology.' In *The Cambridge Companion to Karl Barth.* Edited by John Webster. Cambridge: Cambridge University Press, 2000. 92-110.

____. *Karl Barth's Critically Realistic Dialectical Theology: Its Genesis and Development.* Oxford: Clarendon Press, 1995.

____. *A Scholastic of a Higher Order: The development of Karl Barth's theology, 1921-31.* Unpublished Ph.D. diss., Princeton Theological Seminary, 1989.

____. 'The Sum of the Gospel: The Doctrine of Election in the Theologies of Alexander Schweizer and Karl Barth.' In *Toward the Future of Reformed Theology.* Edited by David Willis and Michael Welker. Grand Rapids: Eerdmans, 1999. 470-493.

____. 'The Unheard Message of Karl Barth.' *Word and World* 14 (1994): 59-66.

McKim, Donald K., editor. *How Karl Barth Changed My Mind.* Grand Rapids: Eerdmans, 1986.

Meier, Kurt. 'Die zeitgeschichtliche Bedeutung volkskirchlicher Konzeptionen im deutchen Protestantismus zwischen 1918 und 1945.' In *Nordische und deutsche Kirchen im 20. Jahrhundert.* Edited by Carsten Nicolaisen. Göttingen: Vandenhoeck & Ruprecht, 1982. 165-197.

Metzger, Paul Louis. *The Word of Christ and the World of Culture: Sacred and Secular through the Theology of Karl Barth.* Grand Rapids: Eerdmans, 2003.

Migliore, Daniel. 'Vinculum Pacis: Barth's Theology of the Holy Spirit.' Unpublished English manuscript. Published in German translation as: 'Vinculum Pacis – Karl Barths Theologie des Heiligen Geistes.' *Evangelische Theologie* 6 (2000): 131-152.

Nicolaisen, Carsten. *Nordische und deutsche Kirchen im 20. Jahrhundert.* Göttingen: Vandenhoeck & Ruprecht, 1982.

O'Grady, Colm. *The Church in Catholic Theology: Dialogue with Karl Barth.* Washington-Cleveland: Corpus Books, 1969.

____. *The Church in the Theology of Karl Barth.* Washington-Cleveland: Corpus Books, 1968.

Palma, Robert J. *Karl Barth's Theology of Culture: The Freedom of Culture for the Praise of God.* Allison Park: Pickwick Publications, 1983.

Rendtorff, Trutz. *Church and Theology: The Systematic Function of the Church Concept in Modern Theology.* Translated by Reginald H. Fuller. Philadelphia: Westminster Press, 1971.

Roberts, R. H. 'Barth's Doctrine of Time: Its Nature and Implications.' In *Karl Barth: Studies of his Theological Method.* Edited by S. W. Sykes. Oxford: Clarendon Press, 1979. 88-146.

Rumscheidt, H. Martin, editor. *Footnotes to a Theology.* Corporation for the Publication of Academic Studies in Religion in Canada, 1974.

____. *Revelation and Theology: An analysis of the Barth-Harnack correspondence of 1923.* Cambridge: Cambridge University Press, 1972.

Schepers, Maurice B. 'The Work of the Holy Spirit: Karl Barth on the Nature of the Church.' *Theological Studies* 23 (1962): 625-636.

Scholder, Klaus. *The Churches and the Third Reich — Volume 1: Preliminary History and the Time of Illusions 1918-1934*. Translated by John Bowden. Philadelphia: Fortress Press, 1988.

_____. *The Churches and the Third Reich — Volume 2: The Year of Disillusionment: 1934 Barmen and Rome*. Translated by John Bowden. Philadelphia: Fortress Press, 1988.

Sharp, Douglas R. *The Hermeneutics of Election: The Significance of the Doctrine in Barth's Church Dogmatics*. Lanham: University Press of America, 1990.

Shults, F. LeRon. 'A Dubious Christological Formula: From Leontius of Byzantium to Karl Barth.' *Theological Studies* 57 (1996): 431-446.

Smart, James D. *The Divided Mind of Modern Theology: Karl Barth and Rudolf Bultmann 1908-1933*. Philadelphia: Westminster Press, 1967.

Sonderegger, Katherine. *That Jesus Christ Was Born A Jew: Karl Barth's 'Doctrine of Israel.'* University Park: Pennsylvania State University Press, 1992.

Sorge, Sheldon W. *Karl Barth's Reception in North America: Ecclesiology as a Case Study*. Unpublished Ph.D. diss., Duke University, 1987.

Sykes, Stephen. *The Identity of Christianity*. Philadelphia: Fortress Press, 1984.

Sykes, S. W. 'Barth on the Centre of Theology.' In *Karl Barth: Studies of his Theological Method*. Edited by S. W. Sykes. Oxford: Clarendon Press, 1979. 17-54.

_____, editor. *Karl Barth: Centenary Essays*. Cambridge: Cambridge University Press, 1989.

_____, editor. *Karl Barth: Studies of his Theological Method*. Oxford: Clarendon Press, 1979.

Thompson, John. 'Christology and Reconciliation in the Theology of Karl Barth.' In *Christ In Our Place*. Edited by Trevor A. Hart and Daniel P. Thimmell. Allison Park/Exeter: Pickwick Publications/Paternoster Press, 1989. 207-223.

_____. *Christ in Perspective: Christological Perspectives in the Theology of Karl Barth*. Edinburgh: Saint Andrew Press, 1978.

_____, editor. *Theology Beyond Christendom*. Allison Park: Pickwick Publications, 1986.

Torrance, Thomas. 'The Atonement and the Oneness of the Church.' *Scottish Journal of Theology* 7 (1954): 245-269.

_____. *Karl Barth: An Introduction to His Early Theology*. London: SCM Press, 1962.

_____. *Karl Barth, Biblical and Evangelical Theologian*. Edinburgh: T & T Clark, 1990.

Von Balthasar, Hans Urs. *The Theology of Karl Barth*. Translated by John Drury. New York: Holt, Rinehart and Winston, 1971.

Webster, John. *Barth's Ethics of Reconciliation*. Cambridge: Cambridge University Press, 1995.

_____. *Barth's Moral Theology: Human Action in Barth's Thought*. Grand Rapids: Eerdmans, 1998.

_____, editor. *The Cambridge Companion to Karl Barth*. Cambridge: Cambridge University Press, 2000.

_____. 'The Christian in Revolt: Some Reflections on *The Christian Life*.' In *Reckoning With Barth*. Edited by Nigel Biggar. London & Oxford: A. R. Mowbray & Co., 1988. 119-144.

_____. *Karl Barth*. London: Continuum, 2000.

Wendebourg, Ernst-Wilhelm. 'Die Christusgemeinde und ihr Herr: Eine kritische Studie zur Ekklesiologie Karl Barths.' *Arbeiten zur Geschichte und Theologie des Luthertums* 17 (Berlin/Hamburg: Lutherisches Verlagshaus, 1967): 1-272.

Werpehowski, William. 'Command and History in the Ethics of Karl Barth.' *Journal of Religious Ethics* 9 (1981): 298-320.

Willems, B. A. *Karl Barth: An Ecumenical Approach to His Theology.* Translated by Matthew J. van Velzen. Glen Rock: Paulist Press, 1965.

Willis, David, and Michael Welker, editors. *Toward the Future of Reformed Theology: Tasks, Topics, Traditions.* Grand Rapids: Eerdmans, 1999.

Willis, Robert E. *The Ethics of Karl Barth.* Leiden: E. J. Brill, 1971.

Yocum, John. *Ecclesial Mediation in Karl Barth.* Hampshire/Burlington: Ashgate Publishing, 2004.

Index

Schleiermacher, debate 37-45
theology, center 110
Tillich, debate 62-3
on the Trinity 68
works
　Church Dogmatics 1, 10, 11,
　23, 37, 55, 65, 67, 78, 79, 80,
　81, 92, 95, 96, 97, 99, 118,
　119, 127, 130, 139, 141, 142,
　160, 162, 168, 196, 224, 253,
　263, 280, 281
　Göttingen Dogmatics, 99, 117,
　118, 127, 154, 158, 160, 173,
　186, 233
　　ecclesiology 66-82
　Romans commentary
　(*Römerbrief*) 25-8, 30, 34, 36,
　37, 42, 56, 59, 60, 61, 62, 66,
　75, 79-82, 86, 99, 120, 127
　141, 168, 173, 177, 273
Biggar, Nigel 165
Bultmann, Rudolf 22, 66, 130, 197

Calvin, John 73, 89-90, 91
　on election doctrine 99
Chalcedonian pattern 7, 10, 11, 63,
　64, 132, 140, 146, 168, 192, 270
　meaning 3-4
　see also Christ, divine/human
　　nature
Christ
　Barth on 41
　church, as body of 198-202, 227
　church law, source of 209-11
　and the community 198-203, 221-
　4
　divine/human nature 4, 64, 65, 66,
　117-18, 120, 149-50, 171, 283-4
　　see also Chalcedonian pattern
　election 112
　　and the church 121-7
　existence, forms of 199-200

Herrmann on 20-1, 21-2
history, and history of the church
　150-2
holiness of 185
Holy Spirit, identification with
　148, 195-8
life, correspondence to
　community 205-8
mission 244-50
obedience/exaltation 131-3
presence 147-9
as *totus Christus* 151-2, 200, 202-
　5
and the world 147, 230-1
Christology
　Barth's 62, 108, 119-20
　and ecclesiology 1, 2, 7, 66-7,
　160, 284
　Herrmann's 42
　　Barth on 42
　logical elements 3-6, 9-10
　as narratology 113-14, 118
　Schleiermacher's 38-9
　theology as 3
church, the
　apostolicity of 69, 190-2
　as article of faith 168-70, 171
　authority, basis 81
　Barth on 8-10, 12-13, 15, 25, 29-
　37, 45, 47-8, 55-6, 67-81, 157-8,
　270-87
　as body of Christ 198-202, 227
　catholicity of 69, 188-90
　and the crucifixion 30
　and discipline 74
　election
　　of Christ 121-7
　　of God 104
　elements 8-10
　of Esau 31, 32, 33, 35
　　see also visible/invisible
　　dialectic

Rendtorff, Trutz 61-2, 66
reprobation 33
revelation
    Barth on 27-8, 34-5, 37-8, 62-3,
        87-8
    and the church 59-61, 67-8
    Feuerer on 83-4
    and preaching 60
    and reconciliation 131
Roman Catholicism 23, 217
    Barth on 96
    the church in 45-58, 104, 179,
        180, 282
    ecclesiology 45-58
    Marian dogma 130, 282
    Protestantism, differences 49-58
Romans commentary, *see under*
    Barth
Römerbrief, see under Barth

sacraments, and the church 74, 78
Schleiermacher, Friedrich 2, 21, 22,
    54, 90, 159, 197
    Barth, debate 37-45
    Celebration of Christmas 40-1
    Christology 38-9
    on the church 39-40, 180
    Holy Spirit/human spirit
        confusion 43
    on peace 42
Scholder, Klaus 91
Scripture
    and the church 73-4, 81, 210
    and history 144
Second Vatican Council 54
Sonderegger, Katherine 126-7
state, and church 257-69, 285
Sykes, S.W. 109-10

theology
    Barth's 110
    as Christology 3
Thompson, John 143-4
Thurneyssen, Eduard 141
Tillich, Paul 21, 66
    Barth, debate 62-3
totus Christus
    Christ as 151-2, 200, 202-5
    meaning 202
Trinity doctrine 63, 110
    Barth on 68
    immanent/economic 102

vocation, Christian 138-9, 141, 225
Volk concept 91

Webster, John 138, 197-8, 274
Wilhelm II 17
Word, the 52, 53
    and the church's mission 247-53
    and the flesh 4, 5, 55, 64, 65, 66-
        7, 77, 111, 149, 174, 199, 202,
        214, 229, 230
world, the
    in abstract 231
    and Christ 147, 230-1
    and the church 9, 33, 226-9, 234,
        235-43, 267-9
    and the community 122-3, 225-9
    God, distinction 25-6, 28, 30, 31,
        36, 60
    history of 231-2
worship
    and the church 213-15
    and the community 206-7